Oratio Obliqua, Oratio Recta

An Essay on Metarepresentation

François Recanati

A Bradford Book
The MIT Press
Cambridge, Massachusetts
London, England

© 2000 Massachusetts Institute of Technology

All rights reserved. No part of this book may be reproduced in any form by any electronic or mechanical means (including photocopying, recording, and information storage and retrieval) without permission in writing from the publisher.

This book was set in Sabon on '3B2' by Asco Typesetters, Hong Kong, and was printed and bound in the United States of America.

First printing, 2000

Library of Congress Cataloging-in-Publication Data
Oratio obliqua, oratio recta : an essay on metarepresentation / François Recanati.
    p.   cm. — (Representation and mind)
"Bradford book."
Includes bibliographical references and index.
ISBN 0-262-18199-1 (alk. paper) — ISBN 0-262-68116-1 (pbk. : alk. paper)
1. Semantics—Psychological aspects. 2. Psycholinguistics. I. Title. II. Series.
P325.5.C63 R47 2000
401'.9—dc21   99-087948

10 0303670 1

Oratio Obliqua, Oratio Recta

DATE DUE FOR RETURN

UNIVERSITY LIBRARY

3 0 JUN 2008 A

ANN HAL 62

This book may be recalled before the above date.

Representation and Mind
Hilary Putnam and Ned Block, editors

Contents

Preface

Utterances and thoughts have content: They represent (actual or imaginary) states of affairs. Those states of affairs consist of entities having properties and standing in relation to other entities. Among the entities which can be linguistically or mentally represented in this manner are linguistic and mental representations themselves. This is the phenomenon known as *metarepresentation*. Thus we can think or talk about speech or thought, whether our own or someone else's, as in the following example:

John believes I want to stay; he would like me to leave, but I don't think he will have the guts to tell me "Leave the room!"

The first sentence, 'John believes I want to stay', describes John as believing something. This is a metarepresentation because the belief which is thus described itself possesses a content and represents a state of affairs (viz. the fact that I want to stay). So we must distinguish two representations. John's belief is the primary representation—the 'object-representation', as I will call it. The utterance 'John believes I want to stay' represents John's belief and is therefore the metarepresentation. Note, however, that the primary representation is not so absolutely, but relatively. If we analyse it we see that it itself is a metarepresentation. The belief represents a state of affairs involving a certain person (myself) having a certain desire (the desire to stay). Now a desire, as much as a belief, is a representation endowed with content. We therefore have three levels of representation in the first sentence. At the bottom level I am represented as staying. This state of affairs is the content of the desire which is ascribed to me. My having that desire is a second state of affairs, which is the content of the belief ascribed to John. John's holding that belief is a third state of affairs, which is the content of the utterance.

The second sentence of the example, 'He would like me to leave', is simpler—it involves only two levels of representation and two states of affairs: my leaving, which is the content of John's desire, and John's so desiring, which is the content of the utterance. But the third sentence ("I don't think he will have the guts to tell me *Leave the room!*") is more complex. It represents the fact that the speaker does not hold a certain belief; the belief in question represents someone having the guts to issue a certain imperative utterance; that utterance itself expresses a desire on the part of its putative utterer; which desire bears on the speaker's leaving the room.

The complexity revealed by the analysis of such examples contrasts with the ease with which we process and understand them. Many take this as evidence that humans are endowed with a specific metarepresentational faculty which enables them, in particular, to ascribe mental states to others and to explain (or predict) their behaviour on that basis. A lot is known concerning the development of that alleged faculty, and there is an active debate in psychology and the philosophy of mind concerning the relation of metarepresentation to pretense and simulation. I will have something to say about that issue shortly. But it seems clear to me that not much theoretical progress can be made in this area until we know more about the very structure of metarepresentations.

As what I have said already makes clear, I take it that there are (at least) two levels of content in metarepresentations. First, there is the content of the object-representation. Second, there is the content of the metarepresentation itself. The former, I claim, is included in the latter: the (meta)representation that John believes that it will rain carries the content of the (object-)representation that it will rain, as well as an extra bit of content. The extra bit is the properly 'meta' part, whereby the object-representation is referred to as an entity on its own right and situated in the order of things.

This is a simple and intuitive idea. Yet if it is taken seriously, a number of consequences follow which are relevant to current debates in philosophy and cognitive science.

The logical form of belief reports such as 'John believes that it will rain' is generally construed as being the same as that of 'Peter loves Mary', viz. $R(a, b)$. This analysis does not do justice to the fact that the content of the metarepresentation includes the content of the object-representation. To be sure, the embedded sentence is nominalized, but its having the grammatical status of a noun-phrase does not entail that it plays the logical role of a singular term. The logical form of belief reports, rather, is $R(a, p)$ where 'p' is a sentence and 'R' a higher-level predicate. There is but a short step from there to $R_a p$, where 'R_a' is a sentential operator; a step which brings belief reports and *oratio obliqua* closer to another form of metarepresentation, which the following examples illustrate:

In the film, Robin Hood meets Sherlock Holmes.

In the picture, Mary is smiling.

Whatever the differences between the two forms of linguistic metarepresentation (*oratio obliqua*, e.g., belief sentences, on the one hand; 'media sentences' as studied in Fauconnier 1985 and Ross 1997 on the other hand) they have in common the dual structure of metarepresentations: their content includes the content of the object-representation as well as the 'extra bit' talked about earlier.

Second, we must reject the traditional view that the object-representation is 'mentioned' rather than 'used', in metarepresentational contexts. On this still popular conception, a representation (e.g., a sentence) can *either* be used transparently to represent something, *or* it can itself be represented. If the latter, the representation becomes 'opaque' and no longer represents. It follows that metarepresentations do not talk about the subject-matter of the object-representation. But if metarepresentations have the basic structure I take them to have, just the opposite is true. Since metarepresentations carry the content of the object-representation they *must* be about whatever the object-representation is about. The object-representation remains 'transparent' even though it is represented.

Another important consequence of the simple and intuitive idea I defend in this book concerns the debate over simulation and its role in metarepresentation. If metarepresentations have the structure I say they have, then they work by replicating/simulating the representation they are about. Metarepresentations thus essentially involve simulation. Yet, I will argue, metarepresentation cannot be reduced to simulation. There is simulation to the extent that the content of the metarepresentation and the content of the object-representation necessarily overlap, but that simulative overlap must be *partial* for there to be metarepresentation rather than sheer simulation.

Note that the basic structure I ascribe to metarepresentations is not specific to them. Metarepresentations share that structure with a host of other representations such as 'In the kitchen, Mary is singing', or 'Two days ago, it rained'. There too we find a primary representation together with an 'extra bit' whereby the fact represented at the primary level (the fact that Mary is singing, or the fact that it rains) is somehow located in the order of things (as a fact holding at a certain place or at a certain time). What distinguishes metarepresentations is their involving, e.g., fictional or hypothetical situations: In metarepresentations, the fact represented at the primary level is located in the *imaginary* realm rather than in the actual world. Following Bühler, however, I claim that simulation is involved as soon as one considers facts holding in remote situations, whether remote in space-time or in 'logical space'. On this view, humdrum representations such as 'Two days ago, it rained' must themselves be seen as resting on two capacities; a simulative capacity whereby we can represent what is not given to our senses, and a reflective capacity whereby we can, at the same time, entertain a representation *and* locate the fact it represents within a higher-level structure. If I am right, metarepresentations exploit (and extend) a complex ability that is already in place for representing the actual world.

The view I hold suggests that metarepresentations are 'semantically innocent'. Replicated in a metarepresentational context the object-representation retains its own content. Thus the sentence 'The Earth is flat' represents the same state of affairs when it is uttered in isolation and when it occurs embedded in 'John believes that the Earth is flat'.

Admittedly there are (prima facie) counterexamples to the thesis of semantic innocence. If a proper name lacks a referent, as the names

'Vulcan' or 'Santa Claus' do, a simple subject-predicate sentence in which the name occurs will lack a truth-value. But if we prefix the sentence with 'Leverrier believed that' or 'My three-year-old son believes that', the complex belief sentence may well be true (it seems). Now it could *not* be true if the constituent sentence lacked a truth-value. It follows that the semantic properties of the constituent sentence must have changed as a result of metarepresentational embedding. Indeed there are reasons to believe that metarepresentational embedding sometimes causes the complement sentence to be evaluated with respect to a *shifted context* distinct from the context with respect to which the global metarepresentation itself (or the object-representation, when taken in isolation) is evaluated. Because of this contextual shift, the content of the embedded sentence turns out to be different from the content of that very sentence, considered in isolation.

This plausible story, which I discuss in the second half of the book, conflicts with the view that metarepresentational embedding is innocent and does not affect the content of the object-representation. It does not really conflict with the general analysis of metarepresentational structure offered in the first half of the book, however. According to that analysis, the content of a metarepresentation includes the content of the object-representation. Thus the metarepresentation 'Leverrier thought that *S*' does not merely talk about but actually *displays* the thought it talks about. Let us call the content thus displayed 'C_L'. One may well admit that the belief report 'Leverrier thought that *S*', which ascribes to Leverrier a thought with the content C_L, actually displays C_L, in accordance with the position defended in the first half of this book; while insisting that the embedded sentence which expresses C_L *in the metarepresentation* has a different content, or no content at all, when it occurs outside the metarepresentation. In other words, the iconicity thesis (the view that the content of the metarepresentation includes the content of the object-representation) does not entail semantic innocence, but merely suggests it.

Be that as it may, I have chosen to defend the view that metarepresentational embedding *is* innocent, in a certain sense at least. Metarepresentational operators ('John believes that', 'In the film') shift the *circumstance* with respect to which the sentence which follows is evaluated. In this respect they are like ordinary intensional operators such as 'It is possible that', 'In the kitchen' or 'Two days ago it was the case that'. They shift the circumstance, but they do not shift the 'context' with respect to which the complement sentence is interpreted. If they did, they would be *hyperintensional* operators, as they have often been said to be: operators in whose scope one expression cannot be substituted for another one with the same content *salva veritate*. I do not deny that such failures of substitution characteristically occur in metarepresentations, nor do I deny that they can be accounted for in terms of context-shift. But I think the explanation should be pragmatic rather than semantic. Metarepresentational operators *per se* are not hyperintensional, but merely intensional; they do not shift the context but only the circumstance of evaluation. Yet they provide an environment hospitable to various *pragmatic* processes such as free enrichment and context-shifting, which generate opacity and induce prima facie violations of semantic innocence. Context-shifts in metarepresentational contexts must therefore be acknowledged, I argue, but they need not be traced to the properly semantic contribution of metarepresentational operators.

The analysis of context-shifts, both in and outside metarepresentations, in the second half of the book is closely associated with the analysis of *oratio recta*. I take it that there are two distinct processes at issue: metarepresentational circumstance-shift, illustrated by *oratio obliqua*, and quotational context-shift, illustrated by *oratio recta*. The major difficulty in this area comes from the fact that the two processes, though distinct, seldom come in pure forms. Thus opacity in *oratio obliqua* often arises from quotational intrusions of various sorts. And the commonest forms of *oratio recta* bring it close to *oratio obliqua*, as Burge once noticed (Burge 1978: 146–50). Precisely to the extent that the two processes often mix, giving rise to all sorts of hybrid, I have tried to go as far as I could in the direction of disentangling them; hence my slightly provocative claim that metarepresentational operators are 'merely intensional'. Those who think it is an empirical fact that metarepresentational operators are hyperintensional and/or act as Kaplanian 'monsters' (context-shifting operators) are invited to construe my claim as an idealization; an idealization which will hopefully shed some light into one of the darkest areas of semantic theorizing.

Just as the capacity for metarepresentational embedding (and, more generally, the capacity for reflective simulation on which it rests) is an important feature of human cognition rather than a linguistic curiosity, I think that the process of context-shifting which underlies many quotational phenomena in natural language ultimately rests on another important cognitive ability: our capacity for *deference*, which plays a central role in learning and theorizing. This view is argued for, much too sketchily I admit, in the last part of the book.

I started working on what was to become this book in the year 1995. I gave several talks on Metarepresentation and Simulation for the 'Metarepresentation' seminar organized by Gloria Origgi at CREA, and in April of the same year I participated in the conference on 'Belief and Acceptance' organized by Pascal Engel in Caen. At the end of the year, I wrote a long manuscript entitled 'The Simulation of Belief', which served as basis for several published papers. A few months later Dan Sperber invited me to participate in the Tenth Vancouver Cognitive Science Conference on 'Metarepresentation', which was to take place in February 1997. At about the same time Alex Orenstein asked me to contribute to a volume on Quine he was co-editing, and Richard Zuber to a Festschrift for Oswald Ducrot. The three forthcoming papers I wrote on these occasions ('The Iconicity of Metarepresentation', for the Vancouver conference; 'Opacity and the Attitudes', for the Quine volume; and 'Context-Shifting in Metarepresentation', for the Ducrot volume) were all huge, and they all concerned the same topic or group of topics. It was evident that a book, this book, had to be written.

In parts I and II I used materials from 'The Iconicity of Metarepresentation' (Recanati forthcoming a); in part III, materials from 'Opacity and the Attitudes' (Recanati forthcoming b); and in parts IV and V, materials from 'Context-Shifting in Metarepresentation'. Materials from several other papers were exploited, namely: in part II, 'The Dynamics of Situations' (Recanati 1997b) and 'Situations and the Structure of Content' (Recanati 1999); in part III, 'Relational Belief Reports' (Recanati forthcoming c); in part V, 'Talk about Belief' (Recanati 1998); and, in Part VI, 'Can We Believe What We Do Not Understand' (Recanati 1997a) and 'Deferential Concepts' (Recanati forthcoming d).

When I decided to write the book, in 1997, I sent a proposal to two publishers, which both accepted it. One of them asked me to change my original title, 'Oratio Obliqua, Oratio Recta', which was found unpalatable. This was one of my reasons for choosing the other publisher. Soon, however, I realized that *everybody* found my Latin title unpalatable and I started looking for a better one. I am very grateful to Kent Bach and Joseph Almog for their excellent suggestions ('Metatalk', from Kent Bach; 'Obliquities', from Joseph Almog); and to many others, including Ned Block, Alvin Goldman, John Perry, and Deirdre Wilson, for ranking the candidates I had shortlisted. But when I informed the MIT Press that the title had been changed, I was surprised to receive a message from the copy-editor, Alan Thwaits, urging me to keep the original title, which *he* found perfectly appropriate! Surprised, but pleased to find someone sharing my old-fashioned taste in these matters.

Many people have had an impact on this work either by influencing me by their ideas, or by asking me to write the papers which served as basis for portions of this book, or by commenting on what I had written. I should start by acknowledging the general influence of Jon Barwise, Gilles Fauconnier, and Dan Sperber on my thinking in the areas covered in this book. I am also indebted to Anne Bezuidenhout, Ned Block, Dick Carter, Benoît de Cornulier, Mark Crimmins, Steven Davis, Jérôme Dokic, Oswald Ducrot, Pascal Engel, Graeme Forbes, Ulli Haas-Spohn, Pierre Jacob, Keith Lehrer, Pascal Ludwig, Brian Loar, Friederike Moltmann, Kevin Mulligan, Alex Orenstein, Gloria Origgi, Jérôme Pelletier, Stefano Predelli, Joëlle Proust, Alberto Voltolini, Marcel Vuillaume, Deirdre Wilson, Andrew Woodfield, and Richard Zuber. Special thanks are due to Isidora Stojanovic for her detailed comments on the second part of the book. Last but not least, I am grateful to my colleagues and students at CREA for many good discussions.

I

Iconicity

1
Three Principles

§1.1 Extensionality

In contemporary philosophy there is a huge body of literature devoted to the analysis of metarepresentations, especially belief reports like

(1)   John believes that kangaroos have tails.

On the face of it, such metarepresentations seem to contain a primary representation, viz. 'Kangaroos have tails', and something like an operator 'John believes (that)' which makes a sentence out of a sentence. In this respect 'John believes that S' appears to be very much like 'It is not the case that S'.

A major difference between 'John believes that' and the sentence-forming operator 'it is not the case that' is that the latter is *extensional*: the truth-value of the complex representation is a function of the truth-value of the primary representation. In this instance, the Principle of Extensionality is respected:

Principle of Extensionality
Given any sentence which contains as a part a sentence S, its truth-value is unchanged if we substitute for S any other sentence S' having the same truth-value as S.[1]

In contrast 'John believes that' is not extensional: the truth-value of the complex statement does not depend merely on the truth-value of the embedded sentence (or, more generally, on the extension of the constituent expressions). John may believe that grass is green without believing that snow is white, even though 'Grass is green' and 'Snow is white' have the same truth-value. Consequently, the Principle of Extensionality is violated.

The Principle of Extensionality is a consequence of a more general principle:

Generalized Principle of Extensionality (GPE)
The truth-value of a sentence is unchanged if we replace a constituent of that sentence by another one with the same extension.

The extension of a singular term (be it a 'genuine singular term', i.e., a name or an indexical, or a definite description) is an object; the extension of a predicate is a class of objects; and the extension of a sentence is a truth-value (i.e., 'true' or 'false', as the case may be). The GPE therefore entails various *replacement principles*, one of which is the Principle of Extensionality:

Extensional replacement principles
• Substitutivity of Co-Denoting Prima Facie Singular Terms
A prima facie singular term t (i.e., a name, an indexical, or a description) can be replaced *salva veritate* by some other term t' provided t and t' have the same extension.
• Substitutivity of Co-Extensive Predicates
A predicative expression F can be replaced *salva veritate* by another predicative expression G if the class of objects which satisfy F is identical to the class of objects which satisfy G.
• Principle of Extensionality (Substitutivity of Equivalent Sentences)
A sentence S can be replaced by a sentence S' in any complex sentence in which S occurs if S and S' have the same truth-value.

The first of these replacement principles should not be confused with another principle, the Principle of Substitutivity of Singular Terms, which concerns only genuine singular terms (names and indexicals), but not descriptions. Someone who rejects the GPE, hence the first extensional replacement principle, will want to retain the Principle of Substitutivity, which holds in many non-extensional contexts (such as the modal context 'It is necessary that ...'). I will return to this distinction between the two principles later (§3.5).

The GPE is more general than the simple Principle of Extensionality, but it can still be generalized much further. First, it is not only the truth-value of a sentence, but *the extension of any sort of expression whatso-*

ever, which is unchanged if, in that expression, a constituent is replaced by another one with the same extension. Second, it is not only the extension of an expression, but its semantic value *at all levels* which arguably is a function of the semantic values of its parts. This last principle, which entails the GPE, I call the Generalized Principle of Compositionality (GPC).

As Frege and Carnap both emphasized, different types (or levels) of semantic value can be ascribed to expressions; the unitary notion of 'meaning' is therefore rather misleading. Beside its extension, a linguistic expression possesses a *content*, which is what determines its extension (with respect to a circumstance of evaluation). Kaplan added a further distinction between 'character' (linguistic meaning) and 'content', in order to account for those cases in which the content of an expression partly depends upon the context in which the expression is tokened (Kaplan 1989a). In Kaplan's framework, which I will adopt in what follows, there are three distinct aspects of 'meaning'. Depending on the level of analysis, the semantic value of an expression can be either its *character*, or its *content*, or its *extension*.[2]

The Generalized Principle of Compositionality can now be stated as consisting of three sub-principles, the third of which is identical to the GPE:

Generalized Principle of Compositionality (GPC)
The semantic value of an expression at all levels is a function of the semantic values of its parts; that is,

(a) the character of an expression is a function of the characters of its parts,
(b) the content of an expression is a function of the contents of its parts,
(c) the extension of an expression is a function of the extensions of its parts (= GPE).

Given that the GPC entails the GPE which entails the Principle of Extensionality, belief reports, which violate the Principle of Extensionality, raise an obvious problem for those who defend the GPE or the GPC. Now the attachment of philosophers and logicians to this group of principles is so great that, more often than not, they have attempted to save the Principle of Extensionality by showing that its violations are 'only apparent', given a particular analysis of belief reports. In building theories to that effect, however, they have been led to sacrifice what, following Davidson, Barwise and Perry have called 'semantic innocence' (Barwise and Perry 1981).

§1.2   Innocence

Most philosophers analyse 'John believes that S' as consisting of a two-place predicate 'believes' and two singular terms, viz. 'John' and 'that S'. The standard argument in favour of that analysis is the validity of certain inferences involving belief sentences, e.g., the following:

John believes that grass is green.
Everything John believes is true.
Therefore, it is true that grass is green.

If we rephrase 'It is true that grass is green', in which there is a dummy subject, into 'That grass is green is true', then the argument can easily be accounted for on the assumption that 'that grass is green' is a term (possibly a definite description). The inference pattern is:

a is F (That grass is green is believed by John.)
Every F is G.   (Everything believed by John is true.)
Therefore, a is G.   (That grass is green is true.)

In this framework the GPE seems to apply, for the truth-value of the belief report is unchanged if we replace either of the singular terms flanking the two-place predicate 'believes' by a codenoting expression. The following inferences are both licensed by one of the replacement principles which the GPE entails, namely, the principle of Substitutivity of Co-Denoting Prima Facie Singular Terms:

John believes that S.
John is the landlord.
Therefore, the landlord believes that S.

John believes that S.
That S is the most crazy thing I have ever heard.
Therefore, John believes the most crazy thing I have ever heard.

However, we still have the problem of analysing the complex singular term 'that S'. It contains the sentence S, but the reference of the 'that'-

clause is *not* a function solely of the extension of the embedded sentence. If we replace the sentence *S* by another one with the same truth-value but a different content, the truth-value of the complex sentence 'John believes that *S*' will possibly shift. Again, John may believe that grass is green without eo ipso believing that snow is white. This is a violation of the GPE.

Many philosophers have dealt with this problem by appealing to the thesis of Semantic Deviance, according to which the extension of an expression is affected when it is embedded within a 'that'-clause. For Frege, who put forward a radical version of the thesis, the extension of a sentence systematically shifts in such circumstances. Once embedded, 'Grass is green' no longer denotes its truth-value (viz. True) but it comes to denote its truth-*condition*, viz. the proposition that grass is green. In other words, the extension of a sentence is not its normal extension, viz. its truth-value, when the sentence is embedded in a belief context; an embedded sentence refers to its (normal) *content*. So if we replace 'Grass is green' by 'Snow is white' in a 'that'-clause, we do *not* replace an expression with another one with the same extension. *In the context of the belief sentence*, 'Grass is green' and 'Snow is white' do not have the same extension. The Principle of Extensionality is therefore respected, appearances notwithstanding.

Some philosophers, like Quine, do not like the idea that the embedded sentence refers to a 'proposition' or 'content', because they are suspicious of such entities. But they stick to the thesis of Semantic Deviance: they maintain that when a sentence is embedded in a belief report its semantic value is affected.[3] 'That'-clauses, in this respect, are similar to quotation contexts: when we put a sentence in quotes, it no longer represents what it ordinarily represents. The sentence is mentioned rather than used. The same thing holds, Quine says, for non-extensional contexts in general. Non-extensional contexts in general are assimilated to quotation contexts, in which words stop behaving in the normal way. Thus,

It is contingent that grass is green

is read as

That grass is green is contingent

and this is construed as similar to

'Grass is green' is contingent

where the sentence occurs within quotation marks. Because the representation is mentioned rather than used, we cannot expect the GPC to apply in those contexts. As Quine says (1951: 26),

From the standpoint of logical analysis each whole quotation must be regarded as a single word or sign, whose parts count no more than serifs or syllables. A quotation is not a *description*, but a *hieroglyph*; it designates its object not by describing it in terms of other objects, but by picturing it. The meaning of the whole does not depend upon the meanings of the constituent words. The personal name buried within the first word of the statement

(1)   'Cicero' has six letters

e.g., is logically no more germane to the statement than is the verb 'let' which is buried within the last word. Otherwise, indeed, the identity of Tully with Cicero would allow us to interchange these personal names, in the context of quotation marks as in any other context; we could thus argue from the truth (1) to the falsehood

(1′)   'Tully' has six letters

By parity of reasoning, 'that S' in 'John believes that S' counts as logically a single word, whose semantic value does not depend upon the semantic values of its parts. (If the words in the embedded sentence did their normal compositional job, in accordance with the GPC, the Principle of Extensionality *would* apply.)

In the case of quotation the thesis of Semantic Deviance is extremely plausible. Do the first word of (2) and (3) below have e.g., the same extension? No, the first one refers to cats, the second one refers to the word 'cats'.

(2)   Cats are nice.

(3)   'Cats' is a four-letter word.

(Note the difference in number between the two words: one is singular, the other one plural.) But what about belief sentences and 'that'-clauses in general? Consider (4):

(4)   John believes that grass is green.

Is it credible to say that the words 'Grass is green' do not represent what they normally represent? In what sense? Does 'grass' in the embedded sentence refer to anything else than grass? As Davidson emphasized,

If we could recover our pre-Fregean semantic innocence, I think it would seem to us plainly incredible that the words 'The earth moves', uttered after the words 'Galileo said that', mean anything different, or refer to anything else, than is their wont when they come in different environments. (Davidson 1968: 108)[4]

I fully agree with Davidson that we should at least try to 'recover our pre-Fregean innocence', that is, to do without the thesis of Semantic Deviance. In an 'innocent' framework, the semantic value of an expression in the embedded part of a belief report is construed as its *normal* semantic value (whatever that may be).

Ironically, many of those who explicitly defend 'semantic innocence' in the analysis of belief reports (e.g., Crimmins and Perry 1989) do so within the standard framework. They hold that 'that'-clauses refer to the proposition which the embedded sentence would express, were it uttered in isolation. But, I will argue (§2.2), that is not 'innocent' in the strong sense in which Davidson and Barwise and Perry talk about pre-Fregean innocence. One way of achieving innocence in that strong sense is to capture a central, though neglected, feature possessed by belief reports and other metarepresentations: the feature of 'iconicity', to which I now turn.

§1.3   Iconicity

Belief sentences belong to a class of sentences which have, or seem to have, the (syntactic) property that they contain other sentences. For example, the sentences

If Peter comes, John will be happy

Peter comes and John will be happy

both contain the sentence 'Peter comes' and the sentence 'John will be happy'. Similarly,

It is true that John will be happy

Peter believes that John will be happy

Later today, John will be happy

all seem to contain the sentence 'John will be happy'.

Whenever we have a complex sentence dS which contains a sentence S in this manner, the following schema yields true instances:

Schema (I)

One cannot entertain the thought that *dS* without entertaining the thought that *S*.

For example:

One cannot entertain the thought that John believes that grass is green without entertaining the thought that grass is green.

One cannot entertain the thought that it is not the case that Peter is smart without entertaining the thought that Peter is smart.

One cannot entertain the thought that if it rains the road will be wet without entertaining the thought that the road will be wet.

Here, like Frege in 'The Thought', I rely on an intuitive understanding of what it is to 'entertain' (or 'grasp' or 'apprehend') a thought, as opposed to asserting it or judging it to be true.

The property I have just mentioned holds for all sentences which contain a sentence as part, with the exception of sentences which contain another sentence in quotation marks.[5] Sentences with 'that'-clauses, in particular, satisfy (I): one cannot entertain the thought such a sentence expresses without entertaining the thought expressed by the embedded sentence. This is true of a belief report such as 'John believes that *S*' as much as of an extensional sentence such as 'It is true that *S*'.

If we want to make sense of this intuitive observation, we will be inclined to take the containment relation seriously. The following principle suggests itself:

Principle of Iconicity

Attitude reports and other metarepresentations contain the object-representation not only syntactically (in the sense that *dS* contains *S*), but also semantically: the proposition *Q* expressed by *dS* 'contains' as a part the proposition *P* expressed by *S*—and that's why one cannot entertain *Q* without entertaining *P*.

This principle itself makes sense only in the context of a certain type of semantic theory—a theory which construes propositions (the contents of utterances) as structured entities; that is indeed the sort of theory I have in mind. I leave it to proponents of the other sorts of semantic theory to decide whether and how they would be willing to account for the intuitive observation noted above.[6]

The Principle of Iconicity is so named because, if it is true, metarepresentations essentially *resemble* the representations they are about—they share a lot of content with them. Indeed that is the intuition I am trying to convey. Consider example (5):

(5) *Tom*   The Moon is made of green cheese.

  Bob   According to Tom, the Moon is made of green cheese.

Tom's utterance represents the Moon as being made of green cheese. Bob's utterance, which is a metarepresentation, has a different subject-matter: it is about Tom's utterance (or the belief it expresses), as the prefix 'According to Tom' makes clear. Yet, via the contained sentence, Bob's metarepresentational utterance displays the content of Tom's utterance and therefore replicates it to some extent. *Both Tom's utterance and Bob's include a representation of the Moon as being made of green cheese.* That representation is offered by Tom as a representation of the way the world actually is; and by Bob as a representation of the way the world is according to Tom.

The Principle of Iconicity goes against the received wisdom concerning metarepresentations. As undergraduates we learn that if a metarepresentation m represents an object-representation r and r is about x, then m is about r and *not* about x. If the Principle of Iconicity is correct, just the opposite is true: Whenever a metarepresentation m represents an object-representation r and r is about x, then m is bound to be about x (as well as about r).[7] In other words, metarepresentations are fundamentally *transparent*.

Before proceeding, let me point out that not all metarepresentations in the general sense of 'representations of representations' fall into the same basket here. There is a difference between, e.g., (6) and (7):

(6) Tom stated Leibniz's Law.

(7) Tom stated that identical objects have all their properties in common.

Both statements are about a statement, namely Tom's statement of Leibniz's Law. However, the content of Tom's statement (viz. Leibniz's

Law) is displayed only in (7).[8] It follows that only (7) is an iconic meta-representation, that is, a metarepresentation which displays the content of the object-representation and thereby replicates it. (6) is not iconic—it does not satisfy schema (I): One *can* entertain the thought that Tom stated Leibniz's Law without entertaining the thought that identical objects have all their properties in common (= Leibniz's Law); but one *cannot* entertain the thought that Tom stated that identical objects have all their properties in common without entertaining the thought that identical objects have all their properties in common. So it makes a big difference whether we use a standard singular term (or description) or a 'that'-clause. This difference is ignored in standard accounts. From now on, I will reserve the term 'metarepresentation' for those representations of representations which *do* satisfy (I) and which, I claim, have the semantic property of iconicity. For example:

According to John, grass is green.

John believes that grass is green.

John says that grass is green.

In the picture, grass is green.

In the film, grass is green.

Etc.

I take those metarepresentations to constitute a natural class, and it is that class which I am trying to characterize via the Principle of Iconicity.

2

'That'-Clauses as Singular Terms

§2.1 Iconic Names

The evidence I gave for the Principle of Iconicity consists of all true instances which can be obtained by appropriately filling out schema (I):

Schema (I)

One cannot entertain the thought that *dS* without entertaining the thought that *S*.

Can we account for that evidence in line with the standard account, according to which 'that'-clauses are singular terms? At least we can try, and that's what I am going to do in this chapter. (In the next chapter, I will question the standard account and explore alternative frameworks.)

Let me first define an *iconic name* as a (genuine) singular term formed from a sentence and denoting the content of that sentence. It is easy to devise an iconic name-forming operator: thus I can decide that square brackets, placed around a sentence, form a term denoting the proposition expressed by the sentence in question. According to this convention, which I will adopt in what follows, [grass is green] is an iconic name of the proposition that grass is green. In order to account for the validity of schema (I), we can make the following assumption: 'that'-clauses, in English, *are* iconic names, and the word 'that' obeys the same convention as I have just described for square brackets—it is an iconic term-forming operator. In that way we can straightforwardly represent the difference between examples (6) and (7) from chapter 1 (repeated below): (6) contains an ordinary name (or a description)[9] of Leibniz's Law while (7) contains an iconic name.

(6)   Tom stated Leibniz's Law.

(7)   Tom stated that identical objects have all their properties in common.

The distinction between iconic and non-iconic ways of denoting contents is similar to the distinction between two ways of denoting words and expressions (§10.1): autonymous mention, as in '*Boston* is disyllabic', and heteronymous mention, as in 'The name of my favourite city is disyllabic' (figure I.1).[10] Autonymous mention is iconic in the sense that what is talked about is actually displayed or exhibited (Searle 1969: 73ff, Davidson 1979).

The iconic term-forming operator [ ] (or 'that', if we accept the view of 'that'-clauses as iconic names) can be given a semantics analogous to that of demonstratives in Kaplan's framework (Kaplan 1989a). For Kaplan, the character of an expression is a function from contexts to contents. Since indexicals are directly referential expressions, the content of an indexical (whether a 'pure' indexical or a demonstrative) is its referent, hence the character of an indexical is the rule which contextually determines its referent. For example, the character of the pure indexical 'I' is the rule that an occurrence of 'I' refers to the producer of that occurrence. In contrast to pure indexicals, "a demonstrative without an associated demonstration is incomplete" (Kaplan 1989a: 490):

[Demonstratives] require, in order to determine their referents, an associated demonstration: typically, though not invariably, a (visual) presentation of a local object discriminated by a pointing.

In other words, a demonstrative has a character only when it is accompanied by a demonstration. The character in question is the rule that the demonstrative refers to the object demonstrated. Similarly, we might say the following concerning iconic names: the iconic term-forming operator [ ] must be completed by a sentence S, and it is the resulting term which

	Iconic	Non-iconic
Mention of form	'Shit'	The four-letter word
Mention of content	That identical objects have all their properties in common	Leibniz's Law

Figure I.1
Varieties of mention

possesses a character. The character of an iconic name $[S]$ is the rule that, in a context c, $[S]$ refers to the content of S in c.

In this theory the character of $[S]$ is such that in order to determine its content, one must grasp the content expressed by S: one must not only think *of* the content of S, but think *it*, in order to think the thought which the complex sentence expresses (viz., the thought that this content is believed by John). Iconic names are distinguished from non-iconic terms by their character, that is, by the *mode of presentation* of the referent. The referent of $[S]$ is presented iconically: we understand which proposition is referred to by *directly grasping that proposition*.[11] That iconic mode of presentation at the character level is filtered out as truth-conditionally irrelevant at the content level: there is no difference as far as content is concerned between (6) and (7). In both cases a certain proposition, viz., Leibniz's Law, is referred to, and what is said is that Tom stated that proposition. The analogy with demonstratives is, again, illuminating. I cannot think 'That mountain is F' without thinking of the mountain under the mode of presentation corresponding to the way the mountain in question is being demonstrated. That mode of presentation is an integral part of the thought. Still, the *content* of the thought is a singular proposition, to the effect that the mountain in question is F. The mode of presentation associated with the demonstration is present in the thought only at the 'character' level; at the 'content' level it is filtered out as truth-conditionally irrelevant (Recanati 1993).

The theory of iconic names bears some similarity to Quine's view of quotation. Remember the passage cited above (§1.2): "A quotation is not a *description*, but a *hieroglyph*; it designates its object not by describing it in terms of other objects, but by picturing it. The meaning of the whole does not depend upon the meanings of the constituent words." The same thing is true of iconic names: the proposition expressed by the embedded sentence S which occurs in the iconic name $[S]$ is involved at the character level but it is not part of the content of the utterance. The reference of the iconic name is not described in terms of other objects (viz., the objects named in S, which are constituents of the proposition that S); rather, it is assigned directly to the name, by the semantic rule which is the character of the iconic name.

§2.2   Innocence Lost

The theory of iconic names accounts for the validity of schema (I) by appealing to the special *character* of 'that'-clauses, but it analyses their *content* in the standard fashion. On this analysis a belief report like 'John believes that Peter likes grass' expresses a singular proposition Q consisting of a dyadic relation and a sequence of two arguments, namely John and a certain proposition P (the proposition that Peter likes grass). That proposition P is referred to by the 'that'-clause, much as John is referred to by the proper name 'John'.

It is unclear that this approach is consistent with the Principle of Iconicity. According to that principle, the content of a complex sentence dS has much in common with the content of the sentence S which it contains. What is common to them is, precisely, the content of S, which the content of dS includes as a part. Now what is common to the above propositions P and Q? Not much, arguably. The latter is the proposition that John believes P; the former is the proposition that Peter likes grass. The relations (believing versus liking) are different, as are the respective *relata* ($\langle$John, $P\rangle$ versus $\langle$Peter, grass$\rangle$). What is common to the two propositions is only the general form aRb.

To be sure, the proposition P itself figures as one of the *relata* in the proposition Q; hence there is an obvious sense in which Q contains P. Is this not sufficient to satisfy the Principle of Iconicity? That is unclear. The proposition P figures as an 'object' in Q. It is referred to, much as it would be if a real name was used instead of a 'that'-clause. Now, what Q must contain in order for the Principle of Iconicity to be really satisfied is arguably not the proposition P construed as an object—the semantic value of a singular term—but the proposition P construed as the semantic value (content) of a sentence. (I will return to that distinction between two ways of construing propositions in section 3.3.)

At this point, a defender of the theory of iconic names may reply as follows. Who cares if the Principle of Iconicity is satisfied? What matters is only the epistemological evidence underlying schema (I), and *that* is accounted for. There is no a priori reason why an account in terms of character should be less acceptable than an account in terms of content; hence there is no reason to insist on respecting the Principle of Iconicity.

I agree. But the Principle of Iconicity is not alone at stake. The Principle of Innocence is also threatened by the theory of iconic names. Indeed, it is far from obvious that that theory—or, for that matter, *any* version of the standard analysis—is semantically innocent in the sense in which Davidson first used that phrase. For the sentential complement is said to *name* a proposition; but that is not what the complement sentence does when it is not embedded. Unembedded, the sentence *expresses* the proposition which, once embedded, it names. Hence, by construing 'that'-clauses as names, it seems that all versions of the standard account, including the theory of iconic names, violate semantic innocence.

Many philosophers (including myself) have attempted to provide innocent versions of the standard account. The usual strategy consists in drawing a distinction between the embedded sentence ('Peter likes grass') and the complete 'that'-clause ('that Peter likes grass'). The embedded sentence, it is said, expresses a proposition, and it is that proposition which is named by the 'that'-clause (consisting of the embedded sentence plus the complementizer 'that'). In this way innocence is allegedly saved: the sentence does the same thing—it expresses a certain proposition— whether it is embedded or not; it never names a proposition, since that is a job for the complete 'that'-clause.

I do not think this strategy works, however. First, the distinction between the embedded sentence and the complete 'that'-clause has no obvious equivalent when we turn to metarepresentations like 'In the film, Peter likes grass' or 'According to John, Peter likes grass'. There is no 'that'-clause in such examples—only the sentence 'Peter likes grass'. Second, even when the distinction makes syntactic sense, it is unclear that it enables us to preserve semantic innocence. I will show that by considering an analogous case: that of quotation.

Faced with an instance of quotation, e.g., *'Cat' is a three-letter word*, we have two options. We can say that the word 'cat' in this context does something different from what it normally does: it is used 'autonymously' (self-referentially). Or we can say that it is the complex expression *'cat'* (consisting of the word 'cat' *and the quotes*) which denotes the word 'cat'. If, by taking the second option, we refrain from ascribing the word 'cat' a deviant function in quotation contexts, we will be led to deny that the word 'cat' really occurs; rather, with Tarski and Quine, we will say that it occurs there only as a 'fragment' of the longer expression, much as 'cat' occurs in 'cattle'. From the semantic point of view, the relevant unit is indeed the complete quotation; the word 'cat' itself thus disappears from the picture. *In this way innocence is lost as surely as it is when we take the first option.* A truly innocent account is one that would *both* acknowledge the occurrence of the expression at issue in the special context under consideration *and* ascribe it, in that context, its normal semantic function. (Of course, there is no reason to expect an account of quotation to be semantically innocent in that sense.)

Similarly, we have two options with regard to attitude reports, in the standard framework. If we say that the complement sentence, once embedded, names the proposition which it would normally express, we accept that the embedded sentence does not do what it normally does. On the other hand, if, in order to protect innocence, we draw a sharp distinction between the embedded sentence (which expresses a proposition) and the 'that'-clause (which names it), *we run the risk of making the former disappear from the logical scene.* For the relevant semantic unit is the complete 'that'-clause. At the level of logical form the sentence 'John believes that *S*' has the form *aRb*—it consists of a two-place predicate and two singular terms. The embedded sentence plays a role only via the 'that'-clause in which it occurs. What role? Arguably a *pre-semantic* role analogous to that of the demonstration which accompanies a demonstrative. For genuine singular terms are semantically simple: they have their referent directly assigned by a semantic rule such as '*Nixon* refers to Nixon' or '*I* refers to the speaker' or '*that* refers to whatever the speaker is demonstrating'.[12] If, therefore, we really want to treat 'that'-clauses as names, we have to ascribe them a purely syntactical complexity. That is the sort of view I sketched: 'that'-clauses consist of the word 'that' and a sentence, but the sentence plays only a pre-semantic role, like the demonstration which accompanies a demonstrative. If that is right, then semantically the complexity of the 'that'-clause matters no more than the pragmatic complexity of a demonstrative-*cum*-demonstration or the pictorial complexity of a quotation.

I conclude that current versions of the standard account, according to which 'that'-clauses are referring expressions, sacrifice semantic innocence to some extent—even those that claim otherwise. In line with this conclusion, I will eventually give up the standard account and explore alternative possibilities (chapter 3).[13] Before proceeding, however, we must briefly consider a couple of attempts to show that the standard analysis is in fact compatible with the Principle of Innocence.

§2.3   Innocence Regained? (1) 'That'-Clauses as Directly Referential Expressions

According to the theory of direct reference, the content of a directly ref-erential expression is its extension. If, therefore, we treat 'that'-clauses as names, hence as directly referential expressions, we will be in a position to regain semantic innocence by arguing as follows:

• The (normal) content of a sentence is the proposition it expresses.
• 'That'-clauses name the proposition expressed by the embedded sentence.
• Since 'that'-clauses are directly referential terms, their content is their extension, viz. the proposition which they name.

It follows that *the content of a 'that'-clause is identical to the content of the embedded sentence*—hence innocence is regained: in an attitude context, the complement sentence makes its normal semantic contribu-tion, viz. the proposition which it expresses. The complex proposition expressed by 'John believes that Peter likes grass' can thus be represented as follows:

⟨BELIEVES, ⟨John, ⟨LIKES, ⟨Peter, grass⟩⟩⟩⟩

As this representation makes clear, the proposition that Peter likes grass is a part of the proposition that John believes that Peter likes grass, in accordance with the Principle of Iconicity.

The problem with this otherwise attractive view is its claim that *the content of a term and that of a sentence can be identical.* That sounds as unacceptable as the claim that the content of a predicate and that of a singular term can be identical. Certainly, if two expressions are of dif-ferent types, their contents should be of different types also. This I call the 'Heterogeneity Principle'.[14]

The difficulty I have just mentioned points to a general difficulty in the theory of direct reference itself; a difficulty which was discussed by

Kaplan (in reference to Russell's discussion of Frege in 'On Denoting').
Here is Kaplan's statement of the difficulty:

Consider the statement expressed by the sentence, 'The center of mass of the
Solar System is a point'. Call the proposition, 'P'. P has in its subject place a
certain complex, expressed by the definite description. Call the complex, 'Plexy'.
We can describe Plexy as "the complex expressed by 'the center of mass of the
solar system'." Can we produce a directly referential term which designates
Plexy? Leaving aside for the moment the controversial question of whether
'Plexy' is such a term, let us imagine, as Russell believed, that we can directly
refer to Plexy by affixing a kind of *meaning marks* (on the analogy of quotation
marks) to the description itself. Now consider the sentence '^{m}The center of mass
of the solar system^m is a point'. Because the subject of this sentence is directly
referential and refers to Plexy, the proposition the sentence expresses will have as
its subject constituent Plexy itself. A moment's reflection will reveal that this
proposition is simply P again. But this is absurd since the two sentences speak
about radically different objects. (Kaplan 1989a: 496 n. 23)

What generates this difficulty is the very move which enabled us to
regain semantic innocence. By directly referring to the content of a non-
directly referential expression A, we produce a directly referential term B
whose content is identical to that of A, but whose extension is different
(since the extension of B is identical to its content while the extension of
A is not identical to its content). Thus 'Plexy' denotes the content of the
description, which denotes the center of mass of the solar system; despite
this difference in their respective extensions, 'Plexy' and the description
'the center of mass of the solar system' are said to have the same content.
This is unacceptable—if two expressions have the same content, they
must have the same extension. Similarly, the sentence 'Peter likes grass'
has a certain content by virtue of which it denotes the value 'true'. The
'that'-clause 'that Peter likes grass' denotes the content in question; if it is
construed as directly referential, then the content of the 'that'-clause is its
extension, hence the 'that'-clause has the same content as the sentence,
despite the fact that their extension is totally different (the extension of
the sentence is the value 'true', the extension of the 'that'-clause is the
proposition it denotes). Evidently, this is incompatible with the claim
that content determines extension.

   This difficulty shows that the embedded sentence and the 'that'-clause
(construed as a directly referential term) cannot really have the same
content. Since, by assumption, the 'that'-clause refers to the content of
the embedded sentence, we must qualify the alleged identity between the

content of a directly referential term and its extension;[15] hence it is unclear that we can 'regain innocence' in the manner suggested above.

§2.4   Innocence Regained? (2) 'That'-Clauses as Complex Singular Terms

Our problem with semantic innocence stemmed from our decision to treat 'that'-clauses as genuine names, construed as semantically simple expressions whose reference is fixed directly by a semantic rule. That entails that the embedded sentence plays only a pre-semantic role, that of a 'reference fixer', active at the level of character but not at the level of content. It is precisely because the embedded sentence is not semantically active at the level of content that it is unclear that we can respect the principles of Innocence and Iconicity in that framework. Let us therefore tentatively give up the claim that 'that'-clauses are semantically simple, and construe them as semantically complex singular terms.

A 'that'-clause is made up from a sentence and the word 'that'. In order to satisfy the Principle of Innocence the difference between the content of the 'that'-clause and the normal content of the sentence must be kept to a minimum. On the other hand, the word 'that' must contribute something to the content of the 'that'-clause. One simple way of achieving these desiderata is to assign the word 'that' the identity function as intension. Thus, according to Cresswell, the word 'that' "functions as a purely syntactic device which converts a sentence into a nominal but does not essentially change its value" (Cresswell 1973: 166). In Cresswell's framework, the intension of the embedded sentence is a function from world-time pairs to truth-values (a 'proposition', in the possible-worlds sense of the term), and that is also the intension of the 'that'-clause: since the word 'that' contributes the identity function, it preserves the intension of the sentence it operates on. On that view the intension of the 'that'-clause is identical to the intension of the embedded sentence.

The sort of view I have just described is obviously consistent with the principles of Innocence and Iconicity. But it seems to flout the Heterogeneity Principle, for it ascribes the same intension to a sentence and to a singular term (the 'that'-clause). Note, however, that I formulated the Heterogeneity Principle in terms of 'content': according to that principle, if two expressions belong to distinct categories, their contents must be different. Now it is the intension of the 'that'-clause which is identical to the intension of the embedded sentence, in Cresswell's framework; and the intension of an expression is not the same thing as its content. If, like Cresswell himself in later work, we draw a systematic distinction between (structured) content and (unstructured) intension, it will turn out that there *is* a minimal difference between the content of the 'that'-clause and that of the embedded sentence.

Following Carnap (1947) and Lewis (1970) Cresswell (1985) suggests that the content of an expression is a structure composed of the intensions of its parts arranged in a manner corresponding to the syntactic structure of the expression. The content of the embedded sentence is a proposition (in the 'structured' sense) consisting of the intensions of its constituents arranged in a certain way. The content of the 'that'-clause is bound to be different because it contains the intension of the word 'that' (viz. the identity function) over and above the intensions that are also involved in the content of the embedded sentence. In such a framework, then, we don't really flout the Heterogeneity Principle, even though the 'that'-clause and the embedded sentence have the same semantic value (i.e., intension, distinct from content). The intension of the embedded sentence is determined by the intensions of its parts and the way they are put together; that intension is a proposition in the possible-worlds, unstructured sense. The intension of the 'that'-clause will, in turn, be determined by the intensions of *its* constituents, namely the embedded sentence and the word 'that'. Since the intension of 'that' is the identity function, the intension of the 'that'-clause is identical to that of the embedded sentence, but that is fine, since their respective contents are different.

On that view a 'that'-clause is treated as a singular term whose content includes the content of the embedded sentence. The Principle of Iconicity is therefore satisfied. Is the Principle of Innocence also satisfied? Up to a point. It is satisfied to the extent that the embedded sentence's contribution to the content of the 'that'-clause is the proposition it normally expresses. Still, there is a residual difference between the content of the embedded sentence and the content of the 'that'-clause—a difference that is ineliminable as long as one construes 'that'-clauses as terms. That difference seems acceptable, and compatible with the Principle of Innocence, because the 'that'-clause contains an extra word (the word 'that'), corresponding to a syntactic operation on the embedded sentence. Insofar as it posits such a difference, however, the analysis of 'that'-clauses as complex singular terms fares no better, with regard to semantic innocence, than their analysis as directly referential terms whose content is simple.

Which analysis should we prefer? I see advantages on both sides. By treating 'that'-clauses as directly referential expressions and accounting for their iconicity in terms of character, one can stick to the view that genuine singular terms—those expressions that are representable as individual constants in first-order predicate calculus—are semantically simple. On the other hand, since 'that'-clauses are syntactically complex, the claim that they are semantically simple conflicts with what I will refer to below as the 'Grammatical Constraint' (§3.1). According to the Grammatical Constraint, logical form should match grammatical form as closely as possible. In this respect the account in terms of content seems preferable to the account in terms of character.

But there is a third option. If we want to maintain both that genuine singular terms are semantically simple, and that 'that'-clauses lack the relevant simplicity, then we should give up the view that 'that'-clauses are singular terms. Giving up the view in question is not such a large step to take. Cresswell himself says that the word 'that' is a "purely syntactic device." Why not, then, analyse 'John believes (that) grass is green' as consisting of the *sentence* 'grass is green' prefixed with an operator 'John believes (that)', directly operating on that sentence? Why not consider 'that' as a syntactic device which we use when a sentence (*not* a name) fills the argument slot of a higher-level predicate? If we take this line, we shall respect the twin principles of Innocence and Iconicity to the point of justifying the structure:

$\langle \text{BELIEVES}, \langle \text{John}, \langle \text{LIKES}, \langle \text{Peter}, \text{grass} \rangle \rangle \rangle \rangle$

We will do so, however, *without* flouting the Heterogeneity Principle. The complement sentence will contribute the content appropriate to a sentence because it *is* a sentence. Embedding a sentence within 'John believes that ...' does not transform it into a name, on the sort of view now to be considered.

3

Metarepresentational Operators

§3.1   Davidson on Quotation and Indirect Speech

Unsurprisingly, Davidson's concern with semantic innocence leads him to accept the Principle of Iconicity. To be sure, he does not explicitly mention that principle, nor the evidence in its favour; but Davidson's account of indirect speech supports the Principle, as we shall see.

Before discussing Davidson's account of indirect speech (Davidson 1968), it is worth considering his theory of quotation (Davidson 1979). The two theories have much in common, but there is a significant difference between them. Davidson's theory of quotation could easily be extended so as to cover indirect speech as well; the resulting theory would be very similar to the theory of iconic names. But (like the theory of iconic names) it would threaten semantic innocence, and that is something Davidson does not want. Davidson is sensitive to the difference between quotation and indirect speech: linguistic material in quotes is 'inert' and does not do its normal semantical work, whereas the words within a 'that'-clause are active and presumably do their normal semantical work. Hence Davidson strives to preserve semantic innocence in his account of indirect speech. That is why he does not merely extend his account of quotation to indirect speech.

Let us start with Davidson's theory of quotation and see what a theory of 'that'-clauses along similar lines would look like. For Davidson, the quoted material is not really part of the sentence in which the quotation occurs; rather, it must be considered as part of the context. The quoted material is the *demonstratum*, in Kaplan's terminology. In contrast to the quoted material (the demonstratum), the quotation marks themselves *are* part of the sentence; they act as a *demonstrative* referring to the demonstratum given in the context. So the sentence

Galileo said 'The Earth moves'

really is the sentence

Galileo said '. . .'

in a context in which the words 'The Earth moves' are being demonstrated. That sentence is more or less synonymous with

Galileo said that

in which 'that' is a demonstrative referring to the demonstrated linguistic material.[16]

'Galileo said that' is a complete sentence, which expresses a proposition as soon as some demonstratum becomes available as referent for the demonstrative. The situation is exactly the same, from a semantical point of view, when quotation marks are used instead of a demonstrative. Indeed quotation marks *are* a particular sort of demonstrative, in Davidson's framework. The difference between quotation marks and other demonstratives is that the quotation marks are governed by the following convention: the demonstratum is conventionally enclosed *within* the quotation marks. Despite this syntactic incorporation, made easy by the fact that the demonstratum is linguistic, the enclosed material is not part of the sentence in the logical sense because it does no semantical work; it is merely an aspect of the context for the semantically active part of the sentence.

If we were to extend this view to 'that'-clauses, we would have to say that *the embedded sentence is not a constituent of the complex sentence from a logical point of view*. The only constituent is the demonstrative 'that'. On this view, directly inspired by Davidson's theory of quotation, the sentence

Galileo said that the Earth moves

really is the sentence

Galileo said that

in which 'that' is a demonstrative. In this theory the embedded sentence, which follows 'Galileo said that', is treated as having only a *pre-semantic* role, like demonstrations in Kaplan's framework. Indeed it *is* a demonstration (display) of the proposition which the demonstrative 'that' refers to.

Davidson's own account of indirect speech departs as little as possible from his account of quotation while respecting semantic innocence. In order not to violate innocence, Davidson refrains from treating the embedded words as semantically inert and active only at a pre-semantic level. Yet he maintains that the embedded sentence is not part of the belief report: the belief report strictly speaking consists of the sentence 'John believes that', where 'that' is a demonstrative.[17]

Davidson's solution, as is well-known, consists in splitting belief reports in two sentences, each with its own semantic contribution. The embedded sentence S expresses the proposition P; the prefixed sentence 'John believes that' expresses the proposition Q which does not contain P as part, but refers to P (via the demonstrative 'that') and says that John believes it.[18]

Davidson's theory straightforwardly accounts for the epistemological facts summarized in schema (I): if the sentence 'John believes that Peter likes grass' is double and expresses two propositions, viz. P (the proposition that Peter likes grass) and Q (the proposition that John believes that), then one cannot entertain the double content of the belief sentence without entertaining the proposition P which is part of that double content. We see that Davidson's theory commits him to accepting the Principle of Iconicity: the total content expressed by 'John believes that S' incorporates the content expressed by S. The Principle of Extensionality is also preserved, on Davidson's account: There no longer are intensional sentences, that is, complex sentences whose truth-value is changed if we replace a constituent sentence by another one with the same truth-value. In Davidson's account, failures of extensionality are merely apparent: thanks to the 'paratactic' analysis, the sentence whose truth-value is affected by the replacement of the embedded sentence is *not* the very sentence in which the replacement occurs. Instead of a complex sentence *containing* another one, we have two sentences, the first of which refers to the content expressed by the second. When the second sentence is replaced by a third one with the same truth-value as the second but a different content, the reference of the demonstrative in the first sentence (hence the truth-value of the latter) is changed. But no violation of Extensionality is thereby achieved. Extensionality is violated only if the truth-value of a sentence is changed by replacing a constituent *of that sentence* by another one with the same extension.

Despite all its merits, however, Davidson's theory is unacceptable. It blatantly violates a methodological constraint which philosophers of language in this century have too often ignored. Since the early days of 'ideal language philosophy', with a few exceptions (like Montague), logically-minded philosophers have been happy to posit 'logical forms' at variance with the superficial 'grammatical forms' of the sentences they were dealing with. This policy was justified by a dubious ideology concerning the 'defects' of natural language—an ideology which so-called 'ordinary language philosophers' were quite right to criticize. Many philosophers still think the policy can be justified even though the ideology has been abandoned. However, it is the opposite policy which is justified—the policy embodied in what Jackendoff (1983: 13) calls the 'Grammatical Constraint':

Grammatical Constraint
One should prefer a semantic theory that explains otherwise arbitrary generalizations about the syntax and the lexicon.

"The Grammatical Constraint," Jackendoff says, "must be imposed on semantic theory for semantics to be an empirically interesting enterprise" (Jackendoff 1983: 15).[19] In contrast to other cognitive semanticists such as Langacker (1987), Jackendoff does not go as far as to say that *every* aspect of syntax should be explained in semantic terms. "The point of the Grammatical Constraint is only to attempt to minimize the differences of syntactic and semantic structure, not to expect to eliminate them altogether" (Jackendoff 1983: 14). Practically, however, whether one interprets the Grammatical Constraint weakly or strongly does not make a big difference. We are always supposed to *try* to eliminate discrepancies between syntactic and semantic structure.

I find Jackendoff's argument in favour of the Grammatical Constraint rather convincing. In particular, I agree that

under the reasonable hypothesis that language serves the purpose of transmitting information, it would be perverse not to take as a working assumption that language is a relatively efficient and accurate encoding of the information it conveys. To give up this assumption is to refuse to look for systematicity in the relationship between syntax and semantics. A theory's deviations from efficient encoding must be rigorously justified, for what appears to be an irregular relationship between syntax and semantics may turn out merely to be a bad theory of one or the other. (Jackendoff 1983: 14)

In line with the Grammatical Constraint, we can hardly accept Davidson's suggestion that 'John believes that *S*' consists of two sentences, because it is clear, on grammatical grounds, that that is not the case. The sentence *S is* contained in the sentence 'John believes that *S*': someone who pretends otherwise is someone who does not accept the Grammatical Constraint. In contrast, there is grammatical evidence that a sentence within quotation marks is not fully integrated to the sentence containing the quotation, where it stands in the manner of a *corps étranger*. (More on this in part IV.)

§3.2   Prior's Adverbial Analysis

The difficulty we are facing is this. We want to say (i) that 'believes' in 'John believes that Peter likes grass' expresses a relation between John and what he believes; and (ii) that what John believes is actually expressed (displayed) by the embedded sentence 'Peter likes grass'. Because of (i), we think that 'believes' is a two-place predicate, that is, an expression which makes a sentence out of two terms. On this construal what follows 'believes' must be a term, not a sentence; hence we view 'that' as converting the embedded sentence into a term. Because of (ii), however, we think the embedded sentence must remain a sentence; it must *not* be converted into a term. The two requirements are reconciled if, like Davidson, we consider that there are two sentences instead of one: the first sentence ('John believes that') expresses the relation and consists of a two-place predicate flanked by two terms; the second sentence ('Peter likes grass') expresses a proposition, viz. that which the first sentence refers to. But if, out of respect for the Grammatical Constraint, we do not take this liberty, what can we say? Are we not forced to sacrifice the second requirement to the first one?

We are not. The difficulty stems from the fact that a predicate, in the logical sense, demands terms to fill its argument places. Since a sentence is not a term, there are *two* options for the analysis of belief reports. Either we say that the embedded sentence is converted into a term which fills the second argument place of the predicate 'believes' (standard analysis); or we say that the embedded sentence is (and remains) a bona fide sentence, and deny that the verb really corresponds to a (first-level) predicate with two argument places. The latter option, suggested by Quine, has been pursued by Arthur Prior.

To make sense of the Quine-Prior suggestion, we must introduce the notion of a functor.[20] A functor makes a sentence out of one or several expressions which can be either terms *or* sentences. In '*Rab*', '*R*' makes a sentence out of two terms, '*a*' and '*b*'; in '&*pq*' (a Polish-like notation for '*p* & *q*'), '&' makes a sentence out of two sentences '*p*' and '*q*'. Both the predicate '*R*' and the connective '&' are functors. There is no reason why there should not exist functors of a mixed variety ('connecticates'), that is, functors making a sentence out of a term and a sentence. 'Believes that' is such a functor, according to Prior: it makes a sentence out of a term (e.g., 'Paul') and a sentence (e.g., 'Grass is green'). When a term is provided, the connecticate becomes a monadic propositional operator 'Paul believes that ...', which makes a sentence out of a sentence. 'Paul believes that' thus belongs to the same logical category as other sentence-forming operators like 'it is not the case that' or 'it is necessary that'.

In this framework we can maintain that the verb is a 'two-place predicate' in the *grammatical* sense, that is, a verb which comes with two 'argument roles' (one of the roles being filled by a sentential argument). Yet it does not function as a predicate in the standard logical sense, but as a connecticate, when the verb takes a sentence as second argument.[21] In such contexts the verb in combination with the first argument contributes an operator, much like a sentential adverb would. Thus 'John believes that grass is green' is more or less equivalent to 'According to John, grass is green'.[22]

In the case of 'believe', the second argument place can be filled by a noun-phrase, as in (1) below, or by a sentence, as in (2). This suggests that in (2) the embedded sentence itself has the status of a noun-phrase. Indeed (2) is only a stylistic variant of (3), which contains a 'that'-clause; and there is but a short step from (3) to (4), in which it can hardly be doubted that the 'that'-clause has the status of a noun-phrase. Note that the relation of (2) to (4) is the same as the relation of (1) to (5):

(1)   John believes that story.

(2)   John believes Peter will come.

(3)   John believes that Peter will come.

(4)   That Peter will come is something which John believes.

(5)   That story is something which John believes.

All this may be taken to show that the standard, relational analysis is correct, and that Prior's proposal is hopeless. But this conclusion is too hasty. To see why, let us consider other attitude verbs than 'believe'.

There are cases in which the second argument place can be filled *only* by a sentence. In such cases we are intuitively much less tempted to treat the sentence as a singular term, and the verb as expressing a relation. Consider 'complain', for example. As Rundle points out,

> You can complain about something or object to something, but you can neither complain nor object something. So, although you can complain or object that *P*, it would seem wrong to regard 'that *P*' as filling the role of object. (Rundle 1979: 283)

Thus (7) is fine, but neither (6) nor (8) is acceptable:

(6)   *John complains that story.

(7)   John complains that Peter will come.

(8)   *That Peter will come is something which John complains.

Even when the verb at issue *can* take a straightforward term as direct object, Rundle points out, there often is no temptation to treat the 'that'-clause as actually filling the object role. Thus in (9),

(9)   John explained that he had been delayed

the proposition that John had been delayed, allegedly denoted by the 'that'-clause, is not *what* John explained. 'That he had been delayed' is not the thing which John explained; rather, it is the explanation itself. (What John explained was the fact that he was late.) The relation, in (9), between the verb and the statement that John had been delayed is similar to what we find either in direct speech or in 'free indirect speech':

(10)   John explained: 'I have been delayed'.

(11)   John explained: he had been delayed.

In neither case should we say that the quoted words provide the direct object of the verb. Contrast (10) with (12):

(12)   John explained 'I have been delayed' by providing a synonym.

In (10) and (11) the verb (together with its first argument) has a prefatory character, similar to that of a parenthetical clause. Likewise, 'John explained that the train had been delayed' is more or less equivalent to 'The train had been delayed, John explained', or to 'According to John's explanation, the train had been delayed'. It is *not* equivalent to 'John explained the proposition that the train had been delayed'.

Similar observations are made by Friederike Moltmann in a couple of recent papers. As she points out,

Many attitude verbs do take referential NPs of the sort *the proposition that S*, but then obtain a different reading, the reading they have when taking ordinary referential NPs:

a. John imagined that he will win.
b. John imagined the proposition that he will win.
c. John imagined Mary.

a. John expects that he will win.
b. John expects the proposition that he will win.
c. John expects Mary.

a. John heard that Mary closed the door.
b. John heard the fact/the proposition that Mary closed the door.
c. John heard Mary.

An attitude verb taking a referential complement, as in the b- or c-examples above, systematically displays a different reading from the one it has when it takes a clausal complement. (Moltmann 1998 §1)

Moltmann concludes that there is "a fundamental distinction between the semantic value of *that*-clauses and *the proposition that S*: The semantic value of a *that*-clause does not act as an object recognized as such by an agent standing in an attitudinal relation to it; rather it acts only as an 'unreflected' content.... It is a semantic value merely expressed, not referred to by the *that*-clause." (Moltmann 1997 §2.1.)

The upshot of these considerations is that a case can be made for a non-relational analysis of attitude sentences and other metarepresentations. We are not forced to parse the complex sentence 'John believes that grass is green' as

John BELIEVES that-grass-is-green.

Instead of construing 'believes' as a two-place predicate expressing a relation between John and the proposition that grass is green, we can construe it as the connecticate 'believes-that':

John BELIEVES THAT grass is green.

On this view, urged by Arthur Prior, 'John believes that' is a unary sentential operator, on a par with the operators used in modal logic: 'it is possible that', 'it is necessary that', etc. (See Hintikka 1962 for a similar treatment.)

§3.3   Higher-Level Predication

The adverbial analysis raises an obvious objection. It does not account for the intuition that 'believes' in 'John believes that grass is green' expresses a relation between John and what he believes. That intuition is supported by the validity of inferences like (13).

(13)   John believes that grass is green.
       Everything John believes is true.
       Therefore, it is true that grass is green.

As we have seen, such inferences can easily be accounted for on the assumption that 'that'-clauses are terms, and verbs like 'say' or 'believe' two-place predicates (§1.2). How will those inferences be accounted for if we give up that assumption?

   To account for (13) we may follow Ramsey and analyse the major premise as 'For all p, if John believes that p, then it is true that p' (Ramsey 1990: 39). That is what Prior does. In support of that move, let us consider another valid inference:

(14a)   Australian deconstructionists are rare.
        Everything rare is precious.
        Therefore, Australian deconstructionists are precious.

There are reasons to believe that 'rare' is not a first-level predicate. If it were, we could reason as follows:

(14b)   Australian deconstructionists are rare.
          John is an Australian deconstructionist.
          Therefore, John is rare.

But this is as nonsensical as the next:

(14c)   Australian deconstructionists are very few/less than fifty.
          John is an Australian deconstructionist.
          Therefore, John is very few/less than fifty.[23]

Following Frege, let us construe '... are rare' and '... are less than fifty' as *second-level* predicates. It is the 'concept' of an Australian deconstructionist which is said to be rarely instantiated, or instantiated by less than fifty persons. A more obvious example of higher-level talk is

(15)   John is something which I am not, namely Australian

which should be analysed as 'For some F, John is F and I am not F'.

If we make room for such higher-level quantification and predication, then (13) raises no problem for the view that 'John believes that' is a sentential operator. If we can quantify predicates, then surely we can quantify sentences.[24] Inference (13) will thus be construed as instantiating the following pattern:

$\delta\sigma$

For every p, if δp then $\delta' p$

Therefore, $\delta'\sigma$

Here 'δ' and 'δ'' respectively stand for two sentential operators (e.g., 'John believes that' and 'It is true that') and 'σ' for a sentence (e.g., 'grass is green'), while 'p' is a sentential variable. This entails, of course, that we reject Quine's claim that quantification is fundamentally 'objectual' and involves existential commitments. When we quantify in predicate or sentence position, we don't quantify objectually.[25] As Prior stressed in many places, a quantified sentence like (15) commits us to no more than the corresponding substitution instance: 'John is Australian but I am not'. If the latter does not carry ontological commitment to properties, neither does the former.

To say that the quantification or predication at issue is not first-level quantification or predication is to say (inter alia) that the properties or propositions talked about are not *objectified*. The gist of the higher-level approach advocated by Frege is this: There are two different ways in which we can talk about concepts. We can reify the concept, construe it as an object and engage in first-level talk about it. That, according to Frege, is what we do when we say things like 'The concept of horse is multiply instantiated' since 'the concept of horse' is (for Frege) a singular term. But we can also engage in higher-level talk about concepts, in which case the concept talked about is 'expressed' rather than 'referred to'. In 'Australian deconstructionists are less than fifty' the concept of an Australian deconstructionist is expressed, it is not referred to.

If we accept Frege's distinction between the two ways of talking about concepts, we can extend it and account for iconicity by construing *oratio obliqua* as another variety of higher-level talk: higher-level talk about propositions (rather than about concepts). On this view propositions are not reified when we use the '*x Vs that p*' construction. Thus we capture the distinction between 'John stated Leibniz's Law' and 'John stated that identical objects have all their properties in common'.

§3.4 To Reify or Not to Reify

The approach I have described raises familiar objections which must be briefly discussed. These objections purport to show that the standard approach is much preferable.

The standard approach is what Bealer (1982) refers to as the "first-order approach," as opposed to the "higher-order approach" advocated in the previous section. On the first-order approach, whenever we quantify or make something (possibly a property or a proposition) the subject of discourse, we *reify* it: we present it as a 'thing', or as 'something'. Thus if I say: 'The concept of Australian deconstructionist is rarely instantiated', I convert the concept in question (expressed by the predicate 'Australian deconstructionist') into an object. Similarly if I say: 'John is something which I am not', I talk about a 'thing', namely that property which John instantiates and which I don't. In the same way, when I say 'That grass is green is something which John believes' I construe the content of his belief as a 'thing'. This is OK since, as is well-known, *everything* is a thing. "Any property or relation can simply be assigned as the value of a first-order variable" (Bealer 1982: 88). If we don't want to count something as a thing, then we must not make it the subject of discourse, nor make it the value of a variable, as we do when we quantify.

A preliminary argument in favour of the first-order approach derives from the very use of phrases like 'something' and 'everything' in alleged higher-order quantification ('There is *something* which John is and which I am not'). This is supposed to show that we are actually talking about 'things', as in ordinary first-order discourse. But the fact that we use a phrase like 'something' in no way shows that the quantification must be understood as first-order. 'Something' may well be construed as idiomatic and neutral. What is more relevant is the linguistic category to which the substituends belong: thus in 'John is something which I am not' the quantification is best seen as second-order because the substituends must be predicates (e.g., adjectives such as 'Australian'). No reification takes place here.[26]

A more pressing objection, voiced by Bealer, relates to "the traditional linguistic distinction between subject and predicate, between noun and verb" (Bealer 1982: 85)—a distinction which is evident in the surface syntax of natural language. If we choose the first-order approach, Bealer suggests, we capture that central distinction. Linguistic predicates (e.g., 'runs') cannot be subjects. If we want to put a predicate in subject position, we have to nominalize it. By thus nominalizing a predicate we make the concept it expresses into an object. That is the gist of the first-order approach. We thereby achieve a strict correspondence between syntax and semantics. If something is 'subject' from the syntactic point of view, its semantical correlate is an object (a thing). Similarly for propositions: 'that'-clauses are not sentences, they are *nominalized* sentences. Through nominalization we refer to abstract objects—objects which, like any others, can be the values of individual variables. On the higher-order approach, in contrast, the grammatical distinction between subjects and predicates is ignored. Linguistic predicates can be subjects. In 'This apple is red, red is a colour, therefore this apple is coloured', the predicate 'red' which occurs in the first premise is said to be subject in the second. In both cases it is said to contribute a concept rather than an object.

I think that objection can be disposed of. It is not true that the distinction between subject and predicate is flouted, on the higher-order approach. Rather, we have two distinctions instead of one. The first distinction is relative rather than absolute: it is the functional distinction between what is talked about and what is said about it. The expression corresponding to what is talked about is the 'subject', the expression corresponding to what is said about it is the 'predicate' (in the *functional* sense). That distinction is relative because the same thing which is predicate in one statement can be subject in another, higher-level statement. There is *also* an absolute distinction between two categories of expression-type: singular terms and predicates. 'Red' is a predicate in that sense. According to the higher-order approach, an expression which belongs to the category of predicates can be subject in the *functional* sense. But neither distinction is lost; nor has the connection between category and function been severed. To be sure, it is no longer possible to provide a direct functional characterization of the category 'predicate', since predicates can function as subjects. But singular terms can be functionally characterized as those expressions which can *only* be subjects; hence the contrast between singular terms and predicates can still be drawn in functional terms.

Still, Bealer's observation that a verb like 'runs' cannot be subject is correct. Bealer concludes that linguistic predicates cannot be subjects. But what is meant by 'linguistic predicate' here? If 'runs' is a prototypical example of linguistic predicate, then a linguistic predicate fulfils two functions (Strawson 1974a, 1974b). On the one hand it specifies or introduces a property, here the property of running, which the subject is said to exemplify. On the other hand, it provides "the symbolism of predicative or propositional coupling" (Strawson 1974b: 76). In the case of a predicate like 'runs', it is the finite ending of the verb that provides that symbolism; in the case of a predicate like 'is Australian', it is the copula. Wiggins once proposed that distinction between the two functions as a "running repair" to Frege's theory of predication, a repair intended to provide a way out of Frege's Paradox:

Let us hold onto the thought that second level quantification is over what it seems to be over, viz. entities like *man, horse, admirer of Hegel, wise, run, walk, sit, work, sleep*. Such entities—let us call them concepts—are not objects, and they are neither saturated nor unsaturated. They are simply the references of grammatical predicates. But let us also take the copula and the finite endings of verbs seriously. What the copula does on this alternative view is to *combine* with a concept-word or predicate to produce an unsaturated expression that will in its turn combine in the fashion Frege himself describes with a saturated expression to produce a complete sentence. (Wiggins 1984: 133)

In this framework the word 'predicate' is ambiguous. It can mean the concept-word, be it a noun, an adjective, or a verb-stem, which serves only the first of the two functions. Or it can mean the "properly unsaturated predicative phrase" (Wiggins 1984: 135) which fulfils the two functions and which consists of a concept-word together with the copula. Now it is only predicates in the first sense which can be subjects; for the symbolism of propositional combination can only go with the expression which serves as predicate in the functional sense, hence it cannot go with the expression which serves as subject. (For an explanation, see Strawson 1974a: 30–1.) So there is a sense in which it is correct to say, as Bealer does, that linguistic predicates cannot be subjects. But there is also a sense (*another* sense) in which it is correct to say, with the higher-order theorist, that linguistic predicates *can* be subjects.

Of course, Bealer will reply that a concept-word, insofar as it functions as subject in a sentence, serves to pick out a *thing*. Among the things we can thus talk about are the properties of being a man, an admirer of Hegel, etc. Strawson seems to agree with this. According to him, predicates in the first sense stand for properties much as singular terms stand for individuals: that is why we can quantify in predicate position as well as in singular term position (Strawson 1974b). Quantification into predicate position thus turns out to be objectual in Quine's sense, thanks to the distinction between the two functions (Strawson 1997: 5). At this point the difference between Bealer's view and Strawson's no longer sounds very substantial, even though Strawson accepts, while Bealer rejects, quantification into predicate position.

Still there is one central issue that should not be forgotten. The point of the higher-order approach as I understand it is the idea that it is the same concept-word 'red' which serves as predicate in 'This apple is red' and as subject in 'Red is a colour' (or, less controversially perhaps, in 'Red is what I thought the Japanese flag was'). *No conversion of a general term into a singular term takes place.*[27] The general term remains a general term. In other words, there can be subjectification without reification.

Of course, there are cases in which reification does take place. It is not part of the higher-order approach as I understand it that we never talk about properties by construing them as objects. For Frege, as I pointed out above, there are two ways in which we can (attempt to) talk about a concept: we can reify it or not. Similarly, I claim, there are two ways of talking (or thinking) about propositions. In *oratio obliqua*, we talk about propositions without reifying them.[28]

§3.5 Substitutivity

From now on I will assume that metarepresentations consist of two components: a sentential operator ('according to John', 'John believes that') and a sentence ('Peter likes grass').

The first thing to note, in connection with that analysis, is that the operators at issue—metarepresentational operators, as I will call them—are not extensional. The Principle of Extensionality is violated: even though the sentence 'John believes that *S*' (under the analysis in question) contains the sentence *S* as a constituent, it is not possible to replace *S* by an equivalent sentence without possibly affecting the truth-value of the complex sentence. This is OK for, as Prior says,

there is no more reason for accepting [the Principle of Extensionality] as true than there is for believing that the earth is flat, and it is in one way a rather similar belief. What we say by our sentences (or better, how we say things are) may vary in innumerable other 'dimensions' than that of truth-value; for any given *p*, it may not only be or not be the case that *p*, but may also be believed by Paul or by Elmer or by everybody or by nobody that *p*, it may be possible or impossible or necessary that *p*, it may be desirable or undesirable or a matter of indifference whether *p*, and so on, and for a given *f*, whether it is or is not the case that *f(p)* may depend solely on whether it is or is not the case that *p*, but it may on the contrary depend on a variety of these other factors in the situation. . . . The so-called law of extensionality was an interesting early effort at generalisation in a scientific logic, and no doubt does hold within the first area to be thoroughly examined—the functions required in the foundations of mathematics —but in no other science that I've heard of do the practitioners cling to the first guesses of their teachers, in the face of the most obvious counter-examples, with the fervour of religious devotees. (Prior 1963: 150–1)

According to Tom Baldwin, Prior's rejection of the Principle of Extensionality merely shows that the significance of that principle was not apparent to him (Baldwin 1982: 256–257). The only thing I can say is that it is not apparent to me either. Like Prior, I think the Principle of Extensionality is false. Hence I reject the GPC:

Generalized Principle of Compositionality (GPC)

The semantic value of an expression at all levels is a function of the semantic values of its parts; that is:

(a) the character of an expression is a function of the characters of its parts,

(b) the content of an expression is a function of the contents of its parts,

(c) the extension of an expression is a function of the extensions of its parts (= GPE).

What I reject is the third part of the GPC, viz. the GPE ('Generalized Principle of Extensionality'). The extension of an expression is *not* in general a function of the extensions of its parts. The reason why that is so is that the extension of an expression primarily depends on its *content* (and the way the world is); now the content of an expression depends on more than merely the extensions of its parts: it depends on their contents. Thus if, in a complex expression, you replace a constituent by another one with the same extension but a different content, you change the content of the complex expression, hence, possibly, its extension. (When we say that the two constituents have the same extension, we mean that they have the same extension *in the current circumstance*. But operators like 'It will be the case that', 'It might have been the case that' or 'John believes that' arguably indicate that the sentence in their scope must be evaluated with respect to a circumstance *distinct from* the current circumstance in which the complex sentence itself is evaluated. It is therefore not surprising that we cannot always substitute an expression for another one in the embedded sentence even though they have the same extension in the *current* circumstance. Substitutability will be guaranteed only if the two expressions have the same extension in *every* possible circumstance of evaluation, that is, if they have the same content.)

Rejecting the GPE leaves us with a more restricted principle of compositionality:

Restricted Principle of Compositionality (RPC)

(a) The character of an expression is a function of the characters of its parts.

(b) The content of an expression is a function of the contents of its parts.

(c) The extension of an expression is *not* a function of the extensions of its parts.

Contrary to the GPC, the RPC does not entail that expressions with the same extension can be substituted *salva veritate*. But it suggests that expressions with the same *content* can be substituted *salva veritate*. This entails various intensional replacement principles, including the Principle of Substitutivity of Singular Terms: that two directly referential terms with the same extension can be substituted *salva veritate* (since two directly referential terms with the same extension have the same content).

Intensional replacement principles

• A genuine singular term *t* (e.g., a name or an indexical) can be replaced *salva veritate* by some other term *t′* provided *t* and *t′* have the same extension (hence the same content).

• A predicative expression *F* can be replaced *salva veritate* by another predicative expression *G* if *F* and *G* express the same concept.

• A sentence *S* can be replaced *salva veritate* by a sentence *S′* in any complex sentence in which *S* occurs if *S* and *S′* express the same proposition.

The problem is that those replacement principles do not seem to be unrestrictedly valid. Like the extensional replacement principles, they have numerous counterexamples. Intensional replacement principles work well for modal sentences such as 'It is necessary that *S*', but apparently they do not work for belief sentences. For even *synonymous* expressions—expressions which certainly have the same content—cannot be substituted *salva veritate* in belief sentences. John can believe that Paul is an ophtalmologist without believing that Paul is an eye-doctor. If that is right, then metarepresentational operators like 'John believes that' are not merely 'intensional'; they are *hyperintensional* in that replacing an expression by another one with the same content may change the truth-value of the sentence in which the change occurs (Cresswell 1975, Bigelow 1978).

Failures of extensionality led us to give up the GPC in favour of the RPC. Should failures of intensional replacement lead us to give up the RPC as well? Are there hyperintensional operators, which violate the RPC, much as there are intensional operators which violate the GPC? I do not think so. If two sentences S and S' have the same content, they express the same proposition. Now if the propositions they respectively express are the same, whatever is true of one proposition must be true of the other. Hence if John believes that S, and the proposition that S is the same as the proposition that S', it must be true that John believes that S'. This seems to show that, if two sentences have the same content, they *must* be substitutable even under the 'John believes that' operator.[29]

Now consider the alleged counterexample to the RPC:

(a)   John believes that Paul is an ophtalmologist.

(b)   'Ophtalmologist' has the same content as 'eye-doctor'.

(c)   John believes that Paul is an eye-doctor.

By virtue of (b), 'Paul is an ophtalmologist' ($= S$) and 'Paul is an eye-doctor' ($= S'$) have the same content and express the same proposition σ. Both (a) and (c) apparently consist of that proposition in the scope of the operator δ corresponding to the phrase 'John believes that'; hence it seems that (a) and (c) must express the same proposition $\delta\sigma$. How then could (a) and (c) differ in truth-value? How, without giving up the RPC, can we account for our clear intuitions that (a) can be true and (c) false?

One way of accounting for our intuitions consists in acknowledging the *context-sensitivity* of the phrase 'John believes that'. By substituting 'Paul is an eye-doctor' for 'Paul is an ophtalmologist', you change the context in which the phrase 'John believes that' is tokened, and that can affect the semantic value of that phrase, if it is context-sensitive. Thus we can imagine that the same phrase 'John believes that' corresponds to distinct (though related) operators depending on the context. In (a) 'John believes that' corresponds to some operator δ. The inference goes through if we *fix* that operator: if δp, and Ipq (the proposition that p is identical to the proposition that q), then δq. But what we have in (c) is not quite the operator δ, but the *phrase* 'John believes that'. That phrase, in (a), corresponds to the operator δ, but if it is context-sensitive it may well change its content in (c) and correspond in that context to a distinct operator δ', in such a way that the inference no longer goes through: from the fact that δp, and the fact that the proposition that p is identical to the proposition that q, it does not follow that $\delta'q$. All that follows is the proposition that δq (but that proposition is arguably *not* what (c) expresses).

On this analysis when a sentence S cannot be replaced *salva veritate* by a sentence S' with the same content within the complex sentence dS, the culprit is the prefix d, whose content changes from context to context. The substitution itself changes the context and causes the shift in semantic value of the prefix. Because of the possible context-sensitivity of the prefix d, all the intensional replacement principles, including the Principle of Substitutivity, are false, strictly speaking. But the RPC (and, of course, the laws of identity) remain true. On this account the intensional replacement principles come out true *only if* the semantic values (contents) of all expressions in the sentence are 'fixed' and prevented from shifting as a result of the replacement itself. Under such artificial conditions, the counterexamples vanish.

To illustrate that point, consider Quine's well-known counterexample to the Principle of Substitutivity of Singular Terms:

Giorgione was so-called because of his size.

'Giorgione' and 'Barbarelli', being co-extensive proper names, presumably have the same content; yet 'Barbarelli' cannot be substituted for 'Giorgione' *salva veritate*. The reason for that failure is that the replacement would change the context for the adverb 'so', whose semantic value is context-sensitive. But if we fix the reference (hence the content) of the adverb 'so', then, evidently, the Principle of Substitutivity unproblematically applies. If Giorgione was so-called, that is, called 'Giorgione', because of his size, and Giorgione = Barbarelli, then, of course, Barbarelli was 'so' called (in the now *fixed* sense: 'called "Giorgione"') because of his size. Similarly, there is no reason to assume that the function expressed by 'John believes that' will be the same irrespective of the sentence which fills the blank after 'that'; but if we artificially fix the function expressed by the prefix, then, evidently, it will be possible to replace the embedded sentence by any other sentence expressing the same proposition, without affecting the truth-value of the complex sentence dS. If we fix the value of d, the complex sentence will express the same proposition δp before and after the replacement, instead of expressing δp before and $\delta' p$ after the replacement.

My aim in this section was not to urge a particular explanation of failures of substitutivity in belief contexts. I merely wanted to show that, unless it is properly qualified,[30] the Principle of Substitutivity is false, so that its failures should cause us no more worry than the failures of the Principle of Extensionality.

II

Simulation 1: Circumstance-Shifting

4

Simulation and Beyond

§4.1 Two Approaches

Iconicity is the property in virtue of which metarepresentations contain the representation they are about (the 'object-representation'), both syntactically and semantically. Among the theories which capture that property of metarepresentations, we can distinguish two groups. Theories of the first group maintain that there is a difference between the content of the metarepresentation and the content of the object-representation; the latter is a proper part of the former. According to theories of the second group, there is no such difference: the metarepresentation has the same content as the object-representation and differs from it only in some other dimension.

Modal theories of metarepresentations belong in the first group. A modal theory analyses a metarepresentation dS as consisting of the object-representation S and a circumstance-shifting prefix d. While S is true in a circumstance c iff a certain condition p obtains, dS is true in a circumstance c iff condition p obtains in a different circumstance c', where c' bears a certain relation R to c. An example of modal representation is: 'It will be the case that grass is green'. It consists of 'grass is green' and a circumstance-shifting prefix 'it will be the case that'. While 'grass is green' is true in a circumstance c iff grass is green in c, 'It will be the case that grass is green' is true in c iff grass is green in a distinct circumstance c' such that c' is later than c. Similarly, the metarepresentation 'John believes that grass is green' is true in c iff grass is green in all possible circumstances c' compatible with what John believes in c. In that framework there is a clear difference between the truth-conditional content of S and that of dS.

Because of that difference between the content of S and the content of dS, it is in general possible to assert the complex proposition that dS (e.g., the proposition that John believes that grass is green) without asserting the component proposition that S (e.g., the proposition that grass is green). In general, the content of a sentence is not asserted unless that sentence occurs in isolation. When it occurs only as a component of a longer sentence, it is the proposition expressed by the complex sentence, not that expressed by the component sentence, which is asserted.

I think the modal approach to metarepresentations is essentially correct. Before actually putting forward a theory along these lines, however, we must consider a theory belonging to the second group: the simulation theory. The basic notion it uses, that of simulation, will turn out to be an essential ingredient of the account to be put forward later.

For theories of the second group, the reason why the proposition that S is not asserted when a metarepresentation dS is issued (i.e., uttered or entertained) is not that S is embedded instead of occurring in isolation. There are well-known cases in which a proposition is not asserted even though the sentence which expresses it is uttered in isolation: that happens whenever the speaker is not seriously attempting to characterize the actual world, but merely evoking some imaginary world. For example, suppose that, misled by unreliable weather reports, we're caught in the middle of a storm and I say, 'The weather is indeed lovely'. My utterance is clearly ironic: I do not *assert* that the weather is lovely—I do not characterize the world as it is but, rather, the world as the weather reports misleadingly depicted it. Irony, here as elsewhere, involves a form of pretense or mimicry.[1] Now the sentence in this example is uttered in isolation, but we can imagine that a certain prefix serves to indicate that the sentence which follows is not really asserted. A good example of that sort of thing is provided by children's games of make-believe. In such a game my son says to my daughter:

On serait un roi et une reine.

This utterance expresses the proposition that my children are King and Queen respectively. That proposition is not asserted because the world of reference is not the actual world, but some imaginary world evoked by the game. The function of the conditional mood in French is precisely to shift the world from the actual world to some imaginary world.[2] Beside the conditional mood (or the 'imparfait', a tense which serves the same function in children's games) there are specific adverbials, such as 'pour de faux', which signal that the utterance is not a serious assertion purporting to characterize the actual world, but a pretend assertion (or question, or request) purporting to characterize the imaginary world of the game. In this type of case—when an adverbial such as 'pour de faux' is used—the proposition expressed by the utterance dS is arguably the very proposition expressed by S; the only function of the prefix is to indicate that the proposition in question is not asserted—that the speaker is merely pretending. So we have a complex sentence dS, but it's not because S is not 'uttered in isolation' that it's not asserted; rather, it's because the sentence is not (seriously) asserted that it's been prefixed with 'pour de faux', to make clear what the speaker is doing.

The simulation theory is the view that metarepresentational prefixes such as 'John believes that' have such a pragmatic function: they indicate that the speaker is not characterizing the actual world, but, say, John's 'belief world', much as the ironist, in our earlier example, playfully (simulatively) describes the world as it would have been had the meteorological predictions been correct. The point of the ironist is to show how much the world thus described differs from the actual world. The point of the belief ascriber is, simply, to show how the world is according to the ascribee. In both cases, according to the theory, the utterance is not a genuine assertion but an instance of pretend assertion. Such a theory clearly belongs to the second group: for the only contribution of the prefix is pragmatic; there is no difference between the content of S and the content of dS—dS expresses the proposition that S while signalling that that proposition is not seriously asserted.

§4.2   The Simulation Theory

The notion of a prefix 'indicating' or 'signalling' the force of an utterance makes sense only with respect to language or communication. But it's an important fact about *thoughts* that we can entertain thoughts either assertively or not. Assertive thoughts are thoughts which we entertain concerning the actual world. But we can also entertain thoughts concerning imaginary worlds. In such a case the representation of a state of affairs is 'de-coupled' from the actual world.[3] This de-coupling is effected through mental simulation.

Mental simulation is the activity we engage in when we imagine some world distinct from the actual world—when we pretend that the world is different from what it actually is (Kahneman and Tversky 1982). In the example of pretend play I gave above (my son saying to my daughter, 'On serait un roi et une reine') the representation that my children are King and Queen respectively is non-assertively entertained, in the sense that the world of reference is not the actual world, but the imaginary world of the game. There is no essential difference between children's pretend play, thus described, and the fictional activity of adults. When an author (or story-teller) says 'Once upon a time, there was a King and a Queen', she deploys an imaginary world, in exactly the same way as my children in their game of make-believe. The pretense in those examples is communicational, but it need not be. What is involved is an act of *mental* simulation: we pretend that the world is different from what it actually is, as we do when we imagine a counterfactual possibility.

According to the simulation theory, when we say or think that John believes that S (or that, according to John, S), we simulate John's mental state and assert that S within the simulation. As Quine says, "we project ourselves into what … we imagine the [ascribee]'s state of mind to [be], and then we say what, in our language, is natural and relevant for us in the state thus feigned" (Quine 1960: 218). Thus the operator in 'John believes that S' really is a 'pretense' operator.

In support of the simulation theory, consider propositions (1) and (2):[4]

(1)   Peter believes that John's phone number is 325-248.

(2)   Peter believes that John has the same phone number as Mary.

From (1) and (2) we have no difficulty inferring (3).

(3)   Peter believes that Mary's phone number is 325-248.

How does the inference proceed? The simulation theory offers a straightforward answer to that question. If to think that John believes that *S* is to think that *S* within a certain pretense, then the subject who is given (1) and (2) as premises holds the following under the pretense in question.

(1*)   John's phone number is 325-248.

(2*)   John has the same phone number as Mary.

The subject is therefore in a position to infer that:

(3*)   Mary's phone number is 325-248.

To be sure, this is inferred 'under the pretense', hence the subject holds (3*) only under the pretense also. But to hold (3*) under the pretense in question *is* to hold (3), according to the simulation theory. The transition from (1) and (2) to (3) is therefore explained.

The simulation theory as I have described it is fairly close to (radical versions of) what is described under that name in the philosophy of mind literature. Thus Gordon says that "to attribute a belief to another person is to make an assertion, to state something as a fact, *within the context of practical simulation*" (Gordon 1986: 168).[5] A merit of that theory is that it is as 'innocent' as a theory of metarepresentations can be. Iconicity is a built-in feature of the simulation theory: if to metarepresent is to simulate the object-representation, then the metarepresentation can only resemble the object-representation.

I think that iconicity can indeed be accounted for by linking metarepresentation to simulation. But the link forged by the simulation theory is too simple and too direct. The simulation theory, I will argue, conflates two different things: the exercise of simulation and its exploitation.[6]

§4.3   Conditionals and Simulation (1)

In the early seventies, two authors—the Oxford philosopher John Mackie and the French linguist Oswald Ducrot—put forward a pragmatic analysis of conditionals which is exactly like the 'simulation theory', and which has the same merits and the same defects as the simulation theory. We may call it the 'simulation theory of conditionals'.

The distinction I want to make between actual simulation and something which presupposes simulation but differs from it ('post-simulation') is best introduced by first considering the case of conditionals.

According to Ducrot and Mackie, a conditional utterance serves to perform two distinct illocutionary acts: (i) the antecedent introduces a *supposition:* it invites the hearer to consider a certain possibility; (ii) the consequent is asserted or put forward *within* that supposition.[7] The two illocutionary acts, therefore, are the act of 'supposing' and the act of 'asserting under a supposition'. The former is typically performed by means of the phrase 'Suppose that ...' or 'Imagine that ...'. Insofar as "the primary function of 'if' is to introduce a supposition, to invite us to consider a possibility," it "can be expanded into 'suppose that', and the consequent can be regarded as being put forward within the scope of that supposition" (Mackie 1973: 98). The conditional 'If Peter comes, he will be tired' is therefore equivalent to a pair of utterances:

(4)   Imagine/suppose that Peter comes.

(5)   He will be tired.

The assertion in (5) is made only 'within the supposition' introduced by (4). We are to imagine a situation in which Peter comes; it is the imaginary situation thus introduced—not the actual world—which we characterize in (5). Utterance (5) therefore is not an assertion *tout court*, but a pretend assertion concerning the imaginary situation which (4) invites us to consider. Such a simulative assertion is similar to the 'On serait un roi et une reine' previously mentioned: for the latter also characterizes some imaginary situation previously evoked.

Even though this is a speech act analysis which "explains conditionals in terms of what would probably be classified [and is indeed classified by Ducrot] as a complex illocutionary speech act, the framing of a supposition and putting something forward within its scope" (Mackie 1973: 100), Mackie insists that the act of supposition in question is not essentially or primarily linguistic:

Supposing some possibility to be realized and associating some further how-things-would-be with it is something that can be done merely by *envisaging* the possibilities and consequences in question. Among the reasons why this is important is that it makes comprehensible the otherwise puzzling fact that animals which seem not to use language—at any rate, not a language with any such grammatical structure as ours—seem capable of reasoning conditionally. (Mackie 1973: 100)

One consequence of the Ducrot-Mackie account is that conditionals are not strictly speaking true or false. The act of supposing is certainly not evaluable in that dimension; and the statement which is made 'under the supposition' is only a pretend assertion, an assertion which can be evaluated only within the pretense that the imaginary situation depicted by the antecedent actually obtains. The theory therefore "abandons the claim that conditionals are in a strict sense statements, that they are in general any sort of descriptions that must either be fulfilled or be not fulfilled by the way things are, and hence that they are in general simply true or false" (Mackie 1973: 93).[8]

The problem is that conditionals often seem to be true or false in a fairly straightforward sense. For example we can say: 'It is true that if Peter comes, he will be tired' (Mackie 1973: 102). What does that mean, if the conditional 'If Peter comes, he will be tired' is not strictly speaking true or false? To be sure, one can invoke the redundancy theory to dispose of this difficulty—by arguing that 'It is true that if P, Q' says no more and no less than 'If P, Q'. But that misses the point. The point is that a conditional such as 'If Peter comes, he will be tired' may legitimately be construed as stating a fact concerning the actual world. Even a counterfactual conditional such as 'If Peter came, he would be tired' can be so construed. As Stalnaker says,

Counterfactuals are often contingent, and contingent statements must be supported by evidence. But evidence can be gathered, by us at least, only in this universe.... It is because counterfactuals are generally about possible worlds which are very much like the actual one, and defined in terms of it, that evidence is so often relevant to their truth.... The conditional provides a set of conventions for selecting possible situations which have a specified relation to what actually happens. *This makes it possible for statements about unrealized possibilities to tell us, not just about the speaker's imagination, but about the world.* (Stalnaker 1968: 44–45; emphasis mine)

And David Lewis:

It is ... the character of our world that makes counterfactuals true.... The other worlds provide a frame of reference whereby we can characterize our world. By placing our world within this frame, we can say just as much about its character as is relevant to the truth of a counterfactual: our world is such as to make an (A-and-C)-world closer to it than any (A-and-not-C)-world [where A and C

correspond to the antecedent and the consequent of the counterfactual]. (Lewis 1986: 22)

What Stalnaker and Lewis say of counterfactuals holds even more clearly for indicative conditionals. If I say:

If John opens the fridge, he will be scared to death

my reason for saying that is that I know John, and I know what is in the fridge. It is John's *actual* character which supports the fact that if he opens the fridge (the actual fridge, with its actual contents) he will be scared to death. Had John's character, or the contents of the fridge, been different, the conditional would not hold. In that sense the conditional is about the actual world.

The simulation theorist might reply as follows. Let us replace the conditional by the corresponding Ducrot-Mackie pair:

Suppose John opens the fridge.

He will be scared to death.

There is no doubt that the simulation theory applies here: a supposition is made, and something is put forward in the scope of that supposition. The 'assertion' that John will be scared to death can be disputed or accepted only by someone who engages in the simulation and imagines John's opening of the fridge. Now, if the pretend assertion is accepted (if the hearer agrees with the speaker), that means that the speaker and the hearer view the imaginary situation in the same way; and they do so presumably because they have the same information concerning John and the fridge in the actual world. So the connection with the actual world exists, yet the utterance does not *say* anything about the actual world. The utterance says something only about an *imaginary* situation, but the suppositional procedure through which that situation is constructed in imagination takes the actual world as its starting point, so that the utterance provides some evidence concerning the actual world, or the way the speaker takes it to be. The same thing holds, arguably, for the conditional: it does not *say* anything about the actual world, even though what it says concerning the imaginary situation depicted by the antecedent is grounded in the speaker's information concerning the actual world. To say that the conditional makes an assertion concerning the actual world simply because it is connected to the actual world in that way would be to fall prey to what Barwise and Perry (1983) call the 'fallacy of misplaced information'.

Well, perhaps; but there is, I will argue, a significant difference between the conditional 'If John opens the fridge, he will be scared to death' and the corresponding Ducrot-Mackie pair. The Ducrot-Mackie pair states something only within the supposition that John will open the fridge; not so with the conditional.

§4.4 Conditionals and Simulation (2)

Note, first, that conditionals can be embedded within, e.g., belief sentences: 'Paul believes that if John opens the fridge, he will be scared to death'.[9] Following Peter Long (1971: 142–3), Mackie himself ultimately accepts that conditionals are, or function as, genuine 'statements' (i.e., express true or false propositions) in such contexts. Peter Long distinguishes between two uses of conditionals: the 'propositional employment' and the 'non-propositional employment'. In the propositional employment, 'If P then Q' means that Q is inferable from P. In its non-propositional employment, the sentence asserts that Q within the supposition that P. Long, followed by Mackie, holds that the non-propositional (simulative) use is primary: the propositional use presupposes the non-propositional use. As Mackie admits, this theory is much weaker than the full-blown simulation theory. It is also, I think, much closer to truth. Be that as it may, what matters for my purposes is the distinction between two things: asserting a proposition within the scope of a supposition; and asserting that a proposition follows (is inferable) from a supposition. I take it that conditionals are typically used to do the latter. If I am right, the simulation theory is guilty of conflating the two things.

To bring that point home, let us consider natural deduction systems of logic, in which we find both conditionals and assertions-within-the-scope-of-a-supposition. Mackie acknowledges that the 'suppositional procedure' is at work in such systems, where we introduce temporary assumptions and reason in terms of them (Mackie 1973: 99). To assume something, in natural deduction, *is* to make a supposition in the Ducrot-Mackie sense: we assume the truth of an auxiliary premise P, and infer from it (and other premises) a certain proposition Q. Q is not asserted, as it is inferred only 'under the assumption'. We only pretend to assert Q, or assert it 'within the scope' of the assumption that P. If Q is self-contradictory, we can discharge the assumption and assert the negation of the auxiliary premise ('Reductio ad absurdum'). If Q is not self-contradictory, we can discharge the assumption and assert the conditional $P \rightarrow Q$ ('Conditional proof'). For example, suppose that we want to prove '$\neg p$' from '$p \rightarrow \neg p$'. We can do it as follows (table II.1). We start with our premise '$p \rightarrow \neg p$' (step 1). Then we assume the negation of the proposition we want to prove (step 2). Within that assumption, we derive a contradiction (steps 3–4). We then discharge the assumption and infer the negation of the auxiliary premise (step 5).[10] What is of interest here is the clear distinction between the propositions which are asserted and those which are merely 'assumed', that is, simulatively asserted. The propositions we find at steps 1 and 5 are asserted; the intermediate propositions are all assumed.

Now let us consider an instance of Conditional proof. Suppose that we want to prove '$\neg q \rightarrow \neg p$' from '$p \rightarrow q$'. We can do it as follows (table II.2). We start with our premise '$p \rightarrow q$' (step 1). We then assume the antecedent of the conditional we want to prove (step 2). This enables us to infer the consequent (step 3). As the antecedent, '$\neg q$', was not really asserted, but merely assumed, the consequent, '$\neg p$', is not asserted either. But the inference rule of Conditional proof enables us to infer the conditional '$\neg q \rightarrow \neg p$' from the fact that, under the assumption that $\neg q$, the proposition that $\neg p$ can be derived.

When we look at the representation of the proof in table II.2, we see very clearly that there is a difference between line 3 and line 4. At line 3,

Table II.1
Reductio ad absurdum: an example

	Assertion	Assumption	By
1	$p \rightarrow \neg p$		premise
2		p	auxiliary premise
3		$\neg p$	1, 2, modus ponens
4		$p \ \& \ \neg p$	2, 3, &-introduction
5	$\neg p$		2, 4, reductio ad absurdum

we find the simulative assertion of the consequent in the scope of the assumption corresponding to the antecedent. That this assertion is fictitious is shown by its occurring in the assumption column. At line 4, however, we find the conditional, which *is* asserted. It occurs in the assertion column. The conditional is not in the scope of the supposition; but it holds because, and to the extent that, the consequent is assertible within the scope of the supposition.

Line 4 corresponds to what I call the 'post-simulative mode': we exploit the simulation effected at the previous level (lines 2–3) to say something about the imaginary situation envisaged at line 2. During the simulation, we (non-assertively) say things within the scope of the supposition; after the simulation, we are in a position to assert *that* the supposition in question supports the consequent. What we say at the post-simulative level we do not say from within the simulation, but from the outside, as it were. The post-simulative mode implies taking a reflective stance toward the simulation which it presupposes.

§4.5　The Post-Simulative Mode

The distinction between the exercise of simulation and its post-simulative exploitation goes some way toward explaining the otherwise puzzling fact that conditionals emerge late in children's development (in the second half of the third year); later than morphosyntactically similar sentences. Presumably, the reason for that is semantic: conditionals are distinguished from e.g., 'when'-sentences by the fact that they talk about *imaginary* situations; hence they are cognitively more complex than formally similar types of sentences used to talk about the actual world. However, Bowerman has argued against that explanation, citing evi-

Table II.2
Conditional proof: an example

	Assertion	Assumption	By
1	$p \rightarrow q$		premise
2		$\neg q$	auxiliary premise
3		$\neg p$	1, 2, modus tollens
4	$\neg q \rightarrow \neg p$		2, 3, conditional proof

dence to the effect that "well before children produce conditionals they appear to be not only capable of entertaining situations contrary to reality but also in some cases of marking them as counterfactual" (Bowerman 1986: 290–1). Hence the puzzle and Bowerman's aporetic conclusion:

> These negative outcomes suggest that further work is needed on our theoretical assumptions about what determines timing of acquisition. (Bowerman 1986: 304)

Bowerman is certainly right, but I think the cognitive complexity hypothesis should not be given up too hastily. As I suggested above, it is one thing to be able to imagine counterfactual situations and to engage into overt pretense; it is quite another to be able to state, from the outside, objective facts concerning the imaginary situations thus evoked.[11] If I am right, there are two types of fact regarding imaginary situations: (i) facts which hold *within* the situations in question, and which can only be simulatively asserted; and (ii) objective facts *about* those situations, to the effect that they support such and such facts of the first type. Those objective facts can be asserted *tout court*, and they are typically expressed by means of conditionals. Conditionals, therefore, are not equivalent to Ducrot-Mackie pairs.

To illustrate the distinction between the two sorts of fact, let us consider a much simpler type of case, involving only real situations. As John Perry (1986b) pointed out, if I say or think 'It is raining', my utterance/thought concerns the place where I am, but the place in question is not represented explicitly (reflectively) in the utterance/thought. The representation that it is raining concerns that particular place because it is the place in which the representation is tokened. In contrast, if I say 'It is raining here' or 'It's raining in Paris', the place where it is raining is articulated *in* the representation. The difference is not merely a difference in wording. The simple assertion that it is raining states a simpler fact (a fact with fewer constituents); that fact, however, is 'relativized' to a particular context, namely the place the speaker is in. (On relativization, see Barwise 1989: 253–4, and Recanati 1999: 125–9). In the other case, when I say 'It is raining here' or 'It's raining in Paris', the place is an explicit constituent of the fact which is stated, but that fact is no longer relativized to the context in question. In other words, what changes from one utterance/thought to the next is both the fact which is explicitly stated and the context relative to which the utterance/thought is interpreted. In Recanati 1997b I analysed the second type of change as follows:

When I say 'In Paris, it is raining', this makes sense only insofar as the location Paris is virtually contrasted with some other location, such as London or the country. This is a point which European 'structuralism' has much insisted on: whatever is singled out in speech is extracted from a 'paradigm' or contrastive set. If no other location was implicitly considered, the specification of the location would play no role and could be omitted. The fact that the location is singled out shows that the situation with respect to which the locationally specific representation is interpreted includes the mentioned location *and others from the same paradigm*. The situation might be, for example, the Continent of Europe (which contains Paris, Rome, Vienna, etc.). But the locationally non-specific 'It is raining' can be interpreted with respect to a smaller situation, viz. Paris itself (to the *exclusion* of any other location). (Recanati 1997b: 54–55)

In that sort of example, we can say that the simple representation 'It is raining' is asserted *within* a particular context or situation, namely the situation which it concerns; while the more complex representation 'It is raining here' or 'It is raining in Paris' is *about* that situation but is not asserted *within* it. In the more complex utterance/thought, the place where it is raining is considered from the outside and explicitly represented. I think we find the same contrast between Ducrot-Mackie pairs and the corresponding conditionals, except that the situation at issue is imaginary rather than real. In a Ducrot-Mackie pair, the 'consequent' (the second member of the pair) is asserted *within* the supposition made by the 'antecedent' (the first member); but a conditional asserts *that* the imaginary situation corresponding to the antecedent supports the consequent.

Similarly, there is a striking contrast between, e.g., the pretend assertions made by the story-teller, *concerning* some imaginary situation, and (serious) metarepresentational assertions *about* the story and the imaginary situation it depicts. The former do not talk about the actual world but are asserted within a context of mental simulation; the latter do talk about the actual world, by explicitly characterizing the imaginary situation depicted by the story. Thus when I say 'In the film, Robin Hood meets Sherlock Holmes', I talk about the actual world and an aspect of it: the film which I saw yesterday. It's an objective fact concerning the actual world that, in the film I saw yesterday, Robin Hood meets (met) Sherlock Holmes. To be sure, the fact that Robin Hood met Sherlock Holmes is only a fact in a certain 'fictional world', but that is not the fact which the metarepresentation states: what the metarepresentation says is that *that fact holds in the world pictured by the film*—and that is a different fact from the fictitious fact in question.

Using that distinction we can reanalyse the simulative solution to the 'phone number problem' mentioned in §4.2 (table II.3). We must not conflate the metarepresentations (1 and 2 in table II.3) and the associated 'assumptions' (3 and 4). In solving the phone number problem by the simulation method, we start from the metarepresentations 1 and 2, which are our premises. By simulatively projecting ourselves into Peter's shoes we assume the ascribed beliefs (auxiliary premises 3 and 4). Having done so we can reason within that assumption and derive 5. Then we discharge the assumption and assert the metarepresentation 6, which results from re-embedding ('retrojecting') 5 into the original matrix.[12]

Table II.3
The phone number problem

	Assertion	Assumption	By
1	Peter believes that John's number = 325-248.		premise
2	Peter believes that John's number = Mary's number.		premise
3		John's number = 325-248.	1, projection
4		John's number = Mary's number.	2, projection
5		Mary's number = 325-248.	3, 4, symmetry and transitivity of =
6	Peter believes that Mary's number = 325-248.		5, retrojection

There is a clear difference between the pretend assertion 5 and the metarepresentation 6, as there was a difference between the pretend assertion of the consequent and the assertion of the conditional in the instance of Conditional proof discussed above (§4.4). The difference between 5 and 6 is the same as the difference between 1 and 3 and between 2 and 4: it is the difference between a metarepresentation *about* a 'belief world' and a simulated assertion made 'from within' a belief world which we assume.

That is not to deny that there is a close connection between simulation and metarepresentation; there is indeed, but the simulation theory much overstates it. Simulative assertions such as 'On serait un roi et une reine' *are not metarepresentations at all*—they are primary representations, just as a film or a novel consists of primary representations of (non-actual) facts. Similarly for irony, free indirect speech etc. In such cases the speaker (thinker) is not making a serious assertion, but only pretending. In metarepresentations something quite different happens: we seriously characterize the actual world by mentioning facts which hold in imaginary situations. The reason why our representations concern the actual world is this: The imaginary situations we talk about are related to things in the actual world (and represented as such), so that to say something about the imaginary situations in question is to say something about the actual world. Thus to say something about what happens to Holmes (in such and such an imaginary situation) is to say something about a real world object, namely the novel in which that situation is described. It is that fundamental insight which modal theories capture when they make the truth-value of the metarepresentation at a given circumstance c depend upon the truth-value of the object-representation at a distinct circumstance c' appropriately related to c.

5

Austinian Semantics

§5.1 Austinian Propositions

I what I have said so far is correct, there are two main distinctions which a proper theory of metarepresentations must draw. First, there is a distinction between saying something about a situation and saying something within (or better: with respect to) a situation. That distinction is illustrated by the contrast between 'It's raining' (said at location l) and 'It's raining at l'. Second, there is a distinction between two sorts of situation: real situations (such as the place l in the above example), and imaginary situations, such as those described by novels, or those which correspond to the antecedents of conditionals. Conditionals and metarepresentations are statements *about* imaginary situations; while simulative assertions are statements made *with respect to* some imaginary situation.

In standard semantic theories the first distinction cannot be represented. 'It's raining' and 'It's raining at l' are taken to express the same proposition, consisting of a two-place relation $Rain(t, p)$ and a sequence of two arguments: a time and a place. The place is not articulated at all in the sentence, while the time presumably is (via the present tense); despite this difference, the content of the utterance is said to be the same in both cases—only the wording is supposed to change.

Dissatisfied with this approach, we can give up standard semantics and opt for the non-standard variety which Barwise and Etchemendy call 'Austinian semantics' (Barwise and Etchemendy 1987; Recanati 1987, 1996, 1997b, 1999). The basic idea is that each statement is interpreted with respect to a particular situation which it 'concerns' (in

the sense of Perry 1986b). The complete content of an utterance, therefore, is an 'Austinian proposition' consisting of two components: the fact
which the utterance explicitly states (the proposition it expresses, in the
standard sense), and the situation which that fact or proposition concerns. An utterance standardly construed as expressing a proposition p
therefore turns out to have a richer content $\langle s, p \rangle$, where s is the situation which the utterance concerns.

In Austinian semantics, an utterance is true if and only if the fact it
states holds in (or 'at') the situation it concerns. Consider the canonical
example (from Barwise and Etchemendy 1987: 121–2). Looking at a
poker game, I say 'Claire has the ace of hearts'. My utterance expresses
the fact that Claire has the ace of hearts, and the situation it concerns is
the poker game I am watching (at a certain time t_1). For the utterance to
be true, it is not sufficient if the fact it expresses obtains; that fact must
hold *in the situation the utterance concerns*, i.e., the poker game in
question at the time in question. As Barwise and Etchemendy point out,
if I am mistaken and Claire is not among the players of the game, my
utterance is not true—even if Claire is playing poker in some other part
of the city and has the ace of hearts there. It is true only if Claire has the
ace of hearts *in that poker game*. Similarly, the utterance 'It is raining',
uttered with respect to a certain location, is true if and only if it is raining *at that location*.

Whenever a fact σ holds in a situation s, or equivalently, whenever a
proposition is true at s, we say that the situation in question *supports*
that fact or proposition. In symbols: $s \models \sigma$. Insofar as an utterance presents the fact which it states as holding in the situation which it concerns,
and is true iff that is the case, its complete Austinian content can be
represented as follows:

$$[s] \models \sigma$$

On the left-hand-side, in square brackets, we find the situation which the
utterance concerns (the 'exercised situation', as I call it). On the right-
hand-side we find the fact which the utterance explicitly states. When the
fact in question is represented by a sentence or a formula instead of a
metavariable, the sentence or formula will be enclosed within double
angle brackets: $[s] \models \langle\!\langle \ldots \rangle\!\rangle$.

In general at least, the situation which an utterance concerns is not a constituent of the fact which the utterance states; it is only a constituent of the global, Austinian proposition. An utterance (or thought) such as 'It's raining' will therefore be represented as follows:

(1)   [Paris] $\models$ 《It is raining》

As the left-hand-side makes clear, that utterance concerns a certain location, namely Paris. That location is represented at the Austinian-proposition level, but it is not a constituent of the fact which the utterance explicitly states. That fact can be analysed as involving a 1-place relation (*Rain*, construed as a property of times) and an appropriate argument (the present time).[13] In contrast, if we say 'It's raining here' or 'It's raining in Paris', the fact which the utterance states will involve a 2-place relation, with the location itself as one of the arguments. In this way, thanks to the distinction between the two levels of content (the fact or proposition on the right-hand-side, and the complete Austinian proposition), we can represent the contrast between saying something about a situation and saying something 'concerning' that situation.

§5.2   Projection and Reflection

Two cognitive mechanisms at work in discourse can be characterized in this framework: *reflection* and *projection* (Recanati 1997b).

Let us consider again our subject who says or thinks: 'It is raining'. If she comes to *reflect on* the situation which the representation concerns, and makes it explicit, she will entertain a more complex representation: the simple representation 'It's raining' will be replaced by 'It is raining here' or 'It is raining in Paris'. As I have just said, the new representation expresses a fact involving the *two-place* relation Rain(t, p) between times and places, instead of the simpler fact involving only a property of times.

When the situation is made explicit in this way, generally by contrast with other possible situations, the situation which the utterance concerns (i.e., that which figures in the left hand side of the Austinian proposition) is correspondingly enlarged. (This point was already made in §4.5.) Thus the subject who says 'Its raining in Paris' or 'It's raining here' normally has in mind other locations (e.g., other capitals of Europe), and is attempting to state a fact concerning not just Paris, but, more globally, the meteorological situation in e.g., continental Europe. The more complex representation ('It's raining in Paris') can therefore be represented as

(2)   [Europe] ⊨ ⟪It's raining in Paris⟫

That is a *minimal* reflection of (1): the only difference between (1) and (2) is that the situation which the representation in (1) concerns is a constituent of the fact stated by the representation in (2); which representation therefore concerns a larger situation. But reflections need not be minimal. Reflection operates whenever we start with a representation concerning a certain situation, for example a situation given in the context, and make that situation explicit in a second representation which is 'about' it but 'concerns' a larger situation. An example of (non-minimal) reflection is provided in the following discourse:

(3)   Look, it's raining! It's always like that in this city.

The first utterance of (3) states a fact concerning the location where the utterance is situated (viz., Paris); the second utterance is explicitly about that location, and concerns a larger situation (one that includes Paris and the other locations with which it is implicitly contrasted).

Instead of representing minimal reflections by increasing the arity of the relation, we can leave the relation as it was prior to reflection and simply copy the pre-reflective Austinian proposition into the right-hand-side of the post-reflective Austinian proposition:

(2*)   [Europe] ⊨ ⟪Paris ⊨ ⟪It's raining⟫⟫

I find that notation more perspicuous and I will use it in what follows. In a formula like (2*), corresponding to what will later be called a 'δ-structure' (§6.4), there are two situations and two support relations: the leftmost situation, represented within square brackets, is that which the utterance concerns. It is that situation which supports the complex fact represented within double angle brackets. The other situation (Paris) is explicitly mentioned and is a constituent of the complex fact in question —the fact stated by the utterance. (It is because there are such cases that we need square brackets to single out the 'exercised situation': the situation which the utterance concerns.)

Projection is very similar to reflection, except that it operates in the other direction. A situation is first mentioned (that is, it is a constituent of some fact which is stated); the speaker then 'projects herself into that situation' or assumes it, and states something with respect to that situation, as if it was given in the external context (while it is only given 'in the discourse'). This phenomenon is illustrated by the following example:

(4)   Berkeley is a nice place. There are bookstores and coffee shops everywhere.

In the second utterance ('There are bookstores and coffee shops everywhere') the quantifier 'everywhere' ranges over locations in Berkeley; yet Berkeley is not represented in the utterance—it's not a constituent of the fact which the utterance states. Nor is Berkeley 'contextually given' in the sense in which Paris was in the previous example: I assume that the above discourse does not take place *in* Berkeley but, say, in London. Berkeley is represented in the *previous* utterance, however, and this enables it to be used as the situation 'with respect to which' the second utterance is interpreted. In Recanati 1997b I analysed the example as follows:

The first sentence of (4) talks directly about Berkeley considered as an object: it states a fact of which Berkeley is a constituent. But the second sentence of (4) does not talk about Berkeley in this manner. The second sentence of (4) expresses a fact internal to Berkeley rather than a fact 'about' Berkeley in the sense of including Berkeley as a constituent. The second sentence of (4) is interpreted with respect to the Berkeley situation without mentioning that situation. That is possible because the Berkeley situation has already been mentioned—in the first sentence. This is a standard instance of projection. (Recanati 1997b: 61)

Because projection operates, the two sentences of (4) do not concern the same situation. The first sentence, which expresses a fact containing Berkeley as a constituent, concerns a situation 'larger than' the Berkeley situation itself; it may concern, e.g., the United States (in which there are many cities, not all of which are nice by European standards), or California, or perhaps the set of cities with big universities, etc. What matters is the contrast with the second utterance, which concerns a much smaller situation: Berkeley itself. It is that smaller situation which provides the domain for the quantifier 'everywhere'. Utterance (4) can therefore be represented thus:

(4a)   [USA] $\models$ 《Berkeley is a nice place》

(4b)   [Berkeley] $\models$ 《There are bookstores and coffee shops everywhere》

§5.3   Situations, Facts, and Worlds

In the Austinian framework, an utterance or a thought is true iff the fact or proposition it states holds in or is true at the situation it concerns. Now what are facts, what are situations, and what do I mean when I say that a fact holds in a situation?

Facts are complexes consisting of objects having properties and standing in relations. Such complexes can be represented as sequences consisting of a n-place relation and a sequence of n appropriate arguments (plus, perhaps, a polarity to distinguish positive from negative facts).[14] The world, Wittgenstein said, is the totality of such facts: all that is the case. Intuitively, situations are portions of the world. It is therefore tempting to represent situations as *sets of facts,* with worlds construed as maximal situations.

There is a problem with this representation, however. If situations are represented as sets of facts, the support relation between situations and facts will be represented in terms of set membership: a situation will be said to support a fact if and only if it contains that fact. Since a set has its members essentially, this will prevent us from representing the contingency of the support relation.[15] For example, it is a contingent fact that it is raining in Chicago; but if the Chicago situation *is* the set of facts it supports, then it cannot be a contingent fact that that situation supports (contains) the fact that it is raining. That is why we must distinguish situations from the sets of facts they are associated with. Situations determine sets of facts *only relative to a world.* Thus, in the actual world, it is raining in Chicago. But the Chicago situation might have been different—it might have contained different facts. For our purposes a world w can be represented as consisting of a domain of entities, $\mathrm{Dom}(w)$; and a function W from entities in that domain to sets of facts concerning those entities. The set of facts (or 'factual set') associated with a situation $s \in \mathrm{Dom}(w)$ is the set $W(s)$. Different worlds can associate different sets of facts with the same situations if the situations in question are in the domains of those worlds.

The support relation can now be tentatively defined as follows:

Support relation

A situation s supports an atomic fact σ with respect to a world w if and only if σ belongs to $W(s)$.

Since the support relation turns out to be relative to a world, instead of '$s \models \sigma$' we must write:

$$s \models_w \sigma$$

By default—in the absence of an explicit subscript—the support relation will be interpreted as relative to @, the actual world.[16]

At this point various questions arise. First, are situations a special sort of entity, alongside, e.g., ordinary objects, or are all entities (including ordinary objects) situations? I opt for the latter view (§6.1). Anything is a situation insofar as it can be associated with a factual set. Thus my right leg is a situation insofar as there are facts concerning it, much as there are facts concerning what is going on here and now.[17]

Second, the facts I have talked about so far are *atomic* facts. What about molecular facts such as the fact that σ & σ'? The definition of the support relation can be extended in the usual way so as to encompass such facts. For example, a situation s will be said to support a conjunctive fact σ & σ' iff s supports σ and s supports σ'. (There may be problems in generalizing this move to, e.g., disjunction,[18] but I do not have to go into these matters here.)

Third, what about the special case in which a situation s' is said to support *the fact that another situation s supports σ*, as in (2*) above? What are the truth-conditions of what I call 'δ-structures'? My answer is the following. For s' to support the fact that $s \models \sigma$ two conditions must be satisfied: (i) s must be accessible from s', and (ii) s must support σ. The accessibility condition has already been illustrated in connection with the poker game example (§5.1). Even if it is a fact that Claire has a good hand (assuming that she is presently playing cards somewhere), still that fact does not hold in the poker game we are watching, for Claire is nowhere to be found in that situation. (We suppose that she is playing somewhere else.) We can construe Claire herself as a situation supporting the 0-adic fact of having a good hand: Claire $\models$ 《has-a-good-hand》. It is not the case that the poker game situation we are watching supports the complex fact $\langle\!\langle$Claire $\models \langle\!\langle$has-a-good-hand$\rangle\!\rangle\rangle\!\rangle$ because the 'situation' Claire is not 'accessible from' that poker game situation:

This poker game $\not\models \langle\!\langle$Claire $\models \langle\!\langle$has-a-good-hand$\rangle\!\rangle\rangle\!\rangle$

I will not have much to say here about the accessibility relation, which the poker game example negatively illustrates. When, as in this example, a situation is or corresponds to a spatio-temporal region in which there are objects having properties and standing in relations to other objects, both the locations included in the region and the objects it contains are accessible—indeed whatever is 'in' a situation is accessible from it. But that is not the only form of accessibility we must consider. In an important type of case, which will play a central role in what follows, a situation s is accessible from a situation s' even though s is not literally 'in' s'. Indeed, in the type of case I have in mind, *s and s' do not even belong to the same world.*

In the actual world there are entities (e.g., books, utterances, pictures, or mental states) which have content. Their having the content which they have is a contingent property of these entities. Through their contents the entities in question give us access to imaginary situations, i.e., they project 'possible worlds' with respect to which the situations which they depict support certain facts. Thus the Sherlock Holmes stories depict certain situations which support certain facts in the fictional world imagined by Conan Doyle. In this type of case a real-world situation s' (involving a certain book) gives us access to an imaginary situation s (that which is depicted in the book)—a situation which belongs to a possible world w distinct from the actual world. Since, in the possible word in question, s supports σ, it follows that

$$[s'] \models_@ \langle\!\langle s \models_w \sigma\rangle\!\rangle$$

Even though the fact $\langle\!\langle s \models_w \sigma\rangle\!\rangle$ is not contingent (because the internal support relation is indexed to a particular world), it is contingent that s' supports that fact; for it is contingent that s' gives us access to the imaginary situation s.

§5.4   Imaginary Situations

What *is* an imaginary situation? Is it a situation which is not in the domain of @? Certainly not. Hypothetical situations are typical cases of imaginary situation in the intended sense, yet they may well belong to Dom(@). Suppose I utter (5):

(5) If John went to Lyons, he took the 1:30 train.

What is at stake here is a hypothetical situation, viz. a situation in which John went to Lyons. Suppose that John indeed went to Lyons. Then the hypothetical situation turns out to be in the domain of @ (in the sense that @ associates a set of facts with that situation). Yet it still is an hypothetical (hence an imaginary) situation. So we cannot define an imaginary situation as a situation which does not belong to the domain of @.

Situations can be in the domain of several worlds; a situation does not essentially belong to the domain of this or that world. When we present a situation as supporting a certain fact, however, the support relation *is* relative to a world. I therefore suggest the following definition: An imaginary situation is a situation which is presented as supporting a certain fact *with respect to a world w different from @.*

The definition I have just given raises a problem. What is the possible world at issue in conditionals? According to Stalnaker, it is "that world in which the antecedent is true which is most similar, in relevant respects, to the actual world" (Stalnaker 1975: 68). But we run into a difficulty if we so characterize the world w with respect to which the imaginary situation mentioned by the antecedent of a conditional is presented as supporting the fact expressed by the consequent. Whenever the antecedent of an indicative conditional turns out to be true, the world w in question turns out to be identical to @: for example, if John actually went to Lyons, then the actual world *is* that world in which the antecedent of (5) is true which is most similar to the actual world. But if that is so, then we cannot appeal to the difference between @ and w to capture the intuitive distinction between real situations and hypothetical situations. In the described circumstances, the hypothetical situation in which John went to Lyons would turn out to be a real situation by the above definition.

The above definition of imaginary situations could perhaps be defended by pointing out that it brings 'modes of presentation' into the picture. Even if the antecedent of an indicative conditional turns out to be true, still the hypothetical situation denoted by that antecedent is not 'presented as' supporting the consequent *with respect to* @, but with respect to a world *w which may, but need not, be identical to* @. The hypothetical situation is hypothetical precisely because one does not know whether or not it is actual. So one appeals to a world *w* possibly distinct from @, and one says that, with respect to that world, the situation denoted by the antecedent supports the consequent. That world may turn out to be the actual world, but it is not presented as such.

Introducing modes of presentation for worlds would hopelessly complicate an already complicated picture, however. A simpler solution consists in acknowledging that *w* need be not a unique world but may be (and typically is) a *class* of worlds. On this view, the hypothetical situation corresponding to the antecedent is said by the conditional to support the consequent with respect to a class of worlds, namely those worlds in which the antecedent is true which are relevantly similar to the actual world. The class of worlds in question may turn out to contain the actual world (if the antecedent turns out to be true simpliciter), but it contains other worlds as well. Thus we can stick to our definition of an imaginary situation, reformulated as follows: An imaginary situation is a situation which is presented as supporting a certain fact with respect to a world *w* different from @, or with respect to a class of worlds containing such a world *w*.

We are now in a position to analyse mental simulation. There is mental simulation whenever a representation *concerns* an imaginary situation, as in (6):

(6) $[s] \models_w \sigma$

In (6) the subject imagines some aspect or portion of a world *w* distinct from the actual world. The imaginary situation *s* thus envisaged she characterizes as supporting the fact that σ. This representation fits all the instances of mental simulation we have mentioned: children's games of make-believe, fiction, irony, supposition, etc.

In discussing the simulation theory of conditionals (§4.3), I mentioned that an act of mental simulation can set up a context for other acts of mental simulation within its scope. That is what happens in Ducrot-Mackie pairs:

Suppose he comes back tonight.

He will be tired.

We won't worry him by mentioning the fire.

'He will be tired' and 'We won't worry him by mentioning the fire' characterize the hypothetical (imaginary) situation in which he comes back tonight. In the initial act of 'supposing', the subject pretends that the world is as supposed; it is the imaginary world w thus deployed through the pretense that indexes the support relations in the subsequent Austinian propositions.

$[s] \models_w$ 《He will be tired》

$[s] \models_w$ 《We won't worry him by mentioning the fire》

In Recanati 1997b I gave the following examples of *projection* involving imaginary situations:

(7)   John is totally paranoid. Everybody spies on him or wants to kill him, including his own mother.

(8)   I did not know you were so much interested in knights. You should read *A Connecticut Yankee in King Arthur's Court*, by Mark Twain. There are a lot of knights.

In (7) the first utterance ('John is totally paranoid') concerns a real situation s'. That situation s' is presented as supporting 《John is paranoid》. Now a paranoid is someone who believes himself to be in a certain type of situation. Let us call the situation John believes himself to be in s. That situation is an aspect of his 'belief world', j, that is, it is part of what John takes to be the actual world.[19] It supports certain 'facts' in John's belief world, but those need not be facts in the actual world. Now the second sentence of (7) concerns that imaginary situation s. The speaker does not seriously assert that everybody spies John or wants to kill him: she expects the hearer to understand that fact as holding in John's belief world, more specifically in the imaginary situation s John believes himself to be in. Such a shift in point of view is constitutive of 'free indirect speech', of which (7) is a typical instance. Free indirect speech generally involves an operation of projection: an imaginary situation is first mentioned, then assumed.

(7a) $[s'] \models_@ \langle\!\langle$ John is paranoid $\rangle\!\rangle$

(7b) $[s] \models_j \langle\!\langle$ Everybody spies on him, etc. $\rangle\!\rangle$

The other example is similar. In the second sentence of (8) Twain's fiction (a portion of the actual world) is mentioned. Now Twain's fiction has a certain content, that is, it describes a certain situation as supporting certain facts. The situation in question is imaginary in the sense that the facts it is presented as supporting only hold in the world of the fiction. The third sentence of (8) is directly interpreted with respect to that imaginary situation. It is in that situation that there are a lot of knights. This is similar to the Berkeley example (§5.2), except that the situation which is assumed is an imaginary situation instead of a real one.

§5.5   The Analysis of Metarepresentations: A First Sketch

The representations from which projection operates in the last two examples are not 'metarepresentations' in the sense in which I have been using this term in part I. They are about 'representations', namely John's belief-system or Twain's book, both of which have a certain content; but they are not metarepresentations because the content of the representations they are about is not actually displayed. We can, however, replace the representations from which projection operates, in those examples, by genuine metarepresentations:

(9)   *John believes that he is being persecuted.* Everybody spies on him and even his mother wants to kill him.

(10)   *In Twain's book, a nineteenth-century man finds himself in King Arthur's England.* There are a lot of knights and funny medieval things.

In those examples the first sentence (italicized) is a metarepresentation. Now most philosophers and linguists would analyse the second sentence in (10) as an *elliptical* metarepresentation. Once the allegedly elided material has been restored, (10) becomes:

(10*)   In Twain's book, a nineteenth-century man finds himself in King Arthur's England. *In that book* there are a lot of knights and funny medieval things.

It is clear, however, that the second sentence of (9) is an instance of 'free' indirect speech. Now, as all students of free indirect speech know, it would be a mistake to construe (9) as merely an elliptical version of

(9*) John believes that he is being persecuted. *He believes that* everybody spies on him and *that* even his mother wants to kill him.[20]

Similarly, (10) is not merely an elliptical version of (10*). There is a semantic difference between the initial metarepresentation in both examples and the pretend assertion that follows. The pretend assertion is no more an elliptical metarepresentation than the metarepresentation is a pretend assertion. The metarepresentation mentions some imaginary situation (viz. that described in Twain's book, or that John believes himself to be in). That situation is simulatively assumed in the pretend assertion that follows.

To account for the difference between the metarepresentation and the pretend assertion that follows, we must apply the distinction between 'concerning' and 'being about' to the special case of imaginary situations. Like all representations, a metarepresentation states a fact concerning a situation. The situation the metarepresentation concerns is a real situation involving, e.g., a certain book or the mental states of a certain person; and the fact it states is about an imaginary situation, namely that which the book or the beliefs depict. The metarepresentation 'John believes that he is being persecuted' therefore expresses the Austinian proposition:

$$[s'] \vDash_@ \langle\!\langle s \vDash_j \text{John is being persecuted} \rangle\!\rangle$$

Here s' is the real situation which the metarepresentation concerns (a situation involving John and his beliefs); and s is the imaginary situation John believes himself to be in.[21] On this analysis a metarepresentation is not an instance of mental simulation, for the situation which it concerns (in this example at least) is a real-world situation, not an imaginary situation.[22] The imaginary situation s is mentioned *in* the metarepresentation, but it is not that situation which the metarepresentation concerns. That is why the metarepresentation gives rise to a serious assertion, rather than a pretend assertion. In (9), however, the metarepresentation is followed by a pretend assertion concerning the imaginary situation which the metarepresentation mentions. (9) can therefore be represented as the following sequence:

(9a) $[s'] \vDash_@ \langle\!\langle s \vDash_j$ John is being persecuted$\rangle\!\rangle$

(9b) $[s] \vDash_j \langle\!\langle$Everybody spies on him, etc.$\rangle\!\rangle$

The same sort of analysis can be offered for (10). The initial metarepresentation 'In Twain's book, a nineteen century man finds himself in King Arthur's England' mentions the situation described in Twain's book as supporting the fact that a nineteen century man finds himself in King Arthur's England. It is that imaginary situation, assumed through projection, which the second sentence of (10) concerns.

On this tentative analysis a metarepresentation states a fact *about* the imaginary situation described by some representation R (a film, a book, a mental state, an utterance, a picture, or whatnot); namely the fact that that situation supports a further fact σ. Hence there are three levels of semantic analysis for metarepresentations. We need to draw a distinction between (i) the fact σ which the imaginary situation is said to support, and (ii) the fact *that* the imaginary situation supports σ. Fact (ii) corresponds to what the metarepresentation states, while fact (i) is internal to the imaginary situation which R represents. A further distinction must be drawn between (ii), the fact which the metarepresentation states, and (iii), the complete Austinian proposition which the metarepresentation expresses, to the effect that the real situation the metarepresentation concerns supports the fact (ii).

6

The Double Nature of Situations

§6.1 A World of Situations

The general picture that emerges is the following. The world contains entities of various sorts (objects, locations, events, etc.). Those entities have properties and stand in relations to other entities. One particular relation is that which holds between an entity e and another one e' when e supports a fact involving e':

$$e \vDash_@ \langle\!\langle \ldots e' \ldots \rangle\!\rangle$$

When that particular relation holds e acquires the status of a *situation* (i.e., a fact-supporting entity), a situation which *comprises* the entity e' in its domain. A situation comprises all the entities which are constituents of some fact in the factual set of that situation.[23]

Every entity is a situation insofar as it supports some fact. Instead of distinguishing situations from other entities, as most philosophers do, I suggest that any entity can be *viewed* either as such (as an entity) or as a situation. When we think of something as an entity we think of it as having properties and standing in relation to other entities. Thus my situation as I am writing this can be thought of as a pleasant one. To say (or to think) that that situation is pleasant is to view it reflectively as an entity having a certain property. But the same situation can be thought of not as an entity having properties and standing in relation to other entities, but as a situation. When we view something as a situation, we think of it as comprising other entities and containing facts involving them; or rather, we don't think of it but we think thoughts concerning it, thoughts about the entities which it comprises.[24] Thus my situation as I am writing this comprises my computer, my cat, and of course myself, and it contains the fact that I am typing on my computer while my cat is trying to attract my attention. This situation is represented as such (*qua* situation) when the entities it comprises and the facts it contains are represented. If the situation itself is represented as having properties and standing in relation to other entities it is no longer construed as situation but as an entity.

The shift from construing something as a situation to construing it as an entity is the process I called 'reflection'. Projection is the inverse process whereby an entity *e* comprised in the current exercised situation *s* (i.e., a constituent of some fact concerning *s*) itself becomes the exercised situation as we mentally focus on *e* and the entities which it comprises. In reflection we step out of the current exercised situation and adopt a reflective stance towards it, construing it as an entity comprised in the new exercised situation. In projection we focus on an entity comprised in the exercised situation up to the point where it becomes the exercised situation and is no longer represented as an entity: only the entities which *it* comprises are represented.

Insofar as it contains facts, each situation is like a micro-universe, closed upon itself and insulated from the other micro-universes. It is insulated because, and to the extent that, the facts which hold within a particular situation do not necessarily hold outside that situation. For example it is a fact concerning this situation that everyone it it (i.e., me and my cat) is happy. That fact does not hold if we extend the situation so as to include other people. (That property is known as 'nonpersistence': nonpersistent facts are those facts which may hold in a situation *s* without holding in a larger situation *s'* extending *s*. Nonpersistence is arguably a property of a certain class of quantificational facts:[25] see Barwise and Cooper 1981 for the relevant classification of quantifiers.)

So the overall structure is that of a world consisting of situations which are both mutually alternative micro-universes *and* entities connected to each other within larger situations. The situations are connected to each other when viewed from outside, that is, when considered as entities. But they are insulated from each other when viewed from inside. The Austinian dynamics I have described in terms of projection and reflection consists in stepping in and outside situations. For example we start with a particular situation *s*, which our thought at a given instant concerns; through reflection we step outside of *s* into a larger situation *s'* comprising both *s* and other entities; then we can project ourselves into some situation *s** which is among the entities comprised in *s'*. In this way we can go from any situation to any other, despite the fact that situations are insulated from each other when considered from inside.

§6.2 Perner's 'Multiple Models'

A similar structure can be discerned in Josef Perner's theory of 'multiple models' as a stage in the child's mental development. The 'models' talked about by Perner are very similar to my 'situations', and Perner himself calls the child in that stage of mental development a 'situation theorist'.

Somewhere around $1^1/_2$ years ... infants acquire a series of skills that require facility with multiple mental models. They come to understand means-end relationships, which require multiple models to project the desired state and the necessary steps to get there. They can infer the location of an invisibly displaced object, which requires extra models for representing past points in the course of displacement. They start to engage in pretend play, which requires an extra model representing the world as different from the way it really is. They learn to interpret representational media, like pictures, language, and mirror images, which require models for representing the information conveyed in these media. (Perner 1991: 47)

While the infant in the previous stage of mental development is constantly updating a single model of reality, the 'situation theorist' uses a number of alternative models at the same time. Multiple models are needed precisely because the information within the models cannot be integrated into a single, coherent picture:

A single model ... has severe limitations, which become apparent when incompatible facts need to be recorded. Incompatibility of new information with the existing state of the model is typically used to update the model. The old information is erased and supplanted by the new. Systematic understanding of temporal change is therefore not possible with a single updating model. A second model is needed to preserve a record of past states. (Perner 1991: 47)

So it is pretty clear that the models Perner is talking about must be construed as *alternatives* to each other. Yet, at the same time, Perner acknowledges the need for *integration* of the models:

So far I have suggested only that different mental models be used to represent different contexts, so that events at different times are not confused with the present and pretense is not confused with reality. For instance, I suggested that Jacqueline represented the sequence of invisible displacements in the following two models,

Model 1

[*past*: "Potato inside the box under the rug."]

Model 2

[*present*: "Box empty. Potato under the rug."]

where the expressions inside quotation marks constitute the representational content of each model and the expressions outside quotation marks are markers that guide how each model is used by the system. In this example these markers could have originated from the fact that the model marked "past" was formed *before* the one marked "present." And these markers serve a useful purpose if they direct the child's action in such a way that actual search for the potato is governed by the model whose content situation is marked "present," whereas the model marked "past" is used for looking up missing information about the present situation.

However, viewing "past" and "present" as implicit codes guiding the use of models provides an adequate account only as long as children merely use these models correctly. But children soon do more.... The infant is aware of the temporal relationship between the immediate past, when the object was visible, and the present, when it has disappeared.... *Explicit modeling of the temporal relationship can be achieved by merging the hitherto separate models into one complex model containing different situations or contexts*:

Complex Temporal Model

["*past*: [Potato inside the box under the rug.]
present: [Box empty. Potato under the rug.]"]

(Perner 1991: 66; emphasis mine)

The alternative models or situations are thus integrated into a single, overarching model or situation which comprises them all. That integration is a central aspect of the multiple-models stage of mental development described by Perner. The situation theorist does not merely use disconnected models for various aspects of reality but connects the models together within an overall picture of the world.

It is because of their dual nature that situations are both connected and disconnected in this manner. *Qua* entities they are connected to each other; *qua* situations they are insulated from each other.

§6.3 Stages in Mental Development: A Digression

The fact that, according to Perner, the multiple models of the early situation theorist are integrated within a complex model goes against a claim implicit in what I said earlier. In chapter 4, I contrasted pretend play, which involves simulation (thought 'concerning' an imaginary situation), and genuine metarepresentation: thought 'about' an imaginary situation, but concerning a real situation.

Pretend play

$$[s] \models_w \sigma$$

Metarepresentation

$$[s'] \models_@ \langle\langle s \models_w \sigma \rangle\rangle$$

That distinction between two representational structures is naturally interpreted as corresponding to the much discussed distinction between two stages in the development of the child's 'theory of mind'. As is well-known, the child engages in pretend play shortly after the age of 1, much before she masters the notion of a representation. Thus two-year old children—Perner's situation theorists—consistently fail the 'false belief task' even though they massively engage in pretend play at that age. It is only later (between 3 and 4) that the child succeeds in that task and can be credited with genuine metarepresentational abilities.

In table II.4 the logical distinction and the developmental distinction are made to correspond to each other. I suggested so much in chapter 4, when discussing the late emergence of conditionals. I pointed out that the ability to state objective facts *about* imaginary situations is cognitively more complex than the ability to entertain imaginary situations 'from within', that is, to engage in mental simulation. This extra complexity, I suggested, might explain why conditionals (and full metarepresentational

Table II.4
From pretense to metarepresentation

Type of activity	Age of emergence	Representational structure
Pretense	Second year	$[s] \models_w \sigma$
Metarepresentation	Fourth year	$[s'] \models_@ \langle\langle s \models_w \sigma \rangle\rangle$

abilities) emerge later than counterfactual thinking. But this will not do. According to Perner, the situation theorist is aware that the pretense is only pretense and is able to compare pretense and reality, much as she is able to compare the past and the present. Thus at one year and three months Piaget's daughter Jacqueline, while pretending that a certain piece of cloth was her pillow, provided many signs that she "fully appreciated the discrepancy between the reality of the object being a piece of cloth and her pretense of treating that object like her pillow" (Perner 1991: 51; for qualifications, see Harris 1989: 60–4). That implies that the models at stake (the reality model and the pretense model) are already integrated within a single, overarching model. As Perner says,

Jacqueline, whose apparent delight ("knowing smile") indicated such awareness, must have been able to form the following complex model:
Pretend-Reality Model
["*real*: [This object in front of me is a piece of cloth.]
pretend: [This object in front of me is my pillow.]"]

(Perner 1991: 66)

In our framework, that means that the child engaging in pretend play is already capable of entertaining complex representations like (1):

(1) $[s'] \vDash_@ \langle\!\langle s \vDash_w \sigma \rangle\!\rangle$

Here s' is the actual situation in which the children are playing a game of make-believe, and s is the imaginary situation they are pretending to be in. In other words, the fact that the representational structure underlying pretend play is distinct from, and simpler than, that which underlies conditionals and metarepresentations does not imply that the early situation theorist engaging in pretend play has, at that time, no access to the more complex representational structure. Quite the opposite seems to be the case. What then distinguishes the early situation theorist from the late metarepresentation theorist? What explains the time-lag noted by developmental psychologists?

A possible answer to this question has been suggested by Perner himself. According to Perner, the child can entertain a complex model encompassing both the real and the imaginary without mastering the notion of representation, that is, without properly understanding the relation between the real and the imaginary. The child masters the elaborate notion of representation when she is able to conceive of both misrepresentation and the availability of several interpretations for a given representation. Before the child can do that, imaginary situations are treated on the pattern of real situations: they are part of the world, but they have special properties which distinguish them from the other situations. Imaginary situations are like ghosts who are part of the actual world but exhibit funny properties (e.g., invisibility and penetrability). Thus, commenting on an experimental set up in which children are asked to compare the situation in a picture with a real situation (both of them containing Snoopy), Perner writes:

> Depending on how much the child knows about "pictorial situations," the child may be aware that in the picture Snoopy does not move, cannot be stroked very rewardingly, does not snap, and so on. This awareness, however, does not show that the child is also aware of the relationship between the picture and the real scene. Snoopy is there twice, once in reality and again in the picture. (Perner 1991: 85).

I find this suggestion plausible. There is indeed a general property which distinguishes imaginary from real situations and to which the child can be sensitive even though she does not master the full-blown notion of representation. The property I have in mind I call *hyperinsulation*. As we have seen, real situations are insulated from each other because the facts which hold in them need not hold outside them. Thus if a fact belongs to the nonpersistent variety, it may hold in a situation s without holding in a situation s' comprising s. Persistent facts which hold in s will necessarily hold in s', however. Thus if there is a man with a hat in this room, there is a man with a hat in the building of which this room is a part. That is because existentially quantified facts are persistent, in contrast to universally quantified facts. (If everybody is happy in this room, it does not follow that everybody is happy in the building.) Now, if we turn to imaginary situations, we see that *even persistent facts holding in such situations need not hold in situations comprising them* (Recanati 1996: §6).

Take a book: that is a real world entity which supports a number of facts hence can (like any other entity) be construed as a situation. Among the facts in question there will be facts concerning who authored the book, when it was issued, and so forth, as well as facts about the content of the book—the situation which it describes. We can therefore distinguish a number of situations ordered by the comprise relation. First we have, say, the reading situation s_1 in which (let us suppose) I presently find myself, with a certain book in my hands. The book in question itself is a situation s_2, supporting a number of facts (e.g., the fact that there are twelve chapters and 156 pages). The imaginary situation described in the book is a third situation s_3. Situation s_1 comprises situation s_2 which comprises situation s_3. Now suppose that, in the imaginary situation described by the book, there is a man who can fly. We have:

(2) $s_1 \vDash_@ \langle\!\langle s_2 \vDash_@ \langle\!\langle s_3 \vDash_w \langle\!\langle \text{There is a man who can fly} \rangle\!\rangle\rangle\!\rangle\rangle\!\rangle$

In other words: it is a fact concerning my present reading situation (s_1) that it contains a book (s_2) which 'contains' a situation (s_3) in which there is a man who can fly. But it does not follow that in my present situation s_1 there is a man who can fly, even though $\langle\!\langle$There is a man who can fly$\rangle\!\rangle$ is a persistent fact. It is because s_3 is an imaginary situation (whose factual set is relative to a world w distinct from @) that the facts it supports, whether 'persistent' or not, do not persist when we move upward from that situation to the situations comprising it. That is the property which I call hyperinsulation.

Whether or not Perner's explanation of the time-lag between the emergence of conscious pretense and success in the false-belief task is correct, it is important to realize that hyperinsulation, as a property of imaginary situations, can be appreciated by children even if they do not fully master the notion of representation (i.e., the relation between imaginary situations and the real situations comprising them). The child can represent imaginary situations as such as soon as she knows that whatever goes on in an imaginary situation is bound to remain there, in isolation from the things that really happen.

§6.4 δ-Structures

So far I have stressed the double nature of situations, which can be viewed either as entities (from outside) or as situations (from inside). The two construals correspond to the following representational structures:

(3) $[e] \models \sigma$

(4) $[e'] \models \langle\!\langle \ldots e \ldots \rangle\!\rangle$

In (3) the situation e is exercised, that is, viewed from inside: what is represented is the *content* of that situation (a portion of its factual set) rather than the situation itself construed as an entity. In (4), however, the situation e is explicitly represented as an entity—as a constituent of some fact concerning some other situation.

Let us now turn to a third representational structure—actually a species of (4)—which has loomed large in our study so far:

(5) $[e'] \models \langle\!\langle e \models \sigma \rangle\!\rangle$

This I call a 'δ-structure'. In a δ-structure a situation is explicitly mentioned as supporting a certain fact. A δ-structure therefore brings into play two situations and two facts. The two situations are: the situation which the complex representation concerns (that represented within square brackets) and that which is explicitly mentioned. The two facts are: the fact which the mentioned situation is explicitly represented as supporting, and the fact *that* the mentioned situation supports that fact. Among the examples of δ-structures we have dealt with so far there were: various utterances/thoughts about spatial locations, such as 'In Paris it is raining'; conditionals, construed as utterances/thoughts about hypothetical situations; and metarepresentations, construed as utterances/thoughts about the imaginary situations represented in various media (films, books, mental states).

The representations in Perner's 'complex models' (the 'complex temporal model' and the 'pretend-reality model') are also δ-structures. Perner's complex temporal model corresponds to a global situation s comprising two sub-situations: a past situation and the present situation, each supporting a certain fact. The present situation supports the fact that the box is empty; the past situation supports the fact that the potato is in the box. It is because these facts cannot be consistenly integrated that different models (corresponding to the two situations) are needed. Integration takes place at the higher level, that of the complex temporal model itself. The situation s supports both the fact that *in the past situation* the potato was in the box, and the fact that *in the present situation* the box is empty.

Complex temporal model

$[s] \vDash_@ \langle\!\langle$ past situation $\vDash_@ \langle\!\langle$ Potato inside the box $\rangle\!\rangle\rangle\!\rangle$

$[s] \vDash_@ \langle\!\langle$ present situation $\vDash_@ \langle\!\langle$ Box empty $\rangle\!\rangle\rangle\!\rangle$

Similarly, the pretend-reality model corresponds to a global situation s' supporting both the fact that *in reality* the object in front of the subject is a piece of cloth and the fact that *in the pretense* that object is her pillow:

Pretend-reality model

$[s'] \vDash_@ \langle\!\langle$ real situation $\vDash_@$
      $\langle\!\langle$ This object in front of me is a piece of cloth $\rangle\!\rangle\rangle\!\rangle$

$[s'] \vDash_@ \langle\!\langle$ pretend situation $\vDash_w$
      $\langle\!\langle$ This object in front of me is my pillow $\rangle\!\rangle\rangle\!\rangle$

What is interesting with δ-structures is that they are intermediate between the two main types we have distinguished (i.e., (3) and (4) above). I said that a situation is construed *as a situation* when the entities it comprises and the facts it contains are represented; while it is construed *as an entity* when the situation itself is represented as having properties and standing in relation to other entities. Now δ-structures involve both construals at once. A situation is simultaneously represented as an entity (having the property that it supports the fact σ, and standing in the comprise relation to the constituents of σ) and as a situation (since the fact σ itself is represented). With δ-structures, we view the mentioned situation both from inside and from outside.

This should remind us of what was said in chapter 3 about 'that'-clauses and higher-level predication. I suggested that in an utterance like 'John believes that grass is green' or 'It will be the case that grass is green' the fact or proposition that grass is green is not reified and named: it is actually expressed. Still, at the same time, we express a (higher-level) fact about that proposition, to the effect that John believes it or that it will hold in the future. This superimposition of levels corresponds to my present claim that the situation mentioned by the prefix in a δ-structure is viewed both as an entity (a constituent of the higher-level fact) and as a situation (containing the lower-level fact). The internal, lower-level fact and the external, higher-level fact are simultaneously expressed, the former being nested within the latter. This hybrid structure is made possible by, and is revelatory of, the double nature of situations.

In view of what has just been said, I must qualify a claim I made earlier (p. 75):

a metarepresentation is not an instance of mental simulation, for the situation which it concerns ... is a real world situation, not an imaginary situation. The imaginary situation *s* is mentioned *in* the metarepresentation, but it is not that situation which the metarepresentation concerns. That is why the metarepresentation gives rise to a serious assertion, rather than a pretend assertion.

When I made that claim, in the course of discussing the simulation theory, it was important to emphasize the difference between straight-forward simulation, as illustrated by games of make-believe, and the (reflective) exploitation of simulation which characterizes conditional statements as well as metarepresentations. Conditionals, metarepresentations, etc., are all δ-structures on the pattern of (1), repeated below:

(1) $[s'] \vDash_@ \langle\!\langle s \vDash_w \sigma \rangle\!\rangle$

This is clearly distinct from instances of straightforward simulation such as

(6) $[s] \vDash_w \sigma$

In (1) the exercised situation is a real situation (the actual world is what indexes the leftmost support relation). In (6) the exercised situation is imaginary.

That distinction is still essential and it holds good. But, given what has just been said concerning δ-structures, the following qualification is in order. Even though in metarepresentational talk we take a reflective stance toward the imaginary situation we are mentioning, still the content of that situation is displayed, and to that extent metarepresentations involve simulation. Not only do we view the imaginary situation from outside—from the point of view of the actual world—as e.g., the situation depicted in such and such a film; we *also* view that situation from inside as a situation in which, say, Robin Hood meets Frankenstein. Two levels coexist here: a simulative representation of the imaginary situation from inside, and a non-simulative representation of that situation from outside (*qua* situation represented in the film). It is because the former representation is subordinated to the latter that the overall representation does not count as an instance of mental simulation, even though it clearly involves one.

§6.5   Circumstance-Shifting as Simulation: Bühler's Theory

According to the psychologist and language-theorist Karl Bühler, simulation is involved not only when we think or talk about imaginary situations, but more generally, whenever we think or talk about a situation that is not given to our senses. Without simulation, therefore, we could not go beyond Perner's 'single-updating model'.

Following Bühler we can distinguish two basic representational modes, or rather two poles. In the *egocentric* mode what we say or think directly concerns the situation in which we presently are: the *hic et nunc* situation, as I will call it. That mode is dominant in what we may call the 'egocentric stage' in the child's linguistic development, when only 'monoremes' or one-word utterances are issued (Sechehaye 1926). Such utterances are holistically predicated of the child's egocentric situation. Not being liable to vary, that situation is not and does not have to be articulated. As Perner says, "the perceiver has no option of representing anything but current reality" (Perner 1991: 67).

The other mode is more complex and involves what Bühler calls 'a liberating step' from the *hic et nunc* situation: the subject freely considers, and characterizes, situations which are not given to his or her senses—for example situations she remembers or imagines. According to Bühler what makes the liberating step possible is mental simulation: the absent situation is *presentified* through an act of the imagination.[26] (Even memory involves such an act.). As a result, the subject both experiences the egocentric situation and, at the same time, simulatively experiences the absent situation, which comes before 'the mind's eye'. Being simulatively presentified, the imagined situation and what occurs in it can be deictically referred to much like the *hic et nunc* situation and what occurs in it can be deictically referred to. Bühler calls this 'imagination-oriented deixis' as opposed to (normal) perceptual deixis and invokes in this connection some of the phenomena I will deal with later in terms of 'context-shift' (see parts IV and V below).

The liberating power of the simulation comes from the fact that the imagined situation can replace the egocentrically given situation as that which the current thought or discourse concerns:

> [If] a proper name such as 'Heidelberg' or 'Lake Constance' ... is dropped as the subject of a sentence in the presence of a hearer who has been there, then an imagination-oriented deixis is at work and the release of the sense of the sentence from the support for understanding provided by the concrete speech situation has been more or less adequately prepared; if one is displaced in imagination to a thing, *one can forget from where one was displaced.* ...
>
> If I hear 'it is raining' without any prelude, I take this to be a diagnosis of the weather in the speech situation; it is raining where the speaker is at the moment. ... The addition of an exposition 'at Lake Constance' brings a releasing step: 'it is raining at Lake Constance'; this extended dictum can be spoken anywhere, its sense is largely liberated from ... the speech situation. (Bühler 1934: 426).

It seems that Bühler is putting forward a simulation theory of utterances like 'At Lake Constance it is raining'. The speaker and the hearer are in a certain situation which they can perceive. Let us assume that, in that situation, the sun is shining. The speaker utters the expositional formula 'At Lake Constance' which Bühler describes as providing 'displacement instructions' (Bühler 1934: 425). Lake Constance is thus pre-sentified and the subject can think, concerning that place: it is raining. Displacement here is the transition from a thought/utterance concerning the *hic et nunc* situation to a thought/utterance concerning another, disjoint situation. In the Austinian framework this can be represented as the transition from (7) to (8):

(7) $[hic\ et\ nunc] \models_@ \langle\!\langle$ The sun is shining $\rangle\!\rangle$

(8) $[\text{Lake Constance}] \models_@ \langle\!\langle$ It is raining $\rangle\!\rangle$

But we need not construe Bühler's theory that way. When Lake Constance is referred to, it is referred to *in connection with the hic et nunc situation*: The speaker and the hearer are aware that the situation they are in is part of a bigger spatio-temporal frame including other places, one of which is Lake Constance.[27] Lake Constance is therefore thought of as attainable from the *hic et nunc* situation: if one moves from here in a certain direction, one will end up in Lake Constance. (The same considerations apply to thoughts about the past or the future.) So it is not true that the mentioned situation (Lake Constance) has *replaced* the *hic et nunc* situation as that which the utterance or thought concerns. The *hic et nunc* situation has not disappeared from the picture.

Does it follow that it is the *hic et nunc* situation which the utterance/thought concerns, in the Lake Constance example? Not quite. Another distinction due to Bühler can be useful at this point. Bühler distinguishes between the *hic et nunc* situation which is 'the point-like origin' of the deictic coordinate system, and various *expansions* of the deictic sphere around that point-like origin. For example:

[The speaker who says 'I'] means more than just the I of the moment ...; he means a role-player who survives the moment of speaking.... That is an expansion of the I-sphere that is just as usual as when a speaker in Berlin says *here* and includes all of Berlin. That alone is enough to remove the sense of a spoken utterance from the realm of ocular demonstration, even if a deictic clue is still indispensable to fulfil its sense. (Bühler 1934: 424)

Bühler also distinguishes that process of 'expansion' of the deictic sphere, from the process of 'displacement', that is, the step from (7) above to (8). In displacement one goes from the *hic et nunc* situation to a *disjoint* situation, that is, a situation which, like Lake Constance in the above example, neither is nor contains the *hic et nunc* situation. In expansion one goes from the *hic et nunc* situation to a larger situation containing it.

Armed with those distinctions, let us resume the analysis of 'At Lake Constance it is raining'. The speaker and hearer find themselves in an initial situation which they perceive and in which, we suppose, the sun is shining. That is the *hic et nunc* situation. The speaker then mentions a disjoint situation by uttering the expositional formula 'At Lake Constance'. As this situation is evoked it becomes available for projection. The shift from the *hic et nunc* situation to the mentioned situation into which speaker and hearer can project themselves is what Bühler calls 'displacement'. But it is not true that the utterance 'At Lake Constance it is raining' itself achieves displacement, if we define the latter as requiring that *the situation which the representation concerns* (the 'exercised situation') be disjoint from the *hic et nunc* situation.

When the subject says or thinks 'At Lake Constance it is raining', what is the exercised situation? Arguably, the exercised situation is neither the *hic et nunc* situation, nor the mentioned situation (Lake Constance), but the relevant expansion of the *hic et nunc* situation; an expansion which contains both the *hic et nunc* situation and the mentioned situation. As I pointed out earlier, Lake Constance can be successfully mentioned only because the speaker and the hearer are mutually aware that that place exists as part of the same spatio-temporal frame to which the *hic et nunc* situation also belongs. 'At Lake Constance it is raining' can therefore be represented as (9), with '*S*' standing for the relevant expansion of the *hic et nunc* situation.

(9) $[S] \models_@ \langle\!\langle$ Lake Constance $\models_@ \langle\!\langle$ It is raining $\rangle\!\rangle\rangle\!\rangle$

To sum up, a crucial feature of displacement is that the exercised situation is disjoint from the *hic et nunc* situation. In (3), however, the exercised situation still is an expansion of the *hic et nunc* situation; hence no displacement is achieved, strictly speaking. The subject keeps an eye on the *hic et nunc* situation and appeals to mental simulation only obliquely, to characterize an expansion of the *hic et nunc* situation. Again, we find that complex representations like (9) have a hybrid, transitory nature, that they involve simultaneously viewing a situation from outside and from inside.

7
World-Shifting

§7.1 Heterogeneous δ-Structures

Let us take stock. The world consists of situations which are both insulated from each other and connected to each other, thanks to their dual nature. In the egocentric stage representations (whether linguistic or mental) concern the *hic et nunc* situation. Simulation enables us to go beyond that stage and to consider other situations: situations remote in space or time, or more radically imaginary situations belonging to some other possible world.

In that framework, what characterizes metarepresentations? So far I have argued that, like conditionals, they are δ-structures on the pattern of (1):

(1) $[s'] \vDash_@ \langle\!\langle s \vDash_w \sigma \rangle\!\rangle$

Such representations 'concern' a real world situation s', but they are 'about' an imaginary situation s, which is represented as supporting the fact that σ. Simulation is involved in shifting from the exercised situation s' to the mentioned situation s, but if Bühler is right, that simulative aspect is not characteristic of metarepresentations and conditionals as opposed to other δ-structures such as 'A moment ago, the potato was in the box' or 'At Lake Constance, it is raining': *whenever* a situation distinct from the *hic et nunc* situation is mentioned, simulation is involved (§6.5).

The most salient difference between metarepresentations and conditionals, on the one hand, and other δ-structures like Bühler's Lake Constance example on the other hand, is that the situation mentioned in a conditional or a metarepresentation is an *imaginary* situation, that is, a situation whose factual set is relative to a world w possibly distinct from the actual world. As we have seen, a δ-structure involves two situations, two facts, and two support relations. In metarepresentations and conditionals the two support relations are indexed to different worlds. When that sort of thing happens, I say that a *world-shift* occurs, resulting in hyperinsulation. A δ-structure like (1), in which a world-shift occurs, I call a *heterogeneous* δ-structure (table II.5).

There is a problem with that picture, however: it does not capture the *difference* between conditionals and metarepresentations. To see that, let us systematically compare a conditional and a metarepresentation involving the same innermost fact, e.g., (2) and (3) below.

(2)   In the book, a third world war has been declared.

(3)   If John is not mistaken, a third world war has been declared.

Both statements characterize an imaginary situation as supporting the fact that a third world war has been declared. In one case the imaginary situation is a hypothetical situation (that which the antecedent of the conditional describes: a situation in which John is not mistaken); in the other case it is the situation depicted in a certain book. But we note an asymmetry between the conditional and the metarepresentation. The

Table II.5
Homogeneous and heterogeneous δ-structures: first analysis

Homogeneous δ-structure

$[s'] \models_@ \langle\!\langle s \models_@ \sigma \rangle\!\rangle$

A moment ago, the potato was in the box.
At Lake Constance it is raining.
When he sees my sister, he will understand.

Heterogeneous δ-structure

$[s'] \models_@ \langle\!\langle s \models_w \sigma \rangle\!\rangle$

Conditionals	Metarepresentations
If he sees my sister, he will understand.	*John believes that S.* *In the book, S.*

book referred to in (2) is a real world object, hence (in my theory) a situation to which a factual set is associated in the actual world. There is no counterpart to that real situation in the case of conditionals. To be sure, conditionals *concern* a real situation, much as metarepresentations do. In that sense they are about the actual world. But metarepresentations do more than that: they *explicitly mention* a real situation, namely the actual world entity which depicts the imaginary situation. If, therefore, we maintain that both conditionals and metarepresentations mention an imaginary situation as supporting a certain fact, we must acknowledge that metarepresentations are *more complex* in that they mention not only that imaginary situation, but also a real entity which stands in the representation relation to that imaginary situation.

The extra complexity of metarepresentations—the fact that they mention a real situation and not merely an imaginary situation—is displayed in table II.6. As we can see on the table, the conditional mentions a hypothetical situation (a situation in which John is not mistaken), and says that it supports the fact that a third world war has been declared;

Table II.6
Conditionals versus metarepresentations

Conditionals		
$[s] \models_@$ $\langle\!\langle s'$	$\models_w$ $\sigma \rangle\!\rangle$	
Hypothetical situation described by the antecedent	Consequent of the conditional	
If John is not mistaken,	*a third world war has been declared.*	

Metarepresentations		
$[s] \models_@$ $\langle\!\langle R$	$\models_@$ $\langle\!\langle s'$	$\models_w$ $\sigma \rangle\!\rangle\rangle\!\rangle$
The book as real-world object	Imaginary situation described in the book	
In the book		*a third world war has been declared.*

while the metarepresentation mentions a real situation (the book) as supporting the fact that an imaginary situation (that which the book depicts) supports the fact that a third world has been declared.

If this analysis is correct, Table II.5 must be revised. (Table II.7 incorporates the needed revisions.) But is the analysis correct? It raises a difficulty of its own. Consider (4) and (5):

(4)   In the book, there is a three-page chapter.

(5)   In the book, there is a winged horse.

Both (4) and (5) mention a real situation, namely the book, but the innermost fact—the fact which is stated by the sentence following the situation-mentioning prefix—holds in the 'world of the book' in (5), and in the actual world in (4). (5) therefore involves a world-shift while (4) does not. This is similar to the difference between (6) and (7):

(6)   When he sees my sister, he will understand.

(7)   If he sees my sister, he will understand.

The difference between an 'if' sentence and the corresponding 'when'-sentence can easily be represented in the framework set up so far. It is the difference between the following:

$[s] \vDash_@ \langle\!\langle s' \vDash_@ \sigma \rangle\!\rangle$

$[s] \vDash_@ \langle\!\langle s' \vDash_w \sigma \rangle\!\rangle$

But the difference between (4) and (5) cannot be represented as simply as that, that is, in terms of a mere world-shift. If metarepresentations dis-

Table II.7
Homogeneous and heterogeneous δ-structures: second analysis

Homogeneous δ-structures
$[s'] \vDash_@ \langle\!\langle s \vDash_@ \sigma \rangle\!\rangle$

Heterogeneous δ-structures	
Simple	Complex
$[s'] \vDash_@ \langle\!\langle s \vDash_w \sigma \rangle\!\rangle$	$[s'] \vDash_@ \langle\!\langle R \vDash_@ \langle\!\langle s \vDash_w \sigma \rangle\!\rangle \rangle\!\rangle$
(Conditionals)	(Metarepresentations)

play the extra complexity I have mentioned, then the difference between (4) and (5) will be represented as the difference between the following:

$[s] \vDash_@ \langle\!\langle$ the book $\vDash_@ \langle\!\langle$ There is a three-page chapter $\rangle\!\rangle\rangle\!\rangle$

$[s] \vDash_@ \langle\!\langle$ the book $\vDash_@$
$\qquad\quad \langle\!\langle$ the imaginary situation it describes $\vDash_w$
$\qquad\quad \langle\!\langle$ There is a winged horse $\rangle\!\rangle\rangle\!\rangle\rangle\!\rangle$

Instead of simply a difference in world-indices, we have a further difference in representational complexity. This sounds like a violation of compositionality: for (4) and (5) are formally very similar, hence perhaps there should not be such a difference in complexity between their respective contents.

To sum up, there are two possible analyses of metarepresentations in the framework set up so far; both raise difficulties. According to the first analysis, metarepresentations are simple heterogeneous δ-structures (table II.5). This analysis does not capture the difference between metarepresentations and conditionals, namely, the fact that in a metarepresentation like (2) a real situation is mentioned (over and above the imaginary situation which supports the innermost fact). The second analysis, which I favour, emphasizes that difference and ascribes a more complex structure to metarepresentations (table II.7). But this leads to an apparent violation of compositionality when we are given a pair of sentences like (4) and (5). What, then, can we do?

§7.2   Conditionals and Metarepresentations

If we are impressed by the compositionality objection to the second analysis, we can retreat to the first analysis, according to which both conditionals and metarepresentations are simple δ-structures on the pattern of (1).

(1) $[s'] \vDash_@ \langle\!\langle s \vDash_w \sigma \rangle\!\rangle$

That analysis itself raises an objection, as we have seen. It does not account for the difference between e.g., (2) and (3):

(2)   In the book, a third world war has been declared.

(3)   If John is not mistaken, a third world war has been declared.

Sentences (2) and (3) differ in that (2) does, while (3) does not, mention a real situation (the book) over and above the imaginary situation which supports the innermost fact. In defense of the first analysis, however, we could argue that the real situation in question is mentioned *only in order to make the imaginary situation talked about identifiable*. On this view, which I will shortly criticize, the real situation which a metarepresentation mentions enters the picture only at the mode of presentation level. At the content level only the imaginary situation occurs. That imaginary situation is *presented as* the situation which the book depicts, but that mode of presentation remains external to the content of the metarepresentation. The content of the metarepresentation therefore is a heterogeneous δ-structure as simple as the content of a conditional: in both cases an imaginary situation is mentioned as supporting the fact that a third world war has been declared.

It was part of the objection to the first analysis that in a conditional like (3) there is no counterpart to the real situation which is mentioned in (2). That too can be disputed. After all, (3) mentions John, and John also is a real situation. Like the book in (2), John is mentioned in (3) in order to identify the hypothetical situation talked about. Admittedly, there remains a difference between (2) and (3); but it is a difference in the ways in which the imaginary situation talked about is presented. In (3) the imaginary situation is described *from inside*, in terms of one of the facts it supports (the fact that John is not mistaken); in (2) the imaginary situation talked about is described *from outside*, in terms of its relation to another entity (the book which depicts it). We find the same sort of contrast between homogeneous δ-structures like (6) and (8):

(6)   When John sees my sister, he will understand.

(8)   Later this afternoon, he will understand.

In (6) the temporal situation talked about is described from inside, in terms of one of the facts it supports (the fact that John sees my sister); in (8) it is described from outside, in terms of its place within a larger temporal situation.

In this way we can defend the first analysis and stick to the picture displayed in table II.5. However that is not what I will do. My reason for not pursuing this line of defense is this: I am not convinced that the real situation mentioned in a metarepresentation can be confined to the mode of presentation level. My skepticism has several sources, but one argument in particular deserves mentioning. It bears on the issue we are debating: the relation between conditionals and metarepresentations.

It take it that there is something metarepresentational about conditionals. What is a conditional? It is a statement which mentions a hypothetical situation and says that it supports such and such a fact. What is a hypothetical situation? It is a situation which one 'hypothetizes', that is, the content of an act of supposing. One thus finds that a conditional is a statement about the imaginary situation which a certain type of mental act represents, much as a metarepresentation is a statement about the imaginary situation which a representation R (possibly a mental act) represents.

On this view conditionals are like metarepresentations. What is the difference? There are two major differences, according to me. First, the mental act of supposing which is at stake in conditionals is not given independently of the conditional, but takes place in the very process of entertaining the conditional. To think conditionally 'If p, then q' *is* to suppose that p and to characterize the imaginary situation which is thus imagined as supporting the fact that q. This reflexivity is absent from metarepresentations, which are about a representation R distinct and independent from (though to some extent mimicked by) the metarepresentation itself. The second major difference between conditionals and metarepresentations is this. The mental act of supposing stands in the representation-relation to the imaginary situation posited by the antecedent, just as the real situation mentioned in a metarepresentation stands in the representation-relation to the imaginary situation supporting the innermost fact; yet in the case of the conditional the act of supposing is not 'mentioned' in the full sense of the term, while the book, the film, or John's beliefs *are* mentioned when we say things like 'In the book ...', 'In the film ...', or 'John believes that ...'. The act of supposing that p is no more mentioned when I say 'If p then q' than the present utterance is mentioned when I say 'I am bald'. There is a sense in which 'I' means 'the producer of this utterance', but whatever 'reference' to the utterance takes place is certainly confined to the mode of presentation level and does not affect the content of what is said. Similarly, I think that whatever 'reference' to the act of supposing occurs in a conditional is confined to the mode of presentation level and does not affect the content of the conditional—which content merely involves the imaginary situation to which the act of supposing stands in the representation-relation. That is all in contrast to what happens in metarepresentations. For as I said, metarepresentations do mention the real situation R which stands in the representation-relation to the imaginary situation supporting the innermost fact. Because this contrast between conditionals and metarepresentations is important, I do not buy the view that the reference to the situation doing the representing is confined to the mode of presentation level in the case of metarepresentations.

§7.3   Compositionality and Polysemy

We are thus back to the second analysis, according to which metarepresentations do, while conditionals do not, mention real situations and not merely imaginary situations (table II.7). That analysis raises the compositionality objection, as we have seen. Metarepresentations such as (5) are ascribed a complex structure: a real situation, say a book, is mentioned as supporting the fact that an imaginary situation (that which is depicted in the book) supports the fact expressed by the internal sentence following the prefix 'in the book'. Now where does that complex structure come from? Since (4) and (5) are formally similar, how can their respective contents be as different as the second analysis assumes?

(4)   In the book, there is a three-page chapter.

   $[s] \vDash_@ \langle\!\langle$ the book $\vDash_@ \langle\!\langle$ There is a three-page chapter $\rangle\!\rangle\rangle\!\rangle$

(5)   In the book, there is a winged horse.

   $[s] \vDash_@ \langle\!\langle$ the book $\vDash_@$

   $\langle\!\langle$ the imaginary situation it describes $\vDash_w$

   $\langle\!\langle$ There is a winged horse $\rangle\!\rangle\rangle\!\rangle\rangle\!\rangle$

Formidable though it seems, the compositionality objection vanishes as soon as we take notice of the pervasiveness of polysemy and meaning-shifts in natural language. Consider, for example, the contrast between (9) and (10).

(9)   John heard the music.

(10)   John heard the piano.

There is a sense in which *only sounds can be heard*. Let us call that 'Principle P'. Insofar as music consists of sounds, (9) respects Principle P. What about (10)? Does it not violate the principle that only sounds can be heard? No: when one talks of hearing the piano, what one means is that one hears *the sounds emitted, or the music produced, by the piano*. How is it possible to mean such a thing by (10)? A widespread theory has it that 'the piano' in (10) is not used literally but metonymically: on that use it does not mean *the piano* but *the sounds emitted by the piano*. A better theory, argued for by Langacker (1984), ascribes to 'hear' two distinct (though related) senses. It is in the *primary* sense of 'hear', $hear_1$, that only sounds can be heard. (Principle P must therefore be rephrased as the principle that only sounds can be $heard_1$.) The second sense, $hear_2$, can be defined in terms of the primary sense: to $hear_2$ an object is to $hear_1$ the sounds emitted by this object. Evidently, 'hear' in (10) is used in the second sense. Sentences (9) and (10) can therefore be paraphrased thus:

(9*)   John $heard_1$ the music.

(10*)   John $heard_2$ the piano.

Now (10*) itself is paraphrasable as (10**):

(10**)   John $heard_1$ the sounds emitted by the piano.

If we compare (9*) and (10**), we notice a difference in semantic complexity. But that difference results from the distinct semantic contributions made by the polysemous verb 'hear' in (9) and (10) respectively. Being located at the 'subatomic' level (Parsons 1990: chapter 1) that difference can be acknowledged consistently with the observation that (9) and (10) are syntactically undistinguishable.

There are well-known cases in which a similar difference in semantic complexity is clearly due to a shift in meaning. Thus consider Nunberg's famous example:

(11)   My car is parked out back.

(12)   I am parked out back.

Nunberg once thought that 'I' in (12) is used metonymically to denote the speaker's car (Nunberg 1979); but that analysis he now considers as misguided and unacceptable. According to his new analysis (Nunberg 1995), 'I' in (12) denotes the speaker—period. To be sure, there is a sense in which *only vehicles can be 'parked out back'*. Let us call that 'Principle Q'. Sentence (12) seems to violate Principle Q, in the same way in which (10) seemed to violate Principle P. But the violation is merely apparent in both cases. In the same way in which 'hear' in (10) assumes a different sense from the sense it has in Principle P, the phrase 'parked out back' does not mean the same thing in (12) and in Principle Q. In Principle Q, 'parked out back' means the same thing as it does in (11). It is used to predicate a certain property (the property of being parked out back) of a *vehicle*. In 'I am parked out back', however, the same phrase is used to predicate a different (and more complex) property: the property of *having a car which is* parked out back. *That* property is predicated of persons. The predicative expression 'is parked out back' thus undergoes a transfer of meaning; a process that is quite systematic, according to Nunberg (Nunberg 1995). In virtue of this process, (12) expresses a more complex proposition that (11).

In the same way in which 'John heard x' or 'x is parked out back' can mean two distinct things, depending on the value we assign to x (which value determines the relevant sense for 'hear' or for 'parked out back'), we can distinguish two possible senses for 'In x, p'. In a first sense, 'In x, p' means, or entails, that x supports the fact that p. In a second, meta-representational sense, 'In x, p' means that x *represents an imaginary situation which* supports the fact that p. These two senses are illustrated by (4) and (5) respectively.

Now the question arises, where in this particular case does the polysemy come from? Which expression, if any, undergoes a meaning shift? There are several options. On one theory it is the phrase 'the book' which can be used metonymically to denote the situation depicted in the book. This is similar to the view that 'the piano' in (10) means 'the sounds (or music) emitted by the piano', or to the view that 'I' in (12) refers to the speaker's car. On another view, it is the relation expressed by 'in' which is different in the two cases. Which theory we favour is relevant to the current issue. For suppose we opt for the metonymy theory. Then we need not ascribe a more complex structure to (5) than to (4). The difference is simply that in (4) we talk about a real world object/situation (the book), whereas in (5) we talk about an imaginary situation, viz. the situation depicted in the book, which we metonymically designate by using the same noun-phrase 'the book' in a different sense. In both cases we ascribe to the subject (the book, or the imaginary situation depicted in the book) the property of supporting a certain fact (the fact that there is a three-page chapter, or the fact that there is a winged horse). On this view the difference between (4) and (5) is exactly similar to the difference between (6) and (7), repeated below:

(6)　When he sees my sister, he will understand.

(7)　If he sees my sister, he will understand.

The difference between (4) and (5), or between (6) and (7), is simply that between a homogeneous and a heterogeneous δ-structure:

$$[s'] \vDash_@ \langle\!\langle s \vDash_@ \sigma \rangle\!\rangle$$

$$[s'] \vDash_@ \langle\!\langle s \vDash_w \sigma \rangle\!\rangle$$

It follows there is no structural difference between metarepresentations and conditionals: both have a simple structure, in accordance with table II.5.

Nunberg's reasons for considering the predicate, rather than the subject, as the locus of meaning transfer fully apply to our case, however. I can say: 'In this book, which was written thirty years ago and contains many chapters, there is a man who can fly'. According to Nunberg, that would not be possible if 'the book' really was used metonymically to refer to the situation depicted in the book. (The situation described in the book is not the sort of thing that can be said to have been written thirty years ago or to contain chapters.) I therefore opt for the view that the property ascribed to the book in (5) is the complex property of *representing a situation which* supports the fact that there is a winged horse, while in (4) the book is ascribed the simpler property of supporting the fact that there is a three-page chapter. The difference between (4) and (5) can thus be represented as that between the following:

$[s] \models_@ \langle\!\langle$ the book $\models_@ \langle\!\langle$ There is a three-page chapter $\rangle\!\rangle\rangle\!\rangle$

$[s] \models_@ \langle\!\langle$ the book $\models_@$

$\qquad\langle\!\langle$ the imaginary situation it describes $\models_w$

$\qquad\qquad\langle\!\langle$ There is a winged horse $\rangle\!\rangle\rangle\!\rangle\rangle\!\rangle$

On this analysis, the sense of (5) is structurally more complex than the sense of (4), even though there is no relevant syntactic difference between the two sentences. This is OK for the difference in complexity can be traced to the different semantic contributions which some expression makes in (4) and (5) respectively. The so-called compositionality principle provides an objection to the analysis summarized in table II.7 only if we assume that linguistic expressions in general are univocal and always make the same semantic contribution; some theorists even consider this assumption to be part and parcel of the compositionality principle. But it is pretty clear that this assumption is false, given the phenomenon known as 'systematic polysemy'.[28] As a result, the objection carries little weight and need not retain us any longer.

§7.4   Revising the Analysis

Even though the compositionality objection carries little weight, I am not ultimately satisfied with our analysis as it stands. I wish to maintain that a metarepresentation mentions a real situation, while downplaying the extra complexity that this seems to imply. That is the gist of the amendment which I am now going to propose.

Let us return to the contrast between 'if'-sentences and 'when'-sentences, as illustrated by (6) and (7):

(6)   When he sees my sister, he will understand.

(7)   If he sees my sister, he will understand.

In (7), a world-shift occurs. While (7) as a whole is interpreted with respect to a real situation, namely that which the utterance concerns, the consequent is interpreted with respect to the imaginary situation mentioned in the antecedent. In (6), no world-shift occurs, for the situation mentioned in the antecedent of a 'when'-sentence is a real situation, in contrast to the situation mentioned in the antecedent of a conditional.

Despite this difference, (6) and (7) have much in common: in both cases a situation is mentioned in the antecedent, and the consequent is evaluated with respect to that situation, according to the general structure:

$$[s'] \vDash \langle\!\langle s \qquad\qquad \vDash \sigma \rangle\!\rangle$$
$$\qquad\quad \text{antecedent} \quad \text{consequent}$$

In both cases also, the situation mentioned by the antecedent is identified 'from inside' as a situation supporting a certain fact. What 'if' and 'when' contrastively determine is whether that situation belongs to @ or to some world w possibly distinct from @. It follows that the protasis 'if he sees my sister' does two things in (7). First, it provides a way of identifying a situation, given a world: we are to look for a situation containing the fact that John sees my sister. Second, it tells us (through the word 'if') that the relevant possible world in which to look for that situation need not be identical to the actual world.

In the case of metarepresentations, can we discern these two functions? It is not obvious that we can. Take belief sentences. The prefix 'John believes that' introduces us into John's 'belief world', and the complement sentence expresses a fact which holds in that world; but no particular situation within that world is specified as supporting that fact. In contrast, the conditional not only gives us a hypothetical world, but, within that world, it gives us a particular situation: that in which John sees my sister. (As usual, when I talk of 'belief world', 'hypothetical world', etc., cautious readers must systematically replace 'world' by 'set of worlds'.)

If what I have just said is correct, then the structure we assigned to metarepresentations, namely (13), may be too complex after all:

$$(13) \quad [s'] \vDash_@ \langle\!\langle R \vDash_@ \langle\!\langle s \vDash_w \sigma \rangle\!\rangle \rangle\!\rangle$$

The right-hand side contains a real situation (the representation R), an imaginary situation (s, the situation depicted by R), and a shifted world w (the 'world of the representation'). But perhaps we can get rid of the imaginary situation s and keep only R and w.

Let us tentatively revise the analysis according to the above suggestion. Let us say that metarepresentational prefixes (i) mention real situations, and (ii) shift the world with respect to which the complement sentence is evaluated. The fact expressed by the complement sentence is thus understood as holding in the shifted world introduced by the meta-representational prefix; but no particular portion of that world is mentioned as supporting the fact in question. On the revised analysis, a metarepresentation mentions a real situation (the book, or John's belief state) as supporting a fact which holds in some imaginary world—an 'imaginary fact', for short. Metarepresentations are therefore ascribed the following structure:

(14) $[s'] \vDash_@ \langle\!\langle R \vDash_@ \sigma^w \rangle\!\rangle$

Here R stands for the real-world entity (book, film, belief state) which represents the world as being thus and so, while the superscript means that the innermost fact σ holds in the possible world w thus deployed through R.

The revised analysis raises an obvious problem of interpretation. If the situation which the metarepresentation mentions (e.g., the book) is a real situation, that is, a portion of the actual world @, how can the fact which that situation supports hold in some other possible world w? What does that possibly mean?

In an earlier paper (Recanati 1999: 140) I made a suggestion which enables us to make sense of (14). The suggestion is summarized in (15):

(15)   A real situation R supports an imaginary fact σ^w just in case (i) R supports σ and (ii) whichever 'support' relation the fact σ *internally* involves is indexed to w, the imaginary world of the representation.

Let us, for example, consider the metarepresentation (16):

(16)   John believes that, in the eighteenth century, kangaroos had tails.

In (16) the complement sentence, 'In the eighteenth century, kangaroos had tails' expresses an *imaginary* fact, a fact which holds in John's 'belief world'. According to the revised analysis, (16) says that John's belief state (a real situation) supports that imaginary fact:

(17) $[s] \vDash_@ \langle\!\langle$ John's belief state $\vDash_@$
            $\langle\!\langle$ In the 18th century, kangaroos had tails $\rangle\!\rangle^i \rangle\!\rangle^{29}$

What does that mean? Thanks to (15), we can analyse (17) as

(18) $[s] \models_@$ 《John's belief state $\models_@$

$\quad\quad\quad$《the 18th century $\models_i$《kangaroos have tails》》》

Admittedly, (18) is a complex heterogeneous δ-structure of the sort posited by our original analysis (§7.3). In that complex structure we find a real situation (John's belief state), an imaginary situation (the eighteenth century *qua* portion of the world as seen by John) and a fact which that imaginary situation supports (the fact that kangaroos have tails). Still, in contrast to the original analysis, metarepresentations are ascribed the simpler structure (14). We get the more complex structure (18) *only because we access the internal structure of the imaginary fact σ* (which itself consists of a situation, a fact, and a support relation). If we leave σ unanalysed, what we get is an instance of (14), namely (17).

On the revised analysis the difference between (4) and (5), repeated below, *can* be assimilated to the difference between an 'if'-sentence and the corresponding 'when'-sentence: it is a mere difference in world-indices.

(4)   In the book, there is a three-page chapter.

$\quad\quad$$[s'] \models_@$ 《the book $\models_@$《There is a three-page chapter》》

(5)   In the book, there is a winged horse.

$\quad\quad$$[s'] \models_@$ 《the book $\models_@$《There is a winged horse》^{w}》

The difference between the revised and the original analysis should not be overestimated, however. Understood in the light of (15), the revised analysis presupposes something dubious: that the fact expressed by the complement sentence (the sentence following the metarepresentational prefix) is internally complex and itself involves the 'support' relation (Recanati 1999: 141). But that need not always be the case. Presumably, there are metarepresentations where the complement sentence expresses a 'thetic' fact, to use the Brentanian terminology: a fact which displays no internal complexity of the required sort. Such facts are expressed by e.g., weather sentences or existential sentences. It follows that a sentence like 'John believes that there are spies' raises a problem in our framework. According to the revised analysis it will be analysed as

(19) $[s] \models_@$ 《John's belief state $\models_@$《There are spies》^{i}》

But the fact that there are spies does not itself involve an internal 'support' relation. How then can we cash out the imaginary nature of that fact? The definition in (15) is unapplicable here. To deal with such cases we must replace (15) by a more complex definition, namely (20):

(20)   A real situation R supports an imaginary fact σ^w just in case

• if the fact σ internally involves a 'support' relation, then R supports σ and the internal 'support' relation is indexed to w, the imaginary world of the representation;

• if the fact σ is internally simple, R supports the fact that some imaginary situation in the domain of w supports the fact that σ; the situation in question is either contextually determined or left unspecified (quantified over).

Understood in the light of (20), the revised analysis is undistinguishable from the original analysis whenever the fact expressed by the complement sentence is simple. They differ only when the fact expressed by the complement sentence is suitably complex.

§7.5   Conclusion

At the beginning of chapter 4, I mentioned two theories (or rather two families of theory) well-suited to capture the iconicity of metarepresentations: modal theories and simulation theories. The view I actually put forward belongs to the first group. The basic idea is that a metarepresentation dS consists of a circumstance-shifting prefix d and a sentence S. The metarepresentation holds in a circumstance c iff the object-representation S holds in a distinct circumstance c' introduced by the circumstance-shifting prefix.

At the beginning of chapter 4, I used the term 'circumstance' without defining it. Afterwards I did not use it much. I talked of 'situations' instead, and also of 'worlds'. Now what is a circumstance? Is it distinct from a situation?

There is a sense in which a circumstance is a situation, but it is not quite the sense in which I used 'situation' in this and previous chapters. Let us define a 'thick' situation as a situation taken together with the factual set which a particular world assigns to it. A thick situation, therefore, is a situation *qua* belonging to a particular world. The situations I talked about so far were 'thin' rather than 'thick': for I explicitly said that situations can occur in distinct worlds and be assigned distinct factual sets. Be that as it may, a circumstance corresponds to what I've just called a thick situation: a situation *qua* belonging to a certain world. To get a circumstance, therefore, we need a possible world, and a particular situation within that world.

A circumstance, then, will typically involve a place p, a time t and a world w. (The place p and the time t give us a particular situation in w.) Let us suppose that a complex representation dS is evaluated with respect to some initial circumstance c, say the circumstance in which the representation is tokened. The circumstance-shifting prefix d need not shift all aspects (time, place, and world) of the initial circumstance c. Suppose, for example, that the representation is an instance of (21):

(21) In the kitchen, S

Only the place component of the circumstance is shifted through the prefix 'in the kitchen'.[30] The time and the world of c remain untouched. With a temporal prefix such as 'Tomorrow (it will be the case that)', it is the time component which will be selectively shifted in that manner.

In some cases, the shift affects the world component of the circumstance. Thus modal operators are traditionally analysed as world-shifters. (22) is said to be true in a world w iff the embedded sentence is true in some possible world w' accessible from w.

(22) It may/might be the case that camels like sugar.

Conditionals also involve a world-shift, as we have seen. While the prefix in (6) shifts the circumstance by introducing a future situation in which John sees your sister, the prefix in (7) additionally shifts the world to which that situation belongs: we are to consider a possible world (or rather, a class of possible worlds) containing a future situation in which John sees your sister.

(6) When he sees my sister, he will understand.

(7) If he sees my sister, he will understand.

In metarepresentations also the prefix shifts the world: 'in the book' introduces a 'fictional world', i.e., the world as described by the book. (Here also, as I pointed out several times, the 'world' in question is best thought of as a set of possible worlds.) 'In the book, p' holds in the actual world iff the complement sentence holds in the 'world of the book'.

Even though we have opted for the modal view rather than the simulation view, there is more than a grain of truth in the simulation theory. For circumstance-shifting in general involves mental simulation. The simulation at issue is especially dramatic when the shift affects the world—as it does in conditionals or sentences about fiction.

What the simulation theory misses is the *partial* nature of the relevant simulation. In entertaining a δ-structure we view things from an alien point of view—that is where simulation comes in—*and* from our point of view at the same time. I have tried to explicate that in terms of the double nature of situations. Situations are entities having properties and standing in relation to other entities, but they are also micro-universes *containing* entities having properties and standing in relation to other entities. Thus we can view a situation from inside (construing it as a micro-universe) or from outside (construing it as an entity). When we say 'In the book, S' or 'In the kitchen, S', we do both things: on the one hand we mention the book or the kitchen as entities (as we also do when we say things like 'The kitchen is larger than the living-room' or 'The book is cheap'). On the other hand (and at the same time) we consider the book or the kitchen 'from inside' and describe what goes on in them; that is, we view (or pretend to view) the situation as it is for someone who is 'in' the book (e.g., the characters)[31] or in the kitchen. This hybrid nature is essential to δ-structures in general and to metarepresentations in particular.

III

Opacity

8

Introduction

§8.1 The Classical View

In their normal use, Russell once said, names are used to stand for their referent; hence the same assertion is made whether we use one name or another one, provided they refer to the same thing. Whenever a name cannot be replaced by a coextensive name *salva veritate*, this is evidence that the name was not used with its normal referential function. For example when we mention a name, as in 'Cicero has six letters', substitution (of 'Tully' for 'Cicero') does not preserve truth-value, because the name in that context is not used to stand for Cicero.

Quine pursued this line of thought and coined the word 'opacity' for the uses of words which do not license the free interchange of coextensive expressions. In 'John believes that Tegucigalpa is the capital of Nicaragua', we cannot replace 'Tegucigalpa' by the coextensive expression 'The Capital of Honduras', because the words 'Tegucigalpa is the Capital of Nicaragua' are *mentioned* as what John believes; they are not used transparently to talk about the world. 'John believes that Tegucigalpa is the Capital of Nicaragua' can be rephrased as: 'John accepts: "Tegucigalpa is the Capital of Nicaragua." '[1]

Frege held a similar view. According to Frege, words in 'oblique' contexts are not used to talk about their normal referents, but about their senses. That is, we talk about the content of the words themselves rather than about what the words (normally) stand for. Thus if I say 'John believes that Tegucigalpa is the Capital of Nicaragua', I don't say anything about Tegucigalpa: what I say is about John's notion of Tegucigalpa. If the sentence was about the real city Tegucigalpa, the name 'Tegucigalpa' could be replaced by another expression referring to the same city (e.g., 'The Capital of Honduras'); but it is about John's notion, hence it cannot be so replaced, since John's notion of Tegucigalpa is distinct from his notion of the Capital of Honduras.

All the authors I have mentioned appeal to the quotational paradigm and accept something like the following view. Words in their normal uses are transparent and serve to talk about some external reality; but they can also be mentioned, in which case they become the subject-matter and are no longer transparent. In such circumstances they do not serve their normal function, that of representing the world. Substitution failures are evidence that the words are used non-transparently, in a quotational or crypto-quotational manner.

The view I have just expounded and ascribed to Frege, Russell, and Quine deserves to be called the Classical View. It has been enormously influential. As a result it is now commonly accepted that metarepresentations are opaque, and that that is so because the object-representation is mentioned rather than used. In the first two parts of this book I have tried to go as far as possible in the opposite direction. Metarepresentations, I claimed, are fundamentally *transparent*. The fact that the meta-representation has the object-representation as its own subject-matter does not prevent it from being about the subject matter of the object-representation as well. On the contrary, if a metarepresentation m represents an object-representation r and r is about x, then m is bound to be about x as well as about r. This transparency is guaranteed by the Principle of Iconicity. Whichever state of affairs is represented by the object-representation is bound to be represented by the metarepresentation also, because the metarepresentation contains the object-representation. The difference between the metarepresentation and the object-representation is simply that the object-representation represents that state of affairs as holding in the current circumstance c (say, in the actual world), while the metarepresentation represents it as holding in a shifted circumstance c' (e.g., a 'fictional world' or a 'belief world').

How, in this framework, can we deal with the well-known fact that metarepresentational contexts are opaque in the technical sense? According to Quine, a linguistic context is opaque if substitution of identicals is not truth-preserving in that context. Now there are two sorts of 'substitution of identicals', hence two sorts of substitution failure. One sort involves the interchange of expressions with the same *extension*. There is no reason to expect such interchange to be always possible, hence, I will argue, the failure of that sort of substitution is utterly non-mysterious and raises no difficulty at all for our account. To account for extensional substitution failures, there is no need to appeal to the quotational paradigm: it is sufficient to invoke the phenomenon of *circumstantial shift*. (More on this in the next section.)

The other sort of substitution involves the interchange of expressions with the same content. When that sort of substitution fails, we must indeed appeal to the quotational paradigm, but I will argue that in many cases that can be done in such a limited manner that the general view sketched in the first two parts of this book is not thereby threatened.

§8.2   Extensional Substitution Failures

The extension of an expression depends upon two factors: its content, and the circumstance in which we evaluate the expression. The extension of an expression always is its extension in or at a circumstance. Thus a description like 'the President' will denote Chirac or Clinton, depending on whether we evaluate it with respect to the French situation or the situation in the U.S.; 'the President of the U.S.' will denote Reagan or Clinton depending on the period with respect to which we evaluate it; and 'the President of the U.S. in 1998' will denote Clinton or Woody Allen depending on the possible world under consideration.

As I pointed out in §3.5, when we say that two expressions (e.g., 'Tegucigalpa' and 'the Capital of Honduras') 'have the same extension', what we mean is that they have the same extension *in the current circumstance*, that is, at the present time and in the actual world. Now the prefix in a metarepresentation indicates that the internal sentence—the sentence which follows the prefix—must be evaluated with respect to a circumstance c' distinct from the current circumstance c in which the metarepresentation itself is evaluated. Hence it is only normal that we cannot always substitute one expression for another in the internal sentence even though they have the same extension *in the current circumstance*; for the current circumstance is irrelevant when we evaluate the internal sentence and the expressions it contains. What is relevant to evaluating the internal sentence is not the current circumstance c, but the shifted circumstance c'.

To sum up, for two expressions to be freely interchangeable in the internal sentence of a metarepresentation, what is required is that they have the same extension in the shifted circumstance c'. This condition is clearly not satisfied in the alleged examples of substitution failure mentioned by Frege and Quine. For example: Tegucigalpa is the Capital of Honduras in the actual world, but not in John's 'belief world'. Since John's 'belief world' is the relevant circumstance for the evaluation of a sentence embedded within 'John believes that . . .', 'Tegucigalpa' and 'the Capital of Honduras' are *not* relevantly coextensional; hence it is only normal that substitution fails. That it fails does not show that the words are used opaquely or deviantly, but only that a circumstantial shift has taken place. (See, e.g., Hintikka 1969, 1975: 117–8.) Such failures are to be expected *whenever* a circumstantial shift occurs. For example, I cannot substitute 'Clinton' for 'the President of the U.S.' in a sentence like 'Some years ago the President of the U.S. was an actor', simply because the prefix 'Some years ago' relevantly shifts the circumstance, in such a way that the so-called identity 'Clinton = the President of the U.S.', which holds in the current circumstance, becomes irrelevant.

In terms of circumstantial shift we account not only for extensional substitution failures, but also for the so-called *de dicto/de re* ambiguity (chapter 9). Since two circumstances c and c' are involved in evaluating a complex sentence headed by a circumstance-shifting prefix, a description like 'the President of the U.S.' in the internal part of such a sentence will be evaluated either with respect to c or with respect to c', depending on whether or not it takes scope over the circumstance-shifting operator. Thus the sentence 'Some years ago the President of the U.S. was an actor' turns out to be ambiguous: it means either that the current President of the U.S. (i.e., the President of the U.S. in c) was an actor in the past situation c' (*de re* reading), or that in the past situation c' an actor was the President of the U.S. (*de dicto* reading). We find the same sort of ambiguity in belief sentences and other metarepresentations: 'John believes that the President of the U.S. is an actor' means either that he believes, of the current President of the U.S., that he is an actor (*de re* reading), or that he believes that an actor is the President of the U.S. (*de dicto* reading). That sort of scope ambiguity will be dealt with extensively in chapter 9. It will be distinguished from another sort of ambiguity— that between the 'transparent' and the 'opaque' reading—which selectively affects metarepresentations and must indeed be accounted for by appealing to the quotational paradigm.

§8.3   Intensional Substitution Failures

Let us now turn to the other, more problematic sort of substitution failure. If two expressions have the same content, they should be interchangeable *salva veritate*, even if the sentence is headed by a circumstance-shifting prefix: for the content of an expression is not circumstance-dependent in the way in which its extension is. The content of an expression is *what* we evaluate in or at a circumstance; hence it is determined prior to the encounter with the circumstance (Kaplan 1989a). For example, the content of the description 'the President' (or 'the President of the U.S.', or 'the President of the U.S. in 1998') can be construed as a function from situations to individuals. Once an appropriate circumstance is given, the function determines the extension of the description in that circumstance, that is, the individual who is the value of the function. The value of the function is circumstance-dependent, but the function itself is not.

  In metarepresentational contexts, however, substituting an expression for another one with the same content possibly affects truth-value. In §3.5 I gave the following example. 'Ophtalmologist' and 'eye-doctor' are synonymous, hence they have the same content (a function from situations to sets of individuals). It follows that the content of a sentence in which one expression occurs will remain the same after substituting the other expression for it. That will be so whether or not a circumstantial shift occurs, since the content of an expression is not circumstance-dependent. Now if the content of the sentence remains the same, its truth-value also will remain the same. Despite all this, it is intuitively evident that substituting 'ophtalmologist' for 'eye-doctor' in (1) can change truth-value: it is possible for John to believe that Peter is an eye-doctor and to disbelieve that he is an opthalmologist. In other words, (1) and (2) can be both true.

(1)   John believes that Peter is an eye-doctor.

(2)   John does not believe that Peter is an ophtalmologist.

How can we account for that puzzling fact?

The puzzle should be taken seriously. If John believes Peter to be an eye-doctor, and an eye-doctor *is* an opthalmologist, it follows logically that John believes Peter to be an opthalmologist. But this consequence of (1) conflicts with the intuitive truth of (2). In such a case, it is very natural to appeal to the quotational paradigm, in order to account for the joint truth of (1) and (2). We have only to assume that in (2) the word 'opthalmologist' is somehow *mentioned*, as if the speaker had said

(2*)   John does not believe Peter to be an 'ophtalmologist'.

That assumption is indeed very plausible, and I will endorse it in what follows.

An analogous problem arises with directly referential expressions. Their extension is fixed directly at the level of content, prior to the encounter with the circumstance of evaluation. Thus proper names refer directly to their actual bearers, irrespective of the situation talked about (Kripke 1980). 'Hitler' refers to Hitler even if we are talking about a situation in which he was called by some other name and someone else was called 'Hitler'. We would say that, in such a situation, *Hitler* is not called 'Hitler'. Even if we are talking about a situation in which Hitler does not exist, the name 'Hitler' still refers to him. We would describe such a situation as a situation in which *Hitler* does not exist. Being directly determined at the content level, the reference of proper names is circumstance-independent. It follows that coreferential proper names should be interchangeable *salva veritate* even in circumstance-shifting contexts. But in metarepresentations they are not. Lois Lane believes that Superman can fly but she does not believe that Clark Kent can fly. How is that possible, given that Clark Kent is Superman? Presumably, because we are not merely using the words but somehow quoting them when we report Lois' beliefs. In saying that she believes that Superman can fly, we do not merely ascribe her a belief concerning the person Superman, but a belief concerning that person *and involving her 'Superman' notion* (Crimmins and Perry 1989). Again, some form of mention seems to take place, which explains how substitution can fail to preserve truth-value. If this is correct the report can be rephrased as

(3)   Lois believes that 'Superman' can fly.

It is important to note that this sort of substitution failure—*intensional* substitution failure—is characteristic of metarepresentations. We do not find it in, say, sentences about the past. 'Some years ago ophtalmologists used to be male' licenses the inference to 'Some years ago eye-doctors used to be male'. This provides confirmation that the opacity at issue is not a side-effect of the circumstance-shifting process.

Faced with intensional substitution failures, we can only acknowledge that some form of 'mention' takes place; this much must be conceded to Frege and Quine. But, I will argue, this is a very minimal concession. In particular, we need not (or not automatically) give up the view that the words in the embedded portion of a belief sentence are used with their normal semantic function and contribute their normal semantic value, in accordance with the Principle of Innocence. To make that point, I will show that three notions are conflated in Quine's celebrated account of opacity (chapter 10). Since they are not even extensionally equivalent, the unitary notion of 'opacity' must be given up, in favour of a family of related but distinct notions. Thus it will turn out that an expression can be used with its normal semantic function and contribute its normal semantic value even though it is not substitutable; that is arguably what happens on the opaque reading of belief sentences (chapter 11).

9

Metarepresentational Ambiguities

§9.1 Relational versus Notional

In his classic paper 'Quantifiers and Propositional Attitudes' (1956), Quine made a distinction between 'two senses of believing', as he then put it: the notional and the relational sense. That is both a distinction between two types of belief report, and a distinction between two types of belief. The distinction is very intuitive, but it faces difficulties. In later writings Quine expressed skepticism toward the distinction, and more or less gave it up (Quine 1977: 10). Contrary to Quine I think the distinction can be saved. What follows is my reconstruction of it.

Let us start with the distinction between two types of belief. Some beliefs are purely general, others are singular and involve particular objects. As an example of a general belief, we have the belief that there are spies, or the belief that all swans are black. As Frege put it, those beliefs are about concepts, if they are about anything at all: the first is the belief that the concept 'spy' is satisfied by at least one object, the second is the belief that whatever satisfies the concept 'swan' satisfies the concept 'black'. But the belief that Kaplan was a student of Carnap is a belief about two individuals: Kaplan and Carnap. Of this belief we can say: There is an x and there is a y such that the belief is true iff x was a student of y. We cannot say anything similar concerning the belief that there are spies: there is no individual object x such that that belief is true iff x satisfies a given predicate.[2]

A singular belief is relational in the sense that the believer believes something *about* some individual. The relation of 'believing about' descends from more basic, informational relations such as the relations of perceiving, of remembering or of hearing about. All these relations are genuine *relations*. If John perceives, remembers, or hears about the table, there is something which he sees, remembers, or hears about. Similarly, if John believes something about Peter, there is someone his belief is about. Singular belief is based on, or grounded in, the basic informational relations from which it inherits its relational character. To have a thought about a particular object, one must be '*en rapport* with' the thing through perception, memory or communication. Pure thinking does not suffice. Thus inferring that there is a shortest spy does not put one in a position to entertain a singular belief about the shortest spy, in the relevant sense.

In terms of this distinction between singular and general beliefs, well-documented and elaborated in the philosophy of mind (see, e.g., Evans 1982), I suggest that we define a *relational belief report* simply as one that reports the having of a singular belief; and a *notional belief report* as one that reports the having of a general belief. (This distinction, of course, can be generalized to all metarepresentations.)

How do we know whether a given sentence reports a singular or a general belief? Can we tell from the form of the sentence, or is each belief sentence ambiguous between the two readings? Quine opts for the latter view. He thinks that a standard belief sentence like (1) is *ambiguous* between the relational and the notional reading.

(1)   Ralph believes that Ortcutt is a spy.

The relational reading can be forced by 'exporting' the singular term: 'Ralph believes *of Ortcutt* that he is a spy'. When exportation is thus possible, existential generalization is also possible: if Ralph believes that Ortcutt is a spy, in the 'exportable' sense (that is, if he believes of Ortcutt that he is a spy), then there is someone Ralph's belief is about.

Even though Quine's claim concerning the ambiguity of belief sentences between the relational and the notional reading has been very popular, I think that it rests, in part, on a confusion; a confusion which is, again in part, responsible for Quine's despair of the distinction. The confusion will be exposed in a later section (§9.4). In the meantime I will argue that standard belief sentences such as (1), where the embedded sentence contains a singular term, are *not* ambiguous between the relational and the notional reading. That ambiguity, I shall argue, is essentially a matter of scope. *Qua* scope ambiguity, it is not specific to meta-representations: it applies to modal and temporal sentences as well as to belief sentences (§9.2). Moreover, it applies to metarepresentations *only when the internal sentence contains a quantified or descriptive phrase which can interact with the metarepresentational operator in the appropriate manner.* Being scopeless, genuine singular terms give rise to no such ambiguity (§9.3). In §9.4, however, we shall see that there *is* an ambiguity specific to metarepresentations. That further ambiguity has nothing to do with scope, and applies to belief sentences whether the embedded sentence contains a description or a genuine singular term.

§9.2 Scope Ambiguities in Belief Sentences

The distinction between genuine singular terms and descriptive or quantified phrases such as 'some man', 'a man', 'no man' or 'the man' goes back to Russell (1905). While Russell wanted to restrict the class of 'logically proper names' (as he called genuine singular terms) to only a couple of natural language devices, contemporary semanticists consider ordinary proper names and demonstratives, in general, as genuine singular terms. *Qua* genuine singular terms, they are purely referential. Definite and even indefinite descriptions can also be *used* purely referentially, according to some authors at least (Donnellan 1966; Chastain 1975); but the purely referential use of descriptions is not their normal semantic function, while it is the normal semantic function of genuine singular terms.

There is a good deal of controversy over the referential use of definite descriptions. Many people believe that it is irrelevant to semantics. I disagree, but we need not be concerned with this issue here. If, as I believe, definite descriptions have a non-deviant referential use,[3] then, when so used, they behave like genuine singular terms: they are purely referential and their semantic value (on that use) is their referent. What I have to say about the behaviour of genuine singular terms in belief contexts will therefore automatically apply to definite descriptions on their referential use. So I will put referential descriptions aside and consider only what Evans called the 'pure' uses of definite descriptions, that is, their attributive uses.

As Russell pointed out in the above-mentioned paper, definite descriptions are very much like quantified phrases. Like them, they serve to make general statements. If John believes or asserts 'The winner will be rich', we cannot say that there is an object x such that John's belief or statement is true iff ... x ..., for the reason which I gave in footnote 2 (in response to Quine's objection): we cannot say that a certain person, namely the winner, is such that John's belief is true iff *she* will be rich; the condition 'being the winner' must also be satisfied by her. Nor can we say that a certain person is such that the belief is true iff she is both rich and the winner. *Any* person's being rich and the winner will make the belief true.

Definite descriptions are similar to quantified phrases in another respect: like them, they induce scope ambiguities in complex sentences. Thus there are two readings for sentences such as (2) or (3):

(2)   Someone will be in danger.

(3)   The President will be in danger.

Sentence (2) says either that someone is such that she will be in danger, or that it will be the case that someone is in danger. The two readings can be represented as follows:

(2a) $(\exists x)$(it will be the case that (x is in danger))

(2b)   It will be the case that $((\exists x)(x$ is in danger))

The same duality of readings can be discerned in the case of (3). Sentence (3) says either that the President is such that he will be in danger, or that it will be the case that: the President is in danger. On the second reading it is the fate of a future president which is at issue, while on the first reading the sentence concerns the present president. Again, the two readings can be represented in terms of relative scope:

(3a) $(\iota x \text{ President } x)$(it will be the case that (x is in danger))

(3b)   It will be the case that $((\iota x \text{ President } x)(x$ is in danger))

In (2a) and (3a), the quantifier or descriptive phrase is given wide scope; thus it seems to reach into the intensional context created by the operator 'it will be the case that'. But, as Kaplan (1968, 1986) and Quine (1977) pointed out, (3a) and (2a) need not be construed as actually violating Quine's prohibition of quantification into intensional contexts. The intensional operator 'it will be the case that', or 'will-be' for short, can be construed in such a way that in (2a) and (3a) it governs only the predicate 'in danger'; while it governs the whole sentence 'someone is in danger' or 'the President is in danger' in (2b) and (3b). That can be made notationally explicit in the manner of Quine 1977:

(2a′) $(\exists x)(\text{will-be(in-danger) } x)$

(2b′) $\text{Will-be}((\exists x)(\text{in-danger } x))$

(3a′) $(\imath x \text{ President } x)(\text{will-be(in-danger) } x)$

(3b′) $\text{Will-be}((\imath x \text{ President } x)(\text{in-danger } x))$

In (2a′) and (3a′) 'will-be' is understood as a predicate functor making a new predicate, 'will be in danger', out of the original predicate 'in danger'. The quantified variable thus falls outside the scope of the intensional operator. When the operator is given wide scope, as in (2b′) and (3b′), it is understood as governing the whole sentence (including the quantifier and the variable). The quantified variable now falls within the scope of the operator, but, as Quine says, the sentence "exhibits only a quantification *within* the [intensional] context, not a quantification *into* it" (1956: 188).

Before proceeding, let us note that genuine singular terms give rise to no such scope ambiguities: they are, as Geach once put it, "essentially scopeless" (Geach 1972: 117). Thus sentence (4) is not ambiguous, contrary to (2) or (3); there is no truth-conditional difference between (4a) and (4b), as there was between (2a) and (2b) or between (3a) and (3b). According to Arthur Prior (1971), the equivalence between forms like (4a) and (4b) is the distinguishing characteristic of genuine singular terms:

(4)   Cicero will be in danger.

(4a)   Will-be(in-danger Cicero)

(4b)   Will-be(in-danger) Cicero

It is time to introduce belief sentences. Belief sentences with descriptive or quantified phrases are ambiguous in a way that exactly parallels the ambiguities we have just observed in temporal sentences with descriptive or quantified phrases. Thus (5) is ambiguous like (2), and (6) is ambiguous like (3):

(5)   John believes that someone is *F*.

(5a)   Someone is such that John believes him to be *F*.
$(\exists x)(B_j(F)\ x)$

(5b)   John believes that: someone is *F*.
$B_j((\exists x)(Fx))$

(6)   John believes that the President is in danger.

(6a)   The President is such that John believes him to be in danger.
$(\iota x\ \text{President}\ x)(B_j(\text{in-danger})\ x)$

(6b)   John believes that: the President is in danger.
$B_j\ ((\iota x\ \text{President}\ x)(\text{in-danger}\ x))$

The quantification is endorsed by the speaker in (5a), while it is ascribed to the believer in (5b). Similarly, the description is endorsed by the speaker in (6a), while it is ascribed to the believer in (6b). The same ambiguity can be found in other metarepresentations (e.g., 'In the film, the President is in danger').

Note that in (3a) and (6a) the description can be read attributively even though it takes wide scope (Kripke 1977: 258). The speaker says that the President, whoever he is, is such that John believes him to be *F*. The description does not behave like a singular term here; it does not contribute an object. Still the *ascribed* belief is singular: the speaker says that there is a particular object such that the believer believes something of that object.

To sum up, when the quantified phrase or the description takes wide scope, belief reports like (5) and (6) have their relational reading: the belief they report is singular, even though the object the belief is about is only described in general terms.[4] In contrast, when the descriptive or quantified phrase takes narrow scope, the belief report is understood notionally. The believer is said to believe that there is an object *x* with such and such properties; that does not entail that there actually is an object *y* such that the believer believes that of *y*. Whatever quantification there is is strictly internal to the ascribed content; it is not endorsed by the speaker.

§9.3   Singular Terms in Belief Sentences

So far, Quine's claim concerning the ambiguity of belief sentences has been vindicated. But quantified phrases and definite descriptions are not genuine singular terms. As soon as what occurs in the embedded sentence is a genuine singular term (or a referential description), the scope ambiguity vanishes.

Since a singular term is purely referential (unless it is used deviantly), a statement in which it occurs is bound to be singular. That is true not only of a simple statement such as 'Cicero is in danger', but also of a complex statement such as 'John believes that Cicero is in danger'. The former is about the individual Cicero; the latter is about two individuals, John and Cicero (Russell 1910: chapter 7). It follows that exportation is always licensed when the embedded sentence contains a genuine singular term.[5] From

(7)   John believes that t is F

we can always go to

(8)   John believes of t that it is F

and, through existential generalization, to

(9) $(\exists x)(B_j(F)x)$

That means that the ascribed belief is always singular, when the belief report contains a singular term. 'Notional' readings are thus ruled out: only relational readings are available.

What I have just said, of course, presupposes that genuine singular terms are used normally (non-deviantly) in attitude contexts. That is, I am assuming semantic innocence (§1.2), and correlatively rejecting the notion that singular terms in metarepresentational contexts refer to something different from their usual referent (Frege) or behave somewhat deviantly, as they do when they occur autonymously (Quine). I take singular terms to be purely referential, in all their non-deviant occurrences; and I assume that their occurrences in metarepresentational contexts are non-deviant.

The picture I am advocating is highly controversial, of course; but at least it is neat. It is organized around two main distinctions:

• The embedded sentence in a belief report contains either a singular term, or a quantified/descriptive phrase.

• A quantified/descriptive phrase can be given either wide scope or narrow scope vis-à-vis the doxastic operator.

Thus there are three possibilities (table III.1): what occurs in the embedded sentence can be a singular term, a quantified/descriptive phrase with narrow scope, or a quantified/descriptive phrase with wide scope. The belief report counts as *relational* if, and only if, the embedded sentence contains either a singular term or a quantified/descriptive phrase with wide scope. Note that there remains a difference between the two types of case. When using a singular term, the speaker himself makes a singular statement about the individual object the belief is about. When using a descriptive/quantified phrase with wide scope, the speaker ascribes a singular belief, but she does not herself express a singular belief, or make a singular statement, about the individual object the ascribed belief is about.

At this point two main objections spring to mind:

First objection   If the above theory were correct, it would always be possible to infer from 'John believes that *t* is *F*' that there is an *x* John believes to be *F*. But what about statements like (10)?

(10)   My three-year-old son believes that Santa Claus will come tonight.

Since Santa Claus does not exist, there is no individual to whom my son is related in the manner required for singular belief. Hence from (10) we cannot infer 'There is an *x* such that my son believes that *x* will come tonight'. That is a counterexample to the theory.

Table III.1
Interpretations for belief sentences

Belief sentence	Expressed belief	Ascribed belief	Type of reading
With genuine singular term	Singular	Singular	Relational
With quantified or descriptive phrase taking wide scope	General	Singular	Relational
With quantified or descriptive phrase taking narrow scope	General	General	Notional

Second objection   I claim that belief sentences with proper names are not ambiguous, in contrast to belief sentences with quantifiers. But they are: the name can be either endorsed by the speaker as his own way of referring to whatever the belief is about, or ascribed to the believer. That is the same old *de re/de dicto* ambiguity which we have observed in the case of belief sentences with quantifiers.

The second objection is especially important; it is the main obstacle on the road to accepting the view I have just sketched. In the next section, I will argue that it rests on a confusion. Belief sentences with singular terms are indeed ambiguous between a 'transparent' and an 'opaque' reading, but that ambiguity is *distinct from*, indeed orthogonal to, the relational/notional ambiguity we have been considering so far. When the two ambiguities are confused under a single heading (the so-called '*de re/de dicto*' distinction broadly understood), the situation becomes intractable and leads one to despair. Once the ambiguities are told apart, however, the apparently intractable problems disappear.

As for the first objection, it can be rebutted as follows. The reason why we can't infer '$(\exists x)$(my son believes that x will come tonight)' from 'My son believes that Santa Claus will come tonight' is the same reason why we can't infer (12) from (11).

(11)   Santa Claus lives in the sky.

(12) $(\exists x)(x$ lives in the sky)

So the objection is not a specific objection to the view that genuine singular terms behave as such in belief reports; rather, it is an objection to the view that fictional names such as 'Santa Claus' *are* genuine singular terms, used in the ordinary way (non-deviantly) and subject to ordinary logical principles. Since that problem is a general problem, it is not incumbent on the attitude theorist to solve it. (I will, however, have a good deal to say about this problem, and the general issue of fictional names, in later sections of this book, especially in part V.)

To be sure, there is an important difference between a fictional statement like (11) and a statement like 'My son believes that Santa Claus will come tonight 'or 'In the story Santa Claus lives in the sky' ('meta-fictional' statements, as Currie (1990) aptly calls them). The author of a fictional statement does not really make assertions, but only pretends to do so. Thus in (11) she only pretends to say of a certain person that he lives in the sky.[6] Since that it so, the failure of existential generalization is unproblematic. (12) cannot really be inferred, because (11) was not really asserted. (Within the pretense, however, the inference goes through: the speaker pretends to be committed to (12), by pretending to assert (11).) In contrast, it seems that metafictional statements are serious and evaluable as true or false (Lewis 1978). Hence it is not obvious that the failure of existential generalization has the same source in both cases.

But it can be maintained that the author of a metafictional statement such as 'In the story, Santa Claus lives in the sky' is also pretending: she pretends to assert of someone that the story says he lives in the sky. Similarly for (10): the speaker pretends to assert of a given individual that her son believes he will come tonight. In neither case does the speaker really make that assertion, as there is no individual the story (or the child's belief) is about. By pretending to do so, however, the speaker communicates something true about the story or about the child's belief —something which could be communicated literally only by means of a lengthy and cumbersome paraphrase (Walton 1990: 396ff; Crimmins 1998; see also Forbes 1996 for discussion of related isues).

A lot more needs to be said to flesh out this proposal. One must detail the mechanism of 'semantic pretense' through which one can, in a more or less conventional manner, convey true things by pretending to say other things. One must also show how fictional statements like (11) can be distinguished from metafictional statements in which, intuitively at least, it seems that a genuine (and true) assertion is made. If pretense is involved in both cases, it is not quite the same sort of pretense; the theory owes an account of how the two kinds connect up with each other. I cannot go into those complex issues now, but they will be dealt with quite extensively in a later chapter (chapter 15).

§9.4   The Ambiguity of the *De Re*/*De Dicto* Distinction

In §9.2 I glossed the relational/notional distinction in terms of the points of view involved. I said that the description (or the quantification) is 'endorsed by the speaker' in relational readings, while it is 'ascribed to the believer' in the notional reading. Now it seems that—contrary to what I claimed—exactly the same distinction can be made with respect to belief sentences containing singular terms instead of descriptions or quantifiers. Thus (13) can be understood in two ways.

(13)   Ralph believes that Cicero denounced Catiline.

On the transparent interpretation, Ralph is said to have a belief concerning the individual Cicero. Since Cicero is Tully, (13) can be rephrased as (14):

(14)   Ralph believes that Tully denounced Catiline.

The transparent reading of sentences like (13) is often rendered by appealing to the exported form, as in (15):

(15)   Ralph believes of Cicero that he denounced Catiline.

But there is another interpretation of (13) and (14), an interpretation in which they are not equivalent and cannot be rendered as (15). This is the 'opaque' interpretation. On that interpretation, Ralph is said by (13) to have a belief such that he would assent to 'Cicero denounced Catiline', but not necessarily to 'Tully denounced Catiline'. On the opaque interpretation, the use of the name 'Cicero' (rather than 'Tully') to refer to Cicero is *ascribed to the believer*. On the transparent reading, the choice of the name is up to the speaker and does not reflect the believer's usage; that is why replacement of 'Cicero' by 'Tully' in (13) on the transparent interpretation does not induce a change in the ascribed belief.

Quine and many philosophers and linguists after him have jumped to the conclusion that a *single* distinction applies to belief sentences whether they contain singular terms or descriptive/quantified phrases. They have equated the relational/notional distinction talked about in previous sections and the transparent/opaque distinction I have just introduced for belief sentences with singular terms. Both are viewed as instances of the so-called '*de re/de dicto*' distinction. The exported form (15) is the mark of the *de re*. Belief sentences on the *de dicto* (opaque, notional) reading resist exportation, because the doxastic operator takes wide scope—it governs the embedded sentence in its entirety. On the *de re* reading, the doxastic operator takes narrow scope and governs only the predicate: the subject expression, be it quantificational or referential, is endorsed by the speaker without being ascribed to the believer. That is the confused doctrine whose untenability led Quine and others to despair of the original relational/notional distinction.

Yet there is a clear difference between the two distinctions—the relational/notional distinction, and the transparent/opaque distinction. Consider the notional reading of a belief sentence. In such a case the believer is said to believe that there is an object *x* with such and such properties; that does not entail that there actually is an object *y* such that the believer believes that of *y*. Whatever quantification there is is strictly internal to the ascribed belief; it is not endorsed by the speaker. But *even on the opaque reading of a belief sentence in which a singular term occurs, reference is made to some particular individual* (Loar 1972). Thus the speaker who utters (13) on its opaque reading is committed to there being an individual *x*, such that Ralph's belief concerns *x* and is true iff ... *x* .... To be sure, the belief which is ascribed to Ralph on the opaque reading of (13) is not merely the belief that that individual denounced Catiline; that would correspond to the transparent reading of (13). On the opaque reading, Ralph is ascribed the belief that *Cicero* denounced Catiline. Cicero is thought of by Ralph not only as having denounced Catiline, but also *as Cicero*. Yet that feature of opacity is compatible with the relational character of the belief report, that is, with the fact that the speaker himself refers to Cicero as the object the ascribed belief is about (Sainsbury 1979: 63–5). We can represent the opaque reading of (13) as follows:

(16)   Ralph believes of Cicero, thought of as 'Cicero', that he denounced Catiline.

The apposition 'thought of as *Cicero*' is sufficient to distinguish the opaque reading from the transparent reading. Both readings are relational: in both cases Ralph believes something of Cicero, and the speaker himself refers to Cicero as what Ralph's belief is about. On the opaque reading, however, the name has a dual role: it serves not only to refer to the object the ascribed belief is about, but also tells us something about how the believer thinks of that object. As Brian Loar pointed out, this dual role is reminiscent of that of 'Giorgione' in Quine's famous example (Loar 1972: 51).

The non-equivalence of (13) and (14) on their opaque readings is clearly compatible with the relational character of these readings. In the same way in which (13), on its opaque reading, is rendered as (16), the opaque reading of (14) can be rendered as (17):

(17)   Ralph believes of Cicero, thought of as 'Tully', that he denounced Catiline.

The name 'Tully' in (14) refers to Cicero even on the opaque reading. The speaker is therefore committed to there being an individual, namely Cicero (= Tully), such that Ralph believes of that individual, thought of as 'Tully', that he denounced Catiline. There is no such existential implication when a belief report (with a descriptive or quantified phrase) is understood notionally.

As we can see, the contrast between cases in which something is ascribed to the believer and cases in which it is endorsed by the speaker is not drawn in quite the same way for the two distinctions. On the notional reading of a belief sentence with a descriptive/quantified phrase, the quantification is ascribed to the believer *without* being endorsed by the speaker; but the reference to the object of belief, and the existential commitment that goes with it, is *both* ascribed to the believer *and* endorsed by the speaker on the opaque reading of a singular belief sentence. The relational/notional distinction articulates a simple contrast between the point of view of the speaker and the point of view of the believer; while the transparent/opaque distinction articulates a quite different contrast, between the point of view of the sole speaker and the point of view of *both* the speaker and the believer. As far as the respective points of view of the speaker and the believer are concerned, opaque readings are thus essentially 'cumulative'.

Far from being identical to the relational/notional distinction, the transparent/opaque distinction which applies to sentences such as (13) turns out to be a distinction between two sorts of *relational* reading. Hence there is no incompatibility between the claim that belief sentences with singular terms can only be understood relationally, and the observation that they have both a transparent and an opaque reading. Yet, precisely because belief reports with genuine singular terms cannot be interpreted notionally, but only relationally, it has seemed to many that a single distinction applies indifferently to all belief sentences: just as belief sentences with descriptive/quantified phrases can be interpreted relationally or notionally, belief sentences with singular terms can be interpreted transparently or opaquely. To dispell the illusion that this is a single distinction under two different names, one has only to notice that belief sentences with descriptive/quantified phrases are subject to *both* ambiguities. They can be interpreted notionally or relationally; and when relational, they can be interpreted transparently or opaquely. Loar gives the following example of a belief sentence with a quantified phrase which is naturally given a relational yet opaque interpretation:

(18)   Ralph believes that a certain cabinet member is a spy.

This does not mean that Ralph has a general belief to the effect that some cabinet member or other is a spy. As the phrase 'a certain' is meant to indicate, there is a particular cabinet member Ralph's belief is about. The belief report, therefore, is relational. However, Loar (1972: 54) points out that (18)

will often be taken to imply more than

(19) $(\exists y)(y$ is a cabinet member & $B($Ralph, "x is a spy," $y)$

Ralph, we may suppose, believes it of the fellow under a certain description; that is,

(20) $(\exists y)(y$ is a cabinet member
        & $B($Ralph, "x is a cabinet member and x is a spy," $y))$

Loar's rendition of (18) as (20) nicely captures the cumulative aspect of opaque readings. Both the speaker and the believer view the person the belief is about as a cabinet member. As Loar pointed out (1972: 54), in a framework such as Quine's, in which the two distinctions are conflated under a single heading, one cannot account for belief reports which, like (18), are both relational and opaque.[7] 'Relational' entails 'transparent', for Quine and his followers. For that reason also, examples like (13) and (14), on their 'opaque' interpretation (corresponding to (16) and (17)), will have to be considered 'notional', while they are clearly relational. Given the extreme confusion that results, it is only natural that Quine eventually gave up the distinction as hopeless. It *is* hopeless, considered as a single distinction covering all the cases.

§9.5   Conclusion

For any sentence *dS*, if *S* contains a description or a quantifier, a scope ambiguity will arise. The sentence will be given the *de dicto* interpretation whenever the quantifier or description falls within the scope of the operator *d*; it will be given the *de re* interpretation otherwise. On the *de dicto* reading, substitution of coextensive expressions will be prohibited whenever the operator at issue is a circumstance-shifting operator; for the fact that the description falls within the scope of a circumstance-shifting operator entails that sameness of extension in the current circumstance is irrelevant; it is the shifted circumstance that counts.

Failure of extensional substitution in circumstance-shifting contexts is a *general* phenomenon. It is not specific to metarepresentations, but extends to modal contexts, temporal contexts, and so forth. We may call that phenomenon 'opacity' if we want to, but that is not 'opacity' in the sense in which opacity, or the possibility of opacity, is a characteristic feature of metarepresentations.

Genuine opacity corresponds to the other sort of substitution failure talked about in chapter 8: intensional substitution failures. That phenomenon can be found only in metarepresentational contexts. In modal or temporal contexts, one can always replace an expression by another one provided the *substituens* has the same content as the *substituendum*. Nor can genuine opacity be accounted for in terms of scope. Having the same content, the *substituens* and the *substituendum* have the same extension *both* in the current circumstance and in the shifted circumstance; hence the circumstance of evaluation, as determined by operator scope, is irrelevant.[8]

To account for opacity, it seems that we must appeal to the quotational paradigm: we must accept that the words in the embedded portion of the report are not used purely referentially, but somehow mentioned. They have, as Loar puts it, a dual use, similar to that of 'Giorgione' in Quine's famous sentence. Without appealing to the quotational paradigm, how could we account for the fact that even synonyms cannot be freely substituted, in metarepresentational contexts (Mates 1952)? If that is right, then we must ultimately give up semantic innocence in dealing with belief sentences and other metarepresentations.

Yet that is a very delicate matter. Before we give up semantic innocence, we shall embark in an in-depth study of the family of notions at issue here: 'mention', 'purely referential use', 'transparency', 'substitutability', and so forth (chapter 10). In particular, we shall scrutinize Quine's 'Giorgione' example. From that study surprising results will emerge. We shall see that, even if some form of mention takes place in a sentence, in such a way that free substitution of expressions with the same content is blocked, that does not entail that the words at issue are not used purely referentially. This will suggest that we can make opacity compatible with semantic innocence after all. (Violations of semantic innocence in metarepresentational contexts will be acknowledged in later chapters, but the general framework set up in the first parts of this book will be shown to be compatible with those cases as well.)

10

Opaque Uses, Transparent Mentions

§10.1   Two Sorts of Mention

The standard contrast between 'use' and 'mention' misleadingly suggests that we do not use an expression when we mention it. But that is not quite right. We can mention an expression *A* by using another expression *B* which names it. In such a case we do not use *A*, but its name. That I will refer to as *heteronymous* mention. But we can also use A itself in '*suppositio materialis*', that is, *autonymously*. That is what is ordinarily called 'mention' as opposed to 'use'. Now it is clear that in autonymous mention (e.g., (1) below), the mentioned word itself is used, though deviantly (Garver 1965: 231). That is the basis for the contrast between autonymous and heteronymous mention; for the mentioned word does not occur at all in sentences such as (2) in which it is *heteronymously* mentioned.

(1)   'Cat' is a three-letter word.

(2)   Wychnevetsky is a three-letter word.[9]

   To be sure, the distinction between the two sorts of mention can be downplayed by arguing, with Quine, that the word 'cat' occurs only accidentally in (1), much as 'nine' occurs in 'canine' or 'cat' in 'cattle'. But that claim is highly implausible if taken at face value. The occurrence of 'cat' in 'cattle' is indeed an accident; so much so that the word 'cat' does not, *qua* word, occur in 'cattle'. A sequence of letters (or a sound) is not a word. Admittedly, the individuation of words raises complex issues, but on any plausible account 'cat' in 'cattle' will not count as an occurrence of a word. In contrast, the occurrence of 'cat' in

(1) will count as an occurrence of the word 'cat', rather than as an orthographic accident. We can go along with Quine and accept that the first word of (1) is not the word 'cat', but a different expression formed from the word 'cat' by appending quotation marks around it.[10] Still, the occurrence of the word 'cat' *within* the complex expression is no accident. The word 'cat' is named by quoting *it*. That is how autonymous mention works. The mechanism of autonymous mention requires that we use *the word itself*, and put it within quotation marks. This is *toto mundo* different from a case of heteronymous mention (the word *A* is named by the word *B*) in which, by accident, *B* contains *A* in the manner in which 'cattle' contains 'cat'. (Thus instead of 'Wychnevetsky' in (2) we might have used another, no less arbitrary name, viz. 'Wychnecatsky', in which by accident the orthographic sequence 'cat' occurs. The difference with a standard case of autonymous mention is obvious.)

The mentioned word is used, but, as I said, it is used *deviantly*. The word is not used according to its normal semantic function. Thus a word whose role is to name a certain object or to "make it the subject of discourse" (as Mill says) will be used to make *itself* the subject of discourse. Deviant uses, in general, are far from uncommon, and come in many varieties. We may not only use the word 'cat' autonymously, to denote that very word, but also to denote, say, a *representation* of a cat. Thus we can say:

(3)   In the middle of the piazza stood a gigantic cat, due to a local sculptor.

This is deviant because a stone cat is not a cat.[11] So the word 'cat', which means *cat*, can be used to mean many other things through the operation of various 'primary pragmatic processes'—pragmatic processes involved in the determination of what is said (Recanati 1993). Autonymy is one such process; metonymy is another. Such processes generate *systematic ambiguities*. Whenever a word denotes a type of thing, we can use it alternatively to denote a representation of that type of thing; whatever a word denotes, we can use it to denote that very word.

Is the autonymous word referential or not? It depends in what sense. If we accept that the word refers to itself, then it is referential after all.[12] Its referentiality can be checked using the Principle of Substitutivity.

Replacing the autonymous word *A*, which refers to itself, by another, *B*, which also refers to *A*, preserves truth-value, as the possible transition from (1) to (2) shows. But the mentioned word is not referential in the *normal* sense: it does not refer to its normal referent. In what follows I will take 'referential' to mean just that: referential in the normal sense. An occurrence of a word is referential, in that sense, if and only if it refers to the normal referent of the word.

§10.2   Hybrid Uses

A term's being referential does not guarantee that the word can be replaced *salva veritate* by an occurrence of another word referring to the same object. For that to be guaranteed, Quine says, the occurrence at issue must be *purely referential*—the term must be used "purely to specify its object" (Quine 1960: 142). This qualification is necessary because Quine thinks there is a continuum of cases from pure non-referentiality, as illustrated by (1), to pure referentiality. Quine gives the following example:

(4)   Giorgione was so-called because of his size.

In such cases, Quine says, the word (here 'Giorgione') has a dual role. It is both mentioned *and* used to refer. It is a mixture of autonymy and referentiality. It is because the word 'Giorgione' is not used purely referentially that substitution of 'Barbarelli' for 'Giorgione' fails to preserve truth, despite the fact that Barbarelli and Giorgione are (were) one and the same person.

I think Quine's analysis of the Giorgione example is mistaken (§10.3), but his insight that there is a continuum of cases between pure autonymy and pure referentiality seems to me correct and important. A good example is

(5)   A 'robin' is a thrush in American English, but not in British English.

Though it is quoted, the word 'robin' here keeps its normal semantic value: it denotes a type of bird. It is a type of bird, not a word, which is said to be a thrush. But (5) also says something about the word 'robin'. For it is the word, not the bird, whose properties vary from one dialect of English to the next. As Austin pointed out, this mixture of mention and use is typical of semantic discourse:

> Although we may sensibly ask 'Do we *ride* the word "elephant" or the animal?' and equally sensibly 'Do we *write* the word or the animal?' it is nonsense to ask 'Do we *define* the word or the animal?' For defining an elephant (supposing we ever do this) is a compendious description of an operation involving both word and animal (do we focus the image or the battleship?). (Austin 1971: 124)

'Echoes' provide another example of mixed use.[13] Often one uses a word while at the same time implicitly ascribing that use to some other person (or group of persons) whose usage one is blatantly echoing or mimicking. Thus one might say:

(6)   That boy is really 'smart'.

In such examples one is quoting, but at the same time using the words with their normal semantic values.

In (6) the fact that a word is quoted while being used does not affect the truth-conditions of the utterance. But sometimes it does. Thus I can refer to some object, *A*, using the name of another object, *B*, in quotes, providing the person I am mimicking uses the name for *B* as a name for *A*. I may well say

(7)   'Quine' has not finished writing his paper

and refer, by the name 'Quine' in quotes, not to Quine but to that person whom our friend James mistakenly identified as Quine the other day. Any word can, by being quoted in this echoic manner, be ascribed a semantic value which is not its normal semantic value, but rather what some other person takes to be its semantic value.[14] Thus we can draw a distinction, within echoic uses, between those that are truth-conditionally deviant and those that are not. That distinction will be appealed to and elaborated in chapters 14, 19, and 20.

§10.3   'Giorgione'

Even though I accept Quine's point that there are intermediate cases between pure autonymy and pure referentiality, I think his classification of the 'Giorgione' example in that category is mistaken; for I take it that the word 'Giorgione' in (4) is used purely referentially. To be sure, the word 'Giorgione' is mentioned in (4). But there is no inconsistency between holding that the word is used purely referentially, and holding that it is mentioned; for it is mentioned *heteronymously* in (4). Far from referring to itself, the word 'Giorgione' is referred to *by means of a different expression*, viz. the demonstrative adverb 'so' in 'so-called'. Hence the word 'Giorgione' itself is not used in two ways (referentially and autonymously); it is used purely referentially. *In contrast to autonymous mention, heteronymous mention is compatible with purely referential use.* This point can be driven home by splitting sentence (4) in two, as Kit Fine has suggested (1989: 253):

(8) A: Giorgione was Italian.
     B: Yes, and he was so-called because of his size.

Who would deny that the occurrence of 'Giorgione' in A's statement is purely referential? The fact that B's statement contains an expression demonstratively referring to the name 'Giorgione' in no way conflicts with the purely referential character of the occurrence thus demonstrated.

Quine appeals to the failure of substitutivity as proof that the occurrence of 'Giorgione' in (4) is not purely referential. For if it were, it would be substitutable. Now, even though Giorgione is Barbarelli, substitution of 'Barbarelli' for 'Giorgione' does not preserve truth. Substitution of 'Barbarelli' for 'Giorgione' in (4) yields (9), which is false:

(9) Barbarelli was so-called because of his size.

But this proof that the occurrence of 'Giorgione' in (4) is not purely referential rests on an equivocation. The fallacy of equivocation is presented as follows in Quine's *Methods of Logic:*

The two conjunctions:

(10) He went to Pawcatuck, and I went along

(11) He went to Saugatuck, but I did not go along

may both be true; yet if we represent them as of the form 'p & q' and 'r & $\neg q$', as seems superficially to fit the case, we come out with an inconsistent combination 'p & q & r & $\neg q$'. Actually of course the 'I went along' in (10) must be distinguished from the 'I went along' whose negation appears in (11); the one is 'I went along to Pawcatuck' and the other is 'I went along to Saugatuck'. When (10) and (11) are completed in this fashion they can no longer be represented as related in the manner of 'p & q' and 'r & $\neg q$', but only in the manner of 'p & q' and 'r & $\neg s$'; and the apparent inconsistency disappears. In general, *the trustworthiness of logical analysis and inference depends on our not giving one and the same expression different interpretations in the course of the reasoning. Violation of this principle was known traditionally as the fallacy of equivocation....*

The fallacy of equivocation arises ... when the interpretation of an ambiguous expression is influenced in varying ways by immediate contexts, as in (10) and (11), so that the expression undergoes changes of meaning within the limits of the argument. In such cases *we have to rephrase before proceeding.* (Quine 1962: 42–43; notation and emphasis mine)

By the same reasoning, it can be shown that the alleged failure of substitutivity exhibited by the occurrence of 'Giorgione' in (4) is merely apparent. Substitutivity fails, Quine says, because, although Giorgione was so-called because of his size, and Giorgione = Barbarelli, Barbarelli was *not* so-called because of his size. Paraphrasing Quine, however, we can respond as follows: The two statements

(4)   Giorgione was so-called because of his size

(12)   Barbarelli was not so-called because of his size

may both be true; yet if we represent them as of the form 'Fa' and '$\neg Fb$', as seems superficially to fit the case, we come out with an inconsistency, since $a = b$. Actually of course the 'so-called' in (4) must be distinguished from the 'so-called' which appears in (12); the one is 'called *Giorgione*' and the other is 'called *Barbarelli*'. When (4) and (12) are rephrased in this fashion they can no longer be represented as related in the manner of 'Fa' and '$\neg Fb$', but only in the manner of 'Fa' and '$\neg Gb$'; and the apparent inconsistency disappears.

What this shows is that the substitution of 'Barbarelli' for 'Giorgione' does preserve truth after all. The appearance that it does not is caused by the fact that "the interpretation of an ambiguous expression is influenced in varying ways by immediate contexts, ... so that the expression undergoes changes of meaning within the limits of the argument." If, following Quine's advice, we "rephrase before proceeding" we must substitute 'called *Giorgione*' for 'so-called' in (4) *before* testing for substitutivity; and of course, if we do so, we see that substitutivity does not fail. From (5) and the identity 'Giorgione = Barbarelli' we can legitimately infer (13):

(5)   Giorgione was called 'Giorgione' because of his size.

(13)   Barbarelli was called 'Giorgione' because of his size.

I conclude that 'Giorgione' in (4) is purely referential: substitution preserves truth, appearances notwithstanding. Yet the substitution which preserves truth is not any old substitution of coreferential singular terms, but substitution *under a uniform interpretation of whatever context-sensitive expression occurs elsewhere in the sentence.*[15] This condition is crucial, for an apparent failure of substitutivity may be caused by the fact that the semantic value of some context-sensitive expression in the sentence changes as a result of the substitution itself. (That will be so in particular when, as in the 'Giorgione' example, the sentence contains an expression demonstratively referring to the singular term which undergoes substitution). When that is the case, the failure of substitutivity is consistent with pure referentiality. Only a failure of substitutivity under conditions of uniform interpretation provides a reasonable criterion of non-purely referential use.

In his discussions of opacity Quine does not adhere to his own policy of 'rephrasing before proceeding' when the sentence at issue is relevantly ambiguous or context-sensitive. Instead of using 'substitutivity' in the sense of 'substitutivity under conditions of uniformity', he uses it in the sense of 'substitutivity *tout court*'. In that sense the occurrence of 'Giorgione' in (4) is indeed not substitutable. I will hereafter follow Quine and use 'substitutable' in this way. My point concerning the 'Giorgione' example can therefore be rephrased as follows: Pure referentiality does not entail substitutability; hence failure of substitutivity cannot be retained as a criterion of non-purely referential occurrence.

§10.4   Pure Referentiality and Transparency

An occurrence of a singular term is *purely referential*, Quine says, just in case the term, on that occurrence, is used "purely to specify its object." In other words, the term's semantic contribution, on that occurrence, is its (normal) referent, and nothing else. To be sure, a singular term does not only contribute its semantic value (its referent), it also shows or displays whatever other properties it has: its shape, its sense, its affective tone, its poetic qualities, and whatnot. But what matters from a semantic point of view is merely that which the term contributes to the truth-conditions of the whole.

What is meant exactly by a term's 'semantic contribution', i.e., its contribution to the truth-conditions? There is an ambiguity here. On a broad reading, the semantic contribution of an expression is *the over-all difference it makes to the truth-conditions of the sentence where it occurs*. In that sense, 'Giorgione' in (4) does not make the same semantic contribution as 'Barbarelli' in (9); for if they did, (4) and (9) would have the same truth-value. But there is a stricter reading, more relevant to semantic theory. From the standpoint of semantic theory, each expression has a semantic value, and the semantic value of the sentence depends upon the semantic values of its parts and the way they are put together. The semantic contribution of an expression, in the narrow sense, is its semantic value—that which, in part, determines the truth-value of the whole. Thus in the 'Giorgione' example, what the word 'Giorgione' contributes is the individual Giorgione, which it names. The name 'Giorgione' serves also as referent for another expression, and affects the truth-conditions of the sentence in that respect too, but that is not part of the name's semantic contribution (in the narrow sense). Mentioning the name 'Giorgione' is something which *another* expression does; hence it is the semantic contribution of that other expression— while the semantic contribution of the name 'Giorgione' is the individual Giorgione, and nothing else.

As I am using it, the notion of a *purely referential occurrence* of a term is defined in terms of its narrow semantic contribution: a singular term is used purely referentially iff its (narrow) semantic contribution is its referent, and nothing else. But there is room for a distinct notion, defined in terms of the 'broader' type of contribution. Let me define a *transparent* occurrence of a singular term as an occurrence such that *the semantic value of the sentence depends only upon the referent of the term, not on its other qualities (its form, its sense, etc.)*. Thus an occurrence is transparent iff its contribution in the broad sense is its referent, and nothing else.

The distinction between the 'broad' and the 'narrow' semantic contribution of a term, and correlatively between pure referentiality and transparency, is important because it is possible for a term to be purely referential in a sentence, i.e., to contribute its referent and nothing else (in the narrow sense), without being transparent, i.e., such that the truth-value of the sentence does not depend upon any other quality of the term. For suppose that the sentence contains another singular term which demonstratively refers to the first one. Then, even if both terms are purely referential, the truth-value of the sentence will depend upon another property of the first term than merely its referent. That will not bar the first term from being purely referential since those aspects of the term, other than its referent, on which the truth-value of the sentence depends will not be part of the (narrow) semantic contribution of *that term*, but part of the semantic contribution of the other term. That is exactly what happens in the 'Giorgione' example, as we have seen: though purely referential the term 'Giorgione' is not transparent; for the semantic value of the sentence depends not only upon the referent of the term, but also on its identity.

This analysis does not depend on my controversial construal of 'so' in 'so-called' as a demonstrative adverb. If we construe it as anaphorically linked to the name, the situation will be exactly the same: the semantic value of the sentence will depend upon the identity of the purely referential singular term *qua* antecedent of the anaphor. A striking example of that situation is provided by the following example, due to Kit Fine. He imagines a situation in which the man behind Fred is the man before Bill. Despite this identity we cannot infer (14) from (15):

(14)   The man behind Fred saw him leave.

(15)   The man before Bill saw him leave.

This does not show that the description 'the man behind Fred' is not used purely referentially; only that the occurrence of the description is not 'transparent', in the sense I have just defined.

To sum up, transparency entails pure referentiality, but not the other way round. There are *two* ways for an occurrence of a singular term not to be transparent.

• It can be non (purely) referential.
• The linguistic context in which the word occurs may be such that, even if it is purely referential, the truth-value of the sentence will depend upon other properties of the term than its referent. In this type of case I will say that the term occurs in a *reflecting context*; where a reflecting context is *a linguistic context containing an expression whose semantic value depends upon the identity of the term.*

In the second type of case, it's not the way the term is used but rather the context in which it is tokened that blocks substitutivity and generates opacity (the lack of transparency). Hence Quine's shift to talk of 'positions' instead of 'uses' or 'occurrences'. Quine defines a *position* as 'non purely referential' just in case the term in that position is not substitutable. This may be because the term itself is not being used in a purely referential manner, *or* because the linguistic context contains some context-sensitive expression whose value depends upon the identity of the singular term. Quine's notion of a non-purely referential *position* thus corresponds to my notion of an *opaque* occurrence. If I am right in my interpretation, Quine's talk of 'positions' was motivated by his realizing that opacity sometimes arises from the context rather than from the term itself. A term, in and of itself, may be as referential as is possible; if that term is demonstratively referred to by some other expression in the sentence, substitutivity will fail.[16]

§10.5   Transparency and Substitutability

We have distinguished between a purely referential occurrence of a term, and a transparent occurrence (or, in Quine's terminology, an 'occurrence in purely referential position'). Now I want to consider a third notion: that of a *substitutable* occurrence of a singular term, that is, an occurrence of a singular term which can be replaced by an occurrence of a coreferential singular term *salva veritate*.

We have seen that a purely referential occurrence may fail the substitutivity test if it is not transparent (if the 'position' is not purely referential). At this point the question arises, whether we can equate substitutability and transparency.

The first thing we must note in this connection is that it is in fact possible for a purely referential term to be substitutable *without* being transparent. An example of that situation is provided by (16):

(16)   The last word of this sentence designates Cicero.

There is no reason to deny that 'Cicero' is purely referential in this sentence. Its semantic value is the individual Cicero, which it names. But the sentence's semantic value results from the contributions of all constituents, including the demonstrative phrase 'this sentence'. Now the reference of the demonstrative phrase itself depends upon the identity of the singular term occurring at the end of the sentence. If you change the singular term, you change the sentence, hence you change the referent of the phrase 'this sentence'. The singular term 'Cicero' is therefore not transparent, because the context in which it occurs is 'reflecting'. Despite this lack of transparency, the singular term is substitutable: if we replace 'Cicero' by 'Tully', we change the truth-conditions, but the truth-value does not change.

In a case like that, the singular term is substitutable for quite extrinsic reasons. Indeed it can be replaced by any other personal name *salva veritate*, whether that name is coreferential with 'Cicero' or not.

That a singular term can be substitutable without being transparent is not actually surprising. For a term can be substitutable without even being referential. Linsky (1967: 102) gives the following example:

(17) 'Cicero' is a designation for Cicero.

In this sentence the first occurrence of 'Cicero' is (purely) autonymous, like the second occurrence of 'Giorgione' in (5). Yet it is substitutable: replacement of 'Cicero' by 'Tully' or any other name of Cicero in (17) is truth-preserving.[17]

Let us grant that transparency cannot be equated with substitutability. Can we at least maintain, following Quine, that transparency *entails* substitutability? It seems that we should. Paraphrasing Quine (1960: 242), we can argue that if an occurrence of a singular term in a true sentence is transparent, i.e., such that the truth-value of the sentence depends only upon the object which the term specifies, then certainly the sentence will stay true when any other singular term is substituted that designates the same object. Yet even that has been (rightly) disputed. What I have in mind is Kaplan's insightful discussion of what he calls "Quine's alleged theorem" in 'Opacity' (Kaplan 1986).

Kaplan argues that, technically, substitutability does not follow from transparency. But the same point can be made in a non-technical framework, by appealing to the same sort of observation which enabled us to draw a distinction between pure referentiality and transparency.

The crucial point, again, is that natural language sentences are context-sensitive to such a degree, that substituting a singular term for another one can affect the interpretation of other expressions in the same sentence. This may block substitutivity and generate opacity even if the terms at issue are purely referential. Now when a singular term is not only purely referential but *transparent*, it seems that no such thing can happen: for the context is (by definition) not reflecting; it does not contain expressions whose semantic values depend upon the identity of the term. How then can the substitution of coreferentials affect the interpretation of the rest of the sentence? It seems that it cannot, yet, I will argue, it can.

Let us imagine a purely referential occurrence of a term t in a sentence $S(t)$, and let us assume that that occurrence is transparent in the sense that the truth-value of $S(t)$ depends upon the referent of t but not on any other property of t. Since the occurrence of t is transparent, the context $S(\ )$ is not reflecting. Since it is not reflecting, it seems that if we replace t by a coreferential term t', and if the occurrence of t' also is purely referential, then t' can only be transparent. The truth-value of $S(t')$ will therefore depend upon the referent of t' but not on any other property of t'. It follows that $S(t')$ will have the same semantic value as $S(t)$: t, therefore, is substitutable in $S(t)$.

But there is a hidden assumption in the above argument, an assumption which is in fact questionable. It is this: that the linguistic context $S(\ )$ is 'stable' in the sense that if it is non-reflecting in $S(t)$, then it is also non-reflecting in $S(t')$. But suppose we lift that assumption; suppose we accept *unstable contexts*, that is, contexts whose interpretation can shift from non-reflecting to reflecting, depending on which singular term occurs in that context. Then we see that a transparent singular term may not be substitutable after all.

Let us, again, assume that the occurrence of t in $S(t)$ is transparent. This entails that, on that occurrence, t is purely referential and $S(\ )$ is non-reflecting. Yet we cannot conclude that $S(\ )$ will remain non-reflecting after we have substituted t' for t. For an unstable context is a context which is ambiguous between a reflecting and a non-reflecting interpretation. If $S(\ )$ is unstable in this way, then it may be that $S(\ )$ is non-reflecting in $S(t)$ but becomes reflecting in $S(t')$. Suppose that is the case; then t' is not transparent in $S(t')$: the truth-value of $S(t')$ will not depend merely upon the referent of t'—it will depend on the identity of the term. The truth-conditions, hence possibly the truth-value, of $S(t')$

will therefore be different from the truth-conditions of $S(t)$. In such a case, therefore, t is not substitutable: replacing it by a purely referential occurrence of a coreferential term t' may result in a change of truth-value.

That is not a purely theoretical possibility. There are reasons to believe that metarepresentational contexts are unstable. A belief sentence like 'John believes that Cicero is bald' has two readings, as we have seen (§9.4): a transparent reading in which it says of John and Cicero that the former believes the latter to be bald, without specifying how (under which 'mode of presentation') John thinks of Cicero; and an opaque reading in which it is further understood that John thinks of Cicero as 'Cicero'. According to several authors, who use the 'Giorgione' example as paradigm, 'John believes that ... is bald' is a reflecting context on the opaque reading;[18] that is, the sentence somehow involves a 'logophoric' or demonstrative reference to the singular term which occurs in the context. Even if the term in question is construed as purely referential, the truth-value of the sentence depends not only on the referent of the term but also on its identity, on the opaque reading. In contrast, the context is non-reflecting on the transparent reading. Now, arguably, which particular singular term occurs in the sentence may affect its interpretation. This blocks substitutivity: even if the occurrence of the singular term t in 'John believes that t is F' is not only purely referential but also transparent, substituting a purely referential occurrence of a coreferential singular term t' for t may shift the interpretation of 'John believes that ... is F' to its reflecting reading, thereby making the occurrence of t' opaque. That is what apparently happens if we replace 'I' by 'François Recanati' in (18):

(18) John, who confuses me with my grandfather Francis, believes that I died twenty years ago.

(19) John, who confuses me with my grandfather Francis, believes that François Recanati died twenty years ago.

In both cases John is said to have a belief concerning François Recanati, to the effect that he died twenty years ago; but in the second case there arguably is a logophoric or demonstrative reference to the singular term. Following Forbes (1990), (19) can be paraphrased as:

(19*)   John ... *so-believes* that François Recanati died twenty years ago.

That opaque interpretation is natural when the singular term is the proper name 'François Recanati', while the pronoun 'I' rules out this interpretation for pragmatic reasons (McKay 1981; Recanati 1993: 399–401). In (18), the truth-value of the sentence depends only upon the referent of 'I'. In (19), it also depends upon the identity of the referring expression (the proper name) used in the embedded sentence: John is said to have a belief concerning François Recanati *qua* 'François Recanati'.

I am not presently defending this analysis of belief sentences; I will do so in chapter 11. That brief anticipation was only meant to illustrate the notion of an unstable context, that is, a context ambiguous between a reflecting and a non-reflecting reading. In the same way in which a purely referential occurrence may not be transparent if it occurs in a reflecting context, a transparent occurrence may not be substitutable if it occurs in an unstable context. Thus in (18) the singular term 'I' is not substitutable even though it is transparent, because the context is unstable.

To be sure, if, following Quine's general methodological recommendations, we get rid of context-sensitivity by suitably rephrasing the sentences we subject to logical treatment, then we automaticaly get rid of both reflecting and unstable contexts. It then becomes possible to equate (as Quine does) pure referentiality, transparency and substitutability. But, as we saw (§10.3), Quine himself does not follow his own recommendations: he treats 'Giorgione' as non-purely referential and non-substitutable in (4), something which is possible only if we take the context-sensitive sentences "as they come" (Quine 1960: 158), without prior rephrasal. It is this policy which enables him to put in the same basket non-referential (autonymous) occurrences of terms and referential occurrences in reflecting contexts. I have shown that if we take this line, then we should draw a principled distinction between pure referentiality, transparency, and substitutability.

11

Metarepresentational Opacity: An Innocent Account

§11.1 Introduction: Looking for a Dependent Expression

According to Brian Loar, a singular term in the embedded portion of an opaque belief report has a dual role. It refers to the object the belief is about, but also determines an aspect of the ascribed belief concerning that object. The ascribed belief is conjunctive, and the first conjunct depends upon the identity of the singular term. For example, if the sentence 'John believes that Cicero is bald' is given the opaque interpretation, it means that John believes of the individual Cicero both that he 'is Cicero' (whatever that means) and that he is bald. Transparently understood, the sentence only means that John believes of that individual that he is bald.

This theory can be understood in two ways. On one interpretation a singular term behaves deviantly in belief contexts. Instead of merely referring to some object, as singular terms normally do, it refers to an object *and* contributes a 'mode of presentation' to the content of the ascribed belief. That theory gives up semantic innocence, even if it does so in a less extreme manner than Frege's. It construes the singular term in a belief report as referential, but not as *purely* referential.

There is another option, though. It consists in preserving semantic innocence and holding that the singular term in an opaque belief report is purely referential, in accordance with its normal semantic function. The opacity of the occurrence can then be explained by construing the context as *reflecting*, in analogy with the above analysis of the 'Giorgione' example (§10.3–4).

A linguistic context for a singular term is reflecting if and only if it contains a *dependent expression*, that is, an expression whose semantic value depends upon the identity (and not merely the semantic value) of the singular term occurring in that context. In the 'Giorgione' example, the dependent expression was the adverb 'so' in 'so-called', which we can construe either as demonstrative or as anaphoric. When we replace 'Giorgione' by a coreferential term, e.g., 'Barbarelli', the semantic value of the dependent expression changes. That accounts for the sentence's change in truth-value.

In the 'Giorgione' example, the dependent expression ('so-called') is part of the *frame* in which the singular term occurs ('... is so-called because of his size').[19] The dependent expression is therefore disjoint (separable) from the singular term itself. But that need not be the case: for a context to be reflecting, it is not necessary that the dependent expression occur as part of the frame, in disjunction from the singular term itself. There are cases in which the singular term itself will be a constituent of the dependent expression. Let me give an example involving, not a singular but a general term.

Consider the demonstrative phrase 'that nag'. The semantic value of 'nag' is the same as that of 'horse'; the difference, as Frege would say, is one of 'colouring' rather than a properly semantic (truth-conditional) difference. Despite their semantic equivalence, 'nag' in 'that nag' cannot be replaced by 'horse', because the reference of a demonstrative phrase is linguistically underdetermined and crucially depends upon the referential intentions of the speaker, as revealed by the context. Now one aspect of the context which may be relevant to the determination of the speaker's referential intentions is the word which the speaker uses. If he uses a word such as 'nag', that provides some evidence that he does not intend to refer to his beloved and much respected horse Pablo, who happens to be otherwise salient in the context, but rather to the deprecated Pedro. If the word 'horse' was used, however, sheer salience would presumably promote Pablo to the status of referent. Substituting 'horse' for 'nag' can therefore change the likely interpretation, hence possibly the truth-value, of the sentence, by affecting the semantic value of the demonstrative phrase.

In general, whenever the semantic value of a phrase is linguistically underdetermined, and depends upon the intentions of the speaker, that phrase is a reflecting context for its constituents. A 'part' of the global phrase cannot be replaced by a semantically equivalent expression without possibly affecting the semantic value of the whole, because any aspect of the context, including the actual words which are used, may be relevant to determining that semantic value.

Let us now go back to belief reports. If singular terms in belief sentences fulfill their ordinary function and are purely referential, substitutivity failures must be accounted for by appealing to the notion of a reflecting context. That means that we must find a dependent expression in the belief report—an expression whose semantic value depends upon the identity of the singular term.

§11.2 'That'-Clauses as Dependent Expressions

One possible candidate for the status of dependent expression is the 'that'-clause itself. Most philosophers consider a 'that'-clause as a referring expression whose reference is the proposition expressed by the embedded sentence. In my book *Direct Reference* (Recanati 1993), I put forward a slightly different proposal, in order to account for the well-known context-sensitivity of belief sentences. I claimed that a 'that'-clause can, but need not, refer to the proposition expressed by the embedded sentence. It can also refer to a proposition obtained by contextually *enriching* the expressed proposition.

The relevant notion of contextual enrichment is that needed to account for examples like the following:

(1) She took out her key and opened the door.

In that example, analysed in Carston (1985), the fact that the door was opened with the key is not linguistically specified, yet it is certainly part of what we understand when we hear that sentence. It is an aspect of the meaning or content of the utterance which is provided through 'contextual enrichment'. John Perry calls that an 'unarticulated constituent' of what is said (Perry 1986b); and he and Crimmins hold that modes of presentation of the objects of belief are unarticulated constituents of the propositions expressed by opaque belief reports (Crimmins and Perry 1989).[20] I agree with the spirit, if not the details, of that analysis.

In my book I took a 'that'-clause to be a demonstrative phrase whose reference is constrained, but not determined, by the proposition which the embedded sentence expresses—much like the reference of the demonstrative phrase 'that horse' is constrained, but not determined, by the general term it contains. In other words, I took the reference of 'that'-clauses to be linguistically *underdetermined*. Underdetermination is to be distinguished from mere context-dependence. The reference of words like 'I' or 'today' is context-dependent, but it does not exhibit the relevant feature of underdetermination. In a given situation, the meaning of a pure indexical like 'I' or 'today' fully determines what the reference is. Not so with demonstratives. The reference of 'he' or 'that' is not determined by any rigid rule; it is determined by answering questions such as, Who or what can the speaker plausibly be taken to be referring to, in that context? The same thing holds, I assumed, for 'that'-clauses. A 'that'-clause refers to a proposition which resembles the proposition expressed by the embedded sentence (Jacob 1987: part V), but need not be identical with it; it can be an enrichment of it. What the reference of a given 'that'-clause actually is will depend upon the speaker's intentions as manifested in the context.

On that theory, when a belief report such as 'Ralph believes that Cicero is a Roman orator' is understood opaquely, the reference of the 'that'-clause 'that Cicero is a Roman orator' is distinct from what it is on the transparent interpretation. On the transparent interpretation the reference is, arguably, the 'singular proposition' which the embedded sentence expresses, viz. a sequence whose first member is the individual Cicero, and whose second member is the property 'Roman orator'. On the opaque interpretation, the reference is a 'quasi-singular' proposition, that is, the same thing except that the first member of the sequence is itself an ordered pair, consisting of the individual Cicero *and another property serving as 'mode of presentation'* (Recanati 1993, 1995b). The quasi-singular proposition is an enrichment of the expressed singular proposition. The extra constituent provided by the context is the mode of presentation under which the reference of the singular term is assumed to be thought of by the believer.

On that view the 'that'-clause turns out to be a dependent expression, whose semantic value can change if a singular term occurring in the 'that'-clause is replaced by a coreferential term. For the reference of the 'that'-clause ultimately depends upon the speaker's communicative intentions as revealed by the context; and any aspect of the context, including the words which the speaker actually uses to report the ascribee's beliefs, may be relevant in figuring out the speaker's referential intention. In some contexts, the speaker's use of the name 'Cicero' will suggest that the believer thinks of Cicero as 'Cicero'. That is no more than a contextual suggestion, accountable perhaps in Gricean terms (McKay 1981; Salmon 1986); yet it may influence the assignment of a particular semantic value to the 'that'-clause, thereby affecting the truth-conditions of the belief report. That will be so whenever the belief report is understood opaquely: the 'that'-clause will then refer to a quasi-singular proposition involving not only the individual Cicero and the property 'Roman orator', but also a further property such as 'called *Cicero*'.

§11.3   Metarepresentational Prefixes as Dependent Expressions

In chapter 2, I argued that any theory which construes 'that'-clauses as referring expressions is bound to give up semantic innocence at some point or other. In a truly innocent account, the embedded sentence must be treated as, logically, a sentence; it must not be converted into a term. In accordance with this prescription, I analysed 'John believes that' as a *world-shifting operator*. It presents the sentence which follows as true in John's 'belief world', rather than in the actual world. If this is correct we can no longer treat the 'that'-clause as a dependent expression, in a sentence like 'John believes that grass is green'; for there no longer is a 'that'-clause. The two constituents in a belief sentence are: the internal sentence, and the metarepresentational prefix. Where, on this analysis, can we find a dependent expression, in order to account for substitution failures without giving up semantic innocence?

Answering this question is easy, given what has been said so far. We know that the following inference is invalid (on a certain interpretation):

(2)   John believes that Emile Ajar wrote *La Vie devant soi*.

(3)   Emile Ajar = Romain Gary.

(4)   John believes that Romain Gary wrote *La Vie devant soi.*

Despite the identity stated in (3), we cannot infer (4) from (2). For it is possible that (2) is true and (4) false. That entails that (2) and (4) have different truth-conditions. Now, in virtue of (3) and the semantics of singular terms, the embedded sentence in (2) and (4) make the same (narrow) contribution to the truth-conditions of the global belief report. Hence it must be the interpretation of the frame 'John believes that ____', that is, its own contribution to the truth-conditions of the global belief report, which changes from (2) to (4).

To emphasize the similarity with Quine's 'Giorgione' example, and borrowing an idea from Graeme Forbes (1990), I suggest that we re-phrase (2) and (4) respectively as

(2′)   John so-believes that Emile Ajar wrote *La Vie devant soi.*

(4′)   John so-believes that Romain Gary wrote *La Vie devant soi.*

In general, I suggest that whenever an attitude sentence, '*a* Ψs that *p*', is interpreted opaquely, we render it as '*a* so-Ψs that *p*', where 'so' is a demonstrative adverb referring to some manner of Ψ-ing demonstrated in the context. Slightly more colloquially, we might use the phrase '*a* Ψs that *p thus*', or '*a* Ψs that *p in that manner*'. For example, '*a* says that *p*', opaquely understood, will be interpreted as tacitly referring to some manner of saying that *p*, as if the speaker had said: '*a* said that *p thus*'. Similarly for '*a* believes that *p*' and the other attitude verbs.

What is a manner of Ψ-ing? Consider the case of 'saying that'. Some-one can say that I am ill by uttering the sentence 'He is ill' (while point-ing to me) or by uttering 'Recanati is not well'. Those are two ways of saying that I am ill. Similarly, there are different ways or manners of believing that I am ill: e.g., by mentally entertaining the thought 'That guy is ill' or by entertaining the thought 'Recanati is not well'.

Let us assume that the speaker utters

(5)   John said that Recanati is not well

and that this is understood opaquely, as somehow reporting (some of) the words which John himself used. I analyse (5) as

(5′)   John so-said that Recanati is not well
     = John said that Recanati is not well *thus*

where the demonstrative adverb, 'so' or 'thus', refers to some manner of saying that I am ill. Which manner of saying that? *The manner of saying which is instantiated by the speaker's utterance of the embedded sentence.*

In that framework the same prefix 'John believes that' makes different semantic contributions in (2) and (4), because the semantic value of the implicit demonstrative shifts when we substitute 'Romain Gary' for 'Emile Ajar'. The difference can be made explicit as follows:

(2″) John believes that Ajar/Gary wrote *La Vie devant soi* in that manner: 'Emile Ajar wrote *La Vie devant soi*'.

(4″) John believes that Ajar/Gary wrote *La Vie devant soi* in that manner: 'Romain Gary wrote *La Vie devant soi*'.

In (2″) and (4″), the adverbial 'in that manner' must of course be interpreted as modifying the main verb 'believes'. That verb itself must be given the 'transparent' interpretation: in (2″) and (4″) 'believes' is *not* equivalent to 'so-believes'.

§11.4   The Context-Sensitivity of Metarepresentational Prefixes

As it stands the analysis is not wholly satisfactory, for not all aspects of the embedded sentence need to play a role in the imputation of a particular manner of believing to the ascribee.[21] To refine the analysis, we can appeal to Nunberg's useful distinction between the *index* and the *referent* of a given occurrence of a demonstrative (Nunberg 1993). The index is what Kaplan (1989a) calls the *demonstratum*—that which is actually pointed to or attended to—but at least in cases of 'deferred ostension' that is distinct from the referent: the referent is the intended object, identifiable in relation to the index. Thus if, pointing to a car key, I say 'This is parked out back', the index (*demonstratum*) is the key, but the referent is the car. If we apply this distinction to our present case, we will say that the implicit demonstrative 'so' or 'thus' *demonstrates* the speaker's current utterance of the embedded sentence (= index), and thereby *refers to* a certain manner of Ψ-ing, namely, that manner of Ψ-ing which would be instantiated if one Ψ-ed by uttering/entertaining that sentence.[22] On this analysis not all aspects of the demonstrated utterance need to be relevant to the determination of the manner of Ψ-ing which the speaker ascribes to the believer.

We can achieve the same result without appealing to Nunberg's distinction, however. Instead of analysing '*a* so-believes that *p*' as '*a* believes that *p* *in that manner*', we can analyse it, more perspicuously perhaps, as: '*a* believes that *p* *like that*', where the demonstrative 'that' refers to the utterance of the embedded sentence. The manner of Ψ-ing denoted by the whole adverbial phrase 'like that' will then depend upon the dimensions of similarity which are contextually relevant.

Whichever method we choose, the prefix turns out to be context-sensitive in two distinct ways, on the opaque interpretation. First, its semantic value depends upon the embedded sentence which follows it; for the *demonstratum* (the index, or the referent of the constituent demonstrative 'that') automatically changes when we substitute one expression for another in the embedded sentence. Second, the manner of Ψ-ing which the demonstrated utterance is taken to instantiate will itself depend upon the aspects of the demonstrated utterance which are considered relevant. Even if we fix the demonstrated utterance, it will still be possible, by changing the context, to change the manner of Ψ-ing ascribed to the Ψ-er, thereby affecting the semantic value of the prefix.

There is, of course, an even more basic dimension of contextual variation: the belief report can be understood as transparent or opaque in the first place. The opaque reading I take to be a contextual enrichment of the transparent reading. Much as 'She opened the door' in (1) is contextually enriched into 'She opened the door *with the key*', 'John believes that *p*' is enriched into 'John believes that *p* *in such and such manner*'. The transparent/opaque ambiguity for belief reports is therefore an ambiguity between the minimal reading and a contextually enriched reading of the sentence.[23] Here as often, the enriched reading entails the minimal reading.[24]

Table III.2 summarizes the three dimensions of contextual variation we have discerned in belief sentences. All these possible shifts in interpretation can be construed as changes in the semantic value of the prefix '*a* Ψs that' (or, more appropriately perhaps, as changes in the content of

Table III.2
Contextual variations in the interpretation of belief sentences

Minimal vs. contextually enriched interpretation	Variation of the demonstratum	Variation of the manner of Ψ-ing taken to be instantiated by the demonstratum
Transparent (minimal) reading: a believes that p		
Opaque (enriched) reading: a so-believes that p (= a believes that p *like that*)	$\left\{\begin{array}{l}\text{believes that } p \\ \text{like } d_1 \\[1em] \text{believes that } p \\ \text{like } d_2 \\[1em] \vdots\end{array}\right.$	$\left\{\begin{array}{l}\text{believes that } p \text{ in manner } m_1 \\ \text{believes that } p \text{ in manner } m_2 \\ \text{believes that } p \text{ in manner } m_3 \\ \vdots\end{array}\right.$ $\left\{\begin{array}{l}\text{believes that } p \text{ in manner } m'_1 \\ \text{believes that } p \text{ in manner } m'_2 \\ \text{believes that } p \text{ in manner } m'_3 \\ \vdots\end{array}\right.$ $\left\{\begin{array}{l}\vdots\end{array}\right.$

the global frame 'a Ψs that ____'). The content of the embedded sentence itself is not affected by the contextual variation. It is the prefix which can be interpreted minimally or in an enriched, opaque manner ('a so-Ψs that'), depending on the context;[25] and it is the semantic value of the prefix which, on the opaque interpretation, varies according to the two further sorts of contextual change I have described. The internal sentence always makes the same contribution; and the contribution it makes is also the same as it makes when uttered in isolation.

It remains to be shown how the difference between the two interpretations of the prefix (the opaque and the transparent interpretation) can be cashed out in the framework set up in part II. In chapter 7 the content of (i.e., the fact stated by) an utterance like 'John believes that p' was analysed as

John's belief state $\models_@ p^j$

where 'j' is John's 'belief world' (§7.4). In a footnote, I suggested that the following analysis might be more appropriate:

$(\exists x)(x$ is a belief-state $\&$ x belongs to John $\&$ $x \models_@ p^j)$

In terms of this analysis, the shift from the transparent to the opaque reading of the prefix can be cashed out as the contextual provision of an extra conjunct. 'John so-believes that S' (where S is an embedded sentence expressing the proposition that p) is thus analysed as

$(\exists x)(x$ is a belief-state $\&$ x belongs to John $\&$ x is like S $\&$ $x \vDash_@ p^j)$

or perhaps as

$(\exists x)(x$ is a belief-state $\&$ x belongs to John $\&$ x is like u $\&$ $x \vDash_@ p^j)$

where 'u' is the speaker's own utterance of the embedded sentence S.

§11.5   Opacity, Substitution, and Quantification

The prefix 'John believes that' is a dependent expression only on the opaque reading, i.e., when it is interpreted as 'John so-believes that'. On the transparent reading it is not a dependent expression. Since the occurrences of singular terms in the embedded sentences are uniformly treated as purely referential, in accordance with their normal semantic function, they come out *transparent*, by the definitions given in chapter 10, whenever the prefix itself is given the transparent reading: for (i) they are purely referential, and (ii) the context in which they occur is not reflecting (since the prefix is not a dependent expression, on the transparent reading). The truth-value of a transparent belief report therefore depends only upon the reference of the term, not on its identity. That strongly suggests that singular terms in transparent belief contexts should be substitutable, that is, freely replaceable by coreferential singular terms. Yet, I shall argue, they are not.

The reason why occurrences of singular terms in transparent belief reports are not substitutable, even though they are transparent, is very simple. Since (i) the prefix can be given an opaque (enriched) as well as a transparent (minimal) interpretation, depending on the context; and (ii) substituting one expression for another in the embedded sentence changes the context in which the prefix is tokened; it follows that the substitution can shift the interpretation of the prefix from transparent to opaque, by making it more likely that the speaker, using *those* words, intends to capture the believer's own way of thinking of the matter. In other words, belief contexts are *unstable* (§10.5). Only if we somehow fix (stabilize) the transparent interpretation of the prefix will substitution of coreferentials be a legitimate move.

Our findings so far can be summarized as follows:

• An occurrence of a singular term in the embedded portion of a belief sentence is purely referential (hence 'innocent'), but not necessarily transparent: it is transparent only if the belief sentence is given a minimal interpretation ('transparent' reading). When the belief sentence is given an enriched interpretation ('opaque' reading), the occurrence of the singular term is not transparent, because the context in which it occurs is reflecting.

• Whether transparent or not, an occurrence of a singular term in the embedded portion of a belief sentence is not substitutable. It is non-substitutable either because the context *is* reflecting (opaque reading) or because the substitution can *make it* reflecting (transparent reading).

A last feature of singular belief reports must now be considered. As we saw in chapter 10, Quine tends to equate pure referentiality, transparency and substitutability. There is a fourth, no less important property on Quine's list: existential generalizability. When a singular term is purely referential (transparent, substitutable), Quine says, existential generalization is possible. When substitutivity fails because of opacity, existential generalization likewise fails. Thus we cannot go from (6) to (7):

(6)   Giorgione was so-called because of his size.

(7) $(\exists x)(x$ was so-called because of his size)

Contrary to Quine, who holds that transparency entails substitutability, I emphasized that even transparent occurrences of singular terms in (transparent) belief reports are not substitutable—unless of course we stabilize the context by fixing the interpretation of all the other expressions in the sentence while we make the substitution. A first question that arises, therefore, is this: Is a transparent occurrence of a singular term in a belief context open to existential generalization? If the answer is, as I claim, 'yes', then, *pace* Quine, substitution and existential generalization do not go hand in hand. I will go much further than that: I will argue that even opaque occurrences of singular terms in belief contexts are open to existential generalization. On the picture I am advocating (table III.3), substitution is *never* possible (even if the occurrence of the

Table III.3
Singular terms in belief reports: their 'Quinean' properties

	Occurrence of singular term	
	in 'opaque' belief report	in 'transparent' belief report
Purely referential?	yes	yes
Transparent?	no	yes
Substitutable?	no	no
Open to existential generalization?	yes	yes

singular term at issue is transparent); while existential generalization is *always* possible (even if the occurrence of the singular term at issue is opaque).

The unstability of the context accounts for the (surprising) failure of substitutivity in transparent belief reports. Substitutivity fails because the substitution can, by changing the context, shift the interpretation of the prefix from transparent to opaque, thereby affecting the truth-conditions of the belief report. It is also the unstability of the context which accounts for the (no less surprising) possibility of existential generalization in opaque belief reports.

Normally, opacity blocks existential generalization. For the truth-value of a sentence containing an opaque occurrence of a singular term depends upon the identity of the term, not merely on its reference. When that term is eliminated through existential generalization, the statement is left incomplete and unevaluable: a reflecting context with nothing to reflect. Thus, Quine observes, (7) "is clearly meaningless, there being no longer any suitable antecedent for 'so-called'" (Quine 1961: 145). There is, however, a crucial difference between an opaque belief sentence and a sentence like (6)—a difference which accounts for the success of existential generalization in opaque belief sentences.

Sentence (6) is a reflecting context for the singular term 'Giorgione', and it is so in a stable manner: the context *remains* reflecting under operations such as substitution of coreferentials or existential generalization. But a belief sentence is a reflecting context for the singular terms occurring in the embedded sentence only when it is given the opaque ('so-believes') interpretation; and that interpretation is a highly context-sensitive hence *unstable* feature of the sentence. As I have repeatedly stressed, replacing a transparent occurrence of a singular term by an occurrence of a coreferential singular term may change the truth-value of the report by shifting the prefix from the transparent to the opaque interpretation. In the other direction, replacing an opaque occurrence of a singular term, that is, an occurrence of a singular term in the embedded portion of an opaquely interpreted belief report, by a variable, automatically shifts the interpretation of the prefix from the opaque ('so-believes') to the transparent interpretation; for it is only on the transparent reading that the quantified statement makes sense. If the context remained reflecting, the statement would become meaningless once the singular term is eliminated. By virtue of this compensatory mechanism, we can go from 'Tom believes that Cicero denounced Catiline', even on the opaque interpretation, to 'Someone is such that Tom believes *he* denounced Catiline'. The opacity of the original sentence is pragmatically filtered out in the very process of existential generalization.

At this point one might argue that, surely, the inference is illegitimate. We can go by existential generalization from '*Fa*' to '$(\exists x)(Fx)$', but not from '*Fa*' to '$(\exists x)(Gx)$'. But in the type of inference I have just described, an expression (viz. the prefix) is interpreted differently in the premise (the opaque belief sentence we start with) and the conclusion (the quantified statement). Logically, therefore, the inference does not take us from '*Fa*' to '$(\exists x)(Fx)$', but from '*Fa*' to '$(\exists x)(Gx)$'. That is an instance of the fallacy of equivocation mentioned in §10.3.

But I think existential generalization from opaque belief reports with singular terms *is* a valid move. As I pointed out earlier, the opaque reading entails the transparent reading. It is therefore legitimate to go from the opaque belief report 'Tom believes$_o$ that Cicero denounced Catiline' to the meaningful quantified statement 'There is someone of whom Tom believed$_t$ he denounced Catiline'; for the latter is entailed by the transparent belief report 'Tom believes$_t$ that Cicero denounced Catiline', and that transparent belief report itself is entailed by the opaque belief report.

IV

Context-Shifting and Oratio Recta

12
Context-Shifting

§12.1 World, Context, and Rigid Designation

As we have seen in part II, a lot of our thought and talk involves *imaginary* situations. Not only do we indulge in phantasy and pretend play; we also exercise the imagination for serious purposes. There are many aspects of the actual world which we can represent only by locating it within the 'frame of reference' provided by other possible worlds (Lewis 1986: 22). Thus counterfactual statements such as 'If he came now, he would be happy' tell us something about the actual world, by characterizing an imaginary situation. Metarepresentations provide another example. In saying 'In the film, a giant spider swallows New York City', we describe a real-world object (the film) by describing an imaginary situation (that which the film itself represents). In saying 'John believes that Morocco is a Republic' (or 'According to John, Morocco is a Republic'), I characterize John by describing the world as it is according to him.

   In the examples I have just given, a representation concerning some possible world distinct from the actual world is incorporated within a representation concerning the actual world. This is to be contrasted with another type of case in which two *distinct* representations are involved. I have in mind examples like:

(1)   John is completely paranoid. Everybody wants to kill him, including his own mother!

(2)   There is a great film showing at the Piazza. A giant spider swallows New York City.

In those examples (already discussed in part II) there are two distinct representations, *A* and *B*, such that *A* concerns the actual world, *B* concerns an imaginary situation, and *B* is functionally subordinated to *A* in the sense that the representation of the imaginary situation in *B* serves to illustrate or elaborate the representation of the actual world provided by *A*. In conditionals or metarepresentations the situation is very similar except that *A* and *B* are not distinct: *B* is a proper part of *A*. Thus *A* is what I called a heterogeneous δ-structure (§7.1). It consists of the representation *B* headed by a prefix ('if he came', 'John believes that', 'in the film') whose function is to shift the world with respect to which the representation is evaluated. The complex representation 'In the film, a giant spider swallows New York City' concerns the actual world @ but the opening part 'in the film' shifts the world in such a way that the embedded portion, 'A giant spider swallows New York City', is interpreted as concerning another world *w*—the 'world of the film'. The complex representation is true in the actual world iff the embedded representation is true in the world introduced by the prefix.

In possible-worlds semantics the extension or denotation of an expression is world-relative: it depends on the world at issue. The set of bald men, which is the extension of the predicate 'bald', is different in different possible worlds; for some of the people who are actually bald might not have been, and some of the people who are not bald might have been. Similarly, the definite description 'the President of France in 1997' denotes Chirac in the actual world, because Chirac actually won the election, but we can easily imagine a world in which Jospin won. With respect to such an imaginary world, 'the President of France in 1997' denotes Jospin rather than Chirac. Now heterogeneous δ-structures involve two worlds: the world in which the complex representation itself is evaluated, and the world in which the embedded representation is evaluated. This generates ambiguities (chapter 9). Consider examples (3) and (4):

(3)   The President [i.e., the President of France in 1997] might have been a Socialist.

(4)   John believes that the President is a Socialist.

Depending on whether or not it takes scope over the world-shifting operator, the description 'the President' will either denote an individual in @ (the world in which the complex representation is evaluated), or an individual in the possible world (or set of possible worlds) introduced by the operator. On the former reading the utterance means that: The President (viz. Chirac) is such that he might have been a Socialist, or such that John believes him to be a Socialist. On the latter reading it means that France might have had a Socialist as President (instead of Chirac), or that, in John's 'belief world', a Socialist is President.

If we replace the description by a proper name or a demonstrative, the ambiguity vanishes:

(5)   John believes that Chirac is a Socialist.

(6)   John believes that he [pointing to Chirac] is a Socialist.

The reason why that is so is that names and demonstratives are 'rigid designators': their denotation does not vary across possible worlds. To be sure, a name like 'Chirac' might have denoted someone else. There certainly are possible worlds in which Jospin is called 'Chirac' and Chirac is called by some other name. Similarly the demonstrative pronoun 'he', and the accompanying gesture, might have demonstrated someone else: someone else than Chirac might have stood in the direction of the pointing finger. In *that* sense, the extension of a name or demonstrative is not invariant across possible worlds. But what the claim that names and demonstratives are rigid designators amounts to is merely this: When, using those expressions, we talk about some imaginary situation, the denotation of the expression on that use is not the person whom the pointing gesture would demonstrate in the imaginary situation, or the person who would be called 'Chirac' in that situation, but the individual who is *actually* pointed to, or the person who is *actually* called 'Chirac'. It is the actual-world denotation that counts, even though we are explicitly dealing with imaginary situations. Since the denotation of the expression is always its actual-world denotation, the world-shift operated by the prefix 'it might have been the case that' or 'John believes that' has no effect on its interpretation.

The aspects of the actual world on which the denotation of names and indexicals depends are aspects of the *context*, that is, of the situation of utterance. The denotation of (a token of) 'I' depends upon who utters it; the denotation of a demonstrative depends upon which individual the speaker is demonstrating while uttering it; the denotation of (a use of) a proper name depends upon which individual stands at the origin of the causal chain leading to that use of the name; and so forth. Had the context of utterance been different, the denotation would have been different, but, given a particular context of utterance, it is that context which fixes the denotation of indexicals and proper names, irrespective of which world is being talked about or described in the utterance. In that sense the denotation of names and indexicals is *context*-relative, but it is not *world*-relative. The distinction thus drawn between 'context' (situation of utterance) and 'world' (described situation) explains why it is not contradictory for me to imagine and talk about a situation in which, say, I do not exist (Kaplan 1989a: 495, 498). In referring to myself as 'I', I exploit the fact that I am speaking, and that certainly presupposes that I exist; but the imaginary situation I am describing (that in which I do not exist) must be sharply distinguished from the situation which determines the denotation of the indexical (the situation of utterance: that in which I am speaking).[1]

§12.2   Imaginary Contexts

As I said at the beginning, we are quite free to consider and talk about imaginary situations—possible worlds—either for fun or for serious purposes. Do we have a similar freedom with respect to contexts? The traditional answer to that question is: No. In a typical passage, Barwise and Perry claim that we cannot exploit imaginary contexts in the way we can describe and talk about imaginary worlds:

> One cannot simply choose which discourse situation to exploit. I cannot exploit a discourse situation with Napoleon as speaker; even if I am fully convinced that I am Napoleon, my use of 'I' designates me, not him. Similarly, I may be fully convinced that it is 1789, but it does not make my use of 'now' about a time in 1789. (Barwise and Perry 1983: 148)[2]

This suggests that no departure from the actual world is accepted as far as the context is concerned. The context of an utterance is fixed by *actual facts* concerning the utterance: who is actually speaking, to whom, etc. If that's right, there is an important asymmetry between worlds and contexts: contexts, contrary to worlds, cannot be shifted at will.

As against this view, Ducrot has insisted that the 'context' of an utterance is *not* fixed by actual facts concerning the utterance: much like the world (the situation talked about), it can be shifted according to the whims of the imagination. Thus a novelist can write:

It's been three years since we left the Earth. A couple of weeks after the Last Day, we lost track of the other spaceships. I still don't know what happened to my twin brother Henry. If he is alive, he probably thinks I died in the collision.

Let's imagine that this is the first paragraph of a novel. What is the context for those sentences? Well, two sorts of 'context' are relevant here. First, there is the actual context of utterance: the novelist writes those sentences at the beginning of her novel. But that is not the 'context' in the ordinary sense, that is, what determines the reference of indexicals. The word 'I', in the third sentence, does not denote the person who, in the actual context, issues the sentence (the novelist); rather, it purports to denote a character *in* the novel: the 'narrator', distinguished from the actual author. In a perfectly good sense, then, the context for those sentences is not the actual context, but an imaginary context. In that imaginary context, the speaker is on board of a spaceship, he or she has a twin brother called 'Henry', etc.

The distinction between context and world is not blurred when we make room for imaginary contexts. There still is a difference between the situation *described* by the text and the (imaginary) situation of utterance. As usual, the latter determines the denotation of the names and indexicals used in describing the former. The difference comes out whenever there is a world-shift. For instance, in the last sentence of the example, a possible world is introduced, corresponding to Henry's hypothetical beliefs. That imaginary world is clearly distinct from the (no less imaginary!) 'actual world' in which the utterance is supposed to take place.

The distinction between the author of a story and its narrator is commonplace in literary theory. Ducrot imported it into linguistics by similarly distinguishing between the empirical 'author' of a linguistic text, and the 'speaker' (*locuteur*) projected by the text itself. He gave several examples supporting the claim that, whenever they are distinguishable, 'I' refers to the speaker in that sense, rather than to the empirical author of the text (Ducrot 1984: 194 ff). Generalizing that contrast, I suggest that we distinguish between the *external context* in which the text is actually produced, and the *internal context* in which it 'presented as' produced—

both being distinct from the 'world' which the text describes.[3] As Ducrot pointed out, it is the internal context which is relevant for fixing the denotation of indexicals.

Using that framework, and still following Ducrot, we can analyse *oratio recta* as involving the same sort of context-shift as the literary example discussed above. When we quote someone else's words, we engage in a form of play-acting: we simulate the person in question by actually making the utterance we're ascribing to her. Herb Clark, whose views on this topic are very similar to Ducrot's, makes that point vivid by means of an example in which someone, quoting Greta Garbo, utters the quoted words in a Swedish accent while clutching his arms to his chest in a Garboesque pose (Clark 1996: 175). The quoter in that example is obviously playing the part of Garbo. According to Ducrot, Clark, and especially Wierzbicka (1974), something similar takes place whenever we quote someone. The quoter simulates the person whose speech or thought he is reporting, much as an actor simulates the character whose part he is playing, or as the novelist simulates the narrator. That account goes a long way toward explaining why 'I', in such contexts, does not refer to the person who quotes, but to the quoted person.

§12.3   Kaplan's Thesis

Let us grant that the context, like the world, can be shifted. Still, it's far from obvious that it can be shifted as liberally as the world can. Thus David Kaplan claims that there are no context-shifting operators: no context-shift can be triggered (governed, controlled) by some operator within the sentence itself.

To borrow one of Kaplan's examples, suppose I say, at time t_0, 'It will soon be the case that all that is now beautiful is faded'. The prefix 'it will soon be the case that' instructs us to interpret the embedded sentence 'all that is now beautiful is faded' as describing a situation in the near future, for example the situation at t_1. What, asks Kaplan, is the relevant time associated with the indexical 'now' in the embedded sentence? Is it t_1, the time of the described situation? "No," he replies, "it is t_0, of course: the time of the context of use" (Kaplan 1989: 498). This follows from the fact that indexicals are rigid designators: their denotation is fixed directly by the context of utterance, irrespective of the situation talked about.

For the sake of the argument, let us suppose that there *is* an operator 'In some context it is true that', which when prefixed to a sentence yields a truth if and only if in some context the contained sentence expresses a truth. If there were such a context-shifting operator, Kaplan says, 'In some context is is true that I am not tired now' would be true in the present context, provided some agent of some context is not tired at the time of *that* context. The utterance, so interpreted, would have "nothing to do with me or the present moment" (Kaplan 1989: 510), contrary to what must be the case if indexicals are rigid designators. Kaplan concludes that there cannot be context-shifting operators: "No operator can control ... the indexicals within its scope, because they will simply leap out of its scope to the front of the operator" (Kaplan 1989a: 510).

I find this argument—if it is one—partly unconvincing. Granted that indexicals are rigid in the sense that their denotation is fixed by the context irrespective of the situation talked about; it does not follow that there is no context-shifting operator, unless we presuppose that such operators would introduce a situation for the remaining part of the sentence to describe. But context-shifting operators, if they exist, do something else: they introduce a new *context* with respect to which the remaining part of the sentence (and especially the indexicals in it) is to be interpreted. To be sure, if we express the fact that indexicals are rigid by saying that they 'always take primary scope', then, of course, it follows that there will be no context-shifting operator. But to say that indexicals always take primary scope is *already* to say (question-beggingly) that there cannot be such operators.—Be that as it may, Kaplan's thesis seems to be confirmed by the facts. Indexicals do seem to take scope over whichever operator occurs in the sentence.[4] And context-shifting operators don't seem to be among the resources available to users of English. As David Lewis observes,

We could speak a language in which 'As for you, I am hungry' is true iff 'I am hungry' is true when the role of speaker is shifted from me to you—in other words, iff you are hungry. We could—but we don't.... We could speak a language in which 'Backward, that one costs too much' is true iff 'That one costs too much' is true under a reversal of the direction the speaker's finger points. But we don't. We could speak a langage in which 'Upside down, Fred came floating up through the hatch of the spaceship and turned left' is true if 'Fred came floating up through the hatch of the spaceship and turned left' is true under a reveral of the orientation established in the original context. But we don't. (Lewis 1980: 84–85)[5]

Kaplan's thesis is not universally accepted, though. First, a few isolated counterexamples have been alleged. In a footnote, Kaplan himself mentions the following example, due to Thomason: 'Never put off until tomorrow what you can do today'. It is clear that in that sentence the indexicals 'tomorrow' and 'today' are relative to the described situation —the situation in which you can do something but put it off—not to the context of use. 'Today' refers to the day in which the situation occurs, 'tomorrow' to the next day.

Geoff Nunberg gives another putative counterexample:

In the movie *The Year of Living Dangerously*, Mel Gibson plays a reporter in Sukarno's Indonesia who is looking for a shipment of arms destined for the local communists; who will kill him if they find out he is on to them. He is interviewing a warehouse manager, who tells him, "I have seen no such shipment. And you should be careful; *I* might have been a communist."

Nunberg insists that "the warehouse manager ... isn't saying of himself that he could have been a communist, but rather that someone who had the property he exemplifies could have been a communist" (Nunberg 1991). In other words 'I' does not pick out an individual (the warehouse manager) in the actual context of use, but rather in the possible world introduced by the modal operator: the individual in question, whose being a communist is envisioned, is the person who is talking to the reporter *in that possible world*.

In Recanati 1993, chapter 16, I criticized Nunberg's analysis of that example. I think it is not a genuine counterexample to Kaplan's thesis; for the warehouse manager is really saying something *of himself*, contrary to what Nunberg claims. Not all alleged counterexamples to Kaplan's thesis can be dismissed in the same way, however. Thus the Thomason counterexample above is genuine.[6] Another example by Nunberg, namely the prisoner saying 'I am usually allowed to order what I want for my last meal', seems to be a genuine counterexample too (Nunberg 1993: 20–23). Yet such counterexamples, genuine though they are, are much too marginal and isolated to constitute a serious threat to Kaplan's theory.

Besides the isolated counterexamples, however, there are *systematic* counterexamples, that is, whole classes of cases which arguably run counter to Kaplan's thesis concerning the non-existence of context-shifting operators. *Oratio recta* constructions ('John said "..."') are a first class of potential counterexamples; another class of alleged counterexamples comprises metarepresentations on their opaque reading.

§12.4   Do Opaque Metarepresentations Shift the Context?

It can be argued that *opacity-inducing operators* in general shift the context with respect to which the sentence that follows is interpreted.[7] For example, the operator 'It is a priori that' seems to behave exactly like the 'impossible' context-shifting operator 'In some context it is true that' discussed by Kaplan. According to Stalnaker (1978: 320), following Kripke (1980), 'it is a priori that' *is* a context-shifting operator meaning 'in every context it is true that'. 'It is a priori that *S*' is therefore true in the present context if and only, if in every context of use, *S* expresses a truth. To use one of Kripke's examples, it is a priori (but certainly not necessary) that quarks are called 'quarks'.[8]

Let us, once again, consider belief sentences on their opaque readings. Suppose that on Saturday I say:

(7) John believes that yesterday was less busy than Friday.

John, of course, does not realize that yesterday *was* Friday. If he did, the belief I ascribe to him would be irrational. To make sense of that sort of belief ascription, one generally invokes two distinct 'modes of presentation' under which the believer thinks of the object (here, a day) to which he ascribes contradictory properties. I will appeal to such an analysis below (§14.3). But there is another possible analysis, in terms of context-shift. We may suppose that words like 'yesterday' or 'Friday' *do not pick out their referent in the context of use, but in the 'belief world' introduced by the operator 'John believes that'*. If that is so, the words 'yesterday' and 'Friday' do not take primary scope in such examples. John is not said to believe, of a certain day *d* (which turns out to be both Friday and yesterday), that it is less busy than itself; rather, he is said to accept 'Yesterday was less busy than Friday', yesterday and Friday being, *for him,* different days. (We may imagine that John *said* 'Yesterday was less busy than Friday', and that this utterance is all the evidence I have for the belief ascription.)

On this analysis, a metarepresentational operator like 'John believes that' not only shifts the circumstance (the world) with respect to which the internal sentence is to be evaluated, but, sometimes, it also shifts the context in which the sentence is interpreted: we are to interpret the sentence in the shifted circumstance of evaluation, instead of first interpreting the sentence with respect to the current context, and then evaluating it with respect to the shifted circumstance.

A powerful argument in favour of that analysis is provided by attitude ascriptions involving empty singular terms. Suppose Jean, under a delusion, thinks there is a little green man named 'Marcel' in the kitchen. I can ascribe attitudes to her concerning Marcel even though Marcel does not exist. I can say: 'She believes that Marcel is sleeping', much as I can say 'My son believes that Santa Claus will come tonight'. How is that possible? In the context of use, 'Marcel' is an empty name: it does not refer to anything. The global utterance should, therefore, be neither true nor false. Yet the ascription seems to be true. One explanation is that a context-shift occurs, triggered by the operator 'John believes that': instead of using the current context to interpret the embedded sentence, we use the ascribee's 'belief world' (introduced by the operator) as context.

The suggestion that attitudinals shift the context as well as the world fits nicely with the threefold distinction between extensional, intensional, and hyperintensional operators (§3.5). Extensional operators permit the substitution of expressions with the same extension in the actual world. For intensional operators, that is not sufficient; in order to be substitutable within the scope of an intensional operator (e.g., 'It is necessary that'), two expressions must have the same intension, that is, determine the same extension in all possible worlds. Even that is not sufficient when the operator is *hyper*intensional: two expressions which have the same extension in all possible worlds—for example two synonyms, or two co-referring proper names—are still not substitutable under, e.g., an attitudinal like 'John believes that'. That fact can be accounted for by arguing that, in contrast to intensional operators, which induce a shift

away from the actual world (and therefore defeat the principle of extensionality: that two expressions with the same extension in the actual
world should be freely substitutable), hyperintensional operators also
shift the context (and therefore defeat the principle of intensionality: that
two expressions which have the same intension in the actual context
should be substitutable).

Is the claim that metarepresentational operators shift the context as
well as the circumstance of evaluation compatible with the analysis presented so far in this book? On the one hand, it comports well with the
suggestion that the opacity of metarepresentations is due to some hidden
element of quotation (§11.3–4). According to the analysis presented in
chapter 11, the opaque reading of metarepresentations is characterized
(and distinguished from the more basic, transparent reading) by a quotational intrusion which accounts for intensional substitution failures. If,
following Ducrot and Clark, we analyse quotation in terms of context-
shift, that means that in (opaque) metarepresentations both the context
and the circumstance shift, while only the circumstance shifts on the
transparent reading.—On the other hand, semantic innocence can be
achieved only if metarepresentational prefixes do *not* shift the context,
even on the opaque reading; for if they do, the semantic value (the content) of expressions in the complement sentence will differ from what it
is when that sentence is interpreted in isolation. Indeed that is how
intensional substitution failures are accounted for in the context-shifting
framework: intensional substitution fails because the two expressions at
issue have the same content *only when interpreted with respect to the
current context;* but in the metarepresentation they are interpreted with
respect to the shifted context, hence they no longer have the same content and are no longer substitutable.

That is very close to the Classical View (§8.1). In the context-shifting
framework, the words in the embedded part of the metarepresentation
do not have the same content as they have outside it. We are thus back
to the notion that the object-representation is 'mentioned' rather than
'used'. The shift effected by the metarepresentational prefix now constitutes, in Quine's words, "an opaque interface between two ontologies,
two worlds: that of the attitudinist, however benighted, and that of our
responsible ascriber" (Quine 1995: 356). Even though the ascriber does

not believe in Santa Claus, he can use the proper name 'Santa Claus' in the embedded portion of his report, for he then puts the words in the mouth of his ascribee and is no longer responsible for them. The view I put forward in the first three parts of this book is radically different. From what I said in part III concerning the behaviour of singular terms (and the validity of existential generalization) in belief contexts, it follows that the ontology remains that of the ascriber all along, even though the 'world' which is described is that of the attitudinist: the objects the ascribee's belief is said to be about are picked out in the speaker's world, that is, in the actual world.

Being radically innocent, the view I sketched in the first three parts of this book entails that metarepresentational operators do not shift the context; hence it can be maintained only if Kaplan's thesis can be maintained. Accordingly, I will attempt to account for the alleged context-shifting properties of metarepresentational operators without giving up Kaplan's thesis. There are two possible strategies to that effect, as we shall see. The 'bold strategy' consists in simply *denying* that the context shifts in metarepresentations: the context does not shift, or if it does, it does not do so *within* the metarepresentation—the internal sentence is not interpreted with respect to a context distinct from that which is exploited in interpreting the global metarepresentation. The 'modest stategy' consists in accepting that the context shifts within metarepresentations, while arguing that the metarepresentational operator *per se* is not responsible for the shift. It is that second strategy which I will ultimately pursue.

§12.5   Kaplan's Thesis and Oratio Recta

In §12.1 I mentioned two types of world-shift, illustrated by (1) and (1*):

(1) John is completely paranoid. Everybody wants to kill him, including his own mother!

(1*) John believes that everybody wants to kill him, including his own mother!

In neither case does the speaker *assert* that everybody wants to kill John; that fact is presented as holding in John's 'belief world' rather than in the actual world. So a world-shift occurs. But the shift is 'free' in (1): nothing in the sentence 'Everybody wants to kill him, including his own mother' indicates that it is to be interpreted with respect to John's 'belief world' rather than with respect to the actual world. Besides free indirect speech, illustrated by the second sentence of (1), irony provides another striking illustration of a free world-shift. In contrast, the world-shift in (1*) is not free: it is governed by the operator 'John believes that', which instructs us to shift the world in which the embedded sentence is to be evaluated. Now it seems that the same contrast can be found on the side of context-shifts. For I can quote someone either implicitly or explicitly. Thus I can say either:

(8)   Stop that John! "Nobody likes me." "I am miserable." Don't you think you exaggerate a bit?

(9)   John keeps crying and saying "Nobody likes me."

In (8) the quoted sentences ('Nobody likes me', 'I am miserable') are uttered in isolation: nothing in the sentences themselves indicates that the context has shifted. It is because of the neighbouring sentences ('Stop that, John', etc.) that one is able to interpret the quoted sentences as such. This is similar to the example of 'free' world-shift above. But in (9), the metalinguistic frame 'John keeps saying ___' forces us to interpret the sentence which fills the blank as a quotation. The quoted sentence is part of a more complex sentence, and something in the complex sentence indicates that the constituent sentence 'Nobody likes me' is quoted. It follows that the context-shift is not free in (9): it is governed or controlled by the metalinguistic frame, much like the world-shift in (1*) is governed by the operator 'John believes that'.

It is this apparent symmetry which Kaplan denies when he claims that context-shifts are *not* controllable from within the sentence itself. Yet Kaplan has not overlooked examples like (9). Concerning them, he says:

There *is* a way to control an indexical, to keep it from taking primary scope, and even to refer it to another context.... Use quotation marks. If we *mention* the indexical rather than *use* it, we can, of course, operate directly on it. (1989a: 510–511)

By putting indexicals in quotation marks, Kaplan admits, we can shift their denotation, and indeed shift their context of interpretation. Thus, to do the work of the 'impossible' context-shifting operator 'In some context it is true that', we can say:

(10)   In some context, 'I am not tired now' is true.

In view of this possibility, Kaplan qualifies his claim concerning the non-existence of context-shifting operators. No such operator can be expressed in English, he says, "without sneaking in a quotation device" (Kaplan 1989a: 511).

Kaplan obviously does not think this type of counterexample threatens his general thesis. If he did, he would give it more than a passing mention. The reason why this type of counterexample does not look threatening to him is that the indexicals in such environments are, as he says, 'mentioned' rather than 'used'. But what sort of reason is that exactly? I can imagine various types of argument in support of Kaplan's dismissal. One might say either of the following:

• Because the quoted material is mentioned rather than used, the prefix 'John says ...' is not a genuine operator, but a metalinguistic predicate; hence (3) is not a counterexample to the claim that there are no context-shifting *operators*.

• Being instances of *mention*, such examples are arguably irrelevant when we theorize about how indexicals are *used*. There is no reason why the semantic rules governing the use of indexicals—the rules which a semantic theory tries to capture—should still apply when they (the indexicals) are mentioned. On the contrary, it is a well-known fact that the semantic rules governing the use of words are suspended when the words in question are mentioned: words within quotation marks are *semantically inert*.

I shall discuss both arguments in the next chapter. The issue is quite important. If Kaplan is right—if *oratio recta* does not constitute a genuine counterexample to Kaplan's thesis—then perhaps 'it is a priori that' and other alleged context-shifting operators can themselves be treated as (covert) 'quotation devices', and dismissed accordingly. We must therefore embark into an in-depth study of *oratio recta*, before returning to the analysis of attitude reports and *oratio obliqua*.

13

Oratio Recta

§13.1 Open and Closed Quotations

In quotation, as Searle (1969) rightly emphasized, the quoted material is *displayed* or *presented*. That means that a token is produced and the attention of the audience is drawn to that token. Moreover, it is presented with a particular, *demonstrative* intention. Here I am using Clark's notion of demonstration rather than Davidson's (Clark and Gerrig 1990; Clark 1996).[9] "The point of demonstrating a thing," Clark says, "is to enable addressees to experience selective parts of what it would be like to perceive the thing directly" (Clark 1996: 174). For example, I can demonstrate to a friend how my sister Elizabeth drinks tea. To that effect I do something which resembles my sister's drinking tea: I hold an imaginary saucer in my hand, lift it to my lips in a certain way, etc. Through my demonstration, my friend "has a partial experience of what it would be like to see Elizabeth herself drinking tea." In quotation, what we selectively demonstrate is a piece of speech. Often we do not merely demonstrate the words, by actually uttering a token of them, but we also "depict all manner of speech characteristics—speed, gender, age, dialect, accent, drunkenness, lisping, anger, surprise, fear, stupidity, hesitancy, power" (Clark 1996: 175).

The feature I have just mentioned is universal: there is no quotation without it. It is that feature which the 'quotation marks' conventionally indicate in writing—they indicate that the enclosed material is demonstrated. But there is a second, optional feature: the demonstrated material (or perhaps the demonstration itself; see below) may acquire the grammatical function of a singular term within the sentence—a singular term autonymously denoting that material, or rather some type which the presented material instantiates.

In the example below, two sentences (a French sentence and an English sentence) are quoted. Both quotations have the first of the two features distinguished above, but only the second quotation has both features and therefore constitutes what I call a 'closed quotation'.

(1) 'Comment allez vous?' That is how you would translate 'How do you do?' in French.

The French sentence 'Comment allez-vous?' is displayed at the beginning. That is an instance of *open* quotation. The material thus displayed is referred to in the sentence that follows ('*that* is how you would translate ...'), but for there to be open quotation the presented material need not be referred to: it needs only to be demonstrated. (See example (2) below, where there is demonstration without reference.) In contrast, closed quotation requires that there be not only demonstration but also reference. That is not sufficient to define closed quotation, however. The distinguishing characteristic of closed quotation is the fact that *it is the presented material itself, or the presentation of that material, which plays the role of the singular term referring to the presented material.* That is what happens in the second quotation of the example: the English sentence 'How do you do?' is also displayed or presented, and it is also referred to, but the reference is *autonymous* rather than *heteronymous* (§10.1–3). The demonstrated material functions as a singular term reflexively denoting that material (or some type which it instantiates).

The distinction I have just made between the two features, and between the quotations which have both (closed quotations) and those which have only the first one (open quotations), corresponds to the contrast between the two sorts of context-shift mentioned above (§12.5):

(2) Stop that John! "Nobody likes me." "I am miserable." Don't you think you exaggerate a bit?

(3) John keeps crying and saying "Nobody likes me."

In (2) a token of 'Nobody likes me' and 'I am miserable' is displayed for demonstrative purposes, but it is not used as a singular term, in contrast to what happens in (3), where the quotation serves as a singular term to complete the sentence 'John keeps crying and saying ____'.

§13.2   The Semantic Inertia of Closed Quotations

In closed quotation the quoted words are semantically inert, or so it seems. There is ample evidence of that semantic inertia. First, it does not matter whether or not the quoted material makes sense on its own. In the metalinguistic frame 'John said "____" ' I can insert a meaningless string without thereby rendering the sentence meaningless. The inserted material can even be ungrammatical—indeed it need not be linguistic material at all.[10] Another feature which provides evidence for the semantic inertia of quoted words is the irrelevance of the (intrinsic) grammatical function of the inserted material to the function of the quotation within the sentence. Thus even if what is inserted is itself a sentence, as in 'John said "It's late," ' or a predicate, as in 'John said "bald" ' the quotation functions as a singular term within the global sentence.

There is also a sense in which closed quotations are *not* semantically inert: they denote something, namely the presented material, hence they make a semantic contribution to the proposition expressed by the sentence in which they occur. But what the closed quotation denotes or contributes is unrelated to the (normal) semantic value of the quoted material.

In order to account for the phenomenon of closed quotation, it seems that we must sacrifice either the Principle of Semantic Innocence or the Principle of Semantic Compositionality. Choosing the first option we can say that in closed quotation the quoted material acquires a new, deviant semantic value which replaces its normal semantic value (if it has one). This is reminiscent of Frege's treatment of oblique contexts. Choosing the second option, we can draw a sharp distinction between the quoted material, with its normal semantic value, and the new expression constituted by that material and the quotation marks. It is the new expression which denotes whichever type the quoted material instantiates; the quoted material can thus retain its standard semantic value. But the semantic value of the new expression is not a function of the semantic value of the quoted material which occurs inside it (Quine 1951: 26). Whichever option we choose, we must acknowledge that the quoted material is semantically inert in the following sense: it does not contribute its (normal) semantic value to the meaning of the sentence in which the quotation occurs. In other words, the meaning of the quoted words is irrelevant to the meaning of the sentence in which the words are quoted.

Beside the two options I have described, Davidson has argued that there is a third one, which permits to maintain both the Principle of Semantic Compositionality and the Principle of Semantic Innocence. A quotation consists of two parts: the quoted material, and the quotation marks. According to the first option, it is the quoted material which denotes itself self-referentially. According to the second option, it is the whole quotation (quoted material plus quotation marks) which denotes the quoted material. According to Davidson's theory (anticipated by Prior; see p. 319, n. 16), it is the quotation marks themselves that refer to the quoted material. That material is displayed, but it is neither identical to, nor a constituent of, the singular term which completes the metalinguistic frame 'John says ____'. As Davidson says,

It is the quotation marks that do all the referring ... On the demonstrative theory, neither the quotation as a whole (quotes plus filling) nor the filling alone is, except by accident, a singular term. The singular term is the quotation marks, which may be read 'the expression a token of which is here'. (Davidson 1979: 90)

A central feature of that theory is that the quoted material is not considered as semantically part of the sentence at all: semantically it lies outside the sentence, which contains a demonstrative (the quotation marks) referring to the displayed material. This neatly captures the semantic inertia of the quoted material: the latter does not contribute to the meaning of the sentence because it is not semantically part of the sentence.

§13.3   Amending Davidson's Analysis

Because it treats the quotation marks as a singular term, Davidson's theory runs into difficulties and cannot satisfactorily account for the phenomenon of open quotation. Thus in example (1), repeated below, the sentence 'Comment allez vous' would be referred to twice, once by means of the quotation marks, another time by means of the demonstrative 'that'. It makes more sense to say that the sentence is first displayed (demonstrated), then demonstratively referred to.

(1) 'Comment allez vous?' That is how you would translate 'How do you do?' in French.

A similar problem arises in connection with the phenomenon of 'mixed quotation'.[11] Davidson considers that in

(4) Quine says that quotation 'has a certain anomalous feature'

the words 'has a certain anomalous feature' are quoted. Now, obviously, there is no singular term referring to those words in (4). If there were, the sentence would be ungrammatical (see Davidson 1979: 81). Davidson's analysis could perhaps be defended by arguing that in mixed quotation two statements are made at the same time. The speaker of (4) means two things: (i) that Quine says that quotation has a certain anomalous feature; and (ii) that Quine says so using the words 'has a certain anomalous feature'. In contrast to the first statement, the second one is not explicit: the speaker refers to the words 'has a certain anomalous feature' (by means of the quotation marks), but what he says about them (that Quine used those words) remains implicit and must be contextually understood. On that analysis, (4) amounts to the conjunction of an explicit statement ('Quine says that quotation has a certain anomalous feature'), and a mostly implicit statement superimposed on it and partially overlapping with it ('Quine used the words "has a certain anomalous feature"'). The singular term referring to the quoted material is to be found in the implicit statement; in the explicit statement, the material keeps its normal semantic function.

The problem is that only one *sentence* is uttered, even if what the speaker *means* by uttering it (and perhaps even what he says) has the complexity which Davidson's analysis suggests. There is only one sentence, and in that sentence, there is no singular term referring to the quoted material. Rather than insist that the sentence is actually 'elliptical for' a longer, conjunctive sentence in which there *is* a singular term referring to the quoted words, we are much better off, I think, if we simply consider the type of quotation exemplified by mixed cases as *open* quotation. Thus we should give up the view that there is a singular term referring to the quoted material, in such cases. The quoted material is displayed (demonstrated, in Clark's sense) while in active use, but it is not referred to—not explicitly, at any rate. Of course, the reason why the speaker demonstrates the words he is using, in a context in which he reports someone's speech, can only be that those words correspond to those used by the reportee. Moreover, there are reasons to believe that this pragmatic suggestion finds its way into the truth-conditions of the utterance. Still there is 'reference' to the words only in the weak sense that the words are displayed and the attention of the audience is drawn to them; but there is no reference in the stronger sense which implies the effective use of a singular term.

Be that as it may, we can retain the essentials of Davidson's theory, while rejecting his treatment of the quotation marks as a singular term. The quotation marks merely indicate that the quoted words are being demonstrated. It is, I suggest, the demonstration itself which assumes the function of singular term, in closed quotations.[12] Thus we can agree that, in closed quotation,

• the quoted material is displayed or presented for demonstrative purposes, as in open quotation;
• the demonstration assumes a grammatical function in the sentence: that of a singular term denoting the presented material;
• the quoted material itself, distinct from the demonstration (i.e., the *presentation* of that material), is not semantically a part of the sentence in which it is presented.

A sentence like 'John said "It is raining"' can therefore be analysed, *à la* Davidson, as:

John said D. It is raining.

where the second sentence corresponds to the displayed material, while the first sentence contains D, the presentation of that material, serving as singular term.

§13.4   How Inert Is the Quoted Material?

Anything can be presented or displayed, whether it is meaningful or not, grammatical or not, linguistic or not. But from the fact that the displayed material need not have a meaning, it does not follow that it *cannot* have one. In many cases of open quotation, it is pretty clear that the presented material has a meaning, and that this meaning is highly relevant to the meaning of the discourse in which the material is presented. Only think of examples like:

The story-teller cleared his throat and started talking. "Once upon a time, there was a beautiful princess named Arabella. She loved snakes and always had a couple of pythons around her...."

The discourse as a whole is, in part, about snakes and about a princess named Arabella. It is also, and primarily, about a story-teller telling a story. Indeed it is about a story-teller telling a story about snakes and a princess named Arabella. The meaning of the sentences within the quotation marks is obviously relevant to the meaning of the whole discourse, to which it undoubtedly contributes. The contention that quoted words are semantically inert must therefore be qualified.

The claim that quoted words are semantically inert has its source in the phenomenon of closed quotation. An utterance like 'John said "___"', with the blank filled with a sequence of words, is true iff John uttered the words in question; whether the words in question have meaning, and which meaning, is an irrelevant matter. Hence the natural conclusion that a quotation denotes the quoted words themselves, whose own meaning or denotation becomes irrelevant. But this conclusion, although true in a sense, is misleading. The proper conclusion to draw is, as Davidson puts it, that the quoted material is not semantically part of the sentence. The sentence is *about* the quoted material, and the latter is displayed alongside the sentence, as it would be if the speaker had made two distinct utterances. But then, the displayed material may well have a meaning, which contributes to the meaning of the whole discourse. There is semantic inertia only to the extent that, strictly speaking, the meaning of the quoted material is not a part of the meaning of the sentence in which the material is quoted. But the discourse contains more than that sentence: it also contains the quoted material. Hence the quoted material is semantically inert only in a *relative* sense. It remains, or can remain, semantically active at the separate level to which it belongs.

In the same way in which the quoted material is semantically active in the example of open quotation above, it can be recognized as semantically active in a closed variant of that example:

The story-teller cleared his throat and said, "Once upon a time, there was a beautiful princess named Arabella, who loved snakes and always had a couple of pythons around her...."

That piece of text too is about a story-teller telling a story about Princess Arabella and her snakes. Clearly, the meaning of the quoted material is relevant to the meaning of the whole. Again, the only semantic inertia there is is relative: the quoted material is semantically inert *in the sentence in which reference is made to that material*—it is not semantically part of that sentence, but must be seen as lying outside it. Yet it is semantically active in the discourse as a whole.

Since the quoted material turns out to be semantically active after all, in many cases at least, there is no reason why, in such cases, it should not function normally and undergo the process which Fillmore calls 'contextualisation' (Fillmore 1981). A text is contextualised when it gets anchored to an appropriate context, in which the denotations of the indexicals of the text can be determined. That context may be an 'internal' context projected by the text itself. Thus the past tense in the above example ('there was a princess') refers to a time prior to the time of utterance in the internal context. The time of utterance in the internal context is the (fictitious) time at which the story is told as known fact;[13] this is, or may be, distinct from the time at which the story is actually told as fiction. In general, there will be a difference between the context relevant to the interpretation of the upper-layer sentence (that in which the quoted material is referred to or somehow introduced), and the context relevant to the interpretation of the quoted material.

To sum up, we have come to the conclusion that the quoted material may retain its standard meaning. In particular we can maintain that 'I' refers to the speaker, 'now' to the time of utterance, etc. (The only thing that changes is that the context which provides a speaker, a time of utterance, etc., is not the actual context of speech but the internal context projected by the quotation.) So it will not do to dismiss quotation contexts as irrelevant, on the grounds that, when we quote, the rules governing the use of words are automatically suspended. They are not. Hence Kaplan's thesis cannot be defended in that way against the metalinguistic counterexamples.

Kaplan's thesis can still be defended, however. For the quoted words don't really belong to the sentence in which they are quoted. In an instance of closed quotation like (3), there are two sentences masquerading as one. Since that is so, such metalinguistic examples do not really contradict Kaplan's thesis that a context-shift cannot be controlled from within the sentence itself. (3) must be analysed as:

John keeps crying and saying **D**. Nobody likes me.

Here **D** is the demonstration of the words that follow. Since the words in question do not really belong to the sentence in which they are referred to, the counterexample to Kaplan's thesis evaporates: context-shift there is, but it is not controlled from within the sentence in which it takes place.

§13.5   The Quotational Pole

The quoted material remains separate from the sentence in which it is quoted: that is the main conclusion of our investigation of the phenomenon of (closed) quotation. We are thus prevented from treating the metalinguistic frame as an operator acting on the sentence which fills the frame.

A (monadic) sentential operator makes a sentence out of a sentence. To make a sentence out of a sentence is a form of *compounding*. Thus 'It is not the case that S' is a compound sentence, containing the sentence S as a constituent; similarly, 'S and S^*' and 'If S then S^*' are compound sentences. But in 'John says "S"' or '"S" is valid' the sentence S is not really a constituent of the complex sentence; it is *mentioned by* a constituent of the complex sentence (viz. the singular term serving as complement for 'say', or as subject for 'is valid'). Thus, Quine says, this is not a form of compounding, but a metalinguistic predication (Quine 1962: 38).

Whenever there is genuine compounding, the Inheritance Principle applies:

Inheritance Principle

The compound sentence inherits whichever grammatical or semantic flaw occurs in the constituent sentence. As Evans puts it (1982: 364):

"If a sentence fails to be properly intelligible when used on its own, the same will hold of any more complex sentence in which it is embedded."

By this principle, if S is ungrammatical, then 'S and S^*' is ungrammatical too. Similarly, if S is ungrammatical, then 'If S, then S^*' is ungrammatical too. In that respect there is a notable difference between 'John says that S' (*oratio obliqua*) and 'John says: "S"' (*oratio recta*). The latter is fine even if S is ungrammatical. But the former is ungrammatical in that situation. This simply reflects the fact that 'John says that' is an operator, making a sentence out of a sentence. The Inheritance Principle therefore applies. But the other statement, 'John says: "S",' is not genuinely compounded from the constituent statement S. The demonstration, serving as a singular term, is an 'opaque interface' which insulates the quoted material from the sentence in which it is quoted.[14] Nonsense can therefore be turned into *oratio recta* without making nonsense of the mentioning sentence.[15]

We see that the genuine difficulty raised for Kaplan's thesis has to do with the attitudinals and, more generally, with *oratio obliqua*. As we have just seen, *oratio obliqua* does *not* exhibit the semantic heterogeneity which permits us to draw a line between the demonstrated material and the quoting sentence within which it is insulated. In other words, the attitudinals seem to be genuine operators. Yet there is some evidence of a context-shift induced by the attitudinals (§12.4). How can we account for that in a framework which ties context-shifting to quotational heterogeneity?

The most obvious option compatible with the framework consists in positing a continuum of cases between compounding and mentioning. This idea of a continuum of cases is implicit in Quine's writings on the topic. Some measure of mention is involved, according to Quine, in apparent compounds like 'He came because I asked him to'. Can we not say, similarly, that the attitudinals are somehow intermediate between genuine operators and quotation devices? Let us suppose that we can make sense of that notion of a continuum of cases. Then, instead of having a bipartition, as in table IV.1, we would construe straightforward quotation as an extreme (a pole), to which at least certain forms of *oratio obliqua* would be very close. The context-shifting effects exhibited

Table IV.1
Compounding versus metalinguistic predication

Compounding	Metalinguistic predication
S & S^*	John says: "S"
If S, then S^*	"S" is valid
It is possible that S	"S" implies "S^*"
John believes that S	"S" is contingent
$\vdots$	$\vdots$

by the attitudinals could then be accounted for as due to the measure of quotation which they involve—to their proximity to the 'quotational pole'.

In order to pursue this strategy, we must try to figure out whether we can make sense of the notion of semi-quotation which it rests upon. Are there sentences which, while not instances of *oratio recta*, nevertheless share some of the features of *oratio recta*? Could *oratio obliqua* sentences, or at least the opaque ones, be considered as falling into that category?

14

Varieties of Semi-Quotation

§14.1 Metalinguistic Negation

Negation is a paradigmatic operator making a sentence out of a sentence. Yet, as Ducrot and Fillmore pointed out (Fillmore 1971: 382, Ducrot 1973: 240), it has 'metalinguistic' uses: it can be used in a quasi-quotational fashion to reject a previous utterance, as in:

(1) The dinner was not good, it was superb.

In his in-depth study of the topic (Horn 1989: ch. 6), Larry Horn stresses the fact that any aspect of the rejected utterance—be it style, speech level, pronunciation, grammar, or implicatures—can serve as ground for the rejection. Now whichever aspect of an utterance turns out to be relevant for its rejection must be demonstrated while rejecting it. Thus a lot of simulation goes on in metalinguistic negation, as the following examples from Horn 1989 show:

(2) He did not call the [pólis], he called the [polís].

(3) I didn't manage to trap two mon*geese*—I managed to trap two mon*gooses*.

(4) Esker too ah coo-pay luh vee-and?
     Non, je n'ai pas 'coo-pay luh vee-and'—j'ai coupé la viande.

This reminds us of Clark's observation that, in quotation, we can "depict all manner of speech characteristics—speed, gender, age, dialect, accent, drunkenness, lisping, anger, surprise, fear, stupidity, hesitancy, power" (Clark 1996: 175). The same thing holds for metalinguistic negation, whose quotational nature is indeed pretty obvious.[16]

Because metalinguistic negation involves a form of quotation (and, often, the explicit use of quotation marks), it has major properties in common with *oratio recta*. In particular, it violates the Inheritance Principle. An utterance can be acceptable even if it contains a linguistic mistake, provided the mistake in question is demonstrated within the scope of metalinguistic negation. Thus I can say:

(5) Je n'ai pas coupé *le* viande, j'ai coupé *la* viande.

This is as acceptable as the explicitly quotational

(6) "J'ai coupé le viande" n'est pas français.

That metalinguistic negation displays the semantic heterogeneity characteristic of *oratio recta* is confirmed by several observations, to the effect that metalinguistic negation (i) neither triggers negative polarity items nor inhibits positive polarity items, and (ii) fails to incorporate prefixally (Horn 1989: 397). All this shows that metalinguistic negation is not "fully integrated," that it "operates ... on another level from that of the clause in which it is superficially situated" (Horn 1989: 392). After stressing those features, Horn quotes Tasmowski-De Ryck who characterizes metalinguistic negation as follows:

Une proposition déjà énoncée est répétée telle quelle, et la négation s'y applique comme à un tout inanalysable, dans lequel elle ne s'intègre pas réellement. (1972: 199, quoted in Horn 1989: 398)

This reminds one of Quine's characterization of quotation in the well-known passage cited in §1.2 ("Each whole quotation must be regarded as a single word or sign," etc.).

Metalinguistic negation also has context-shifting properties. This is apparent when we consider the behaviour of *presuppositions* under metalinguistic negation. As Stalnaker (1974) pointed out, presuppositions can be construed as constraints on the context: an expression can be felicitously used only in a context in which its presuppositions are satisfied. Since they are *context*-relative rather than *world*-relative, presuppositions share with indexicals the property that, to use Kaplan's words, 'no operator can control [them] within its scope, because they will simply leap out of its scope to the front of the operator'. Yet in metalinguistic negation, the presuppositions of the constituent sentence (that on which negation operates) do not constrain the actual context in which the 'compound' is uttered: rather, they constrain the internal context projected by the rejected assertion, and fall *within* the scope of metalinguistic negation. As a result, the presuppositions of the constituent sentence are rejected under metalinguistic negation, while normal negation is known to maintain the presuppositions of the negated sentence. Thus while (8), like (7), normally presupposes (9), (10) does not:

(7)   He has stopped beating his dog.

(8)   He hasn't stopped beating his dog. *(Ordinary negation)*

(9)   He used to beat his dog. *(Presupposition)*

(10)   He hasn't stopped beating his dog—he never did. *(Metalinguistic negation)*

Is it possible to similarly control indexicals within the scope of metalinguistic negation? Perhaps, though much less easily. If John, a non-native speaker of French, utters (11), his French girlfriend Marie will correct him by uttering (12):

(11)   *John:*   Je suis contente.

(12)   *Marie:*   Tu n'es pas *contente*, tu es *content*.

Even though this is metalinguistic negation, the personal pronoun 'tu' ('you') is still controlled by the actual context of use, that is, by the context of (12) rather than by the context of the rejected assertion (11). In order to make a context-shift possible, we must make the utterance more explicitly quotational:

(11)   *John:*   Je suis contente.

(13)   *Marie:*   "Je suis contente"! Non: Je suis *content*.

In (13), the speaker saying 'Je suis content' (Marie) uses 'je' ('I') to refer to the addressee (John). Thus a context-shift occurs, prepared by the open quotation that comes first. Although more difficult, it is, I think, not impossible to do the same thing directly under metalinguistic negation, as in (14):

(11)   *John:*   Je suis contente.

(14)   *Marie:*   Je ne suis pas contente, je suis content.

Be that as it may, we can acknowledge that some form of context-shift can occur under metalinguistic negation. As Ducrot puts it, the rejected assertion is ascribed to a "speaker" (*locuteur*) distinct from the author of the negative statement.[17]

All the features I have listed point to the fact that metalinguistic negation is a covert 'quotation device'. Horn insists that on its metalinguistic use, negation is no longer a genuine operator making a sentence out of a sentence. What it applies to is not a sentence, but an echoic demonstration of the rejected utterance.

Apparent sentence negation represents either a descriptive truth-functional operator, taking a proposition *p* into a proposition not-*p* (or a predicate *P* into a predicate not-*P*), or a metalinguistic operator which can be glossed 'I object to *U*', where *U* is crucially a linguistic utterance or utterance type rather than an abstract proposition (Horn 1989: 377).[18]

Other authors (e.g., Carston, quoted by Horn) take metalinguistic negation to be like ordinary negation, except that it applies not to the proposition expressed by the sentence *S* within its scope, but to a metalinguistic proposition about that sentence. Whichever theory we accept, it is clear that in metalinguistic negation the speaker does two things: he demonstrates an objectionable utterance, and rejects it as objectionable. It has therefore the force of a metalinguistic statement about a quoted utterance, even though it masquerades as a compound.

§14.2   Do the Attitudinals Have a Metalinguistic Use?

As Horn points out, other operators than negation can also be used metalinguistically. The following are examples of *metalinguistic disjunction*:

(15)   New Haven, or the Elm City, is the pearl of the Quinnipiac Valley.

(16)   Is the conductor Bernst[íʸ]n or Bernsta[áʸ]n?

This suggests that the attitudinals, too, might have a metalinguistic use.

An utterance like 'John believes that *S*' has two readings: one reading where the complement sentence *S* merely expresses the content of John's belief—the proposition which John believes (transparent reading); and another one where *S* is a sentence which John himself accepts, that is, is disposed to assent to. The latter is the opaque reading, where 'John believes that *S*' means or entails something like: John accepts "*S*." The difference comes out in cases in which the proposition which the believer is said to believe can be expressed in different manners, only some of which correspond to the believer's own way of thinking. For example, since Emile Ajar and Romain Gary are the same person, (17) and (18) arguably express the same proposition (if the theory of direct reference is correct):

(17)   Romain Gary wrote *La Vie devant soi*.

(18)   Emile Ajar wrote *La Vie devant soi*.

Yet only (18) would be assented to by someone who has read the book, but does not know that 'Emile Ajar' was a pseudonym used by Romain Gary. Let us suppose that John is in exactly that situation. Then the belief report (19) will come out true only on its transparent reading:

(19)   John believes that Romain Gary wrote *La Vie devant soi*.

John indeed believes the proposition expressed by (17). But he would not assent to (17)—he would not accept that sentence as expressing the belief which he holds. (19), therefore, is false on the opaque reading. On the other hand, (20) is true on both readings:

(20)   John believes that Emile Ajar wrote *La Vie devant soi*.

In other words, it is not only true that John believes of Ajar (= Gary) that he wrote *La Vie devant soi* (transparent reading), but also that he would accept the sentence 'Ajar wrote *La Vie devant soi*' (opaque reading).

It is on the opaque reading that the alleged context-shifting effects described in §12.4 manifest themselves. Transparently interpreted, 'John believes that yesterday was busier than Friday', uttered in a context in which Friday = yesterday, absurdly ascribes to John the belief that a certain day *d* was busier than itself. This prompts us to interpret the belief ascription as opaque and ascribing to John acceptance of the sentence 'Yesterday was busier than Friday'. The suggestion is that, on the opaque reading, 'yesterday' and 'Friday' are not interpreted with respect to the *external* context of the reporter, in which they both denote *d*;

rather, they are interpreted with respect to John's 'belief world' (internal context), in which they denote different days.

The idea that the opaque reading of belief sentences and other *oratio obliqua* constructions arises from a metalinguistic use of the operator has attracted several influential authors. It is implicit in, e.g., Partee (1973) and Stalnaker (1976, 1978). Yet there are two significant differences between metalinguistic uses of operators like negation and opaque uses of attitudinals.

• Even on their opaque reading attitudinals seem to be genuine operators. Except in rather exceptional cases (§17.5), there is no evidence of that lack of integration characteristic of (overt or covert) quotation. This is in sharp contrast to metalinguistic negation, which, as Horn puts it, "does not operate on the same rhetorical or grammatical level as the clause in which it occurs" and fails to display "those traits which are characteristic of the more fully integrated object-level negator" (Horn 1989: 397).

• Opaque readings are not 'marked' as metalinguistic uses of negation are. Let us quote Horn again: "The descriptive use of negation is primary; the nonlogical metalinguistic understanding is typically available only on a 'second pass', when the descriptive reading self-destructs" (Horn 1989: 444). Metalinguistic negation must therefore be explicit: a correction must follow, as in the paradigmatic construction 'Not *X* but *Y*'. Without such a correction, a simple negative statement can only be understood descriptively (or, at any rate, non-metalinguistically).[19] But the opaque reading of attitudinals is as standard as the transparent reading. If attitudinals have a metalinguistic use, it's an interpretation that is much more readily available than for other operators.

How important are those differences? Maybe not very much. But the fact that opaque *oratio obliqua* seems to be *less* quotational, i.e., not as close to *oratio recta*, as metalinguistic negation, naturally leads us to consider other forms of semi-quotation, further away from the quotational pole.

§14.3   Opacity and Mixed Quotation: The Cumulative Account

In §13.3 we touched upon the phenomenon of 'mixed quotation'. In mixed quotation the demonstrated material is, at the same time, in active use, instead of being issued for the sole purposes of the demonstration.

The presented material thus plays a dual role, as Davidson rightly emphasized:

I said that for the demonstrative theory the quoted material was no part, semantically, of the quoting sentence. But this was stronger than necessary or desirable. The device of pointing can be used on whatever is in range of the pointer, and there is no reason why an inscription in active use can't be ostended in the process of mentioning an expression.... Any token may serve as target for the arrows of quotation, so in particular a quoting sentence may after all by chance contain a token with the shape needed for the purposes of quotation. Such tokens do double duty, once as meaningful cogs in the machine of the sentence, once as semantically neutral objects with a useful form. Thus

Quine says that quotation '. . . has a certain anomalous feature'.

may be rendered more explicitly:

Quine says, using words of which these are a token, that quotation has a certain anomalous feature.

(Davidson 1979: 91–92)

This suggests another possible analysis of the attitudinals—that, in effect, which I put forward in chapter 11. Instead of saying that the attitudinals are used metalinguistically on the opaque reading, we can account for their duality of use as follows. On the transparent reading, the words in the complement sentence are used to express the content of the ascribee's belief; they are *not* mentioned. On the opaque reading, they are, at the same time, used to express the content of the ascribee's belief *and* mentioned as words which the ascribee would accept. The speaker thus says something concerning the content of the ascribed attitudes, while drawing the hearer's attention to the form of words he uses. The opaque interpretation of (20) can therefore be rephrased in mixed-quotational terms as:

(21)   John believes that 'Ajar wrote *La Vie devant soi*'.

More generally, the transparent/opaque ambiguity can be represented as follows.

Transparent

John says that *p*.

Opaque

John says that '*p*'.

At this point someone may well wonder what the difference consists in between the two theories: the theory which treats the opaque reading as a form of *metalinguistic use*, and the theory which treats it as an instance of *mixed quotation*. In both cases some form of mention takes place. So, what is the difference?

The difference is this. When, using metalinguistic negation, I say, 'The dinner was not good, it was superb', I do not really deny that the dinner was good: what I deny is the metalinguistic proposition that 'the dinner was good' is an appropriate utterance. The negation is metalinguistic because it applies *not* to the proposition expressed by the sentence it superficially operates on, but, *instead*, to a previous utterance of that sentence or to a metalinguistic proposition about that utterance. But in mixed quotation, the fact that the material in the scope of the operator is mentioned (demonstrated) adds something to, *but does not substract anything from*, its normal import. The material is both used *and* mentioned. Mixed quotation, therefore, is 'cumulative', while metalinguistic uses are not.[20]

The cumulative nature of mixed quotation has the following consequence: *A mixed-quoting sentence S entails the sentence S' which results from suppressing the quotation marks in S*. Thus (22), on Davidson's theory, entails (22*):

(22)   Quine said that quotation 'has a certain anomalous feature'.

(22*)   Quine said that quotation has a certain anomalous feature.

By this test, metalinguistic negation is clearly not cumulative. Again, (1) does not entail (23):

(1)   The dinner was not good, it was superb.

(23)   The dinner was not good.

The cumulative nature of mixed quotation permits to attenuate the contrast between opaque and transparent uses. The opaque use is nothing but an enriched version of the transparent use, according to the following schema (§11.3):

John believes$_{opaque}$ that S =
John believes$_{transparent}$ that S *in that manner*

Here 'in that manner' demonstratively refers to the very sentence *S* used by the reporter to express the content of John's belief. It is this analysis of belief reports, reminiscent of the 'hidden indexical theory', which I argued for in chapter 11.

The difference between the two accounts can be summarized by saying that the opaque reading is *wholly* metalinguistic on one account (the 'metalinguistic' account), while it is *partly* metalinguistic on the other account (the 'cumulative' account). The metalinguistic account therefore dramatizes the difference between the opaque and the transparent reading, which the cumulative account attenuates:

Metalinguistic account

On the transparent reading, the ascribee's belief is said to have a certain objective content. On the opaque reading it is not the objective content of the representation but rather the form of the representation (the accepted sentence) which is specified.

Cumulative account

The opaque reading merely *enriches* the transparent reading with a further specification. In both cases (transparent and opaque), the content of the belief is specified. On the opaque reading both the content *and* the form of the representation are specified.

To see the two accounts at work, let us return to the Friday/yesterday example which seemed to provide evidence of a context-shift within the scope of an attitudinal (§12.4). On Saturday, the speaker reports John's belief by saying:

(24)   John believes that yesterday was less busy than Friday.

In fact, yesterday *was* Friday. It is therefore impossible for yesterday to exhibit a property which Friday does not have. Does this mean that John is said to believe a logical impossibility? On the metalinguistic account, the answer is 'no'. On the cumulative account, it is 'yes'.

On the metalinguistic account, the speaker who utters (24) and means it *de dicto* merely says that the ascribee accepts or would accept the sentence 'Yesterday was less busy than Friday'. He ascribes to John a belief in the truth of the sentence. To be sure, the content sentence 'Yesterday was less busy than Friday' expresses a logical impossibility *for the speaker* (who knows that yesterday = Friday); but on the *de dicto* reading the content sentence does not have to be interpreted with respect to the speaker's actual context, but only from the point of view of the believer himself. So a context-shift occurs, and John's rationality is not impugned: he is not said to believe a logical impossibility.

On the cumulative account, the situation is completely different. No context-shift occurs. On both the transparent and the opaque reading the content sentence is interpreted with respect to *the speaker's* actual context and serves to ascribe a belief in the proposition which the sentence expresses with respect to *that* context. On both the opaque and the transparent reading, therefore, the believer is said to believe that *d* was less busy than *d*. That is indeed logically impossible. But on the opaque reading it is further specified that this impossibility was not represented as such: the believer had two ways of thinking of *d*, once as 'yesterday', another time as 'Friday'. Since he did not realize that both modes of presentation were modes of presentation of the same day, John's belief is not irrational, even though the objective content of the belief turns out to be contradictory. John's rationality therefore is not in question, even though he (unwittingly) believes a logical impossibility.

§14.4   Non-cumulative Instances of Mixed Quotation

The cumulative account forbids context-shifts from occurring in mixed quotation. If a context-shift occurred, the mixed-quoting sentence *S* would no longer entail the sentence that results from removing the quotation marks; but in general at least, the entailment holds. For example, suppose that Quine actually wrote: 'Quotation has a certain anomalous feature which I find puzzling'. Davidson cannot, using mixed quotation, report Quine's statement by saying:

(25)   Quine says that quotation '... has a certain anomalous feature which I find puzzling'.

If he did, 'I' would refer to Davidson, or at least (25) would entail:

(26)   Quine says that quotation has a certain anomalous feature which I find puzzling.

Here the occurrence of 'I' clearly refers to Davidson (whom we assume to be the speaker). But of course Quine never said that *Davidson* finds the said feature puzzling! To adequately report Quine's statement, Davidson must therefore use a form of words like (27) or (28), in which no indexical occurs within the quotation marks:

(27) Quine says that quotation '... has a certain anomalous feature' which he finds 'puzzling'.

(28) Quine says that quotation '... has a certain anomalous feature which [he] find[s] puzzling'.

To be sure, if a sentence like (25) *could* be used by Davidson to report Quine's statement without distorting it, that would entail that the cumulative account is incorrect. In (25) so interpreted, 'I' would not refer to the speaker of (25), namely Davidson, but to the agent of the internal context, namely Quine. A context-shift would occur. It is clear, however, that (25) cannot be so interpreted. That fact certainly supports the cumulative account.

The problem is that there are examples very much like (25) in which a context-shift seems to occur. Thus Cappelen and Lepore (1997: 429) mention the following example of mixed quotation (without noticing the surprising context-shift):

(29) Mr Greespan said he agreed with Labor Secretary R. B. Reich "on quite a lot of things." Their accord on this issue, he said, has proved "quite a surprise to both of us."

The word 'us' here refers to Mr Greenspan and Mr Reich. It does not refer to a group including the speaker of (29). The passage in (29) therefore is a counterexample to the cumulative account, according to which no context-shift occurs in *oratio obliqua*.

We have a similar problem in connection with the Inheritance Principle. Indirect speech in general satisfies that principle; this is neatly captured by the cumulative account. But aren't there exceptions? For example:

(30) My three-year-old son believes that I am a 'philtosopher'.[21]

Since 'philtosopher' is a non-word (as experimental psychologists say), (30) should be considered as ill-formed. But it is fine: we understand the word 'philtosopher' as mentioned, and ascribed to my son. This is like mixed quotation, except that it is not cumulative. In uttering (30) I am not using the word 'philtosopher' as a word of my language while *simultaneously* ascribing the use of that word to my son. I am *merely* ascribing the use of that word to my son.

Other examples in which the Inheritance Principle is violated are not difficult to find:

(31)   John dit qu'il a fini de manger *le* viande.

There has to be a context-shift here too: the speaker must be seen as using John's own language to report what John said. For the sentence would be ungrammatical if it was interpreted with respect to the speaker's context (in which 'viande' is masculine).[22]

These examples show that context-shifts do occur within *oratio obliqua* constructions, contrary to what the cumulative account entails. It is not only the cumulative account of opacity that is put into question, but, more generally, the cumulative account of mixed quotation. It turns out that there are two forms of mixed quotation. One form is the cumulative variety talked about so far. It is characterized by the fact that the mixed-quoting sentence entails the same sentence without the quotation marks. But there is also a non-cumulative variety, illustrated by the examples above.

At this point we must clarify the notion of 'mixed quotation'. By 'mixed quotation' Cappelen and Lepore mean a mixture of *oratio obliqua* and *oratio recta*, characterized by the use of quotation marks in the sentential complement of an indirect-speech construction. They use Davidson's own example as a paradigm ('Quine says that quotation "has a certain anomalous feature"'). But when Davidson introduced that example, he presented it as a "mixed case of use and mention," that is, as a case in which the mentioned words are, at the same time, in active use. There are many cases of that sort which do not involve *oratio obliqua* at all. Let us follow Sperber and Wilson (1986) and talk of 'echoic uses' (or 'echoes') to refer to the broader category, i.e., to the whole class of cases in which, as I said earlier, "one uses a word while at the same time implicitly ascribing that use to some other person" (p. 140). Following Cappelen and Lepore, we shall restrict the phrase 'mixed quotation' to the sub-class of echoic uses occurring in the sentential complement of an *oratio obliqua* construction.[23]

When I first introduced echoic uses, in chapter 10, I mentioned the existence of two distinct varieties:

Often one uses a word while at the same time implicitly ascribing that use to some other person (or group of persons) whose usage one is blatantly echoing or mimicking. Thus one might say:

(32)   That boy is really 'smart'.

In such examples one is quoting, but at the same time using the words with their normal semantic values.

In (32) the fact that a word is quoted while being used does not affect the truth-conditions of the utterance. But sometimes it does. Thus I can refer to some object, *A*, using the name of another object, *B*, in quotes, providing the person I am mimicking uses the name for *B* as a name for *A*. I may well say

(33)   'Quine' has not finished writing his paper

and refer, by the name 'Quine' in quotes, not to Quine but to that person whom our friend James mistakenly identified as Quine the other day. Any word can, by being quoted in this echoic manner, be ascribed a semantic value which is not its normal semantic value, but rather what some other person takes to be its semantic value.

The distinction I made in that passage is that between *cumulative* and *non-cumulative* echoes. When we restrict ourselves to the sub-class of mixed-quotational echoes, it is the distinction between cumulative and non-cumulative instances of mixed quotation.

It may seem that the notion of a non-cumulative instance of mixed quotation, or more generally of a non-cumulative echo, is self-contradictory. Echoic uses in general, and mixed-quotational uses in particular, are cases in which some expression is used and mentioned at the same time. But what does the cumulative account say? That those expressions are used and mentioned at the same time! It seems that the way in which, following Davidson, I define mixed quotation (as a particular type of echo) implies the truth of the cumulative account.

But there is an equivocation here. When we say that in mixed quotation the mentioned word is at the same time 'in active use', we mean that it is not semantically inert in the mentioning sentence; and that is equivalent to saying that the quotation is not of the 'closed' variety. The word is semantically active in the sentence in which it is mentioned: that is what characterizes mixed quotation (and echoic uses more generally). But the cumulative account does not merely say that the quoted word remains semantically active. It says that, while mentioned, the quoted word is at the same time 'used by the speaker' *and therefore interpreted with respect to the speaker's external context.* What I am now urging is recognition of non-cumulative cases of mixed quotation, that is, such that the mentioned word is not 'used by the speaker' in the sense which implies that it is interpreted with respect to the speaker's external context. In non-cumulative cases of mixed quotation, the mentioned word is to be interpreted exclusively with respect to the ascribee's internal context. The quoted words remain semantically active because they do contribute their semantic value to the proposition expressed by the sentence; but that semantic value is deviant, as a result of the context-shift. The words are used with a deviant semantic value and at the same time they are demonstrated so as to signal that there is something special about that use.

Once it is admitted that there are non-cumulative instances of mixed quotation, we can account for the most recalcitrant cases: those in which a belief is reported concerning a non-existent object which the believer (but not the speaker) takes to exist.

(34)   My son believes that Santa Claus will come tonight.

(35)   Jean believes that Marcel is sleeping in the kitchen.

In the context of use, neither Marcel nor Santa Claus exist. (34) and (35) should therefore be neither true nor false. But those belief ascriptions seem to be true. A possible solution, as I pointed out earlier, is to consider that the names are interpreted with respect to the internal context, viz. the 'belief word' of the ascribee, in which *there is* someone named 'Santa Claus' (or 'Marcel'). (See Predelli 1997 for an analogous suggestion.) We are therefore back to what I called the metalinguistic account.

Instead of having to choose between the two accounts (the metalinguistic account and the cumulative account) it turns out that we can appeal to both, depending on the case at issue. Thus we can stick to the 'cumulative' analysis of the Friday/yesterday example, in accordance with the theory presented in chapter 11, while opting for a metalinguistic account in other cases such as (34) and (35). The analysis of opaque *oratio obliqua* on the pattern of mixed quotation gives us such freedom, because there are two varieties of mixed quotation.

§14.5   Failure of a Strategy

Let us take stock. We have seen that *oratio obliqua* per se is not quotational. In its pure form, *oratio obliqua* is transparent. Opaque *oratio obliqua* is a more complex phenomenon: it involves some measure of quotation in addition to the basic pattern. That complexity is displayed by hidden-indexical theories of opacity, which analyse

John believes$_{opaque}$ that *S*

as

John believes$_{transparent}$ that *S in that manner*

where 'in that manner' reflexively refers to the way the content of the belief is expressed in that very sentence. More precisely, I suggested that, in opaque *oratio obliqua*, the words used in the complement sentence to specify the ascribed content are, at the same time, *demonstrated* (open quotation). It is because of that element of quotation that the attitudinals (opaquely construed) are hyperintensional and do not license substitution of intensionally equivalent expressions. For intensionally equivalent expressions are still different expressions, hence the quotational demonstratum changes when the substitution takes place.[24]

According to hidden indexical theories, the words in the complement sentence are used with their *normal* semantic values (Principle of Semantic Innocence); opacity arises merely from the fact that the words thus used with their normal semantic values are, at the same time, demonstrated. But we have just seen that the words in the complement sentence can also be used with a deviant semantic value: that is what happens in non-cumulative instances. In such cases the words are used with a deviant, shifted semantic value and they are demonstrated at the same time. (The role of the demonstration is then precisely to signal that the words are used with a shifted semantic value.) Those cases are the cases in which a context-shift takes place. Neither the Principle of Semantic Innocence nor the Inheritance Principle applies, in such cases.

Table IV.2
When is context-shifting possible?

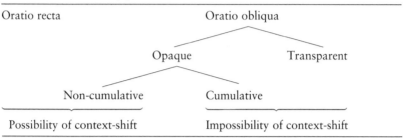

Oratio recta	Oratio obliqua	
	Opaque	Transparent
Non-cumulative	Cumulative	
Possibility of context-shift	Impossibility of context-shift	

As regards the possibility or impossibility of context-shifting, the relevant distinction turns out to be neither that between *oratio obliqua* and *oratio recta*, nor that between opaque and transparent readings of *oratio obliqua* constructions; rather, the dividing line passes between cumulative and non-cumulative opaque readings (table IV.2).

What about Kaplan's thesis, in this framework? Can it still be upheld? Following the line of defense sketched in §13.5, we may try to preserve it by arguing as follows: The closer we get to the quotational pole (*oratio recta*), the more we are entitled to interpret the complement sentence with respect to a shifted context. This way of putting the matter is a graded version of Kaplan's claim that operators can't shift the context "without sneaking in a quotation device."

But the line of defense sketched in §13.5 raises a decisive objection. The intermediate values between pure (transparent) *oratio obliqua* and pure *oratio recta* are cases of 'mixed quotation'. Non-cumulative instances of mixed quotation are supposed to be closer to the quotational pole than cumulative instances, which are themselves supposed to be closer to the quotational pole than transparent instances of *oratio obliqua*. Now the line of defense adumbrated in §13.5 consisted in extending to the most 'quotational' instances of *oratio obliqua* the treatment of *oratio recta* offered in chapter 13. Since *oratio recta* is not a genuine counterexample to Kaplan's thesis, in virtue of the considerations adduced in §13.4; and since the most quotational instances of *oratio obliqua* are mixtures of *oratio obliqua* and *oratio recta*; it follows that such instances are not a counterexample to Kaplan's thesis either—their context-shifting properties can be accounted for in terms of the measure of *oratio recta* which they involve. So was the argument supposed to run. But there is a major flaw in this argument. It is *closed quotation* that has been shown not to constitute a counterexample to Kaplan's thesis, in virtue of the Davidsonian separation of the quoted material from the mentioning sentence. But mixed quotation is a variety of *open* quotation, and *the Davidsonian separation does not apply to it.* That is so even if the instance of mixed quotation we are talking about is very close to the quotational pole in the sense of involving many properties of *oratio recta* (use of quotation marks, context-shift, violation of the Inheritance Principle).

The Davidsonian separation is not characteristic of quotation in general, but only of a particular variety, namely closed quotation. In an instance of closed quotation such as 'He said: "I am tired,"' the demonstration of the quoted material acts as a singular term, and the quoted material itself remains semantically external to the sentence in which that singular term occurs. It is in virtue of this specific feature that closed quotation is not a counterexample to Kaplan's thesis (§13.4). In open quotation, however, the demonstration does not assume the role of a singular term in the mentioning sentence. In standard cases of open quotation, no distinction can be drawn between the quoted material and the sentence in which it is quoted, because the demonstrated material occurs in isolation, as in (36):

(36)   "I am miserable." "Nobody likes me." Don't you think you exaggerate a bit?

In other cases (mixed quotation), a distinction can be drawn between the demonstrated material and the sentence in which it is demonstrated, but the Davidsonian separation still does not obtain because the demonstrated material remains semantically active in the mentioning sentence, and is *not* supplanted by the demonstration promoted to the status of singular term.

I conclude that Kaplan's thesis cannot be defended in the manner suggested in §13.5, that is, by appealing to (i) the fact that there is a continuum of cases between pure (i.e., transparent) *oratio obliqua* and pure *oratio recta*, and (ii) the fact that the quoted material does not really belong to the sentence in which it is quoted. The first premise is correct but the second is not, resulting as it does from an over-generalization. Since that is so, we must find another way of defending Kaplan's thesis.

V

Simulation 2: Context-Shifting as Pretense

15

Metafictional Statements

Let us reconsider the non-cumulative echoes mentioned in §14.4. Not all of them involve *oratio obliqua*. Thus I gave the following example:

(1)   'Quine' has not finished writing his paper.

That example involves a context-shift: the name 'Quine' is interpreted not with respect to the actual context of use (in which 'Quine' names Quine) but with respect to James' 'belief world' (in which 'Quine' names a philosopher distinct from Quine). The speaker ironically mimicks James and uses the name 'Quine' the way James does. That is a deviant use: the speaker uses the name 'Quine' to refer to someone else than Quine. Now the context-shift that occurs in that example is obviously 'free': it is not controlled by an attitudinal such as 'James believes that', for there is no such attitudinal in the sentence.

The same analysis applies to more complex examples in which the sentence does occur as a constituent in a compound:

(2)   The conference cannot start because 'Quine' has not finished writing his paper.

Here again the context-shift is free, even though the sentence in which it occurs is itself in the scope of the operator 'The conference cannot start because ____'. Let us suppose that the real name of the philosopher whom James mistakes for Quine is 'McPherson'. Then what goes on is this: the speaker wants to say that the conference cannot start because McPherson has not finished his paper; and he also wants to mock James for mistaking McPherson for Quine. Given his ancillary goal (mocking

James), the speaker does not utter a sentence which, in the actual context of use, expresses the proposition he wants to get across (the proposition that the conference cannot start because McPherson is not ready); instead he chooses a sentence which expresses that proposition in a different context, corresponding to James' erroneous beliefs. By talking in this way, he ironically pretends that the context is as James sees it.

What is important here is the fact that the speaker's pretense (characteristic of irony) *takes scope over the operator.* In Kaplan's framework, the linguistic meaning, or 'character', of a sentence is a function from contexts to propositions. In the actual context of use, k, (2) expresses the proposition that the conference cannot start because Quine has not finished his paper; but in k', the shifted context of the pretense (in which 'Quine' refers to McPherson), it expresses the proposition that the conference cannot start because McPherson hasn't finished his paper. The speaker pretends that he is in k', and he utters a compound sentence which, in that context, expresses the proposition he wishes to convey, viz. the proposition that the conference cannot start because McPherson has not finished his paper. The context-shifting pretense therefore governs the interpretation of the entire compound sentence.[1]

That analysis also applies if the operator at issue is an attitudinal. Thus we might have:

(3)   The chairperson believes that 'Quine' has not finished writing his paper.

Let us suppose that the chairperson does not mistake McPherson for Quine and does not know that James (or anybody else) mistakes McPherson for Quine. Then the report has to be understood as transparent: the chairperson is reported as believing of McPherson that he has not finished writing his paper. The way McPherson is designated is up to the speaker, and in no way captures an aspect of the ascribed belief. Again, the speaker chooses to refer to McPherson as 'Quine' in order to mock James, who (unbeknownst to the chairperson) mistakes him for Quine. It is pretty clear that the context-shifting pretense, here as previously, affects the context with respect to which the entire compound sentence is interpreted. The context-shift, therefore, is of the 'free' variety, even though an operator is involved.

Now it is important to realize that that sort of analysis can be maintained *even if the reportee is James himself*, the person whom the speaker is ironically mocking.

(4) James believes that 'Quine' has not finished writing his paper.

Again, the speaker mockingly pretends that McPherson is Quine (as James believes), and says *of* him (designated as 'Quine', within the pretense) that James believes he has not finished his paper. On this view, context-shift there is, but it does not occur *within the scope of* the attitudinal. Rather it is the attitudinal which is uttered within the scope of a pretense.

In view of that theoretical possibility, the counterexamples to Kaplan's thesis can be explained away by arguing that whichever context-shift takes place is not controlled by the metarepresentational operator, even though it coincides with the world-shift effected through the latter.

§15.2 Empty Singular Terms: The McDowell Analysis

A great merit of that analysis is that it applies to the hard cases—the cases in which the object the reported attitude is about does not exist. Thus consider

(5) Santa Claus can't come until we're all asleep.

(6) We must go to bed now because Santa Claus can't come until we're all asleep.

(7) My children believe that Santa Claus can't come until we're all asleep.

Let us suppose that Mary says (5) to her children. The analysis of (5) is easy and obvious: Mary does not really refer to Santa Claus, as Santa Claus does not exist; but she pretends that he exists and refers to him (or should we say: quasi-refers) 'within the pretense'. This is like the fictional example discussed in §12.2: in the fictional context of the pretense, there is a person to whom the name 'Santa Claus' refers. With respect to that fictional context, (5) expresses the proposition that that person can't come until everybody is asleep.[2] Of course, with respect to the actual context of use, (5) expresses no proposition at all.

The same analysis obviously applies to (6). Again, Mary pretends that Santa Claus exists, and her entire utterance is to be interpreted with respect to the shifted context of the pretense. Now I claim that the analysis also applies to (7), appearances to the contrary notwithstanding.

Since Santa Claus does not exist, Mary cannot really assert that her children believe *him* to have such and such properties: she cannot ascribe her children a singular belief concerning Santa Claus, for that would commit her to the existence of Santa Claus. This is a straightforward application of the Inheritance Principle: if (5) is truth-valueless because Santa Claus does not exist, then (7) is bound to be truth-valueless too. But what Mary can do, and what she does, is engage into pretense and shift the context: she temporarily pretends that Santa Claus exists, and within that pretense ascribes her children the belief that *he* can't come until they are all asleep.

This analysis of statements like (7) was first put forward by John McDowell twenty years ago, in the following passage:

> Suppose an interpreter finds an expression—say, 'Mumbo-Jumbo'—which functions, syntactically, like other expressions which he can construe as names, but for which he can find no bearer, and reasonably believes there is no bearer.... A sincere assertive utterance of a sentence containing a name with a bearer can be understood as expressing a belief correctly describable as a belief, concerning the bearer, that it satisfies some specified condition. If the name has no bearer (in the interpreter's view), he cannot describe any suitably related belief in that transparent style.... In practice, an interpreter might say things like 'This man is saying that Mumbo-Jumbo brings thunder', and might explain an utterance which he described that way as expressing the belief that Mumbo-Jumbo brings thunder. That is no real objection. *Such an interpreter is simply playing along with his deluded subject—putting things his way.* (McDowell 1977: 124–127; emphasis mine)

According to McDowell, the interpreter's assertion, to the effect that the subject says/believes that Mumbo-Jumbo brings thunder, is a pretend assertion. In virtue of the Inheritance Principle, such an assertion presupposes, and can be made seriously only if the speaker believes, that Mumbo-Jumbo exists. If the interpreter takes the name 'Mumbo Jumbo' to have no bearer, he must either refrain from reporting the belief in the same style in which it is expressed (that is, using a simple subject-predicate sentence: 'Mumbo-Jumbo brings thunder'), or, 'playing along with his deluded subject', he must temporarily pretend that Mumbo

Jumbo exists. Through that pretense the context is shifted. In the actual context of use the speaker does not believe (let alone presuppose) that Mumbo Jumbo exists; interpreted with respect to the actual context, the utterance would therefore violate the principle that "if a sentence x semantically presupposes a proposition ϕ..., then ϕ is presupposed by the speaker" (Stalnaker 1978: 326). In interpreting the utterance we are therefore led to shift the context and interpret the utterance with respect to some imaginary context in which the speaker does believe in Mumbo Jumbo. That mechanism of context-shift corresponds to Stalnaker's description: From "an apparent violation of the rule ... one may conclude that the context is not as it seems" (Stalnaker 1978: 326). The context-shift at issue is of the *free* variety: it is not controlled by the operator.

At this point, however, an obvious objection arises. When I say that my son believes Santa Claus will come tonight, I say something *true:* my son actually believes that. But on the McDowell type of analysis, the utterance is true only 'in the pretense'; outside the pretense, it is neither true nor false, as it contains a singular term which does not refer. This consequence of the account certainly clashes with our intuitions.

Two authors have pursued and elaborated the McDowell type of analysis in recent times: Evans (1982) and Walton (1990). (See also Crimmins 1998.) In response to the above objection, they claim that "pretense can be exploited for serious purposes" (Evans 1982: 364). As Walton says,

It is not uncommon for one to pretend to say one thing by way of actually saying something else. A diner jokingly remarks that he could eat a rhinoceros, in order to indicate, seriously, that he is hungry. Smith declares in a sarcastic tone of voice, "Jones is a superhero", thereby implying or suggesting or asserting that Jones thinks thus of himself. (Walton 1990: 394)

In particular, Evans and Walton insist that we can make a serious claim *about* a fiction by making a pretend assertion *within* the fiction: the utterance counts as true of the fiction if and only if it is pretend-true in the fiction (Evans 1982: 363–364; Walton 1990: 399). Thus I can say

(8)   Santa Claus has a white beard and red clothes

(9)   Sherlock Holmes is clever and Watson is modest

and thereby convey something true concerning the respective stories. The mechanism at work here, Walton says, is fairly general. One can indicate that a certain behaviour is appropriate by actually engaging in that behaviour.[3] Now, the appropriate use to make of a fiction consists in pretending-to-believe propositions true in the fiction. By expressing such a pretend-belief, as in (8) and (9), one indirectly conveys that it is appropriate to so pretend, hence that (8) and (9) are true in the fiction.

On this analysis there are many utterances which, literally, are only pretend assertions, but which nevertheless serve indirectly to make genuine assertions—assertions that are true or false *simpliciter*. That goes some way toward explaining why we have the feeling that 'My son believes that Santa Claus will come tonight', or 'In the Conan Doyle stories, Holmes smokes opium from time to time' are really true rather than merely pretend-true. The speaker offers a true characterization of the Holmes story, or of her children's belief, by uttering something which is not literally true, and does not even express a proposition.

§15.3   The Meinongian Pretense

The Evans-Walton defense of the McDowell analysis raises a serious difficulty. We can perhaps admit that, by uttering (9), one makes a true assertion about the story indirectly, by making a pretend-assertion true within the story. But when we make it *explicit* that we are talking about the story, as in

(10)   *In the Conan Doyle stories* Holmes is clever and Watson is modest

are we still characterizing the story indirectly? In what sense is the genuine assertion made only via a pretend assertion? There no longer is intuitive support for the claim that the genuine assertion about the story is an indirect speech act, in such cases. And the same thing holds for

(7)   *My children believe that* Santa Claus can't come until we're all asleep.

Not only is this a genuine assertion concerning my children's belief; it appears to be also a literal one—much more literal, at any rate, than 'I could eat a rhinoceros' or 'Jones is a super-hero' (§15.2).

There is a second, more theoretical problem. If we hold that metafictional sentences like (7) and (10) literally make only pretend assertions, we must say which pretend assertion it is which they make. Such sentences consist of a *prefix* ('In the Conan Doyle stories', 'My children believe that') and a *fictional sentence* ('Holmes is clever and Watson is modest', 'Santa Claus can't come until we're all asleep'). The fictional sentence expresses only a pretend-truth, i.e., something that would count as true if uttered in the context of the fiction but may well be neither true nor false in reality. (It is neither true nor false when an empty name occurs in it.) Assuming that the metafictional sentence itself expresses a pretend-truth, could it be the same pretend-truth as that expressed by the fictional sentence? Hardly. Sentence (10) explicitly mentions the Conan Doyle stories, that is, the fiction itself. Now the fiction does not exist in the fiction: hence it cannot be true in the fiction that in the fiction Holmes is clever. What is true in the fiction is that Holmes is clever, period. But if what the metafictional sentence expresses is not true in the fiction, in what sense is it a pretend-truth? Is it not, rather, a real truth concerning the fiction *qua* real-world object? Drawing that conclusion would at least enable us to account for our intuitions that such examples are ordinary assertions, rather than non-literal assertions on a par with, e.g., ironical utterances.

As Walton points out, the utterance of the fictional sentence is a piece of pretense, which is demonstrated and presented as an appropriate move (one that 'makes it fictional that one is speaking truly') in a game of make believe licensed by the Conan Doyle stories. The compound itself does not seem to be an instance of pretense:[4] it is, or at least contains, a genuine metalinguistic statement concerning (the appropriateness of) an act of pretense, which act of pretense is exemplified only by a constituent of the compound (the embedded sentence).

That analysis is quite incompatible with the McDowell line, however. If we want to stick to that line, we must insist that *the metafictional sentence itself* literally expresses only a pretend-truth. If we say that, however, we must say which pretend-truth it is that the metafictional sentence expresses. We are thus back to the problem I raised above: if the metafictional sentence literally expresses a pretend-truth, that can't be the same as the pretend-truth expressed by the fictional sentence, insofar as the latter expresses something which is true 'in the fiction'.

Fortunately, the pretense licensed by the fiction—that which a normal consumer of the Conan Doyle stories engages in—is not the only one that can be appealed to in connection with examples like (10). There is, Walton suggests (1990: 422ff, 429), a secondary pretense at play here, which we may call the 'Meinongian pretense'. The content of the Meinongian pretense is this: we pretend that the world contains not only real objects and situations, but also, located in some extra dimension, imaginary objects and situations. On this view, although Holmes is an imaginary person who does not really exist, still *there is* such a person, in the imaginary realm. Since there is such a person, we can refer to him. It is therefore a feature common to the primary pretense (that which is internal to the Holmes story) and to the secondary, Meinongian pretense (which takes the Holmes story to describe an outlandish portion of the universe), that Holmes 'has being' and can be referred to.

To account for utterances like (9), we can appeal to either form of pretense; but to account for utterances like (10), we can only appeal to the secondary pretense. We can't appeal to the primary pretense because, as we have seen, it is not true in the fiction that in the fiction Holmes is clever. But we can appeal to the secondary, Meinongian pretense: The speaker who says 'In the Conan Doyle stories, Holmes is clever' pretends that the universe contains not only Conan Doyle and the fiction authored by him, but also ('in' the fiction in question) an imaginary individual, Holmes, who does not exist 'outside' that fiction. Existence—or should we say: real existence—is treated as a property which some objects have and others don't have. As Walton remarks,

> What we pretend to be the case—that there are things that have a property expressed by the predicate "is a merely fictional character", for instance, and that "exists" expresses a property some things lack—is just what some theorists of a realist persuasion claim actually to be the case. Their mistake is one of excessive literal-mindedness, one of mistaking pretense for what is pretended. (Walton 1990: 424)

On this analysis an explicitly metafictional utterance is not literally true or false; it expresses a truth only in if we indulge in the Meinongian pretense. Why, then, does it not sound 'non-literal' or at least special, as, e.g., ironical utterances do? The main reason is that the Meinongian pretense corresponds to a deeply entrenched way of thinking, comparable to, for instance, our construal of time as a moving object. That metaphor informs a lot of our thought and talk about time, as when we talk of the weeks 'ahead of us' (Fillmore 1975: 28–9, Lakoff and Johnson 1980: 41–43). Since that is the way, or one of the ways, we *normally* think about time, we don't even notice it. Similarly, the Meinongian pretense so permeates our thinking of the imaginary that we don't notice its various manifestations.

The Meinongian pretense arguably corresponds to a particular stage in cognitive development. According to Perner, whose views I discussed in §6.2–3, the child is able to think and talk about the imaginary much before he or she masters the full-fledged notion of a 'representation'. The child first acquires the capacity of simultaneously entertaining several 'models' of the world. This capacity is manifested in the child's mastery of temporal concepts (which requires representing the past and the future as well as the present) and of counterfactual thinking (as exemplified in pretend play, which requires thinking simultaneously of the actual and the imaginary). Appropriately using several models, e.g., a model of the past and a model of the present, is not sufficient, Perner argues: the child must integrate them within a single, complex model, so as to be able to represent the *relations* between the past and the present (as when the child says that an object which has disappeared from view 'is gone'), or between the real and the imaginary (as when the child says that her mother is 'only pretending') (Perner 1991: 65–66). Now this notion of a single, complex model encompassing both the real and the imaginary while keeping track of their distinction closely corresponds to the Meinongian pretense. The domain of objects is divided between those that are real and those that are not. Further properties of the objects follow from their classification as real or imaginary. All the objects in question are part of the domain: they all have being, and are simply distinguished by their properties (including the property of being 'real' or 'imaginary').

§15.4 A Pretense-Theoretic Perspective

Let us take stock. I said that metafictional utterances such as (7) or (10)—repeated below—are true or false only under the Meinongian pretense; outside the pretense, they are (literally) neither true nor false.

(7)   My children believe that Santa Claus can't come until we're all asleep.

(10)   In the Conan Doyle stories Holmes is clever and Watson is modest.

Now intuitively such utterances seem to be true or false *simpliciter*. To account for that intuition, I said that the Meinongian pretense corresponds to a deeply entrenched way of thinking, comparable to our construal of time as a moving object. That metaphor informs a lot of our thought and talk about time, and we don't even notice it. Similarly, I said, the Meinongian pretense so permeates our thinking of the imaginary that we don't notice its various manifestations.

On this view the literal/non-literal distinction still applies, even though the non-literal meaning of the utterance is what we normally grasp. There is a layer of literal meaning, which we hardly notice, and a further layer of meaning which corresponds to what we normally mean (or understand) when we utter (or interpret) the sentence.

There is a more radical view, however. According to Lakoff and Johnson, "our ordinary conceptual system ... is fundamentally metaphorical in nature" (Lakoff and Johnson 1980: 3), and there often is no non-metaphorical way of saying or thinking something. That does not prevent our utterances/thoughts from being evaluable as true or false. It follows that we must reject the view that "metaphors cannot directly state truths, and [that], if they can state truths at all, it is only indirectly, via some non-metaphorical 'literal' paraphrase" (Lakoff and Johnson 1980: 159). They go further and talk as if they rejected the literal/ non-literal distinction itself. Thus they claim that when we metaphorically talk of argument in terms of war, we talk literally, since it is our very concepts that are metaphorical (Lakoff and Johnson 1980: 5). And Lakoff explicitly repudiates the view that, in metaphor, we "say one thing (with a literal meaning) and mean something else (with a different, but nonetheless literal, meaning)" (Lakoff 1993: 248).

Yet we must be more careful and distinguish three issues. First, there is the question, whether we can always find a literal paraphrase for a metaphor; second, there is the question, whether we can maintain the contrast between the literal and the metaphorical; finally, there is a third question concerning the role of the metaphorical component of meaning in our assessments of truth and falsity. Only the second and third questions matter for our purposes. Now, with respect to these questions, I think the more radical view defended by Lakoff can and must be resisted.

According to Len Talmy, one of the contemporary advocates of 'fictivity theory' in cognitive science, metaphor is cognitive pretense, and there is no pretense, in the relevant sense, without some realization that the pretense in question is *merely* pretense, that is, without a contrasting, non-fictive (i.e., literal) representation in the background. As he says,

> The very characteristic that renders an expression metaphoric—what metaphoricity depends on—is that speakers or hearers have somewhere within their cognition a belief about the target domain contrary to their cognitive representation of what is being stated about it, and have somewhere in their cognition an understanding of the discrepancy between these two representations. (Talmy 1996: 269)

Lakoff and Johnson themselves admit that "arguments and wars are different kinds of things" (1980: 5), even though they hold that our metaphorical construal of argument in terms of war is the normal way for us to think and talk about it. This confirms Talmy's observation that "any of the Lakoff and Johnson's three-term formulas—for example, 'Love is a journey,' 'Argument is war,' 'Seeing is touching'—is actually a cover term for a pair of complementary formulas, one of them factive and the other fictive, as represented in the following:

Fictive: *X* is *Y*

Factive: *X* is not *Y*

Thus, factively, love is *not* a journey, while in some fictive expressions, love *is* a journey" (Talmy 1996: 269).

We are therefore entitled to draw a distinction between the 'factive' truth-conditions of a metaphorical utterance and its 'fictive' truth-conditions. When we talk of the weeks 'ahead of us', it may be that the form of words we use implies that time is a moving object, as Lakoff and Johnson put it; still, the expression 'weeks ahead of us' can easily be ascribed a definite extension, and the sentence a definite truth-value, quite independent of the metaphor in terms of which we think of the weeks in question. In such cases the metaphor is confined to the 'mode of presentation' level and does not affect the evaluation of the utterance as true or false. Or consider Talmy's own example:

(11)   That mountain range lies between Canada and Mexico.

(12)   That mountain range goes from Canada to Mexico.

The second form of words posits a 'fictive motion' which is absent from the first example: we talk as if the mountain range moved, by using the verb 'go'. Still there is a sense in which (11) and (12) *say the same thing*, and are true in the same conditions. Let us say that (11) and (12) have the same factive truth-conditions, even though (12) has a superimposed layer of *fictive* truth-conditions which determines our cognitive construal of the state of affairs it depicts.

Even though the pretense is confined to the mode of presentation level, it must be acknowledged because it is closely tied to, and explains, the particular form of words which we use (e.g., the verb 'go' in (12)). As Talmy says, the fictivity pattern is typically exhibited when

one of the discrepant representations is the belief held by the speaker or hearer about the real nature of the referent of a sentence, and the other representation is the literal reference of the linguistic forms that make up the sentence. Here the literal representation is assessed as less veridical than the representation based on belief. Accordingly, the literal representation is fictive, while the representation based on belief is factive. (Talmy 1996: 213)

In general, pretense theory is helpful when there is a mismatch between the truth-conditions which (in virtue of its form) a sentence should have, and the (factive) truth-conditions which it actually has.[5] Whenever we postulate semantic pretense, therefore, we must identify two sets of truth-conditions for the utterance: its fictive truth-conditions and its factive truth-conditions. Accordingly, we must enquire into what the factive truth-conditions of metafictional statements are.

§15.5   The Truth-Conditions of Metafictional Statements

The first answer that comes to mind is this. A metafictional statement like (10) is (factively) true just in case, in the relevant story, there is a person named 'Holmes', with such and such properties, who is clever, and a person named 'Watson', with such and such properties, who is modest. If that is right, the content of the embedded sentence in a metafictional utterance turns out to be general rather than singular, at the factive level.[6] Still, this analysis is compatible with the view that fictional names are genuine names even in metafictional utterances. For, at the fictive level, the name refers and is used to express a singular proposition.

Yet I do not think that answer is quite right. The factive content of (7) is not adequately captured by any of the following statements:

(13)   My children believe that there is an old, bearded man called 'Santa Claus', who wears a red dress, lives in the sky, etc., and cannot come until we're all asleep.

(14)   My children believe that the old, bearded man called 'Santa Claus', who wears a red dress, lives in the sky, etc., can't come until we're all asleep.

These statements ascribe to my children a *general* belief, while the belief which is ascribed to them in (7) is, or at least purports to be, *singular*. As we shall see, it is the nature of the belief we want to ascribe which explains why, in (7), we have recourse to pretense in ascribing it.

The distinction between singular and general beliefs is reasonably clear (§9.1). The singular belief that Clinton is F is distinct from the general belief that someone with such and such properties (Clinton-properties) is F. To be sure, a singular belief pragmatically implies a corresponding general belief. To have a singular belief about a given individual one must have a singular or *de re* concept, that is, a 'dossier' containing various pieces of information putatively concerning that individual (Recanati 1993). Now one cannot have such a dossier without believing that *there is* an individual x satisfying the material in the dossier. Still, the singular belief that t is F (where 't' is the mental singular term associated with the dossier) and the general belief that someone who is G is F (where 'G' is a conjunction of all the predicates in the dossier) are clearly distinct: one is general, the other is singular.

Now consider the case in which the believer is mistaken and there is no object the dossier is about. For example the believer has heard of a promising young philosopher called 'John Martins', and has accumulated information concerning him; but it turns out that there is no such person—no one at the source of the informational chain which reached the believer. As Donnellan says, the informational chain 'ends in a block' (Donnellan 1974). The believer can no longer be said to believe the singular proposition that Martins is *F*, for there is no such proposition. But he still can be said to believe the associated general proposition, to the effect that there is an individual with such and such properties (the Martins-properties), who is *F*.

In such a complex situation the subject entertains what I call a *pseudo-singular belief*. She has a singular mental sentence tokened in her belief box, but no singular proposition is thereby believed, because the sentence in question fails to express any proposition. How can we ascribe such a pseudo-singular belief to the believer? We cannot express the singular proposition she takes herself to believe, for there is no such proposition. If we express the associated general proposition and ascribe *it* to the believer, what we ascribe is not the pseudo-singular belief; for a pseudo-singular belief is no more a general belief than a singular belief is.

In such a case, there are only two options for the ascriber. He can describe the situation from outside, as it were; that is, he can describe the believer as taking herself to believe a singular proposition (that is, as having a singular sentence tokened in her belief box), while in fact there is no such proposition (the singular sentence fails to determine a content). Or he can exploit the Meinongian pretense and do *as if* there was such an object as Martins, Holmes or Santa Claus; that is, he can fictively ascribe to the believer a singular belief concerning Martins, Holmes, or Santa Claus. Since it is clear that the pretense is pretense and that, in fact, there is no such individual, the fictive ascription of a singular belief concerning that individual amounts to the factive ascription of a pseudo-singular belief—an ascription which (in contrast to the ascription of both singular and general beliefs) is not directly expressible save by appealing to the pretense.

16
Untransposed Indexicals in (Free) Indirect Speech

§16.1   The Szuyska Counterexample

In chapter 15, I tried to defend Kaplan's thesis that there are no context-shifting operators, by providing an alternative analysis of the most threatening type of counterexample. Kaplan insists that the indexicals are controlled by the context, rather than by whichever operator occurs in the sentence. As Ducrot points out, the context in question need not be the actual context; it can be an imaginary context. Putting the two points together, I suggested that, in some cases, the utterance will be interpreted with respect to a shifted, imaginary context, *which coincides with the possible world (or set of possible worlds) introduced by some operator in the sentence*. Even in such cases it is not the operator which shifts the context. The context in which the global sentence (operator plus internal sentence) is interpreted is shifted as 'freely' as it would be if the sentence was simple rather than complex.

As usual, however, there are complications and counterexamples, which oblige us to modify the analysis. There are clear cases in which shifted context and shifted world coincide, but which cannot be handled by giving the context-shifting pretense scope over the world-shifting operator. Here is one such example, in French (I quote extensively, as it is an enjoyable *pastiche* in Proustian style):

J'aimais les soutenances de thèse, je les adorais, j'en raffolais, je ne pouvais m'en passer et je déplorais qu'elles fussent aussi rares, qu'il fallût attendre si long-temps, à partir du moment où elles s'étaient annoncées, pour qu'arrivât l'instant unique de goûter à ce plaisir subtil auquel je n'aurais pas cessé de penser tout au long des mois, des semaines, quelquefois des années, qui avaient précédé et qui m'avaient paru interminables, insupportables mais éclairés tout de même par la pensée réconfortante et qui parvenait de temps à autre à mettre du baume sur mon coeur angoissé à force d'impatience: le moment viendra enfin ... *Dès le matin, la tête encore tournée contre le mur et avant d'avoir vu la date et l'heure à ma montre Swatch, je savais que c'était pour aujourd'hui.* (E. Szuyska, *Textes Choisis*; emphasis mine)

In the underlined sentence, 'aujourd'hui' (today) refers not to the day of utterance, but to the day on which the person talked about had the thought *reported by* the utterance. The person in question had the following thought: 'Today is the day' (or in French: 'C'est pour aujourd'hui'). That thought is reported by saying that she 'knew that today was the day'. It cannot be said that the speaker pretends that the thought is reported on the very day on which it is entertained—the past tense forbids that interpretation. It is clear therefore that the context-shifting pretense has narrow scope here: it falls within the scope of the operator 'I knew that'. Or, to put it another way: two distinct contexts are involved in the interpretation of the utterance. The world-shifting operator, 'je savais que' ('I knew that'), is interpreted with respect to the context of utterance: the thought episode is presented as having taken place in the past with respect to the time of utterance. But the context for the interpretation of the embedded sentence is shifted. It is not the context of utterance but the context of the reported thought which is relevant for fixing the reference of 'today' in the embedded sentence.

While occurrences of 'untransposed' indexicals in indirect speech are rare, they are fairly common in 'free' indirect speech. The difference between indirect speech and free indirect speech is simply that the world-shift is free in one case, controlled in the other. That is the difference between, e.g., (1) and (1*):

(1) John is completely paranoid. Everybody wants to kill him, including his own mother! *(Free indirect speech)*

(1*) John believes that everybody wants to kill him, including his own mother! *(Indirect speech)*

In both cases someone's speech or thought is reported: there is a shift from the actual world to the world as conceived of by the ascribee. When the shift is implicit, as in (1), it is common for certain varieties of indexicals to be interpreted with respect to the 'internal' context of the reported thought/speech, rather than with respect to the context of utterance. Now, precisely because the world-shift at issue is free, such occurrences of untransposed indexicals seem, and to some extent are, easier to account for than similar occurrences of untransposed indexicals in indirect speech. We shall therefore consider the former first, and turn to the latter only after we have gained some insight into the function of such occurrences in free indirect speech.

§16.2 Context-Shifting in Free Indirect Speech

There is a particular class of indexicals, which I propose to call *orientational* indexicals, whose instances in free indirect speech are often to be interpreted with respect to the context of the person whose speech or thought is reported, rather than with respect to the context of the reporter. That class includes spatial and temporal indexicals such as 'here', 'there', 'now', 'today', 'tomorrow' etc., as well as demonstratives which, like 'this' or 'that', indicate relative proximity. In contrast to other indexicals, e.g., personal pronouns, which are typically transposed in free indirect speech, orientational indexicals often occur untransposed, as in *oratio recta*. Here are a couple of examples involving 'tomorrow' (from Banfield 1982, §2.4):

(2)   To-morrow was Monday, Monday, the beginning of another schoolweek! (Lawrence, *Women in Love*)

(3)   That could be remedied to-morrow. If it were fine, they should go for a picnic. (Woolf, *To the Lighthouse*).

The contrast between orientational indexicals and personal pronouns appears clearly in the following example in which we have occurrences from both categories:

(4)   After a while, she gave her response. Tomorrow, she would meet me with pleasure; but she was too busy now.

The speaker, say John, reports an utterance by Mary in response to John's earlier query. 'Tomorrow' refers to the day following that of the reported utterance, not to the day following that of the report; but 'me' refers to the utterer of the report, not to that of the reported utterance. That distribution is typical of free indirect speech. It is, however, also possible to find examples of free indirect speech in which a pronoun occurs untransposed, as in this quotation from Dan Sperber:

(5)   What if I [Sperber] had expressed doubts that such an animal exists? He [Filate] would have told me what he knew: they were golden all over; whether it was real gold or just the way they looked, he didn't know. Yes, their heart was of gold, real gold. How should he know if a heart of gold could beat? He was merely quoting what people who had killed these animals were reported to have said, and they know better than any of us. (Sperber, *On Anthropological Knowledge*)

I think the word 'us', in the last sentence, is best interpreted with respect to the reportee's context (viz. Filate's), not with respect to the reporter's context (viz. Sperber's).[7] This is in contrast to 'he' and 'I', which are still interpreted with respect to the reporter's context in that passage.

The occurrence of untransposed orientational indexicals is often considered a distinguishing characteristic of free indirect speech. It is not, however. The Szuyska example above shows that such things can happen even in indirect speech. More important, an utterance like (1) is a standard example of free indirect speech[8] but it does not involve any untransposed occurrence of an orientational indexical. So I think we should draw a distinction between two related phenomena. (i) An utterance in free indirect style purports to describe, not the actual world, but the world as it is for someone whose speech or thought is being implicitly reported. What distinguishes free indirect speech from standard indirect speech is the fact that the world-shift is free, while it is controlled (explicit) in indirect speech. (ii) The untransposed occurrence of orientational indexicals is an *additional* feature, characteristic of literary narratives. When that feature is present, the world-shift is accompanied and reinforced by an associated context-shift.

At this point two questions must be answered. First, why is the world-shift accompanied by an associated context-shift? In what sense does the latter reinforce the former? Second, why is this association more common when the world-shift is free than when it is controlled by an operator?

§16.3 Providing an Internal Perspective

In both free and standard indirect speech, there is a shift from the actual world to the reportee's world, that is, to the world as it is for the person whose speech or thought is being explicitly or implicitly reported. In (1) and (1*), the fact that everybody wants to kill John is presented as holding in John's 'belief world', not in the actual world. Now the reportee's world, like the actual world, can be described 'from within', by imposing a subjective orientation on it. (A world together with such an orientation is sometimes called a 'centered world'.) It is such an *internal perspective* which I think we gain when the world-shift is accompanied by an associated context-shift.

Let us consider the actual world first. If I say 'I am here now, but I will be there tomorrow', I state a fact, say, the fact that François Recanati is in Paris on October 2 but will be in Bordeaux the next day. Insofar as I am making a serious assertion, that fact is presented as holding in the actual world. Now the fact which I state, and which concerns the actual world, is presented under a *subjective* mode: I exploit my own situation in the world I am describing and use it as the 'origin' of a system of coordinates in terms of which I frame my description. Thus I refer to Paris as 'here' because I am presently in Paris, I refer to October 2 as 'now' because that is the current day, etc. Again, I can describe the actual world in such terms only because I am myself situated in that world and can therefore use my own situation as origin or deictic source.

When the world we describe is not the actual world but the reportee's 'belief world', we still frame our description using our situation in the actual world as deictic source. Thus I can say:

(6)   Yesterday Mary thought that Peter would come today.

The reference of both 'yesterday' and 'today' is determined with respect to the day of utterance. Even though the embedded sentence describes the world as seen by Mary yesterday, rather than the world as it actually is, we do not use *her* situation in *that* world, but our situation in the actual world, as deictic source. This is as expected (§12.1). But we can also do *as if* the description we provide originated from Mary herself. That is what happens in free indirect speech when the world-shift is accompanied by an associated context-shift:

(7)   Mary felt relieved. If Peter came tomorrow, she would be saved.

'Tomorrow' is now interpreted with respect to Mary's own point of view. We use her situation as coordinate source in describing the world as it is for her, thereby providing an internal perspective on that world. This is not different from the other sorts of context-shift we have considered so far—quotation, fiction, and so forth.

Since the context-shift, here as elsewhere, is a form of pretense, it is not surprising that it is much more common in free indirect speech than it is in indirect speech. Like context-shifts, free world-shifts rest on pretense. In (1), for example, we temporarily pretend that John's belief world is actual, and within that pretense we make a (pretend) statement. The same mechanism is at work in irony, and whenever a free world-shift occurs. Now there is but a short step from *temporarily pretending that the ascribee's world is actual* (free world-shift) to *using that pretend-world as context for the interpretation of the utterance* (associated context-shift). When the world-shift is free, shifting the context is merely a way of *extending* or *generalizing* the ongoing pretense. For the context is part of the actual world (§12.1); if therefore we pretend that the actual world is different from what it is, it is natural to pretend also that the context is different from what it actually is.

When the world-shift is explicit and controlled by an operator in the sentence, the pretense is 'betrayed' or 'disavowed', to use Walton's words: it is encapsulated within a serious assertion (chapter 5), and the pretend world is insulated from the context in which that assertion is interpreted. We are thus presented with two worlds: the actual world (in which the fact stated by the compound holds) and the shifted world (in which the fact expressed by the embedded sentence holds). Since the shifted world is explicitly presented as distinct from the actual world, the speaker can hardly pretend that it is actual and use it as context. That explains why associated context-shifts are uncommon when the world-shift is not free.

§16.4   Pretense-*cum*-Betrayal

The analysis of associated context-shifts which I have just provided is a bit too simple. It tells us what the rationale is for combining the shifts (that is, for shifting the context as we shift the world): by so doing we provide an internal perspective on the world at issue. But the mechanism it appeals to works only in a limited number of cases.

I said that the pretense underlying the world-shift is extended or generalized: the shifted world, which the speaker temporarily pretends is actual, is used as context. When the world-shift is controlled, the pretense is betrayed and that blocks the generalization. That account is too simple for two reasons. First, as the Szuyska example shows, there are instances of controlled world-shift with associated context-shift. The notion of generalized pretense does not apply (since the pretense should be blocked by the betrayal), yet an associated context-shift occurs and we must say what is going on. Second, the problem raised by the Szuyska example is more general than I have just suggested. In examples like (7), repeated below, the world-shift is free, in the sense that there is no doxastic operator making explicit the fact that the speaker is characterizing a 'belief world' rather than the actual world. The speaker *pretends* that the 'belief world' she is characterizing is actual.

(7)   Mary felt relieved. If Peter came tomorrow, she would be saved.

But the pretense in question is betrayed to some extent, though not as explicitly as it would if a doxastic operator was present. It is betrayed by the use of transposed pronouns, and by the tenses. Thus in (7) both the past tense (*would*) and the third person (*she*) are interpreted with respect to the speaker's actual context: they reflect his or her situation in the actual world. At the same time, the *untransposed* orientational indexicals are interpreted with respect to the context of the reportee and reflect his or her situation in the shifted world. The pretense which underlies the free world-shift is therefore not truly generalized: we do not use the shifted world as context for the interpretation of the complete sentence. Only some parts of the sentence are interpreted with respect to such a pretend context—other parts are interpreted with respect to the actual context.

If that is right, then there are three sorts of case to distinguish, not two. First, there are cases in which we *can* account for an associated context-shift by saying that the pretense which underlies the world-shift is generalized: we use the shifted world as (pretend) context for the interpretation of the whole utterance. That account does not work when the world-shift is controlled since we are then presented with two worlds: the actual world (in which the fact stated by the compound holds) and the shifted world (in which the fact expressed by the embedded sentence holds). Since the shifted world is explicitly presented as distinct from the actual world, the speaker can hardly pretend that it is actual and use it as context. Now the 'generalized pretense' idea cannot account for the third type of case either, that is, for standard instances of free indirect speech such as (7) above. In such examples, the fact which the utterance states is presented as holding in the shifted world, which the speaker temporarily pretends to be actual; but at the same time the speaker betrays this as a pretense by using indexicals whose semantic values depend upon her situation in the actual world. The betrayal is less direct than when the world-shift is controlled rather than free, but it raises the same problem as the Szuyska example: we can't account for that sort of case by saying that the pretense is generalized, since obviously it is not. In typical instances of free indirect speech, as in the Szuyska example, *the pretense is only partial.*

Still, we can maintain that the reason why associated context-shifts are less common in indirect speech than in free indirect speech is that the conflict between the (partial) pretense underlying the context-shift and the betrayal of that pretense is less direct in one case than in the other. So we can consider that we have answered our initial questions: why is the world-shift accompanied by an associated context-shift? And, why is this association more common when the world-shift is free than when it is controlled by an operator? But we now have a third and crucial question to answer: how can we accommodate the partial nature of the pretense? To say that the pretense is partial is to say that it does not govern the interpretation of the entire sentence. Thus in the Szuyska example, the pretense occurs *within* the scope of the epistemic operator. That is a prima facie counterexample to Kaplan's thesis.

§16.5   Quotational Intrusions Again

As it name indicates, free indirect speech is often considered as a (somewhat exotic) variety of indirect speech. Yet there is no doubt that it exhibits many properties characteristic of *oratio recta*. Banfield 1982 lists an impressive number of features which show the proximity of free indirect speech to direct speech. In free indirect speech we can find exclamations, (direct) questions, hesitations, repetitions, incomplete sentences, and modifications of word-order characteristic of *oratio recta*. Here are a few typical examples:

Why then should he be sitting in the bathroom? Was he asleep? dead? passed out? Was he in the bathroom now or half an hour ago? (Lowrie, *Under the Volcano*)

Absurd she was—very absurd. (Woolf, *Mrs Dalloway*)

For they might be parted for hundreds of years, she and Peter. (Woolf, *Mrs Dalloway*)

Ah! That in itself was a relief, like being given another life: to be free of the strange dominion and obsession of *other women*. How awful they were, women! (Lawrence, *Lady Chatterley's Lover*)

Yes, this was love, this ridiculous bouncing of the buttocks. (Lawrence, *Lady Chatterley's Lover*)

Christ, how it heightened the torture ... to be aware of all this. (Lowrie, *Under the Volcano*)

His wife still loved him, physically. But, but—he was almost the unnecessary party in the affair. (Lawrence, *England, My England*)

Something had happened—he forgot what—in the smoking room. He had insulted her—kissed her? Incredible! Nobody believed a word against Hugh, of course. Who could? Kissing Sally in the smoking room! (Woolf, *Mrs Dalloway*)

Many of these constructions would not be acceptable in indirect speech. From that point of view the name 'semi-direct speech', which some theorists use, is less misleading than 'free indirect speech'. Though it shares some features with it, free indirect speech cannot be construed as merely an elliptical form of indirect speech. It really is a mixture of direct and indirect speech. Note that the limit between free indirect speech and *oratio recta* is very tenuous and vanishes when the sentence contains no feature which betrays the world-shift. In (5), the last sentence of the passage in free indirect speech, which contains no such feature, could be construed as a direct quotation from Filate's speech. Filate might well have said: 'They know better than any of us'.[9]

This suggests a tentative solution to our problem. We might argue as follows:

In an utterance such as 'He said "I am tired,"' two distinct perspectives are at work. The same person is referred to first as 'he' and then as 'I' because the context has shifted from the mentioning sentence 'He said D' to the mentioned sentence 'I am tired'. Such a coexistence of conflicting perspectives is made possible by the heterogeneity of quotation. We can extend this analysis to free indirect speech since there is ample evidence that it is quotational to a large extent. Precisely to that extent, free indirect speech tolerates the copresence of conflicting perspectives. Thus we can account for the partial context-shift illustrated by the occurrence of untransposed indexicals in (free) indirect speech by appealing to the notion of quotational intrusion.

Before criticizing that line of argument, let me adduce some evidence in its favour.

That sometimes a sample of *oratio recta* can intrude into an utterance in indirect speech is illustrated by Davidson's example of mixed quotation:

Quine says that quotation 'has a certain anomalous feature'.

Because that instance of mixed quotation is cumulative, it gives us no idea of the sort of conflict that may arise between the two contexts simultaneously at work in the interpretation of a semi-quotational utterance. A better example of quotational intrusion is provided in this passage from the French novelist Barbey d'Aurevilly:

(8)   Prévenue sans doute par la sauvage petite créature, une vieille femme, verte et rugueuse comme un bâton de houx durci au feu (et pour elle ç'avait été peut-être le feu de l'adversité), vint au seuil et me demanda *qué que j'voulais*, d'une voix traînante et hargneuse. (Barbey d'Aurevilly, *L'Ensorcelée*)

There is a sort of inconsistency here. On the one hand the indexicals are transposed as they must be in indirect speech, so it is the speaker's actual context that controls them (thus the narrator refers to himself as 'je'); at the same time the speaker quotationally mimics the old woman whose speech he is reporting, thus shifting the context to hers. But of course, the old woman could not have said: 'Qué que j'voulais?' (first person, past tense). She could only have said: 'Qué qu'vous voulez?' (second person, present tense). There is a conflict which is similar to that generated by the simultaneous use of transposed and untransposed indexicals.

Another example of quotational intrusion worth mentioning is due to Barbara Partee (1973: 326):

(9) She giggled that she would feel just too, too liberated if she drank another of those naughty martinis.

This contains a repetition, like Banfield's example of free indirect speech mentioned earlier:

(10) His wife still loved him, physically. But, but—he was almost the unnecessary party in the affair.

Now Banfield claims that that sort of construction is 'impossible' in indirect speech. Was she wrong to make such a claim? Not necessarily. Insofar as the Partee example involves a quotational intrusion—and it clearly does—Banfield could argue that it is actually a mixture of indirect speech *and* direct speech.

Exactly the same strategy seems to be available to dispose of the Szuyska counterexample to Kaplan's thesis. By stressing the analogy between the Szuyska counterexample and examples of untransposed indexicals in free indirect speech, we can argue that the former also involves a form of quotational intrusion. The context-shift it displays can thus be straightforwardly accounted for, by appealing to the pattern of 'He said: *I am tired*'. That is the gist of the above argument.

That, however, is precisely the line of reasoning I criticized earlier as flawed (§14.5). The Davidsonian account of quotation as involving a separation of the quoted material from the mentioning sentence applies only to *closed* quotation; it does not straightforwardly apply to *mixed* quotation. (In mixed quotation there is only one sentence, a portion of which is demonstrated.) Now all that has been shown in this section is that the examples involving untransposed indexicals, including the Szuyska counterexample, are a mixture of *oratio obliqua* and *oratio recta*. That would be sufficient to dispose of the Szuyska counterexample if we admitted the following thesis:

Whenever there is quotation (*oratio recta*), the Davidsonian separation of the quoted material from the mentioning sentence is operative.

But we don't accept that thesis. The Davidsonian analysis does not apply to mixed quotation; hence the fact that the alleged counterexample to

Kaplan's thesis really is a mixture of *oratio obliqua* and *oratio recta* in no way implies that it is not a genuine counterexample to Kaplan's thesis.

To be sure, the notion of 'quotational heterogeneity' appealed to in the argument can be understood in a broad sense—a sense in which it applies to *all* forms of quotation, including mixed quotation. But quotational heterogeneity in that broad sense cannot be invoked in order to explain the possibility of context-shifts, because it cannot be characterized on independent grounds. One of the criteria for quotational heterogeneity in the broad sense is precisely that intra-sentential context-shifts can occur. So the heterogeneity in question does not explain the possibility of context-shifts—it is, in part, constituted by it. The above argument, to the effect that the coexistence of conflicting perspectives in our examples is 'made possible by' the heterogeneity of quotation, is therefore unacceptable.

Let us take stock. The context-shifting effects we were originally trying to account for arise in non-cumulative instances of mixed quotation. The examples we have considered in this chapter turn out to belong to broadly the same category. In chapter 15, I sketched a pretense-theoretic account of such instances, compatible with Kaplan's thesis; but that account, based on the notion of wide-scope pretense, has been shown to fail when the pretense is partial—when the context-shift is local rather than global, as in the Szuyska example and the examples of pretense-*cum*-betrayal from §16.4. What we urgently need, therefore, is an account of those forms of mixed quotation—or, more generally, of echoic use—which are both non-cumulative and partial in the sense that the context-shifting pretense they involve cannot be considered as governing the entire sentence, but only a restricted portion of it.

A simple example, involving neither free indirect speech nor untransposed indexicals, can easily be constructed:

(11)   Your friend 'Quine' is not Quine, he is only McPherson.

Here the speaker addresses James, the man who mistakes McPherson for Quine, and ironically mimics his deviant use. As in the other examples, the speaker temporarily pretends that McPherson is Quine, but here he does so only during the very brief moment when, at the beginning of the sentence, he uses the name 'Quine' to refer to McPherson. The pretense is local and concerns only the portion of the sentence delimited by the quotation marks. If the pretense was global and governed the entire sentence, the speaker would be (simulatively) asserting a contradiction, namely that Quine is not Quine but someone else.

Can we account for such examples, consistently with Kaplan's thesis? I think we can, and I will attempt to do so in chapter 17.

17

Partial Pretense

§17.1 Intra-Sentential Context-Shifts

In chapter 15, I attempted to account for metarepresentational context-shifts in pragmatic terms. In a purely pragmatic framework context-shifting is a matter of the speaker's pretending that the context is different from what it is. That is similar to what happens in irony. Indeed many examples of context-shift I have given are instances of irony. In those cases everything is normal from the strictly *semantic* point of view: the sentence has its normal character, and the same thing holds of its constituents. The proposition which the utterance expresses is not that which the sentence's character determines with respect to the actual context of utterance, however, but that which it determines with respect to the pretend context. For example, sentence (1) arguably retains its ordinary character, but instead of expressing the proposition that Quine has not finished writing his paper, it expresses a different proposition, namely the proposition that McPherson has not finished writing his paper.

(1) 'Quine' has not finished writing his paper.

That is possible because the speaker of (1) pretends that the context is different from what it is—she ironically pretends that McPherson is the famous philosopher named 'Quine' (as James indeed believes).[10]

Note that the pretense in question is confined to the 'locutionary' level and does not affect the illocutionary act of assertion which the speaker performs in uttering (1). The speaker is not 'serious' when she pretends that the context is different from what it actually is (when she ironically pretends that McPherson is Quine), but she *is* serious when she asserts the proposition expressed by the sentence with respect to *that* context (the proposition that McPherson has not finished writing his paper). Thus we must draw a distinction between two forms of pretense. There is *illocutionary* pretense when we don't seriously assert (but pretend to assert) the proposition which our utterance actually expresses. In *locutionary* pretense, we do as if the utterance expressed a certain proposition, and it is that proposition which we *actually* assert. Corresponding to these two forms of pretense, there are two forms of irony. In (1) the irony is locutionary: I mock James by mimicking his deviant use, but I seriously assert the proposition expressed by the sentence with respect to the deviant context. In standard cases of irony, like the usual weather example, the utterance is ironical in a different sense or, rather, at a different level. In saying 'The weather is indeed lovely' while trying to protect myself from the rain, I don't seriously assert the proposition which the sentence expresses. Rather, I simulate that assertion in order to mock the person who mistakenly claimed that the weather would be lovely. In the first type of case what I simulate is a locutionary act and by thus simulatively performing a locutionary act I actually perform the illocutionary act of asserting the proposition it determines. In the second type of case I seriously perform a locutionary act but I merely simulate the illocutionary act of asserting the proposition which it determines.

The problem with the partial pretense exemplified by (2) below (the example I devised at the end of Chapter 16) is that the sentence can hardly be said to retain its customary character.

(2)   Your friend 'Quine' is not Quine, he is only McPherson.

For the sake of the argument, let us assume that the pretense at work in that example does not affect the character of the sentence but only the context with respect to which it is interpreted. Then the character of the sentence is the same as that of (3):

(3)   Your friend Quine is not Quine, he is only McPherson.

Now, whether we interpret this sentence with respect to the actual context or with respect to the pretend context, in both cases we get a contradiction: the sentence ascribes to a certain person (the actual or pretend referent of 'Quine') the property of not being that person. The fact that, in the pretend context, the referent of 'Quine' is not the same person as in reality changes nothing to the fact that we express a contradictory proposition.

To remove the contradiction, we must draw a distinction between the context in which the global sentence is interpreted and the context with respect to which a specific constituent, namely the subject of the sentence, is interpreted: we have to assume that a context-shift occurs *in the course of interpreting the sentence*. The quotation marks in (2) precisely mark the extent of the context-shifting pretense: it concerns only the first occurrence of the name 'Quine'.

This move, however, raises a problem. The character of a sentence is supposed to be a function from contexts to propositions; but here we can't be satisfied with a single context. Whatever the context is—whether the actual context or the pretend context—the sentence expresses a contradiction, which can be removed only if, in lieu of a single context, we interpret the sentence with respect to a pair of contexts.

If we don't want to give up the standard notion of the character of a complete sentence as a function from (single) contexts to propositions, we have two options:

- Exploiting Kaplan's distinction between 'utterance' and 'occurrence', we can deny that (2) counts as a single *occurrence*, that is, as a single sentence interpreted in a single context.[11] If (2) is interpreted with respect to a pair of contexts instead of a single context, its being a true *utterance* is compatible with the fact that every *occurrence* of that sentence must express a contradiction. On this view (2) does not count as a true occurrence, though it counts as a true utterance.
- Alternatively, we can maintain that (2) counts as a single occurrence (i.e., a single sentence, interpreted in a single context), if we are prepared to admit that the character of that occurrence is affected by the context-shifting pretense. On this view the contextual shift is *built into the character of the occurrence*. Our problem is therefore solved: The character of (3) is such that, whatever the context, that sentence can only express a contradiction; but the character of (2) is different, thanks to the ironical interpretation of the first occurrence of the name 'Quine'.

In sections 17.2–3, I will pursue the second option, which I find most promising. But in §17.4 I will show that the resulting analysis can be made compatible with the first option by appealing to the familiar (though objectionable) distinction between literal and nonliteral meaning. Thus we can deny that (2) is, literally, a true occurrence, while maintaining that the context-shifting process maps the literal character of that occurrence onto a distinct, nonliteral character, in virtue of which it can express a noncontradictory proposition (that which the speaker of (2) actually states).

§17.2 Mapping Characters onto Characters

According to the second option, the contextual shift modifies the character of the sentence, in partial-pretense cases. That claim may seem to conflict with something I said earlier, namely that words like 'today', 'I' etc. retain their ordinary meaning when the context is shifted. If the character of the expressions is modified when a partial shift of context occurs, how can we say that the words retain their ordinary meaning? To answer that question, we must turn to another type of example which provides a useful analogy.

In a certain reading of (4) the word 'lion' is used deviantly:

(4)   There is a lion in the courtyard.

'Lion' can be used here in the sense which it has in 'stone lion'. In that metonymic reading 'lion' means something like: *'representation of* lion'. That special, metonymic reading is deviant (it is not the normal reading), but it is only mildly so: for, clearly, the special, metonymic meaning is a function of the normal meaning. 'Lion', in that use, means 'representation of *lion*'. Hence it seems that the word 'lion' still makes its ordinary contribution. How can we account for that intuition?

Following Richard Grandy (1990: 566–567), we can say that it is the character of the *sentence* which deviates. The character of the sentence is a function of the characters of its parts. In the normal reading of (4), when it is a real lion that is said to be in the courtyard, the function is:

f("there is", "a lion", "in the courtyard")

where expressions within double quotes denote the normal characters of the expressions in question. Now when the context suggests the metonymical reading, the individual words arguably keep their normal characters but it is the composition function, hence the resulting character of the *sentence*, which is affected (Grandy 1990: 567). The function becomes:

g("there is", "a lion", "in the courtyard") =
f("there is", r("a lion"), "in the courtyard")

where 'r' itself is a function mapping the normal character of 'a lion' onto the character of 'a lion representation'. We can therefore consider that the word 'lion' has its normal character in (4). On this view, the word 'lion' keeps its ordinary character, but the character of the sentence is affected by the metonymy.

I propose that we adapt this analysis to our examples of partial pretense. The analogy is, to my mind, fully legitimate. For (4) itself involves a partial pretense. Like any representation, a statue of a lion licenses a game of make-believe in which we pretend that the statue is a lion (Walton 1990). It is that pretense which makes the metonymic use of 'lion' possible: for, in the pretense, the statue *is* a lion.[12] We can therefore analyse (4) as

(5)   There is a 'lion' in the courtyard

where the quotation marks indicate the operation of a function r which maps the character of 'lion' onto the character of 'lion-in-the-pretense'. As a result of that operation, the character of the sentence is no longer the normal character of (4). The normal character of (4) is a function from contexts in which there is a unique salient courtyard, to the proposition that something which is a lion is in that courtyard. The character of (5) is different: it is a function from contexts in which there is a unique salient courtyard, to the proposition that something which is a lion *in a representational game of make-believe*, that is, something which is a lion-representation, is in that courtyard.

The same sort of analysis applies to (2). This sentence no longer needs a pair of contexts to be interpretable. It can now be construed as having a definite character, distinct from the normal character which the sentence would have if, removing the quotation marks, we abstracted from the context-shift which their interpretation requires. Thus the character of (2) turns out to be different from the character of (3) even though in both sentences the name 'Quine' has its normal character.

(2)   Your friend 'Quine' is not Quine, he is only McPherson.

(3)   Your friend Quine is not Quine, he is only McPherson.

The character of (3) is such that, in any context, it expresses a contradiction. But the character of (2) makes it fit for expressing a true proposition, namely the proposition that a certain person whom the adressee mistakes for Quine is not Quine but only McPherson. The difference between (2) and (3) is due to the operation of a *context-shifting function*: a function mapping the character of 'Quine' onto a distinct character, which we can paraphrase by means of the description 'person named "Quine" by the adressee'.

In general, a context-shifting function d maps a character ch—a function from contexts to contents—onto a distinct character ch^* such that, for any context k in its domain, $ch^*(k) = ch(k')$, where k' is a context obtained by shifting some aspect of the initial context k. Thus d shifts the context from k to k'. In example (2), the content of the name 'Quine' with respect to the actual context k_i is Quine himself; but with respect to the pretend context k_j the content of the name 'Quine' is McPherson. Putting the name 'Quine' within quotation marks indicates that a context-shifting function d is at work. The resulting character is such that the content of the complex expression (name plus quotation marks), in the actual context of utterance, is McPherson, even though the content of the name (without the quotation marks) is Quine. Thus (2) can be represented as (6):

(6) d(Quine) is not Quine but McPherson

where the letter d stands for the appropriate context-shifting function.

The examples of untransposed indexicals discussed in Chapter 16 can be represented in the same way:

(7)   I knew that d(today) was the day.

(8)   Mary felt relieved. If Peter came d(tomorrow), she would be saved.

In (7), 'd(today)' refers to the day on which the narrator had the thought expressed by the embedded sentence. The relevant function d shifts the context from the actual situation of utterance to the past situation described by the utterance. The context is shifted, hence the reference of 'today' changes; but the mode of presentation (the character) also changes. The day in question is presented by 'd(today)' neither as *today* nor as *that day*, but as *the day then thought of as 'today'*. The character of 'd(today)' is therefore metalinguistic. Similarly, the character of 'd(Quine)' is metalinguistic: 'd(Quine)' in (6) means: *the person named 'Quine' by James*. That metalinguistic feature is not surprising, since d is what the quotation marks contribute, in this example.[13] But the important fact is that only the character is metalinguistic: the content of the expression in quotes is not metalinguistic—it is a person (McPherson) or a day (the day on which Elisabeth Szuyska had the thought). The proposition expressed by (2) is about a person, McPherson, not about the name 'Quine', even if, at the level of character, the person in question is presented as the person named 'Quine' by James.

I have just shown how we can account for cases of partial pretense, that is, cases in which the context-shift cannot be considered as affecting the entire sentence. Can this account be extended to the other cases—the cases that *can* be handled in terms of global pretense? If those cases can be handled either way, then we should generalize the partial-pretense account so as to achieve uniformity. And indeed we can.

On the global-pretense account, the speaker pretends that the context is different from what it actually is and intends the hearer to interpret the sentence with respect to that pretend context. It is the proposition expressed by the sentence with respect to that context which is asserted (locutionary pretense). Now it turns out that, in an example like (1), there is only one relevant difference between the actual context and the pretend context: in the actual context, 'Quine' refers to Quine, while in the pretend context, 'Quine' refers to McPherson. All the other words have the same content in both contexts. Since that is the only relevant difference, the proposition expressed is the same whether we consider that it is the entire sentence, or only the word 'Quine', that is interpreted with respect to the pretend context. Given that alleged global-pretense cases can in fact be accounted for both ways, we should extend the partial-pretense account in such a way that (1) is analysed as

(9) d(Quine) has not finished writing his paper

where 'd' maps the character of 'Quine' onto the character of 'person named "Quine"' in the pretend context', and the pretend context is James 'belief world' (or the relevant portion of that world).

§17.3   The Modest Strategy

Turning from a purely pragmatic account of context-shift to a partly semantic account in terms of character amounts to giving up the 'bold strategy' as far as the defense of Kaplan's thesis is concerned (§12.4). We can no longer deny that context-shifts occur within metarepresentations. For instance, I have just represented the Szuyska example as

(7)   I knew that d(today) was the day.

The context-shifting function d maps the character of 'today' onto a metalinguistic character paraphrasable by the description 'the day then thought of as *today*'. The context-shift clearly occurs within the scope of the metarepresentational operator 'I knew that'. That operator introduces a circumstance c, viz. the 'centered world' (or worlds) corresponding to the speaker's epistemic state when she had the thought she is reporting. It is that circumstance c which serves as (shifted) context for the interpretation of 'today'. In other words, the relevant function d shifts the context for the interpretation of 'today' from the current context (the context of utterance) to the circumstance c introduced by the operator 'I knew that'. That is similar to what we have in the Thomason example cited by Kaplan:

(10)   Never put off until tomorrow what you can do today.

In that example too the indexical 'today' is interpreted not with respect to the context of utterance but with respect to the described situation.

Concerning that sort of counterexample I said in §12.3 that they were too marginal to threaten Kaplan's thesis. Now the Szuyska counterexample is very marginal too. Untransposed indexicals are extremely rare in indirect speech. They are common in free indirect speech, but only within literary narratives. According to Marcel Vuillaume (1990: 49), free indirect speech with untransposed indexicals cannot be found in oral conversation.[14] So perhaps we should not be overly concerned with those cases either.

What is neither marginal nor exceptional, however, are all the 'echoic' uses of words mentioned in §10.2. The 'Quine' examples fall into that category. Echoic uses are much too common to be dismissed in the way it is perphaps possible to dismiss the literary examples of free indirect speech with untransposed indexicals. Now to account for echoic uses we must appeal to something like context-shifting functions. Whenever such functions operate within the scope of a metarepresentational operator, we have a prima facie counterexample to Kaplan's thesis. Should we, therefore, flatly give up the thesis?

I don't think we should. We can still defend Kaplan's thesis, by turning to what I called the 'modest strategy'. It consists in biting the bullet and accepting that there are intra-metarepresentational context-shifts, while denying that the metarepresentational operator *per se* is responsible for the shift. The crucial point is that a context-shift in the scope of an operator need not be controlled by that operator.

For both contexts and circumstances I distinguished two sorts of shift: *free* and *controlled*. The context, or the circumstance, can be shifted 'freely', on pragmatic grounds. Circumstance-shifts can also be 'controlled' by some operator which makes it mandatory to evaluate the material in its scope with respect to a shifted circumstance. According to Kaplan's thesis, context-shifts cannot be similarly controlled: there are no context-shifting operators. Now there is another distinction, between *global* and *local*. A shift (whether contextual or circumstantial) is global if it affects the entire sentence, and local if it affects only a part of the sentence. The two distinctions are linked because, *whenever a shift is controlled, it is bound to be local:* a controlled shift affects only the part of the sentence which falls within the scope of the controlling operator. By contraposition, *a global shift can only be free*. In chapter 15, in order to defend Kaplan's thesis, I set out to demonstrate that the context-shift which takes place in metafictional statements is global rather than local: its being global entails that the shift is free rather than controlled. That line of argument could unfortunately not be generalized because of the partial-pretense cases. But it would be fallacious to conclude that the context-shift is sometimes controlled by an operator, because sometimes it is local and takes place in the scope of an operator. A controlled shift can only be local, and a global one can only be free; but that leaves open the possibility for a shift to be local *and* free. Arguably, that is what happens in our examples of partial pretense: the shift is local—in the prima facie counterexamples to Kaplan's thesis, it takes place in the scope of the metarepresentational operator—but it is free nonetheless.

I have analysed the prima facie counterexamples to Kaplan's thesis as instances of the following schema:

$\delta(\dots d \dots)$

Here δ is a metarepresentational operator, the parentheses indicate the scope of that operator, and d is a context-shifting function applying to some constituent within the scope of the metarepresentational operator. Even though the context-shift clearly occurs in the scope of the meta-representational operator, we can still defend Kaplan's thesis by treating the metarepresentational operator itself as semantically innocent. In line with the account put forward in parts II and III, we can insist that the metarepresentational operator's sole contribution to the semantic content of the sentence in which it occurs is a circumstance-shifting function. Quite independently from the metarepresentational operator, a context-shifting function operates within the internal sentence. That function maps the character of the expression in its scope onto a distinct charac-ter, thereby affecting the character, hence also the content, of the internal sentence. The important point is that the circumstance-shifting function applies to the content *resulting from* the context-shift. On this view there are *two semantically independent processes:* the circumstance-shift effected through the metarepresentational operator, and the context-shift. These processes are independent in the sense at least that each can take place in the absence of the other. In (1) and (2), for example, the context-shift takes place in the absence of circumstance-shift; and in transparent metarepresentations, a circumstance-shift takes place in the absence of context-shift.

To be sure, there is a form of linkage between the two processes: the context-shift is often parasitic on the circumstance-shift effected through the metarepresentational operator. That is how I analysed the prima facie counterexamples to Kaplan's thesis: the context shifts from the situation of utterance to the circumstance introduced by the operator. But the link thus established between the two processes is pragmatic. *It is never semantically mandatory to shift the context as we shift the circumstance.* The circumstance-shift merely provides an *opportunity* for context-shifting. Kaplan's thesis that there is no context-shifting opera-tor can therefore be reformulated as follows:

Kaplan's thesis (revised)

There is no circumstance-shifting operator which makes it mandatory to use the shifted circumstance as context for interpreting the internal sentence.

By thus reformulating the thesis, we grant that the context may shift in accord with the shift in circumstances. Yet we maintain that, semantically, the metarepresentational operator does nothing but shift the circumstance of evaluation for the internal sentence.

The revised thesis is weaker than the original thesis. It denies that there are circumstance-shifting operators which conventionally shift the context; in particular, it denies that metarepresentational operators fall into that category. But Kaplan's original thesis denied that there were context-shifting operators, period. Can we maintain the stronger thesis? It seems that we cannot. We have granted that the quotation marks, in the 'Quine' examples, shift the context: they contribute a context-shifting function, much like metarepresentational operators contribute a circumstance-shifting function. Hence the quotation marks around an expression (in the sort of example we discussed) function as a context-shifting operator—the very sort of thing which Kaplan's original thesis says does not exist.

We are thus back to the question I raised in §12.5. Kaplan himself admits that, by appealing to quotation marks, we can shift the context. Why is this not a counterexample to his thesis? Why can it not be argued that there is at least one context-shifting operator, namely the quotation marks? I discussed various possible answers to that question, but none proved convincing. At this point we could give up Kaplan's original thesis and adopt the revised thesis instead; for the revised thesis is all we need to protect the innocent approach presented in the first half of this book. But I think we can and should defend Kaplan's original thesis. In the next section I show how.

§17.4   Partial Pretense: Semantics or Pragmatics?

There is an obvious temptation to say that the context-shifting function *d* in our examples is contributed by the quotation marks, which can therefore be construed as a context-shifting operator. Thus in example (2) the word 'Quine' contributes its (normal) character ch, the quotation marks contribute a context-shifting function d, and as a result of these contributions the complex expression—name plus quotation marks—is compositionally endowed with a character ch^* such that the content of the complex expression in the actual context is the same as the content of the name (without quotation marks) in the pretend context.

Neat and attractive though it is, this view misconstrues the role of quotation marks in the sort of case we are concerned with. Note, first, that partial context-shifts can take place in the absence of quotation marks. Thus in our examples of untransposed indexicals no quotation marks occur. A context-shift takes place, but the context-shifting function is not 'contributed' by any expression in the sentence. It is a purely contextual aspect of the interpretation. That is very similar to the metonymy example: in 'There is a lion in the courtyard', the function r which maps the character of 'lion' onto the character of 'representation of lion' is pragmatic and contextual; it is not contributed by a linguistic expression.

When there *are* quotation marks, as in the 'Quine' examples, they serve as danger-signal, drawing the addressee's attention to the expression in quotes and suggesting that there is something special about the way it is used. The same sort of signal can be provided orally through intonation, or in any other way (e.g., by a smile). Such a signal helps the hearer to interpret the sentence properly, but it is not part of the sentence —no more than an ironical smile is. What leads us to think that the signal is part of the sentence is the fact that it corresponds to some constituent in *the interpretation of* the sentence, namely the context-shifting function. We (wrongly) assume that every constituent in the interpretation of the sentence must be 'articulated' by some constituent in the sentence itself. Let us call what is thereby assumed the Articulation Principle:

Articulation Principle

Every constituent in the interpretation of the sentence must be 'articulated' by some constituent in the sentence itself.

John Perry has insisted that the Articulation Principle is false: when I say 'It is raining', the place where it is raining is not 'articulated', yet it is an aspect of the interpretation, which is obviously relevant to evaluating the utterance as true or false. Given our present concerns, the metonymy example is a better illustration of the fact that there are aspects of the interpretation that are not articulated. Again, the function r which maps the character of 'lion' onto the character of 'lion-representation' is not contributed by anything in the sentence—it is a purely contextual aspect of the interpretation. Arguably the context-shifting function in our examples is not articulated either. The ironical use of the name 'Quine' can be indicated orally through intonation or, in writing, by the quotation marks; it does not follow that the context-shift is thereby articulated (hence controlled), for we can provide the same sort of indication when the shift is global (hence free). In a standard example of irony such as 'The weather is lovely', a global shift takes place, but nothing prevents the speaker, through intonation or behaviour, to indicate that he speaks ironically.

We seem to be back to the notion that the context-shift is a pragmatic affair. Is this not incompatible with the claim that the context-shift is semantic and affects the character of the sentence (§17.2)? I do not think it is—at least not if we reject the Articulation Principle. The context-shifting function is a semantic constituent in the interpretation *of* the sentence, which is not contributed by some expression *in* the sentence. Hence it is both semantic (*qua* constituent of the interpretation) and pragmatic (*qua* unarticulated constituent). As Grandy's analysis of (4) shows, the semantic interpretation of a sentence may involve contextual components not only at the level of 'what is said' but also at the level of character. That the character of a sentence may depend upon pragmatic considerations should come as no surprise, for we know already that the character of a sentence containing demonstratives is linguistically underdetermined (§11.2).[15]

The problem is that most semantic theorists still adhere to the Articulation Principle, and I do not want to rest my claim about context-shift on a highly controversial position. Fortunately, my point concerning context-shift and the role of quotation marks can be made even if we take the Articulation Principle for granted. Let us assume that that principle is correct. It follows that the function r in 'There is a lion in the courtyard' *cannot* be part of the literal interpretation of that sentence, since it is not articulated. Literally 'There is a lion in the courtyard' says that there is a *lion* in the courtyard. That is literally false if all there is in the courtyard is a *representation of* lion. It's only at the level of speaker's meaning that the metonymical interpretation of 'lion' becomes relevant. Similarly, we shall have to say that the specific place which the utterance 'It is raining' concerns cannot be an aspect of the literal interpretation of that sentence since it is not articulated. Literally, 'it is raining' is true iff it's raining *somewhere*. It is only when we take into consideration *what the speaker means* that the place she means to characterize through her utterance becomes relevant.

This strategy is applicable to our examples also. From the Articulation Principle, plus my claim that the context-shifting function d is not linguistically articulated, it follows that sentence (2) literally expresses a contradiction: its (literal) character is the same as that of sentence (3). It is only at the non-literal level that, accessing what the speaker means, we must acknowledge the operation of a context-shifting function. On this view, the quotation marks in (2) indicate that what the speaker means departs from what he literally says.

In that framework, we can still accept the two main points I made: (i) that there is some aspect of the interpretation of utterances like (2) which involves a context-shifting function d, and (ii) that that aspect of the interpretation is pragmatic and contextual in the sense of not being linguistically articulated. What we have to reject if we accept the Articulation Principle is only the claim that the relevant level of meaning (where the context-shifting function operates) is literal and concerns semantics proper. More precisely, we must reject both the claim that what is literally said by means of (2) involves McPherson, and the claim that the (literal) character of the sentence is affected by the ironical interpretation of the name 'Quine'. The proposition literally expressed by (2) will be said to contain Quine as a constituent, not McPherson. It is the proposition which *the speaker asserts* ('what is stated' as opposed to 'what is literally said', to use Bach's useful terminology) which contains McPherson as a constituent. Similarly, it is not the (literal) character of the sentence which is affected by the context-shift, but only the (non-literal) character generated through the operation of the context-shifting

Table V.1
Context-shifting in a literalist framework

Example (4): There is a lion in the courtyard	
Literal character	f("there is", "a lion", "in the courtyard")
What is literally said	that there is a lion in the courtyard
Nonliteral character	f("there is", r("a lion"), "in the courtyard")
What is stated	that there is a representation of lion in the courtyard

Example (2): 'Quine' is not Quine	
Literal character	f("Quine", "is", "not", "Quine")
What is literally said	that Quine is not Quine
Nonliteral character	f(d("Quine"), "is", "not", "Quine")
What is stated	that McPherson is not Quine

function. The view we arrive at if we accept the Articulation Principle is given in table V.1.

Whichever strategy we choose—that based on the Articulation Principle or that based on its rejection—we reach the following conclusion. The context-shifting function is *not* contributed by some expression in the sentence. It is a pragmatic aspect of the interpretation of the utterance—at whichever level we locate it—hence the context-shift is free rather than controlled. Thus the partial-pretense cases are compatible with Kaplan's claim that, in contrast to circumstance-shifts, context-shifts cannot be controlled by some operator in the sentence.

§17.5   Context-Shifting versus Circumstance-Shifting

Now that we've shown Kaplan's thesis to be defensible, even in the face of the most blatant prima facie counterexamples, an essential question remains: *Why* is there such an asymmetry between context-shifts and circumstance-shifts? Why are circumstance-shifts controllable and context-shifts uncontrollable? Essential though it is, this question is not directly relevant to my argument in this book. The only thing that matters as far as my argument is concerned is that Kaplan's thesis is actually defensible. Still, I think I owe the reader at least a brief indication of how I think that question should be answered.

Let us go back to the distinction between (pure) indexicals and demonstratives. With each indexical a linguistic rule is associated which contextually determines it reference: the rule that 'I' refers to the speaker, 'today' to the day of utterance, etc. That rule is lexically encoded and constitutes the character of the indexical. But a demonstrative *qua* linguistic expression (type) does not possess a character. According to Kaplan, a demonstrative is semantically incomplete and acquires a full-fledged character only when it is associated with a demonstration or, more simply, a 'directing intention' which may or may not be externalised. In other words: the reference of a demonstrative is *underdetermined* by the linguistic meaning of the expression type, which merely constrains it. To actually determine the reference the speaker's intentions must be adverted to. This is a property which demonstratives share with a host of other 'contextual expressions' (Clark 1992: chapter 10). In all such cases the referent of the expression (token) is that entity which satisfies whichever condition happens to be lexically encoded by the expression (type) *and* to which it is contextually manifest that the speaker intends to refer.[16]

The speaker can make his or her intention manifest in whichever way seems appropriate or convenient. One particular way of making one's intention manifest is by explicitly *declaring* one's intention. For example, the speaker can say: 'He is really clever—I mean Jim'. The clause 'I mean Jim' guarantees that Jim is the referent of the demonstrative 'he'. Or the speaker may say: 'You, George, are very tall', thereby declaring George as his addressee and making him the referent of the demonstrative 'you' (even if George is not in a position to hear the utterance). As these examples show, the reference of a demonstrative is essentially *stipulable*. In contrast, the reference of a pure indexical is not stipulable: it depends upon an objective feature of the context, something which must be *given*. Thus who I mean when I say 'I' is not stipulable—it's got to be the speaker, that is, myself.

Now remember what I said in chapter 5: that the (complete) content of an utterance or thought contains two components—a fact or state of affairs and a situation in which that fact is presented as holding. The situation in question is the circumstance in which the utterance/thought is to be evaluated. That may be the situation of utterance (or the situation in which the thought is tokened), but that need not be: the relevant circumstance for evaluating an utterance/thought is whichever situation the speaker/thinker is implicitly or explicitly referring to. One can say 'It is raining' and refer to what is going on in San Francisco even though the utterance takes place in Paris. It may be contextually manifest that one is talking about the situation in San Francisco. One way of making that manifest, without heavily relying on context, is by explicitly declaring one's intention: one can say 'In San Francisco, it is raining', or 'It is raining—I mean, in San Francisco'. This shows that the type of reference at issue is very much like demonstrative reference—it shares with it the property of being essentially stipulable. That is why circumstance-shifts are controllable: to shift the circumstance of evaluation from the situation of utterance to some other situation, one has only to *say* that the latter is the relevant situation. In other words, the prefix 'in San Francisco' shifts the circumstance *because* the circumstance of evaluation is essentially stipulable, in the Austinian-semantic framework.

In contrast the context is *not* stipulable. Far from being an aspect of content determined by the intentions of the speaker, the context is not even an aspect of content: it is a determinant of content, and as such it must be given. It follows that one cannot change the context at will. The only thing one can do is to *pretend* that the context is different from what it is.

Even though, in contrast to circumstances, the context cannot be shifted 'at will', through a mere stipulation, still it must be acknowledged that context-shifts are surprisingly easy to manage and do not require a lot of stage-setting. It is very common to use a word in a way which mimicks someone else's use. With the exception of untransposed indexicals, which are rare,[17] echoic uses are all over the place. Moreover, they can be as local as we wish. That shows that the sort of pretense at issue can be very superficial and automatic. Because of that property of echoic uses, many theorists are reluctant to use the word 'pretense' in that connection, for they find it too strong.

What I will say in part VI will provide the beginning of an explanation for that particular feature. I will root the context-shifting process in a basic cognitive capacity: the capacity for deference, which I take to be a central aspect of our cognitive endowment. Thanks to deference we can, as David Kaplan puts it, "entertain thoughts *through the language* that would not otherwise be accessible to us" (Kaplan 1989b: 604). The connection I will establish in part VI between context-shifting and deference goes some way toward accounting for our facility and profusion at context-shifting.

VI

Deference and Metarepresentation

18

Deferential Belief

§18.1   Translinguistic Context-Shifts

The analysis of (non-cumulative) echoes in terms of context-shifting functions presented in chapter 17 has a serious drawback. It cannot be extended to cases in which an expression is used with a deviant *character*.

If James has a poor mastery of English and uses 'paper' in lieu of 'poster', I can ironically use (1) to mean (2):

(1)   Quine has not finished writing his 'paper'.

(2)   Quine has not finished writing his poster.

I can also use a non-word provided it belongs to the lexicon of the person whose usage I am mimicking, as in (3):

(3)   My three-year-old son believes that I am a 'philtosopher'.

In all such cases Innocence is violated, but the violation is more serious than in the examples dealt with in Chapter 17. We cannot maintain that the word in quotes retains its normal character, which character applies to a shifted context. Here, the shift affects the character of the expression as well as the context in the narrow sense (i.e., the context *qua* argument to the character function). Thus we cannot represent cases like (1) and (3) as (4) and (5) respectively:

(1)   Quine has not finished writing his 'paper'.

(4)   Quine has not finished writing his d(paper).

(3)   My three-year-old son believes that I am a 'philtosopher'.

(5)   My three-year-old son believes that I am a *d*(philtosopher).

The words 'paper' in (1) and 'philtosopher' in (3) are not used with their ordinary meanings (characters). That is especially clear in the latter case since 'philtosopher' has no meaning at all in English. As for the word 'paper', it has a meaning in English, but that meaning is irrelevant to the meaning it acquires when put in the mouth of someone who merely conflates that word with 'poster' because they sound alike. Clearly, we need something other than the context-shifting function *d* if we want to account for such examples.

In the cases I have just mentioned a context-shift takes place but it is *translinguistic*. It takes us from the actual context (in which the normal rules of English apply) to a pretend context in which deviant semantic rules apply. In a closely related type of case, which I will focus on in what follows, the linguistic norms are on the other side: the speaker (or thinker) does not fully master the rules of the public language but defers to some authority who does. In Burge's most famous example (Burge 1979), someone complains that she has arthritis in her thigh. Since arthritis is an inflammation in the joints, that cannot be the case. But the person who so complains does not know the exact meaning of the word 'arthritis'—she has only a partial and incorrect idea. That does not prevent her from using the word deferentially. In virtue of what Putnam has called 'the division of linguistic labor' (Putnam 1975), she succeeds in expressing the proposition that she has arthritis in the thigh—a proposition which, of course, cannot be true.

Instead of ironically mimicking a deviant use, as in (1) and (3), the speaker in Burge's example mimicks the use of those who, unlike her, do master the concept. Despite the differences, I take it as intuitively evident that the same sort of context-shift is involved in both cases. In both cases the speaker uses someone else's language. For that reason, it will be useful to look at the phenomenon of imperfect mastery in some detail. Another reason for studying that phenomenon is that it goes beyond language and concerns thought as well, or at least our doxastic attitudes. For many of our *beliefs* are deferential. Consider, for example, the belief that Cicero's prose is full of synecdoches, entertained by someone who has only a vague idea of what synecdoches are, but who trusts the teacher. Or, to use an example from Dan Sperber, consider the

Lacanians, who believe that the unconscious is structured like a language. They are not sure what this means, but they trust Lacan, who said so. In such cases the subject deferentially believes something without properly understanding it.

(There is a significant difference between the two examples I have just given. In Sperber's example there is no publicly accepted interpretation for the Lacanian dictum. Opinions widely diverge concerning the correct interpretation,[1] and many, like Sperber himself, assume there is no 'correct interpretation' for that vague and cryptic statement. In contrast, there is a public interpretation of 'synecdoche', on which experts in rhetorics converge. I will henceforth contrast standard *Burgean* cases, such as the 'arthritis' or the 'synecdoche' example, and *Sperberian* cases, whose peculiarity is that the sentence at issue may lack a proper interpretation even at the public level.)

The sort of belief illustrated by the above examples is important. It is involved in education, in religion, and in many other human activities. But it is rather different from what philosophers ordinarily call 'belief'. How different exactly? That is one of the questions I will try to answer in this chapter. To avoid begging the question, I will use a technical term: 'quasi-belief'. The Lacanians, despite their uncertainty as to what Lacan means, 'quasi-believe' that the unconscious is structured like a language (i.e., they accept this sentence and are prepared to assert it, even though they do not fully understand it).

Dan Sperber, whose views I will present and discuss, is one of the first theorists to have extensively dealt with the phenomenon of quasi-belief. I will use his account as a foil, because he characteristically neglects the central distinction I have been at pains to emphasize: that between metarepresentational circumstance-shift and quotational context-shift. As a result he is led to deny that quasi-beliefs are beliefs in the strict sense of the term. Showing why this denial is unwarranted will enable me to reinforce my point concerning the difference between the two processes.

I choose to focus on quasi-belief because I find this phenomenon intrinsically interesting, but the analysis I will offer is meant to account for all cases of translinguistic context-shift. More than that, I will argue in Chapter 19 that the analysis, suitably generalized, works for all cases of context-shifts—including those which can be accounted for by means of simple context-shifting functions.

§18.2   Sperber on Quasi-Belief

In his book *Rethinking Symbolism* (Sperber 1975) Sperber distinguished between two modes of evaluation for sentences. In the normal, descriptive mode we first determine which proposition the sentence expresses; then we evaluate the resulting proposition as true or false. Interpretation precedes truth-evaluation. In the symbolic or hermeneutic mode, truth-evaluation takes place first: The sentence is assigned the value 'true' before interpretation. Arguably, that is what happens in our cases. The Lacanian sentence is believed to be true because it has been uttered by Lacan, who is believed to be a truth-teller. But the Lacanians who accept this sentence do not (yet) understand what it says, if indeed it says something. Similarly, the student accepts the sentence about synecdoches because she trusts the teacher who made the utterance, and she accepts it *before* understanding what it means.

In Sperber's later paper, 'Apparently Irrational Beliefs' (1985), the distinction between the two modes of evaluation is cashed out in terms of a distinction between two ways of being stored in the mind—a distinction that was already present in *Rethinking Symbolism*. A representation, for example the sentence 'Turtles lay eggs', can be directly fed into the 'belief box', or it can be embedded within a metarepresentation which itself figures in the belief box. In the first case the representation interacts with other representations in the mind and this interaction yields action: mental action (inference) or bodily action caused by beliefs in conjunction with desires. In the metarepresentational case the representation is insulated from other representations. Thus I can believe that *John said that* turtles lay eggs, without actually believing that turtles lay eggs: The sentence 'Turtles lay eggs' occurs in the belief box via the metarepresentation in which it is embedded, but it does not occur in isolation, hence it does not give rise to a belief. It does not freely interact with the other representations in the belief box and the rest of the system.

An insulated representation can be emancipated, if the metarepresentational frame within which it is embedded is a validating frame: a frame such as 'It is true that ...'. If we believe that it is true that turtles lay eggs, we are automatically justified in believing that turtles lay eggs. Sometimes, however, emancipation is blocked because the object-representation is semantically 'ill-formed'. That is what happens in quasi-belief, according to Sperber: the representation which is embedded in a validating metarepresentation ('Lacan says that ...' or 'The teacher says that ...') is 'semi-propositional' and cannot be fully interpreted within the mental idiolect of the subject. Often this is because the embedded sentence itself contains some uninterpreted symbol. That a symbol is uninterpreted in this way (whether uninterpreted *tout court* or uninterpreted in the idiolect of the subject) can be indicated by putting quotation marks around it, as in:

(6)   Cicero's prose is full of 'synecdoches'.

Its containing an uninterpreted symbol prevents (6) from being fed into the belief box. Such a representation can only be entertained metarepresentationally. One can have beliefs *about* a representation which one does not fully understand (e.g., one can believe that it is true), but that is all one can do with such a representation, according to Sperber. In order to give rise to a belief in the strict sense, a representation must be fully understood. I will call this 'Sperber's constraint'.[2]

Why should semi-propositional representations be prevented from going into the belief box? In 'Apparently Irrational Beliefs', Sperber gives an evolutionary argument in support of his constraint: there would be too great a risk of inconsistency if semi-propositional representations were admitted into the belief box (Sperber 1985: 54–5). Semi-propositional representations are not fully understood, hence we are unable to determine whether or not they are compatible with other representations in the belief box. To avoid contradictions, it is better to store in the belief box only representations which we fully understand, i.e., representations such that we can, in principle, check whether or not they contradict other representations in the belief box.

To sum up, quasi-belief involves two components, in Sperber's framework:

• The subject has a validating meta-belief, to the effect that a certain representation is true.

• Yet that representation cannot be emancipated and give rise to a plain belief, because it is 'semi-propositional'.

In what follows I will discuss three aspects of this treatment of quasi-belief. I will first consider the relation between the quasi-belief and the validating meta-belief. According to Sperber, the only *belief* the quasi-believer entertains corresponds to the metarepresentation; the object-representation itself does not give rise to a genuine belief because it is ill-formed. Beside the meta-belief, however, Sperber ascribes to the subject a genuine attitude, distinct from belief, directed toward the object-representation. Sperber's position thus stands in contrast to a more extreme view, according to which a quasi-belief is nothing other than, and can be reduced to, the associated meta-belief. In §18.3 I will argue in favour of Sperber's view that quasi-belief cannot be so reduced.

The second aspect I want to discuss concerns the content of quasi-belief (§18.4). Sperber says that the representation which the quasi-believer accepts is semantically indeterminate. Following Burge I will argue that it need not be. Except in rather special cases, deferential representations have both a determinate character and a determinate content. They are not semantically but epistemically indeterminate.

The third issue to be dealt with concerns Sperber's constraint. Is it true that the representations which are the object of quasi-belief are prevented from going into the belief box because they are not fully understood? More generally, is quasi-belief a credal attitude distinct from belief (in the strict sense), as Sperber holds, or is it merely a species of belief? I will discuss Sperber's most recent justification of his constraint, as well as his earlier evolutionary argument; both of them will be found wanting. In particular, I will show that Sperber's argument collapses as soon as one accepts the major point I made in the second half of this book, namely, that metarepresentational circumstance-shift and quotational context-shift are two independent processes.

§18.3   Belief and Acceptance

Many philosophers take the proper objects of propositional attitudes such as belief to be 'propositions', construed either as sequences of semantic values (objects, properties, etc.) or as sets of possible worlds. If we take this *propositionalist* stance, we are almost irresistibly led to the view that quasi-belief is reducible to meta-belief, because of the following argument.

As Sperber puts it, the representation which the quasi-believer accepts is not fully interpreted within her mental idiolect. Thus the student who holds that Cicero's prose is full of 'synecdoches' does not know what synecdoches are. There are also representations which are (partly) 'uninterpreted' not only within the mental idiolect of the subject but equally at the public level. What I dubbed 'Sperberian cases' (as opposed to Burgean cases) fall into that category. In both types of case the subject entertains a validating meta-belief, to the effect that some representation is true; but the object-representation (i.e., the half-understood representation the meta-belief is about) does not possess a definite content, either for the subject or in general. That is the case, evidently, in the Lacanian example: as Sperber emphasizes, it is far from obvious that a sentence like 'The unconscious is structured like a language' expresses a definite proposition. It follows (on the propositionalist view) that there is no attitude whose content corresponds to that of the object-representation. The only genuine attitude involved in such a case is the attitude whose content corresponds to the *meta*representation; for the latter is fully propositional, in contrast to the object-representation.[3] Thus the Lacanian holds a genuine belief, namely the belief that Lacan says that (hence it is true that) the unconscious is structured like a language: the Lacanian's quasi-belief is nothing other than that meta-belief. The same thing holds for Burgean cases. As Donnellan suggests in a recent paper,

When the person in Burge's most well-known example says to the doctor, "I think I have arthritis in my thigh," ... what is really believed is only that the speaker has in the thigh the condition called 'arthritis', or something like that. (Donnellan 1993: 167)

Another position is available, however. It is reasonable to assume that the object of the attitudes—and the attitudes themselves—can be split in two. According to the *representationalist* view, put forward in the seventies (e.g., Harman 1973, Fodor 1975, Field 1978) and endorsed by Sperber, to believe that *p* is to accept a representation *r* which means that *p*. This suggests that there are two distinct relations at work: a primary relation (acceptance) between a cognitive agent and a representation, and a secondary relation (belief) between the agent and the proposition which the representation expresses. That theory, which takes representations to be the primary objects of the attitudes, has received considerable support from more recent studies concerning indexical belief and the puzzles of cognitive significance. As Perry has shown, the puzzles evaporate as soon as we draw a principled distinction between the accepted representation and the proposition thereby believed (Perry 1993). Thus a rational subject may believe and disbelieve the same thing, provided she does so under different 'modes of presentation', i.e., by accepting different representations.

Once we take the representationalist line and grant the dual aspect of the attitudes, it becomes possible to treat quasi-belief as a genuine attitude toward the object-representation. What, according to Sperber, characterizes quasi-belief is the fact that the accepted representation does not uniquely determine a proposition (Sperber 1985: 51), either at the individual or at the public level. This is compatible with there being a genuine attitude toward that representation. Plain belief and quasi-belief can be construed as *two distinct attitudes towards representations—two varieties of 'acceptance':*

- One believes that p iff one accepts a representation which means that p.
- One quasi-believes that p iff one accepts a representation whose meaning is partly indeterminate (in a sense to be discussed).

Both types of attitude are instantiated in the quasi-belief situation: the subject holds a plain belief directed toward the metarepresentation (she believes that Lacan says that the unconscious is structured like a language) as well as a quasi-belief directed toward the object-representation (she quasi-believes that the unconscious is structured like a language).

There is a good reason for maintaining that the quasi-believer holds a genuine attitude towards the object-representation, distinct from the attitude she holds toward the metarepresentation. Unless we make that assumption, we cannot properly account for the continuity between quasi-belief and (plain) belief. That continuity is especially manifest in learning, or rather in education.

In education, quasi-belief gradually turns into plain belief (Sperber 1985: 53). We start by quasi-believing something which the teacher tells us, but which we do not fully understand. Still, we have partial understanding, and this enables us to use the representation in reasoning and to establish connections between the ill-understood representation which we accept and other things which we believe. Exploring those connections sometimes leads us to genuine understanding, hence to belief.

Consider the synecdoche example. In the representation (6), repeated here,

(6)   Cicero's prose is full of 'synecdoches'

only one symbol is partly 'unanalysed' (as Sperber puts it). We understand the representation, except for one particular constituent. Even that constituent we partly understand, however. For example we know that a 'synecdoche' is a trope, distinct from metaphor, irony, litote, and hyperbole. But we do not know exactly which trope it is. We may also be aware of a few examples of synecdoches which the teacher gave. From the general definition of a trope, plus the semi-propositional knowledge about 'synecdoches' (including the fact that such and such examples are examples of 'synecdoche'), plus propositional knowledge about other tropes, we may sometimes gather what a synecdoche is. As a result, the semi-propositional knowledge that a 'synecdoche' is a trope, and that Cicero's prose is full of 'synecdoches', becomes fully propositional: quasi-belief gives way to belief.

I do not see how we can account for this continuity without acknowledging a genuine attitude of 'acceptance without understanding' (quasi-belief). In the situation I have described, learning consists in manipulating a representation which one does not fully understand, up to the point where one understands it. We start by accepting a representation without understanding it; this attitude of acceptance leads us to use the representation in a certain way; and by so using the representation we end up understanding it. What makes learning possible is the use to which the representation is put, and that use itself depends on the initial attitude of acceptance which motivates it.

Could we say that what motivates our use of the representation in learning is 'nothing other than' the validating meta-belief? No: without an appropriate attitude *toward the object-representation* (rather than merely an attitude toward the metarepresentation), there would not be the appropriate use of it which eventually makes understanding possible. This attitude is *caused by* the meta-belief, but it is distinct from it. When emancipation is possible the validating meta-belief (e.g., 'The teacher says that Frege died in 1925') causes the corresponding belief ('Frege died in 1925'). When emancipation is not possible, the validating meta-belief does not lose all causal power; it still causes *acceptance* of the half-understood representation. Acceptance, under such conditions, is what I call 'quasi-belief'.

§18.4   The Deferential Operator

In §18.3, I stressed the dual nature of objects of thought. A primary attitude of acceptance, directed toward representations, is involved both in (plain) belief and in quasi-belief. According to Sperber, the difference between belief and quasi-belief lies in the semantic status of the accepted representation. To believe that p is to accept a representation r which is semantically determinate and expresses the proposition that p. In quasi-belief, according to Sperber, the accepted representation does not uniquely determine a proposition. The representation is partly uninterpreted—at least from an individualistic point of view.

There are two possible interpretations of Sperber's claim that the accepted representation is semantically indeterminate. When we accept a representation which expresses the proposition that p, that proposition is the 'content' of the representation. But the accepted representation also possesses a 'character' over and above its propositional content. Hence a representation can be semantically indeterminate in two different ways: either it has a determinate character but that character fails to determine a content (in the context at hand); or it lacks a determinate character in the first place.

It is well-known that the character of a representation may fail to determine a content, in certain contexts. That is, it is possible for a representation to be endowed with a character but no content, if the context is inappropriate. If I say 'He is tall', but the man I take myself to be demonstrating does not exist, no proposition is expressed, even though the uttered sentence has a definite character. Another example is Austin's (1975: 96–7):

(7)   He said I was to go to 'the minister', but he did not say which minister.

The speech act which (7) reports is 'rhetically' defective (i.e., defective at the content level)[4] because a particular constituent (viz. the incomplete definite description) is contextually uninterpretable. The quotation marks, here as in the synecdoche example, indicate that a constituent of the representation remains uninterpreted.

There is a clear difference between the Austinian example and the synecdoche example, however. In the Austinian example the relevant constituent remains 'uninterpreted' at the *content* level; the representation possesses a (phatic) meaning, but part of its (rhetic) content cannot be computed for lack of contextual information (viz. which minister the speaker is referring to). In the synecdoche case, it is less obvious that the representation possesses a determinate meaning. Compare (7) with (8):

(8)   He said that Cicero's prose is full of 'synecdoches', but he did not say what a synecdoche is.

In (7), the meaning of 'the minister' is clear, but its contextual application is unclear. As a result, there is an indeterminacy at the content level. In (8) it is the meaning itself which is unclear: the hearer does not know what 'synecdoche' means.

What I have just said suggests a radical interpretation of Sperber's claim concerning the semantic indeterminacy of the accepted representation, in quasi-belief. According to that interpretation, the accepted sentence contains a symbol which is not even interpreted at the character level.

Thus interpreted, Sperber's claim faces the following objection. The accepted representation is supposed to be *mentally entertained*; but it is hard to think of a symbol being mentally entertained without being 'interpreted' in some fashion or other. There is a sense in which all mental entertaining *is* 'interpretation'; hence it is not obvious that we can talk of mentally entertaining uninterpreted symbols. In contrast perhaps to what happens in public language, if a mental sentence is well-formed, it *must* possess a definite meaning—a character—even if it falls short of expressing a definite content. This may well be the intuition that underlies Sperber's constraint: a sentence cannot go into the belief box if it contains uninterpreted symbols. With this I wholeheartedly agree—I would even go farther: a sentence cannot make its way into the mind, whether into the belief box or elsewhere, if it contains uninterpreted symbols. This I will refer to later as the 'Interpretation Principle' (see the appendix to this chapter).

Because of this objection, I think we ought to reject Sperber's claim on its radical interpretation; that is, we should maintain that the sentences accepted by the quasi-believer are endowed at least with a character. But which character? What is the character of 'The unconscious is structured like a language'? What about even worse examples of quasi-belief in which it is pretty clear that the accepted sentences are virtually meaningless? Shall we maintain that they, too, have a character?

Even with respect to standard Burgean cases, we have difficulties specifying the character of the accepted sentence. What is the character of (6)? The sentence 'Cicero's prose is full of synecdoches' has a definite character in English, but that 'public' character is irrelevant. Remember what I said above: *In order to be entertained, a mental representation must be endowed with a character.* Now the character in question—that which a mental sentence *must* possess in order to be entertained—must be accessible to the thinker: it must be a character which the subject herself grasps. The public character of the sentence is not sufficient if the subject does not grasp it.

Despite those difficulties, I think we can maintain that the accepted representation is endowed with an appropriate character, even in the Sperberian type of case. The accepted representation must be allowed to include a specific constituent which I call the *deferential operator.* The deferential operator is translinguistic. It belongs to a certain language, say L, but applies to any symbol σ whether or not σ also belongs to L. The result of applying the deferential operator to a symbol σ, whether or not that symbol exists in L, is a well-formed expression of L, which I write as '$R_x[\sigma]$', where x is a user of the symbol σ (see below). The deferential operator is governed by the following conventions:

• If σ is a symbol of category α, then $R_x[\sigma]$ is also of category α.
• A use of the deferential operator is felicitous only in a context in which there is tacit or explicit reference to a user x of σ. (The user in question may be indefinite or collective; it may be the community of users of a given language L'.)
• The character of $R_x[\sigma]$ is that function from contexts in which the felicity condition is satisfied, to the contents which the symbol σ has for

the relevant users (the values of 'x'), given the character which *they* attach to σ.

In Burgean cases, the complex symbol $R_x[\sigma]$ has both a character and a content. What is special with the expression $R_x[\sigma]$ is that its content is determined 'deferentially', via the content which another cognitive agent, contextually referred to, attaches or would attach to σ in the context of utterance. In

(6)   Cicero's prose is full of 'synecdoches'

the last constituent is a deferential symbol whose character is a function from contexts in which users of the symbol 'synecdoche' are being referred to, to the contents which the symbol 'synecdoche' has for those users. In the particular context in which we imagine this representation to be tokened, the relevant user (the x who is being tacitly referred to) is the teacher; hence the symbol's content, in this context, is the content which the symbol 'synecdoche' has for the teacher. Which content it is, the student does not know; but she trusts the teacher and therefore quasi-believes the proposition, whatever it is, which the accepted sentence expresses.

In Sperberian cases the accepted sentence possesses a deferential character but the attempted deference fails: No user x has the cognitive resources for determining the content of the expression to which the deferential operator applies, hence no content is expressed, in that context. Such failure occurs whenever a term is used deferentially by everybody, in a mutual or circular manner.

In each type of case we must draw a distinction between (i) the character, if any, of the symbol σ and (ii) the character of the deferential symbol $R_x[\sigma]$. In Burgean cases σ has a public character, which the subject does not grasp; but the sentence which the subject accepts contains the deferential symbol $R_x[\sigma]$, whose character she grasps. In Sperberian cases σ may well be publicly meaningless: the only character available in the linguistic community is that of the deferential symbol $R_x[\sigma]$. The subject does not grasp the character of σ, because there is no such character for her to grasp. What she grasps is the character of the deferential symbol.

Since the content of the deferential symbol $R_x[\sigma]$ is that which the character of σ itself determines, $R_x[\sigma]$ has a content only if σ has a character. It follows that, in Sperberian cases, the accepted sentence expresses no definite content. In Burgean cases it does: a determinate content is expressed, even though it is unknown to the quasi-believer. Thus the speaker who utters

(9)   I have 'arthritis' in the thigh

expresses the proposition that she has arthritis in the thigh, even if she does not know what arthritis is. Her use is deferential. In the same way, the student accepts a representation, viz. (6), which by virtue of the semantics of the deferential operator expresses the proposition that Cicero's prose is full of synecdoches.

On this view, the object of acceptance in quasi-belief is not a semi-propositional representation (i.e., a representation incompletely interpreted, at whatever level) but a deferential representation (i.e., a representation containing the deferential operator). Hence we must not only reject Sperber's claim on its radical interpretation (according to which the accepted sentence lacks a determinate character), but also on its weaker interpretation (according to which the accepted sentence lacks a determinate content). In Burgean cases the deferential representation has both a character and a content.

Sperber's intuition of indeterminacy can still be captured, however. Even when they have both a character and a content, deferential representations, though semantically determinate, are *epistemically* indeterminate: the subject does not know which proposition the sentence she accepts expresses. Sperber's claim concerning semi-propositionality can therefore be construed as a claim concerning the epistemical state of the user, rather than a claim about semantic content.

§18.5   Are Quasi-Beliefs Real Beliefs?

Beside the question, whether or not a determinate proposition is expressed (in Burgean cases), there is a further question: whether that proposition can be believed. The two issues are orthogonal. One can side with Burge and argue that a definite proposition is expressed, while simultaneously holding, with Sperber, that that proposition, being deferentially expressed, cannot be 'believed' in the strict sense of the term.

The first issue is semantic, the second psychological. It is the psychological question which we must now address.

Sperber is a 'dualist': he holds the view that plain belief and quasi-belief are two distinct (if related) attitudes. As he puts it, "There are at least two cognitively distinct manners of holding true," corresponding to belief and quasi-belief (Sperber 1997: 76). To believe that p is to have in one's belief box a representation which means that p. When someone quasi-believes that p, she does *not* have such a representation in her belief box. What she has in her belief box is a metarepresentation *about* the accepted representation. It is possible to follow Sperber here even if one opts for the analysis sketched in §18.4. According to that analysis, deferential representations may well express determinate propositions. Still, one might hold that such representations cannot go into the belief box. Sperber's constraint, to the effect that whatever is believed must be fully understood, implies that deferential representations (insofar as they are epistemically indeterminate, i.e., not fully understood) cannot give rise to beliefs in the strict sense. They can be accepted but cannot be believed.

Sperber's constraint, and Sperber's evolutionary argument for it, can easily be restated in our framework. Deferential representations (representations containing the deferential operator) are highly risky: the believer has no control over which proposition is expressed, and inconsistencies can proliferate. Hence the policy of banning deferential representations from the belief box can only be profitable to the cognitive system.

What are we to think of this argument? Clearly, it presupposes Cartesian individualism. Sperber assumes that cognitive agents have their beliefs under control, in the sense that they know what they believe. Deferential representations are banned from the belief box precisely because, in their case, the subject does not know the semantic content of the representations which she accepts. But there is a clear sense in which cognitive agents do not, in general, 'know' the propositional contents of the representations which they accept: that is the lesson of externalism. There is nothing exceptionable about deferential representations, in that respect. As research on cognitive significance has shown, whenever the accepted representation is indexical, or includes a name-like constituent, there is a possibility of referential mistake and/or lack of understanding. So the basis of Sperber's argument—cognitive individualism—is extremely shaky.

There is another objection to the claim that deferential representations are banned from the belief box. In §18.3, following Sperber himself, I stressed the continuity between quasi-belief and ordinary belief. This continuity suggests that deferentiality is a matter of degree. Instead of a sharp demarcation of ordinary beliefs from quasi-beliefs, as that which results from Sperber's constraint, we should rather posit a continuum of cases.

In his most recent contribution to the topic (Sperber 1997) Sperber gives another argument in favour of his dualist position. Let us start with a quotation from that paper:

> To accept the existence of a data-base [a belief box] is to assume some representational capacity by means of which data are represented in the data base. I will, for expository purposes, describe this capacity as a language of thought, a 'mentalese', and I will focus on the conceptual repertoire, the lexicon of this mentalese. (Sperber 1997: 74)

The mental lexicon must have limits, Sperber goes on to argue, hence there must be contents which cannot be (directly) expressed using that lexicon, because we lack the appropriate concepts. Contents which can be expressed using the basic conceptual repertoire are called 'intuitive'; contents which cannot are said to be 'non-intuitive'. In quasi-belief, according to Sperber, the content to which a credal attitude is directed is non-intuitive. That content cannot be articulated within the mental vocabulary of the cognitive agent: but the agent can express it *indirectly* via a process of semantic ascent. To that effect she has to use some mental place-holder for the unavailable concept—some uninterpreted symbol σ. The resulting representation, including the place-holder, is semantically ill-formed (incomplete), hence it cannot go into the belief box; but the agent can embed it into a validating metarepresentation. As the object-representation cannot be disquoted (because it does not have the right semantic format and includes a dummy symbol σ), no genuine belief is generated, but instead there is a quasi-belief: a validating metarepresentation is believed but emancipation is blocked.—On this view dualism is true *a priori*. The belief box is *defined* as a repository for the outputs of a certain representational capacity: what exceeds that capacity (non-intuitive representations) cannot go into that box, by definition.

There is a prima facie difficulty for Sperber's position. How is it possible for a metarepresentation to be fully interpreted when the object-representation itself is partly uninterpreted? Sperber apparently thinks that prefixing 'It is true that' (or 'Lacan believes that') to a semantically indeterminate representation can yield a semantically determinate metarepresentation. It is hard to see how this view can be compatible with Semantic Innocence. If Semantic Innocence holds, the semantic incompleteness of the object-representation can hardly fail to entail the semantic incompleteness of the metarepresentation (see e.g., Prior 1963: 153–54). That I referred to earlier as the Inheritance Principle (§13.5).

Sperber could reply that the Inheritance Principle applies to 'oblique' constructions such as 'It is true that ...' or 'Lacan says that ...', but not to *direct quotation*. Thus, if 'glive' is a non-word and 'John kept gliving' is ill-formed, 'It is true that John kept gliving' (or 'Lacan said that John kept gliving') is bound to be ill-formed too; but the direct quotation 'Lacan said: "John kept gliving"' is well-formed. The same thing holds for 'Lacan said that John kept "gliving,"' which is a mixture of oblique construction and direct quotation. For we have seen that not all instances of mixed quotation are cumulative and therefore innocent: some are non-cumulative and involve a deviant use of the expression in quotes (§14.4). In particular, there are instances of mixed quotation (such as the 'philtosopher' example) in which the expression in quotes is a non-word. Since quotation marks can turn non-words into words, both in closed quotation and in (non-cumulative) mixed quotation, why not accept that there are mental quotation marks with the same power? That is, in effect, Sperber's suggestion. That suggestion is in harmony with my own analysis in terms of the deferential operator. Even if a symbol σ is unavailable to the subject, the deferential symbol $R_x[\sigma]$ *is* available. The deferential operator makes a concept out of an empty symbol.

Still, I find Sperber's new argument for his constraint unacceptable. According to Sperber's argument, the only representation which can go into the belief box is the metarepresentation, for the object-representation is ill-formed. *This argument presupposes that in quasi-belief there are only two representations available:* the object-representation, which is ill-formed and cannot go into the belief box, and the metarepresentation, which includes that object-representation in quotes and which is well-formed. But that assumption is unwarranted. Arguably, there are three distinguishable representations in the type of case we are considering. There is the 'disquoted' representation including some uninterpreted symbol; the 'deferential representation' including that symbol in quotes (that is, in the scope of the deferential operator); and the meta-representation in which the deferential representation can be embedded, and which contains some explicit reference to the cognitive agent (or the community of users) to whom the subject defers.

Let us go back to the synecdoche example. The three-prong distinction I am trying to make is that between (6), (10), and (11):

(6)   Cicero's prose is full of 'synecdoches'.

(10)   Cicero's prose is full of synecdoches.

(11)   The teacher said that Cicero's prose is full of 'synecdoches'.

In a cognitive system which lacks the concept of synecdoche, (10) is unexpressible (non-intuitive), hence it cannot be 'believed'. Thus far I follow Sperber. But Sperber argues from there that the only belief available to the subject in that situation is metarepresentational: it is a belief corresponding to (11). I agree that a meta-belief like (11) is in the belief box, in most instances of quasi-belief; but I deny that that is *the only belief there is* in the quasi-belief situation. (6) corresponds to the third representation available: the deferential representation itself, including materials 'in quotes'. That representation is distinct both from the ill-formed object-representation (10) *and* from the metarepresentation (11). In contrast to (10), it is well-formed (since the dummy symbol occurs 'in quotes'), hence it *can* go into the belief box. In contrast to (11), it is metarepresentational only at the character level: the content of the deferential representation (6) is *not* metarepresentational.

Deferential representations are metarepresentational at the level of character but not at the level of content.[5] As an analogy, consider the pronoun 'I'. As Reichenbach pointed out, the meaning of token-reflexive expressions like 'I' is metarepresentational—it conveys an implicit reference to the expression itself (Reichenbach 1947). 'I' means 'the person who utters this utterance'. But the proposition expressed by 'I am bald' is *not* metarepresentational. That is because 'I' is directly referential: its metarepresentational character determines its content but is not part of it (Kaplan 1989a). In the same way, I construe deferential symbols as directly referential. The semantic value of $R_x[\sigma]$ *is* the semantic value which σ has for x. That semantic value is the content of $R_x[\sigma]$. The metarepresentational reference to x's use of σ is not part of the content of $R_x[\sigma]$: it contextually determines that content.

Sperber does not acknowledge the existence of the deferential representation (6). He recognizes only two representations: the ill-formed object-representation (10), and the metarepresentation (11) in which it is embedded in quotes. For Sperber, (11) is analysed not as

(12)   The teacher believes that + Cicero's prose is full of 'synecdoches'

but as

(13)   The teacher believes that … '…' + Cicero's prose is full of synecdoches.

He considers the quotes around the non-word as necessarily part and parcel of a complex metarepresentational frame such as that of (11). That is precisely what I am denying. I think the deferential operator can occur in simpler representations like (6)—no well-formedness constraint rules out such simple deferential representations. If I am right, deferential representations such as (6) need not be embedded into an explicit metarepresentational frame such as (11) in order to go into the belief box. 'Simple' deferential representations are semantically well-formed and can go into the belief box on their own.

Sperber's analysis of (11) as (13) presupposes that the context-shifting process is inseparable from metarepresentational embedding. In this book, however, I argued that the two processes are independent. To embed a sentence within a metarepresentational frame amounts to shifting the circumstance for the evaluation of that sentence. That process may or may not be accompanied by a context-shift. The same thing holds in the other direction: for a context-shift to occur in the interpretation of a sentence, that sentence does not have to be embedded within a metarepresentational frame. If we use 'δ' as a dummy metarepresentational prefix, 'p' as a dummy sentence, and single quotation marks around a sentence to indicate that a context-shift takes place in the inter-

Table VI.1
Metarepresentational embedding and context-shift: four possibilities

		Metarepresentational embedding	Context-shift
A	δp	+	−
B	$\delta` p$'	+	+
C	p	−	−
D	`p'	−	+

pretation of that sentence, there are four distinct possibilities, displayed in table VI.1.

In this chapter we have been concerned with a particular sort of (translinguistic) context-shift, that which is operative in quasi-belief. Sperber's denial that deferential representations can go into the belief box ultimately rests on his neglect of option (D) in table VI.1, which he reduces to option (B). If I am right, however, it is a mistake to hold that deferential representations can occur only within metarepresentations. They can occur within metarepresentations, but they can also occur autonomously. That follows from the fact that context-shift and metarepresentational circumstance-shift are two independent processes.

To be sure, a simple deferential representation such as (6) makes sense only 'in the context of' metarepresentations such as (11). But that dependence of simple deferential representations on associated metarepresentations can be treated by construing the deferential operator as 'indexical', that is, as constraining the context in which it is tokened. There is a constraint on the use of a deferential symbol such as $R_x[\sigma]$: the user of $R_x[\sigma]$ must entertain appropriate metarepresentational attitudes, viz. the belief that some agent x uses σ with a certain content, and the intention to use $R_x[\sigma]$ with precisely that content. The deferential symbol expresses a determinate content only if that constraint is contextually satisfied.[6] For it to be satisfied, there must be some metarepresentation like (11) in the belief box. Still, (6) also occurs in the belief box as a separate representation. Appropriately using a deferential representation implies having a meta-belief, but the deferential representation is otherwise independent of the metarepresentation: it is well-formed in its own right (as an indexical sentence is well-formed), and its content is distinct from the content of the metarepresentation.[7]

In this framework, what is prevented from going into the belief box is not the deferential representation, containing the place-holder σ in the scope of the deferential operator $R_x[\ ]$, but the 'disquoted' representation which results from emancipating σ. The deferential representation itself can go into the belief box. Since that is so, there is no reason to deny that quasi-beliefs are beliefs. The person who quasi-believes that p has, in her belief box, a certain representation (the deferential representation) expressing the proposition that p. If to believe that p is to have in one's belief box a representation which means that p, then the person who quasi-believes that p believes that p.

Appendix: Reply to Woodfield

Andrew Woodfield has put forward the following criticism of my view (Woodfield, forthcoming). He accepts that there is a deferential operator which works in more or less the way I describe, but not my claim that it is at work in examples like the 'arthritis' example. The cases that support my view, according to Woodfield, are the cases in which we consciously use a word which we do not understand, in quotation marks as it were. In contrast to Donnellan, who holds that in such cases what is believed is a metalinguistic proposition (Donnellan 1993), I hold that the content of the thought or utterance is the same as it would be if no quotation marks occurred and no deference took place: The metalinguistic component is located at the character level. Woodfield accepts all this. But my theory explains "a rather specialized range of phenomena," he holds. It was a mistake on my part to extend it to cases of imperfect mastery, like Burge's 'arthritis' example. Woodfield thus rejects my claim that "children, language-learners, indeed anyone, when they pick up words that they do not fully understand, normally bind such words inside deferential operators" (Woodfield, forthcoming).

Not only is there a phenomenological difference between self-conscious deference and imperfect mastery; there is, Woodfield points out, a good theoretical reason for not putting them in the same basket. Imperfect mastery is a matter of degree—one's mastery of a concept is more or less imperfect. In section 18.2, I myself insisted that deferentiality is a matter of degree: there is, I said, a continuum of cases between the deferential use of a symbol which we do not understand and its normal use, between full mastery of a concept and total lack of that concept. In between we find instances of partial mastery—as in Burge's original example. Now this raises a problem for my account, Woodfield says, because

> It seems impossible that there should be a gradual process of moving out of quasi-quotes. It's clearly not a process of bit-by-bit removal (like taking one's clothes off), nor it is a process of decay (like quotation-marks fading away on a page as the ink loses its colour). The learner starts off using mental symbols like R_x['*synecdoches*'] and R_x['*kachna*'] and ends up using completely distinct symbols like *synecdoches* and *duck*.[8] Prima facie, there has to be a saltation—a switch of symbol-*type*—at some point. (Woodfield, forthcoming)

I grant Woodfield both points: first, that there is a difference between self-conscious deference and imperfect mastery; second, that the gradual nature of imperfect mastery makes it hard, if not impossible, to account for the transition from imperfect to full mastery in terms of a switch of symbol-type. The problem for my account is that such a switch is precisely what adding or removing the deferential operator brings about.

Faced with those difficulties, we might allow for the following possibility. Whenever we mentally entertain a sentence containing a symbol we do not properly understand, the deferential mechanism operates *as if* we had used the deferential operator, that is, as if we had put that symbol within quotation marks and deferred to some authority for its interpretation. But we don't have to actually use the deferential operator—the deferential interpretation can be provided by default, simply because no direct interpretation for the symbol is available to the subject. On this account the difference between conscious deference and incomplete mastery is syntactic, not semantic. In ordinary cases of incomplete mastery, the deferential shift takes place without being syntactically articulated.[9] Since that is so the continuum from incomplete to complete mastery no longer raises a problem. No saltation needs to be involved because the difference between normal and deferential use no longer lies at the level of the symbol-type. One and the same symbol-type is tokened in both cases. If that symbol is appropriately connected to some concept in the subject's repertoire, it expresses that concept and conveys its content. If the symbol is not appropriately connected to some concept in the subject's repertoire, the concept that is expressed is that which would be expressed by applying the deferential operator to that symbol. On this account, it is only to be expected that the process of connecting up a symbol with concepts in one's repertoire, hence the transition from deference to full mastery, will be gradual.

Though it is a step in the right direction, the foregoing account is not ultimately satisfactory, for it violates a principle which I put forward in §18.3:

Interpretation Principle

A mental sentence must possess a definite meaning (a character) even if it falls short of expressing a definite content.

If we accept this principle, then there is an incoherence in the revised account I have just sketched. We are to suppose that the subject entertains a mental sentence in which a symbol σ occurs. Whenever that symbol turns out to be uninterpreted by the subject's own lights, it receives a deferential interpretation by default. This violates the Interpretation Principle: for the so-called mental sentence will not be well-formed in the first place—it will *not* be a *mental* sentence—if it contains some uninterpreted symbol. Mental sentences must be constituted out of the right material—conceptual material. The symbols used in thought must be potential conveyors of content: they must be interpreted at least at the character level. That is what the Interpretation Principle requires. The role of the deferential operator was precisely to guarantee satisfaction of the Interpretation Principle. In the same way in which quotation marks can turn a non-word into a well-formed expression of English, the deferential operator can turn the uninterpreted symbol σ into a complex symbol $R_x[\sigma]$, which has a character and possibly a content. On the revised account, however, the uninterpreted symbol σ will acquire a character only when the deferential interpretation is provided by default. But this is too late: how will the uninterpreted symbol σ come to occur as a constituent in the subject's thought, unless it is already interpreted? This is a serious worry for anyone who accepts the Interpretation Principle.

I suggest that we revise the revised account so as to satisfy the Interpretation Principle. Let us not say that the deferential interpretation is provided by default when an uninterpreted symbol occurs in thought. According to the Interpretation Principle, no uninterpreted symbol *ever* occurs in thought. Still, we want to capture the fact that sometimes, in our thinking, we use a public word which we do not understand. In line with the Interpretation Principle, we want the word in question to receive a deferential interpretation from the very start; and we do not want this interpretation to affect the identity of the symbol-type, as the use of the deferential operator would do. These are the desiderata. To satisfy them, we must give up the Aristotelian view that words are labels associated with concepts. We must *construe words themselves as concepts*, which we can associate with other concepts (e.g., recognitional concepts). Thus, when we acquire a public word, whose use we do not yet fully master, we automatically acquire a concept.[10] The concept in question is deferential: its content is determined via the users whom we get the word from (or via the community in general). When we use a word we do not understand in our thinking, it is the deferential concept which occurs in our thought—hence the Interpretation Principle is satisfied. Again, the public word, insofar as we use it in thought, *is* the deferential concept, it does not have to be associated with a deferential or any other type of concept. In this account there no longer is a gap between the public word which occurs in thought and the deferential interpretation it receives: the deferential interpretation is a built-in feature of public words *qua* thought constituents.

What happens when (gradually) we come to understand the word in a non-deferential manner—when, for example, we get acquainted with what it applies to? We must not think of this process as the association of the word with a concept—an association which was lacking beforehand. Rather it is the association of two concepts: a deferential concept and another type of concept. This is the same sort of process which takes place when we recognize an object we have seen before: then a past-oriented demonstrative concept 'that object [which I saw the other day]' gets associated with a standard demonstrative concept based on current perception: 'that object [in front of me]'.[11] In such a situation typically the two concepts coalesce, are merged into a single recognitional concept, with a distinct character. Similarly, when a deferential concept —for example, Putnam's concept of an elm—gets associated with a non-deferential concept (e.g., the demonstrative concept 'that type of tree'), and that association stabilizes, a new concept results, with a distinct character. How is the merging process to be properly described? Does it, or does it not, involve a switch of symbol-type? However these questions are answered, there is no doubt that the merging process can be gradual, and that is all that matters for us.

19

Echoic Uses: A Unified Account

§19.1 Three Types of Echo

If I am right, metarepresentational embedding *per se* is innocent; it is a form of compounding, subject to the Inheritance Principle. That does not mean that the words in the embedded portion always take their normal semantic value: sometimes, I suggested, they take deviant semantic values. When that happens, however, that is because an independent process of context-shift has taken place, over and above the circumstance-shift effected through the metarepresentational operator.

In developing this view, our paradigm has been that of *mixed quotation*. In the formula

$\delta 'p'$

'δ' stands for a metarepresentational operator ('John believes that', 'In the film'), 'p' for a sentence, and the quotation marks indicate that the sentence in question, or a part of it, is mentioned (demonstrated) while in active use. Two distinct phenomena are thus brought together: metarepresentational compounding and echoic use.

Since mixed quotation is our paradigm, we'd better get clear how exactly echoic uses are to be analysed. Clarification is needed especially because three forms of echo, with strikingly different properties, have been distinguished so far. Corresponding to these three forms of echo, there are three varieties of mixed quotation.

First, we must distinguish between *cumulative* and *non-cumulative* echoes. In cumulative echoes the quoted material retains its ordinary semantic value in the echoic sentence, which entails the sentence obtained by removing the quotation marks. Thus (1) entails (1*), and (2) entails (2*):

(1)   That boy is really 'smart'.

(1*)   That boy is really smart.

(2)   Quine said that quotation 'has a certain anomalous feature'.

(2*)   Quine said that quotation has a certain anomalous feature.

Non-cumulative echoes are characterized by the fact that the echoic sentence does not entail the sentence which results from removing the quotation marks. In such cases the quoted material, though in active use, is not used with its normal semantic value but with a deviant semantic value. It is that deviant use which the quotation marks indicate. When we remove the quotation marks, we return to the ordinary interpretation: that blocks the inference from the echoic sentence to the disquoted variant.

The first example I gave of a non-cumulative echo is

(3)   'Quine' has not finished writing his paper

in which the name 'Quine' is not ascribed its normal semantic value (viz. Quine), but what some other person wrongly takes to be its semantic value. Thus interpreted, the sentence does not entail (4):

(4)   Quine has not finished writing his paper.

Sentence (3) means that *the person whom James mistakes for Quine* (viz. McPherson) has not finished writing his paper. This is obviously compatible with *Quine's* having finished writing his own paper. As I said in the chapter from which the example is extracted, "any word can, by being quoted in this echoic manner, be ascribed a semantic value which is not its normal semantic value" (p. 140). If James has a poor mastery of English and uses 'paper' in lieu of 'poster', I can ironically use (5) in the sense of (6):

(5)   Quine has not finished writing his 'paper'.

(6)   Quine has not finished writing his poster.

In the same category we find example (7), borrowed from Cappelen and Lepore:

(7)   My three-year-old son believes that I am a 'philtosopher'.

Since the echo occurs in the internal sentence within a metarepresentation, (7) is an instance of mixed quotation. As in the previous examples, the echo is non-cumulative; (7) therefore belongs to the category of non-cumulative instances of mixed quotation, characterized by the fact that the mixed-quoting sentence does not entail the sentence resulting from removing the quotation marks. (In the case at hand, the sentence which results from removing the quotation marks is not even grammatical—it contains a non-word).

Within the category of non-cumulative echoes, we must draw a distinction between two sub-categories. Examples like (5) or (7) are very different from examples like (8) below—also borrowed from Cappelen and Lepore (1997: 429).

(8)   Mr Greespan said he agreed with Labor Secretary R. B. Reich "on quite a lot of things." Their accord on this issue, he said, has proved "quite a surprise to both of us."

When I first came across that example, I found it somewhat infelicitous. Soon, however, I realized that it was structurally similar to a type of example commonly found in literary narratives—the type of example analysed in chapter 16. Sentence (9) below is a case in point:

(9)   Tomorrow, she thought, she would be relieved.

Examples like (9) do not contain quotation marks, yet they do involve some form of quotational intrusion (§16.5). Be that as it may, there is a lot in common between such cases and examples like (8). In both types of case a shift takes us from the actual context to a pretend context corresponding to the perspective of another agent. The indexicals 'us' or 'tomorrow' are interpreted with respect to the shifted context. Because of the contextual shift, these instances of mixed quotation are unambiguously non-cumulative. Thus the second sentence of (8) does not entail the disquoted form (10):

(10)   Their accord on this issue, Mr Greenspan said, has proved quite a surprise to both of us.

In (10) 'us' must refer to a group of people containing the speaker of (10). But (8) does not entail anything concerning the speaker of (10), nor of (8), for that matter.

Even though (8) and (9) are non-cumulative, they differ from (5) and (7) in that the quoted words—'tomorrow' in (9), and 'us' in (8)—retain their customary meanings: only the context of interpretation changes. These examples at least support a claim I made on p. 188 (with too much confidence) about quotation contexts in general:

> The quoted material ... retain[s] its standard meaning. In particular ... 'I' refers to the speaker, 'now' to the time of utterance, etc. (The only thing that changes is that the context which provides a speaker, a time of utterance, etc., is not the actual context of speech but the internal context projected by the quotation.)

Still, we can maintain that the examples in question, like non-cumulative echoes generally, exhibit some form of deviance. Let me define an echoic use as *weakly deviant* whenever the expression has its normal character but a deviant content. The reason why the content of the expression is not its normal content in such cases is that the context appealed to in determining the content is not the actual context of use but a pretend context. In contrast, an echoic use will be said to be *strongly deviant* whenever the expression does not even have its normal character; and *innocent* whenever it has both its normal character and its normal content.

Cumulative echoes are or at least seem to be innocent.[12] 'Trans-linguistic' cases such as those discussed in §18.1 are strongly deviant. Thus in (5) and (7), the word takes up a new meaning: 'paper' is used with the sense of 'poster', and 'philtosopher' is used in the sense of 'philosopher' (a sense which it does not have in English, since it is a non-word in that language). In both cases a shift takes us from the actual context (in which the ordinary rules of English apply) to a pretend context in which deviant semantic rules apply. This is in contrast to (8) or (9), where the words retain their normal character and only the content deviates as a result of context-shift.[13] Such cases I call 'conservative'.

Our task is to provide a unified account of the three sorts of echo, and of the three varieties of mixed quotation corresponding to them: cumulative, translinguistic, and conservative. This involves two subtasks. First, we must provide a unified analysis for the two non-cumulative varieties, namely translinguistic and conservative echoes. Second, we must show that that analysis can be extended to cumulative echoes as well.

To account for conservative cases I posited a context-shifting function d which maps the original character ch of the expression onto a distinct character ch^* such that, for any context k in its domain, $ch^*(k) = ch(k')$, where k' is a context obtained by shifting some aspect of the initial context k (§17.2). When the context-shifting function operates, the content of the expression in context k is determined by running its character against the shifted context k'. Since $k \neq k'$, the content thus determined is usually not the normal content of the expression (with respect to k), i.e., the content that would be determined by running the character directly against k. It is a deviant content.

As I pointed out in §18.1, that analysis does *not* apply to translinguistic cases. In translinguistic cases the actual character of the expression does not matter: we don't evaluate the actual character against a shifted context (as we do in conservative cases), but we evaluate a deviant, shifted character against the actual context. To account for those cases we must appeal to the *deferential operator* (§18.4). Thus (5) and (7) can be represented as:

(5*)   Quine has not finished writing his $R_{\text{James}}[\text{paper}]$.

(7*)   My three-year-old son believes that I am a $R_{\text{my son}}[\text{philtosopher}]$.

The expression in the scope of the deferential operator assumes a deviant character, namely the character which that expression has for the person to whom the speaker defers (James in (5), the speaker's son in (7)). It is that character which determines the content of the expression, in the context at hand. Since the character in question is distinct from the normal character of the expression in ordinary English (*if* the expression has a character in ordinary English), the content thus determined will, in all likelihood, also deviate from the normal content of the expression.

The contrast between conservative and translinguistic cases can be described in two ways. We can say (as I have done) that in conservative cases we shift the context and run the normal character of the expression against the shifted context; whereas in translinguistic cases we shift the character and run it against the normal context. Or we can say the following: In both conservative and translinguistic cases a context-shift occurs, but in translinguistic cases the shifted feature of the context is the language itself. Both descriptions are legitimate, and there is no contradiction in accepting both of them. The appearance of conflict betwen the two descriptions vanishes when we realize that two distinct notions of context are involved. The notion of context appealed to in the second description is broader than the notion of context used in the first description. The main advantage of the second description is precisely that, by suitably enlarging the notion of context, it gives us what we need to arrive at a unified analysis of non-cumulative echoes in terms of context-shift. Such a unified analysis will be offered in §19.4, after defending the enlarged notion of context against its critics (§19.2–3).

The next step regards cumulative echoes. They have been contrasted with non-cumulative echoes by the fact that they do not involve a context-shift and are therefore innocent. But there is a tension between that characterization of cumulative echoes, and the general character-ization of quotation (*oratio recta*) in terms of context-shift (§12.2). For echoic uses in general, and instances of mixed quotation in particular, are evidently quotational. How, then, could they not involve a context-shift? That difficulty will be addressed in §19.5. It will be argued that even in cumulative echoes, a context-shift occurs, which leaves the con-tent of the expression untouched. That shift will be accounted for within the unified framework set up for dealing with conservative and trans-linguistic cases.

§19.2   Real Contexts and Kaplanian Contexts

I have suggested that in both conservative and translinguistic cases, a context-shift occurs. In conservative cases the context at issue is the context in the standard sense familiar from semantic theory: it consists of a speaker, a place and a time of utterance, etc. In translinguistic cases the shift takes us from the actual context of use to a pretend context in which different semantic rules apply. The context at issue therefore con-tains the language used by the speaker in issuing the relevant expression. (The word 'translinguistic' itself means that we move from one language to another.) According to some semantic theorists, these are two distinct notions of context which should not be conflated in theorizing about how utterances are interpreted. In this section I present their argument; I will reply in the next section.

A context of utterance, in a first, *pragmatic* sense, is a (thick) situation in which a linguistic expression is issued for communicative purposes. In such a situation, there is an agent who issues the expression, an addressee, a place and a time of utterance, etc. but there are also an indefinite number of features which the situation possesses, as any concrete situation does. Among these additional features some, like the beliefs and other attitudes of both the speaker and the addressee and the language spoken, are directly relevant to the interpretation of the utterance. Many other features, like the colour of the speaker's shirt, may be quite irrelevant—they simply happen to be aspects of the situation of utterance.

A second notion of context is that which is relevant to semantic theorizing. The context in that second sense (the semantic sense) is that in virtue of which *an expression already endowed with a linguistic meaning* expresses a definite content. Here we presuppose a particular language and the meaning which that language bestows upon the expression. Which language that is depends upon the context (in the first, pragmatic sense) but when dealing with context in the semantic sense we take that aspect of the richer context for granted and we look for those aspects of context which specifically take us from linguistic meaning to truth-conditional content.

Many semanticists hold that the context in the semantic sense is less rich than the context in the pragmatic sense: it is not a complete situation of utterance, but something more abstract, a package of those features of the pragmatic context which determine the contents of expressions, on the basis of their conventional meanings (Kaplan 1989b: 591). Such a package I call a 'Kaplanian context' because I interpret Kaplan as actually propounding such an abstract view of contexts.[14] A Kaplanian context contains a speaker (since we must know who the speaker is to determine the reference, hence the content, of the word 'I' in English), a place and time of utterance (because those factors determine the content of the English words 'here' and 'now'), a possible world (because the modal adverb 'actually' is likewise indexical), and perhaps a few other features of the context in the pragmatic sense, necessary to determine the content of indexical expressions in the language. Just as there is a finite list of expressions whose content is not fixed directly by the conventions of the language but depend upon the context, there is a list of those contextual features on which the content of these expressions depend. The context in the semantic sense can be equated with such a list or package, that is, with a Kaplanian context—so the argument goes.

Kaplanian contexts are not concrete situations of utterance, but they bear a close enough relation to them. A proper Kaplanian context exhibits certain patterns or satisfy certain constraints without which it would not be suitably related to actual situations of utterance and would not qualify as 'context' in the first place. (Those constraints are the basis for Kaplan's distinction between contexts and circumstances; for circumstances of evaluation are not so constrained.) Thus Kaplanian contexts, for the reasons I mentioned, contain an agent, a place, a time, and a possible world. Such a context will be 'proper', Kaplan says, only if the agent is located at the place and time in question in the possible world in question. For the agent is supposed to be the speaker, the place the place of utterance, the time the time of utterance, etc., and there can be no context in which the person who utters the sentence is not located at the place where the sentence is uttered when it is uttered. By virtue of this a priori constraint on Kaplanian contexts, a sentence like 'I am here now' turns out to be a logical truth in Kaplan's system. It is true with respect to all Kaplanian contexts.

Even though Kaplanian contexts exhibit certain patterns without which they would not qualify as contexts, however, they are not intended to capture *all* the regularities which are characteristic or even constitutive of situations of utterance. For example, there is no context in the pragmatic sense if the 'agent' does not make an utterance, but Kaplan does not attempt to capture that regularity by suitably constraining his abstract contexts: on the contrary, he explicitly accepts as proper contexts in which no utterance is made (1989b: 584–585). As a result the sentence 'I say nothing' does not count as 'false in every context', in Kaplan's system. (Though it *is* false in every context in the pragmatic sense.) This reflects the more abstract nature of Kaplanian contexts, which mimick only certain aspects of pragmatic contexts.

What about the language to which the uttered expression belongs? Is it a feature of the Kaplanian context? Obviously not. Kaplanian contexts contain only aspects of the pragmatic context on which the reference of indexical expressions specifically depend, and the language being spoken is not among those aspects. As a result 'There is no language' no more counts as false in every context, in Kaplan's system, than 'I say nothing' does.

To sum up, if Kaplan is right there are two distinct notions of context: the context in the pragmatic sense, which is a concrete situation of utterance, and the context in the semantic sense, or Kaplanian context, which is a package of contextual factors extracted from the context in the first sense. While conservative context-shifts can be handled by appealing to the semantic notion of context, translinguistic context-shifts cannot be so handled. So it is unclear that we can work with a unified notion of 'context-shift' in dealing with both translinguistic and conservative cases.

§19.3   The Context-Dependence of Context-Dependence

I agree that there are two distinct notions of context—the full situation of utterance (context in the pragmatic sense) and whatever takes us from the linguistic meaning of a sentence-type to its truth-conditional content (context in the semantic sense). Yet that distinction should not be overstated. It is a distinction at the *conceptual* level. The two *notions* of context are different; but that does not prevent the two contexts themselves from being identical. Just as the difference between our respective notions of Hesperus and Phosphorus does not prevent Hesperus from being Phosphorus, it may turn out, as a matter of empirical investigation, that the context in the semantic sense *is* the context in the pragmatic sense. In other words, we may discover that what we need in order to go from the meaning of a sentence-type to whichever content it expresses is nothing short of the full situation of utterance, with all it concreteness. That is precisely the view I hold. It is an alternative to the standard view according to which contexts in the semantic sense are Kaplanian contexts. It follows that there are *three* distinct notions—the context in the pragmatic sense, the context in the semantic sense, and the Kaplanian context—and two opposing views: one which equates context in the semantic sense and Kaplanian context, and another one which equates context in the semantic sense and context in the pragmatic sense.

Yet the theorists who equate context in the semantic sense and Kaplanian context tend to think of that identity as more or less a priori —they think the two *notions* are identical. Remember how I defined the context in the semantic sense: it is that in virtue of which an expression *already endowed with a linguistic meaning* expresses a definite content. The language to which the expression belongs is an aspect of the context in the rich, pragmatic sense, but when dealing with context in the semantic sense we take it for granted. There may be other aspects of the context in the pragmatic sense which we thus take for granted, while indefinitely many other aspects are simply ignored as irrelevant to the determination of content. Since the context in the semantic sense is, by definition, what we get when we consider *only* those aspects of the richer context which take us from the linguistic meaning of the sentence (considered as fixed) to its truth-conditions, the notion of context in the semantic sense arguably reduces to that of Kaplanian context. The context in the semantic sense consists of those aspects of the richer context on which the content of indexical expressions depend, and nothing else: now what is a Kaplanian context, if not a package of precisely those contextual factors?

But there is a hidden presupposition behind that conflation of the two notions. It is this: that we can *selectively list* the features of the richer context on which the contents of expressions depend. That presupposition is encapsulated in the following statement, which I made above in presenting what I take to be Kaplan's view:

Definiteness Assumption

Just as there is a finite list of expressions whose content is not fixed directly by the conventions of the language but depend upon the context, there is a list of those contextual features on which the content of these expressions depend.

Now this is quite wrong. The content of an expression already endowed with a linguistic meaning can depend upon *any* feature of the rich pragmatic situation. Hence, even if it is true by definition that the context in the semantic sense is what we get when we consider *only* those aspects of the pragmatic context which take us from linguistic meaning to content, still it can be argued that the context in the semantic sense is the context in the full pragmatic sense: for *every* aspect of the richer context can be relevant in determining the content of an expression (already endowed with a conventional meaning).

What I have just said does not conflict with the obvious point I made earlier: that some aspects of the pragmatic context, for example the colour of the speaker's shirt, may be quite irrelevant to the interpretation of the utterance. Certainly, in most contexts, the colour of the speaker's shirt will play no role in fixing the content of the speaker's utterance. But in some contexts that contextual feature will possibly play such a content-fixing role. That is crucial: we don't know in advance, and certainly we cannot list, those aspects of pragmatic context on which the contents of expressions can still depend, once their meaning has been fixed. Why is that so? Because *the features of context which are relevant to content-determination themselves depend upon the context.* That is the main point which partisans of Kaplanian contexts systematically overlook. Charles Travis, who made it forcefully by means of a plethora of examples, argues that the Kaplanian view rests on an illegitimate interchange of quantifiers (Travis 1981: 50). We shift from

(11)   For every utterance *u*, there is a proper subset of features of the pragmatic situation in which *u* occurs ('contextual features', for short) such that the content of *u* is a function of those features

which is correct as far as it goes, to

(12)   There is a proper subset of contextual features such that, for every utterance *u*, the content of *u* is a function of those features

which is not.

What Travis' examples show is that the contextual parameters on which content depends are not determined solely by the conventions of the language. In some cases they are: there is no doubt that for indexical expressions, the dependence of the content of the expression on some aspect of context is encoded in the linguistic meaning of the expression itself. But context-dependence goes well beyond indexicality in that sense. Contrary to what the Definiteness Assumption presupposes, it is not true that "there is a finite list of those expressions whose content is not fixed directly by the conventions of the language but depend upon the context." There is no such list. *Any* expression is such that its truth-conditional content can vary according to context. In some cases (indexical expressions) that context-dependence of content is encoded. But if we fix the reference, hence the content, of indexical expressions in a sentence endowed with a linguistic meaning, the content of that sentence will still depend upon the context in ways which are not encoded in the meaning of the sentence but which themselves depend upon peculiarities of the context.

I know that the claims I have just made will sound extraordinary and perhaps unbelievable to many semantic theorists who may not have considered the issue of context-sensitivity in natural language seriously enough. I cannot attempt to argue for those claims here, for that would require detailed analyses of examples and would therefore take us too far afield. I can only refer the readers to the work of Charles Travis (1975, 1981), John Searle (1978, 1980), Julius Moravcsik (1998), and others who have made similar points. Also relevant here are the arguments of Cresswell (1973) and others (including especially Lewis 1980) to the effect that the contextual features on which content depends cannot be listed in advance. The Cresswell-Lewis conclusion is that we need full contexts—contexts in the pragmatic sense—to adequately account for the context-dependence of content.

Assuming that what I have said is right, there are two things we can do with Kaplanian contexts to make them palatable. First, we can *relativize them to context*, in accordance with (11) above. Thus relativizing Kaplanian contexts amounts to holding (against Kaplan) that characters themselves are not fixed by the conventions of the language but somehow depend upon the context. That is indeed a conclusion which I accept: there is a principled distinction to be made between the linguistic meaning of a sentence-type and its character (or rather, the character of an utterance of the sentence). The character of an utterance depends upon which parameters are relevant to fixing the content of that utterance and that, I have claimed, itself depends upon the context. Note that Kaplan himself is willing to decouple linguistic meaning from character when the sentence at issue contains a demonstrative: he holds that a sentence in which a demonstrative occurs has no character (though it has a linguistic meaning in the traditional sense) before it has been completed by a demonstration.

In order to forestall confusion I will call relativized Kaplanian contexts 'contextual indices'. The problem with contextual indices is their lack of uniformity. Different parameters occur in different contextual indices. If we find uniformity desirable for theoretical purposes, we can stick to (unrelativized) Kaplanian contexts and use them as 'pointers' to real contexts. Thus a Kaplanian context consisting of an agent a, a time t, and a possible world w will stand for a concrete situation, namely a situation in which some utterance is made by a at t in w (Lewis 1980: 85–86; Haas-Spohn, forthcoming, §1.2). *That* situation will possess countless other features. Understood in this way, Kaplanian contexts are fine. But then it can no longer be argued that a context in that sense does not contain a language parameter: it does contain such a feature, since it is only a stand-in for a concrete situation of utterance which does.

§19.4   Deference and Context-Shift

Let us take stock. There are three distinct functions which the pragmatic context plays in providing a (literal) interpretation for an utterance:[15]

i. It determines which language is spoken and thereby fixes the *linguistic meaning* of the utterance.

ii. It determines the parameters of context which are relevant to content-determination (i.e., the contextual index) and thereby fixes the *character* of the utterance.

iii. It provides values for those parameters and thereby fixes the *content* of the utterance.

As I have no more to say about the distinction between linguistic meaning and character in this chapter than I have already said, I will simplify matters by lumping (i) and (ii) together under the heading of 'character determination'. Context will therefore be considered as playing two roles: character determination and (given a character) content determination.

When an expression σ is uttered in a context c in a normal communication situation, there is a pragmatic function P which determines the character of σ (with respect to c): $P(\sigma, c) =$ character. To get the content of the utterance we apply the resulting character to the context, which therefore comes into the picture a second time: $P(\sigma, c)(c) =$ content. In this formula there are two occurrences of the letter 'c' corresponding to the two functions of the context: character-determination and content-determination.[16]

We can abbreviate the above formula '$P(\sigma, c)(c)$' as follows: $P^*(\sigma, c)$. The function P^* takes an expression and a context as arguments, and applies to the context the character which the expression has (or would have) in that context. In terms of P^*, we can easily define a *context-shifting operator* O such that

(13) $P^*(O\sigma, c) = P^*(\sigma, c')$

where c' is a pretend context. (13) says that the content of the expression $O\sigma$ in a context c is the same as the content of σ in the context c'. To determine the content of $O\sigma$ in c we must shift the context from c to c' and evaluate σ in c'.

The context-shifting operator O works like the deferential operator, with one difference. The deferential operator as it has been characterized in chapter 18 shifts the context only in its character-determining role. To interpret an expression σ in the scope of the deferential operator, in a context c, we shift the context to c' (a pretend context in which deviant semantic rules apply), take the character which σ has in c', and *apply it to the initial context c*. That is,

(14) $P^*(R_x[\sigma], c) = P(\sigma, c')(c)$

This is very different from the context-shift which occurs in (13). By our definition of P^*

(15) $P^*(\sigma, c') = P(\sigma, c')(c')$

Equations (13) and (15) entail

(16) $P^*(O\sigma, c) = P(\sigma, c')(c')$

We see that O is a *generalized* context-shifting operator. It shifts the context in its two roles (as the replacement of both occurrences of 'c' in the right hand side of the equation shows). But that is not what we want. What we want, in order to arrive at a unified analysis of context-shift, is an operator which shifts the context *either* in the manner of d (as in conservative cases), *or* in the manner of the deferential operator (as in translinguistic cases). In the first type of case, we take the character which σ has in the actual context, and determine the content by applying that character to the shifted context. With the deferential operator, we do just the opposite: we take the character which the expression has in the shifted context and run that character against the actual context.

What we need, therefore, is a *selective* context-shifting operator D. With such an operator, there will be two ways of getting from an expression σ in its scope and a context c to the content of $D[\sigma]$ in c: either by shifting c in its character-determining capacity, or by shifting it in its content-determining capacity. That means that no unique content will be determined unless we have specified the relevant aspect of the context which must be shifted.

Since the function P^* takes only two arguments (an expression and a context) we provide the required aspect parameter by subscripting the selective context-shifting operator itself in the same way in which we subscripted the deferential operator with a variable standing for the person to whom we defer. Indeed we can consider the selective context-shifting operator D as a variant of the deferential operator. Or rather, the original deferential operator is only a special case of D, where it is the character-determining aspect of the context which is specified as relevant. What I am putting forward, therefore, is a reanalysis of the deferential operator, which makes it fit to account for conservative cases as well as for translinguistic cases.[17] From now on, when I use the phrase 'the deferential operator', I mean the operator D. Whatever was said in terms of the original deferential operator R can be said by means of D: we have only to set the aspect parameter of D so as to indicate that it is the character-determining features of the pragmatic context that are shifted.

The new deferential operator can be characterized by means of two clauses, a pragmatic clause and a semantic clause. Let us consider them in turn.

Pragmatic clause

A use of the deferential operator $D_{x,m}$ is felicitous only in a context in which there is tacit or explicit reference to some agent's way of using the expression σ in its scope.

I define a 'way of using' an expression σ as a *class of contexts* characterized by some feature m which contexts in that class possess—language spoken, spatio-temporal location of the agent, or whatnot. The way of using σ contextually referred to is given through one of the two parameters which subscript the operator D. The other parameter corresponds to the person x to whom we defer, that is, to the person whose way of using σ is in question.[18]

As I have suggested, the two sorts of context-shift are to be accounted for in terms of the relevant feature m: $P^*(D_{x,m}[\sigma], c) = P(\sigma, c')(c)$ or $P(\sigma, c)(c')$, depending on how we instantiate the variable m. In translinguistic cases the class of contexts is defined by the language spoken in those contexts; in conservative cases it is defined by the spatio-temporal location of the agent (table VI.2).

Let us now turn to the other clause:

Semantic clause

The character of $D_{x,m}[\sigma]$ is that function from contexts in which the felicity condition is satisfied, to the contents which the symbol σ has when used in the relevant ways.

There is an obvious problem with that clause. It mentions 'the' content which the expression has when used in the relevant way. But how is that content determined? Since a 'way of using' an expression is a *class* of contexts, characterized only through some feature which contexts in that class possess, it is not determinate enough to fix the content of the expression used in that way. What is needed to fix content is a full context, not a class of contexts (§19.3).

To solve this problem, we have only to reflect that the shifted context c' is arrived at through counterfactual thinking: c' is the context as it

Table VI.2
Translinguistic versus conservative cases

Translinguistic cases	Conservative cases
$P^*(D_{x,L}[\sigma], c) = P(\sigma, c')(c)$	$P^*(D_{x,k}[\sigma], c) = P(\sigma, c)(c')$
('L' is the language feature of the context)	('k' is the spatio-temporal location feature of the context)

would be if σ was used in the relevant way. Now it is a general feature of counterfactual suppositions that, in making and interpreting them, we massively rely on the actual state of affairs to flesh them out. In the present case, we can gain determinacy by appealing to the actual context wherever needed. The way of using σ referred to by the speaker provides *some* contextual features—that which is specified through the subscript *m*, together with those which follow from it; the other features necessary to fix content are inherited from the actual context. In other words: we start with some initial context c and shift some feature(s) of c in accordance with x's way of using σ. That is how we get to c'.

§19.5 Cumulative Echoes: A Reanalysis

Using the new deferential operator, we can construct a fully general account of mixed quotation and other echoic uses. So far I have shown how non-cumulative echoes, whether strongly or weakly deviant, can be dealt with in terms of it. We must now turn to *cumulative* echoes to see whether and how they can be accounted for.

In cumulative echoes the content of the demonstrated expression does not deviate. Thus in

(1) Quine said that quotation 'has a certain anomalous feature'

the words within quotation marks contribute the same thing as they would if we removed the quotation marks. The demonstration also contributes something over and above what is contributed by the demonstrated expression, but that is an *additional* component of meaning, on the 'cumulative account' presented earlier (§14.3): it does not substract anything from the normal import of the demonstrated words. That is why the mixed-quoting sentence entails the disquoted variant.

In §19.1 I jumped to the conclusion that cumulative echoes are innocent. In so doing I assumed that the threefold distinction I then made was exhaustive:

Innocent: Neither the character of the expression nor its content deviates.
Weakly deviant: The content deviates but not the character.
Strongly deviant: The character and (therefore) the content deviate.

If we assume that this threefold classification of uses is indeed exhaustive, we are led to infer that a use is innocent whenever the content of the expression does not deviate. But is the assumption of exhaustivity correct? I do not think so. There is a fourth option, which should be seriously considered: the character of the expression may deviate while its content remains normal.

Suppose we apply the deferential operator D to a symbol σ of our own language, thereby mapping the character of σ onto a metalinguistic character, while referring to a user x whose way of using σ is not relevantly different from ours. That is, suppose the class of contexts corresponding to x's way of using σ is characterized by a property m which the actual context happens to possess. In such a case the shift will be vacuous: we defer to an agent x who uses the words in such a way that they express the same content in x's mouth as they would in ours, if we used them non-deferentially. The content of $D_{x,m}[\sigma]$ is therefore the normal content of σ—there is no deviance at the content level. Yet *that content is expressed under a metalinguistic character*—the character of $D_{x,m}[\sigma]$.

That is arguably what happens in cumulative echoes. Our only reason for maintaining that no context-shift occurs in cumulative echoes was the fact that the content of the relevant expression is non-deviant. On the other hand, the claim that no context-shift occurs in such cases is inconsistent with the general characterization of quotation in terms of context-shift. We now see a way out: context-shift there is, but it is vacuous—it does not affect the content of the utterance.[19] What it affects is its character. The character of $D_{x,m}[\sigma]$ is different from the character of σ even if they determine the same content in the actual context c. The two characters are different because there are counterfactual contexts with respect to which they do *not* determine the same contents. Such would be contexts in which the agent x to whom the speaker defers does not use σ in the way he or she actually does, i.e., in conformity to the speaker's own usage, but in a deviant manner.

20
Mixed Quotation and Opacity

§20.1 Cumulative Mixed Quotation: Two Analyses

The analysis of cumulative echoes offered in §19.5 straightforwardly applies to cumulative mixed quotation—indeed the example of cumulative echo I used in that section was an instance of mixed quotation. But the resulting approach to cumulative mixed quotation is significantly different from that which I advocated in earlier chapters. A detailed comparison is in order, which will shed new light on the phenomenon of opacity.

Earlier I approached cumulative mixed quotation in terms of *contextual enrichment*. Contextual enrichment is what takes place in interpreting an utterance like (1):

(1) She took out her key and opened the door.

We naturally understand the second conjunct of (1), 'she opened the door', as meaning that she opened the door with the key mentioned in the first conjunct. Let us assume a context in which that is indeed the right interpretation. The use of the key is not explicitly mentioned in the second conjunct; it is only contextually implied. Although pragmatic and contextual, however, that aspect of the meaning of the utterance is truth-conditionally relevant; or so I would argue. I take the truth-conditions of an utterance to be what those who understand the utterance in question *recognize* as being its truth-conditions.[20] In the case of (1), whoever understands the utterance (on the intended interpretation) recognizes that it is true iff the person referred to took out her key and opened the door with that key. What I call 'contextual enrichment' is the same phenomenon which others call 'unarticulated constituency' and still others 'pragmatic intrusion'[21]: sometimes a contextual implication of an utterance—something which is contextually suggested without being linguistically encoded—finds its way into the truth-conditions of the utterance and becomes an aspect of 'what is said'. Contextual enrichment in that sense is to be distinguished from conversational implicatures, which remain external to what is said and do not affect truth-conditions (Recanati 1989, 1993, 1995a).

Let us see how the notion of contextual enrichment applies to cumulative mixed quotation. In our paradigm example,

(2)   Quine said that quotation 'has a certain anomalous feature'

the words 'has a certain anomalous feature' are demonstrated while they are used. *Pace* Davidson, they are not referred to by means of a singular term—they are merely demonstrated, i.e., the speaker draws the hearer's attention to them while using them (§13.3). The words themselves (demonstration aside) express a certain proposition, namely the proposition that Quine said that quotation has a certain anomalous feature. To that basic meaning the demonstration adds something more. By stressing the words he uses in phrasing his report, the speaker implies that the reportee (Quine) used those very words. As with (1), this aspect of meaning, although to a large extent pragmatic and contextual, finds its way into the truth-conditions of the utterance. The utterance will not be true if Quine said something to that effect but used very different words.

It is that analysis which I applied to opaque belief reports. On the opaque reading 'John believes that *S*' is enriched into 'John believes that *S in this manner*'. A particular 'way of believing', closely related to the words used in phrasing the report, is implicitly ascribed to the believer (§11.4). The transparent/opaque ambiguity for belief reports is therefore an ambiguity between the minimal reading and a contextually enriched reading of the sentence. As I pointed out earlier, this analysis of opacity in terms of contextual enrichment is similar to the so-called 'hidden-indexical theory' (Schiffer 1977, Crimmins and Perry 1989).

An interesting consequence of that analysis is that, even though the content of the demonstrated expression is non-deviant, the content of the global utterance *is* affected by the demonstration: it is contextually enriched. Thus the truth-conditions of (2) are not the same as the truth-conditions of the disquoted variant, even though the words in the sentence have the same content whether or not the demonstration occurs. As I stressed above, (2) is not true if Quine said that quotation has an anomalous feature but used totally different words to say it. Sentence (2) implies that Quine said that *in that manner*—using those very words. A similar enrichment of truth-conditional content is responsible for failures of (intensional) substitution in opaque attitude reports.

Let us now turn to the new analysis of mixed quotation—that which follows from the proposal in §19.5. The notion of a contextual enrichment of content is no longer appropriate, or so it seems. What the demonstration contributes is *a context-shift which affects only the character of the utterance*. On the new analysis, the mixed-quoting sentence expresses the *same* proposition as the disquoted variant, but under a metalinguistic character. Similarly for opaque belief reports, construed as cumulative instances of mixed quotation: the content of the report is the same on both readings of the report, only the character changes.

Which analysis should we prefer? That is a difficult choice. In §19.5, I gave reasons to favour the new analysis. The notion of a vacuous context-shift is what we need to unify the analysis of echoic uses. On the other hand, there are good reasons for considering the contextual implication as constitutive of truth-conditional content in cases like (2) or opaque belief reports as well as in the case of (1). In support of that view there is not only my doctrine concerning the 'availability' of what is said, but also and especially what happens when we embed the utterance under some operator like negation. The relevant aspect of meaning then *is* part of the proposition which is negated. Thus if I say 'Lois does not believe that Clark Kent can fly' the way of believing associated with the name 'Clark Kent' is clearly part of the content which Lois is said not to believe. Similarly, I may negate (2) and thereby deny that Quine used those very words. Such facts are straightforwardly explained on the contextual enrichment picture.

Fortunately, there is no necessity for us to choose between the two analyses; we can accept them both. It is not because we realize that the demonstration affects the character of the utterance (new analysis) that we must give up the view that it also affects its content (earlier analysis).[22] The view we arrive at if we accept both analyses is the following: in cumulative mixed quotation, the normal content—i.e., the content which is shared with the 'disquoted' or 'minimal' variant—is expressed under a metalinguistic character (as the new analysis has it) *and at the same time* contextually enriched (as in the earlier analysis).

The view I have just adumbrated rests on a still more complex analysis of the phenomenon of echoic use than I have offered so far. Beside the distinctions between cumulative and non-cumulative echoes, and between weakly and strongly deviant non-cumulative echoes, it turns out that we can and should appeal to a third distinction, between echoes with enrichment and echoes without enrichment.

§20.2   Echoes with and without Enrichment

In cumulative echoes, the content of the echoic utterance is the same as that of the disquoted variant, but it is expressed under a metalinguistic character. On the more complex view I am now putting forward, two sorts of case must be distinguished within that category: in some cases the context-shift which affects character will be accompanied by an enrichment of content, in other cases it will not (table VI.3).

When I first introduced echoic uses, in Chapter 10, I implicitly characterized cumulative cases—cases in which the demonstrated expression is used with its normal semantic value—as cases in which the truth-conditions of the utterance are not affected by the demonstration (in

Table VI.3
Echoic uses and truth-conditions

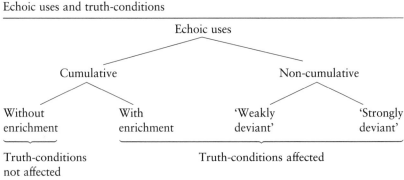

contrast to what happens in non-cumulative cases). The example I gave was

(3)   That boy is really 'smart'

in which the adjective 'smart' is used echoically. The truth-conditions of this utterance are arguably the same as the truth-conditions of the disquoted variant (3*):

(3*)   That boy is really smart.

In Frege's terms, the difference beween (3) and (3*) is one in 'colouring': (3) *evokes* something which (3*) does not, yet they *say the same thing*. But it is not true that cumulative echoes in general do not affect truth-conditions. (3) is an example of a particular sort of cumulative echo, namely cumulative echoes without enrichment. Yet there is another sub-category: cumulative echoes where the truth-conditions of the utterance are affected by the demonstration, as a result of contextual enrichment. Davidson's example (2) is a case in point.

It may seem that there is a contradiction between saying that echoic uses of the cumulative variety affect only the character of the demonstrated expression (§19.5), and saying that, in some cases of cumulative echo, the truth-conditions (hence the content) of the utterance are affected. But the apparent contradiction vanishes as soon as one draws a distinction between the content of the expression at issue and the content of the utterance in which it occurs. Cumulative echoes affect only the character of the demonstrated expression: the character of the demonstrated expression is mapped onto a metalinguistic character which (in the context at hand) determines the same content—hence the content of the expression is *not* affected. Still, the content of the global utterance may be affected. That is so whenever the content of the global utterance is enriched as a result of the demonstration. Thus in (2), the demonstration suggests that Quine used those very words, and that suggestion gets incorporated into the truth-conditional content of the utterance.

The classification in Table VI.3 is still to be completed. Not only are there two types of cumulative echo: with or without enrichment; we find exactly the same contrast between two types of non-cumulative echoes, for example between (4) and (5) (from Chapter 15):

(4) 'Quine' has not finished his paper.

(5) James says that 'Quine' has not finished his paper.

In both cases the demonstrated name 'Quine' is used in James' manner and deferentially refers to McPherson. Both (4) and (5) are non-cumulative echoes, with a deviant content. But in (5) the truth-conditions of the utterance are affected by the echo, not only, as in (4), through the deviant use of the demonstrated expression, but also through some form of enrichment. The deviant use of the name 'Quine' which the speaker of (5) deferentially echoes is understood as part and parcel of the reported utterance. As a result, James' actually saying that McPherson has not finished his paper is not sufficient to make (5) true. (5) will be true only if James said so *using the name 'Quine' to refer to McPherson.*

Since the contrast between two types of echo (with or without enrichment) applies both to cumulative and non-cumulative echoes, our classification takes the form of a matrix: it turns out that there are *four types of echo* (figure VI.1). Now mixed quotation is a particular case of echoic use, namely the case in which the echo occurs in the internal sentence of a metarepresentation. As examples (2) and (5) show, mixed quotation can be either cumulative or non-cumulative. What about the other distinction, between echoes with enrichment and echoes without enrichment? Can it be found also in connection with mixed quotation? Are there instances of mixed quotation that are of types 1 and 3, just as there are instances of type 2 and 4? How we answer that question depends on how we define mixed quotation. If we define it strictly—more strictly than I have just done—I think the answer must be negative: There are no instances of mixed quotation (strictly understood) of types 1 and 3.

On a strict definition, mixed quotation is not merely an instance of echo occurring in the internal sentence of a metarepresentation. For there to be mixed quotation in the strict sense, *the echoed person must be the same person to whom a thought or utterance is ascribed in*

	Without enrichment	With enrichment
Cumulative	Type 1	Type 2
Non-cumulative	Type 3	Type 4

Figure VI.1
Four types of echoes

the metarepresentation. That condition is not satisfied in the following example from chapter 15:

(6) The chairman believes that 'Quine' has not finished his paper.

Here the echoed person is James (who mistakes McPherson for Quine), while the ascribee is the chairman (who does not mistake McPherson for Quine and does not even know that James does). This is not an instance of mixed quotation in the strict sense. But (5) is one, because the believer is also the person whom the speaker echoes when he uses the name 'Quine' to refer to McPherson.

I think that there is no mixed quotation in the strict sense without an enrichment of content. When the target of the echo—the x to whom the speaker defers in using a particular expression σ in quotes—is the ascribee, e.g., the person who is reported to have said that p, two things happen. First, it is suggested that the expression σ was used by x in making the reported utterance. Second, that pragmatic suggestion gets incorporated into the content of the utterance: the utterance is understood as true if and only if x said that p using the expression σ. Why is the suggestion automatically incorporated into the (intuitive) truth-conditional content of the utterance in this type of case, but not in others, is a difficult question which cannot be addressed, let alone answered, in passing. Here I simply record what I take to be a fact concerning mixed quotation—a fact which a proper theory of enrichment should explain.

§20.3 Opacity without Echo

According to our final account two things happen in (cumulative) mixed quotation. First, an expression is used echoically in the internal sentence of a metarepresentation. The speaker defers to the ascribee and uses the expression in his or her manner. The character of the expression is thereby affected and made metalinguistic. Second, that echoic use triggers a process of pragmatic enrichment affecting the overall content of the metarepresentation. This generates opacity. If we replace the relevant expression by another one with the same semantic value, at least the *demonstratum* will be changed, and the suggestion concerning the ascribee's way of thinking or speaking will accordingly be modified. Since that suggestion has been incorporated into the report's truth-conditional content, the truth-value of the report will itself change.

The two processes we have distinguished must be kept separate even though in mixed quotation they come together; for they are independent processes. Not only can there be echoes without enrichment, as we have seen. There can also be metarepresentational enrichment without echo.

Sometimes enrichment takes place because it is *contextually clear* what the ascribee's way of thinking is. As I put it in *Direct Reference*,

Very often, when someone's belief about a particular object is reported, it is contextually manifest which representation (or 'notion') of that object the belief involves—how the believer thinks of that object; it is therefore possible for the speaker to ascribe a belief content which includes that notion, without explicitly specifying the notion in question, simply because the context supplies it. (Recanati 1993: 372)

In such cases enrichment takes place *without being triggered by the speaker's demonstrating some expression which he or she uses.* It takes place simply because it is contextually manifest what the ascribee's way of thinking/speaking is, without there being any need for the speaker's demonstratively replicating that mode of presentation in her own speech.

If this is right, enrichment can proceed from several sources. One likely source is the linguistic expressions which the speaker uses in reporting the belief or utterance. It is that source which is tapped when the speaker demonstrates an expression: she thereby suggests that that expression captures the ascribee's way of thinking or speaking. But the extralinguistic context may be sufficient by itself to make manifest what the ascribee's way of thinking/speaking is. It is examples of the latter sort that have been focussed on by Richard and Crimmins and Perry in their insightful discussions of belief reports.

It might be replied that no *opacity* can be generated by thus tapping extralinguistic sources of enrichment. The argument runs as follows. Whenever the suggestion which gets incorporated into the utterance's truth-conditional content is independent from the expressions used in phrasing the report, those expressions must be freely substitutable, since they merely serve to express the content of the ascribed belief without being responsible for the pragmatic suggestion concerning the vehicle of the belief. The pragmatic suggestion concerning the vehicle arises from the context, not from the words, hence it must survive a change of words. It follows that whenever opacity arises—whenever substitutivity fails—the enrichment at issue must be echoic and have a linguistic source.

But that argument is flawed. Remember what I said earlier about the context-dependence of context-dependence (§19.3): not only does the content of particular utterances depend upon specific features of the context, but which aspect of the context the content of a particular utterance depends on also depends upon the context. Now which expression the speaker chooses to use is an aspect of the context understood in the broad sense (the pragmatic context). If we change the context under that aspect, that may well have an effect on the features which will be relevant to determining the content of the utterance. So, even if in the actual context it is not the referring expression used by the speaker (say, the pronoun 'he') but some aspect g of the extralinguistic context which is primarily responsible for the pragmatic suggestion concerning the vehicle of the ascribed belief, that fact itself—the fact that g has a pragmatic effect on content, which the choice of a particular referring expression does not have—is context-dependent and may no longer hold if we change the context by changing the expression. Thus if we replace the pronoun 'he' by a coreferential expression like 'Prince Tudor', it will perhaps no longer be the case that the contextual feature responsible for whatever is suggested concerning the vehicle of the belief is g rather than the referring expression used by the speaker. That shows that pragmatic enrichment is likely to cause failures of substitutivity even if the source of enrichment is extralinguistic.

I conclude that we do not have to treat as echoic all cases in which a (truth-conditionally relevant) suggestion is made concerning the original vehicle of the ascribed content. We may even go further and refrain from systematically treating as echoic cases in which the suggestion concerning the vehicle is borne by the words used by the speaker in expressing the ascribed content. We should rather distinguish between two sorts of case within that category: cases in which the words used by the speaker, by themselves, are sufficient in that context to trigger the enrichment process, and cases in which *the speaker* draws the hearer's attention to the words he uses by demonstrating them. It is only in the last type of case that the notion of mixed quotation applies.

§20.4   Sources of Opacity

In Chapter 8, I distinguished two sorts of substitution failure in meta-representations, hence two sorts of opacity in the broad sense. One sort involves the interchange of expressions with the same extension. That such substitution should fail in metarepresentational environments is not surprising. Since the metarepresentational prefix shifts the circumstance with respect to which the internal sentence is evaluated, there is no reason why an expression within the internal sentence should be freely replaceable by another expression having the same extension in the *current* circumstance (i.e., the circumstance of evaluation for the whole metarepresentation). What is relevant for evaluating the internal sentence is not the current circumstance, but the shifted circumstance introduced by the prefix.

The form of 'opacity' I have just mentioned is displayed by all sentences introduced by a circumstance-shifting prefix. The other sort of opacity involves the interchange of expressions with the same *content*. The failure of that type of substitution is characteristic of metarepresentations as opposed to other sentences introduced by circumstance-shifting prefixes. Because that is so, it has been argued that metarepresentational prefixes are such that the semantic value of expressions in their scope is not their normal semantic values. The analogy, stressed by Quine, is with quotation marks.

As against this traditional view, I argued that metarepresentational prefixes are semantically innocent: they do not impose a special reading on the expressions in their scope. There is no difference in that respect between metarepresentational prefixes and other circumstance-shifting prefixes. This claim seems to conflict with the observation that the second type of opacity characterizes metarepresentations as opposed to other circumstance-shifting environments; but it does not really. Meta-representational prefixes are like other circumstance-shifting prefixes from the *semantic* point of view: they shift the circumstance for the evaluation of the internal sentence, and do only that. What is specific to metarepresentations is the fact that they provide an environment hospitable to various pragmatic processes affecting the interpretation of the utterance. These processes often take place in connection with metarepresentations (as opposed to other circumstance-shifting environments), but they are not part of the semantic contribution of the metarepresentational prefix. If they were, they would always take place in metarepresentations, hence metarepresentations would always be understood as opaque. But that is not the case. Metarepresentations can be (understood as) fully transparent. Moreover, opaque readings are never imposed by the sentence itself, in virtue of its linguistic meaning. Even if it is wildly implausible, there is always the possibility of a transparent reading for any given metarepresentation.[23]

I mentioned two pragmatic processes jointly or singly responsible for the second sort of opacity. First, there is free enrichment. Among the theories of opacity competing on the philosophical market, the so-called hidden indexical theory appeals to an equivalent notion: that of an 'unarticulated constituent' (Crimmins and Perry 1989). The expressions in the scope of the metarepresentational prefix have their normal contents; but the content of the global utterance is enriched by incorporation of a pragmatic suggestion. As free enrichment is a highly context-sensitive process, substitution failures are easy to account for. Substituting an expression for another one with the same content changes the context for the interpretation of the sentence—since the words used by the speaker are as much part of the context of utterance as anything else. That change in the context of utterance may have an effect on the aspect of meaning generated through free enrichment.

The second pragmatic process responsible for opacity is deference. By deferring to others we shift the context for the interpretation of some expression we use. Unless the shift is vacuous (as in cumulative mixed quotation), it will affect the content of the expression at issue. This generates opacity: Deferentially interpreted, an expression has the content it would have in the shifted context; hence it cannot be replaced by an expression which has the same content in the *current* context.

Pragmatic enrichment brings about opacity without any violation of innocence. Deference (in non-vacuous cases) brings about a violation of semantic innocence, but that violation cannot be blamed on the metarepresentational prefix. In both cases, the pragmatic process responsible for opacity is distinct and independent from the semantic process of circumstance-shifting effected by the metarepresentational operator.

Notes

Part I

1. This formulation is adapted from Russell 1940: 260.

2. Actually we need even more levels than that. Contents (Fregean senses) can be interpreted in two different ways: as unstructured 'intensions', in the sense of contemporary model-theoretic semantics, or in the sense of 'structured contents' (see footnote 6). As Cresswell (1985) has shown, structured contents themselves can be analysed as structures made up of intensions. In what follows I will generally use 'content' in the sense of 'structured content'. We need a further distinction between 'linguistic meaning' and 'character', for in many cases (e.g., demonstratives) the linguistic meaning of an expression underdetermines its character in Kaplan's sense (functions from contexts to contents). So we really need (at least) five levels: linguistic meaning, character, intension, content, and extension.

3. In 'Opacity' (1986), Kaplan stresses the similarities between Frege's and Quine's respective strategies.

4. A similar worry was expressed by Jonathan Cohen in his first book (Cohen 1962: 186): "How unfortunate it would be if, as Frege's theory implies, we could never report exactly what a man said! How unfortunate if somehow, through the very act of trying to report him in indirect speech, our words were forced to bear a different meaning from his!"

5. This gives some support to Arthur Prior's claim that "nothing could be more misleading and erroneous than to treat sentences containing ... other sentences in quotations-marks as a paradigm case to which the things that we are really interested in (thinking that, fearing that, bringing it about that) should be assimilated" (Prior 1971: 61). See footnote 16 below.

6. David Lewis, who treats propositions as unstructured 'intensions' in a possible-worlds framework, constructs a distinct notion, that of 'meaning', in terms of which iconicity can be captured. Meanings *are* structured entities, in Lewis's framework (Lewis 1970). A similar move is made in Cresswell (1985).

7. It follows that "thinking about others' thoughts requires us ... to think about the states of affairs which are the subject-matter of those thoughts" (Heal 1998: 484).

8. In Dummett's terminology, a phrase like 'Leibniz's Law', which picks out a thought, "does not *express* that thought, since it is possible to understand the phrase without knowing which thought it picks out" (Dummett 1993: 173). Dummett does not mention 'that'-clauses in that passage, but I don't see how he could deny that a 'that'-clause expresses the thought it picks out. Mark Richard similarly argues that 'that'-clauses *articulate* the propositions they refer to, while phrases like 'Leibniz's Law' do not (Richard 1993).

9. Phrases like 'Leibniz's Law'—"substantival phrases which have grown capital letters," as Strawson says—are somehow intermediate between names and descriptions (Strawson 1977: 21). Their semantics raises interesting problems which I will presently ignore.

10. The distinction beween mention of form and mention of content appealed to in figure I.1 is due to Sperber and Wilson (1981: 305). Their distinction between 'interpretation' and 'description' corresponds to the distinction between iconic and non-iconic representation (see, e.g., Sperber and Wilson 1986: 224–231).

11. It can be argued that genuine names of propositions are bound to be iconic, for the only way of being 'acquainted with' a proposition is by grasping it (see Recanati 1986: 227–33).

12. If an expression is semantically complex, then arguably it is not a genuine singular term but a quantifier (Neale 1993; see also Lepore and Ludwig 2000, where it is claimed that complex demonstratives are best treated as restricted existential quantifiers in which a demonstrative appears in the nominal restriction). For a contrary view see Richard 1993.

13. Of course that is not the only option available: we may also elaborate the account and make it more and more sophisticated. In this book, however, I want to start with our iconicity intuitions, and build an account which pays due regard to them, rather than start with the standard account and make whatever amendments are needed to pay lip-service to these intuitions.

14. Because of an analogous principle at the level of reference, Frege was led to embrace the paradoxical thesis that "the concept of horse is not a concept" (Frege 1970: 45–48). "A concept is the reference of a predicate," not the reference of a singular term, Frege says; hence the reference of the singular term 'the concept of horse' cannot be a concept—it must be an object. Frege's view will be discussed in §3.3–4.

In contemporary formal semantics in the tradition of Montague, the Heterogeneity Principle does not seem to play any role. To be sure, the semantic values (or 'intensions') of names, predicates, sentences etc. are said to fall into distinct domains: for example, the semantic value of a name will be a thing, the semantic value of a predicate a function from world-time pairs to sets of things, the semantic value of a sentence a function from world-time pairs to truth-values, etc. But the distinction between these domains is not ultimate, because *everything is a thing*, including functions from world-time pairs to sets of things or to truth-values. Nothing, therefore, prevents a name from referring to (hence from having as semantic value) the very thing which is the semantic value of a sentence. That is precisely what happens with 'that'-clauses, according to standard model-theoretic accounts: the intension of a 'that'-clause is the same as the intension of the embedded sentence. (See below, §2.4.)

15. Kaplan suggests that, whenever the reference of a directly referential term B is the content m of a non-directly referential term A, the content of B is not m, but $\{m\}$. Thus the reference of B (and the content of A) is m, but the content of B is $\{m\}$. This amounts to 'marking' the object places of a singular proposition by some operation which cannot mark a complex (Kaplan 1989a: 496). In this way we guarantee that the content of a genuine singular term will always be simple, even if that term directly refers to a complex content.

16. This approach to quotation was first mentioned (with approval) by Arthur Prior (1971: 60–61). He writes:

Some ... would say that the quotation-marks are *demonstratives* which point to their interior, so that ' "The cat sat on the mat" has nineteen letters' is rather like 'The cat sat on the mat ← This has nineteen letters'. I incline to this view myself; and certainly if it is the correct view it is easy to classify the illusion involved in treating ' "The cat sat on the mat" has nineteen letters' or ' "The cat sat on the mat" was uttered by John' as compound sentences with 'The cat sat on the mat' as a component. This is simply the illusion of seeing two sentences as one, because they happen to stand in an interesting relation to one another.

Note that, for Prior, *oratio obliqua* sentences like 'John says that the cat sat on the mat' *are* genuine compounds with 'The cat sat on the mat' as a component. (See §13.5 below.) Hence Prior's conclusion, mentioned above (note 5), to the effect that "nothing could be more misleading and erroneous than to treat sentences containing ... other sentences in quotations-marks as a paradigm case to which the things that we are really interested in (thinking that, fearing that, bringing it about that) should be assimilated" (Prior 1971: 61). In that respect Davidson's extension of the 'two-sentence theory' to *oratio obliqua* sentences is rather unfortunate.

17. According to Schiffer (1987: 133–5), that already goes too far. If Davidson's analysis was correct, Schiffer argues, it would be possible to understand a belief report without understanding the complement sentence.

18. This, of course, is not exactly what Davidson says. According to Davidson, the demonstrative 'that' in 'John believes that S' does not refer to the *content* of the utterance which follows the demonstrative, but to the utterance itself. Yet, for Davidson (as I understand him), to say that 'John believes that', where 'that' refers to the utterance, *is* to say that a certain belief of John's *has the same content as* the utterance in question.

19. This means, in particular, that logical form should match grammatical form as closely as possible. Jackendoff mentions traditional (first-order) quantificational renderings of natural language sentences as an example where the Grammatical Constraint is blatantly violated (Jackendoff 1983: 14).

20. In this paragraph I rely on Orenstein (forthcoming).

21. This should be qualified. 'Believes' *can* be construed as a two-place predicate in the logical sense, if it is a higher-level predicate. See §3.3 below.

22. The analogy should not be pushed too far. There is an obvious grammatical difference between the two sentences 'John believes that grass is green' and 'According to John, grass is green'. Only in the latter is 'grass is green' the main clause. A proper semantic treatment, respectful of the Grammatical Constraint, should account for this difference; but that does not mean that we should go back to the treatment of 'that'-clauses as straightforward singular terms filling an argument slot in a first-level predicate.

23. See Russell (1956: 233) for discussion of an analogous example.

24. The reason for that is not that sentences can themselves be construed as 0-place predicates. Sentences are no more predicates than they are singular terms referring to truth-values. As Dummett pointed out, there is something "unique" about sentences, and Frege's doctrine that they are a species of complex name was "desastrous" (Dummett 1973: 196). Tarski's doctrine that sentences are a species of predicate fares no better in that respect (Evans 1977: 262). Rather than attempt to reduce sentences to either names or predicates, we should admit that there are three basic categories: terms, predicates, and sentences. In such a framework, once it is accepted that quantification extends to predicates and need not be objectual, there are no good reasons to reject Prior's suggestion that sentences too can be quantified. (For a detailed presentation, and a defense, of Prior's views regarding quantification, see Hugly and Sayward 1996; see also Williams 1981: chapter 8. For a contemporary elaboration, see Grover 1992. For a critique, see Richard 1996.)

25. Strawson denies this, as we shall see. But the higher-order approach, interpreted *à la* Strawson, is undistinguishable from Bealer's first-order approach (§3.4).

26. As Moltmann points out, "NPs with *thing* are exempt from the objectivization effect. Such NPs can always refer to or quantify over semantic values that are merely expressed and do not act as proper objects" (Moltmann 1997: §4). Thus we can say 'John is something which I am not, namely Australian', without reifying ('objectivizing', in her terminology) the property of being Australian. That is clearly not equivalent to 'John is *some property* which I am not, namely Australian'. In the same spirit, Moltmann emphasizes the fact that NPs with *thing* can always replace a 'that'-clause *that S* even when it cannot be replaced by the corresponding nominal *the proposition that S* (see §3.2). Thus we can say 'He expected that grass would grow', and 'he expected something' (or 'he expected the same thing as me'), but not (or not in the same sense) 'He expected the proposition that grass would grow'.

27. Surprisingly, it seems that Bealer himself accepts that point or something very similar. To see that, let us compare his first-order representation of the statement '*x* is red and red differs from blue' with the standard higher-order representation (Bealer 1982: 90):

Higher-order: $R(x)$ and $R \neq B$
First-order: $x\Delta r$ and $r \neq b$

In Bealer's first-order approach the copulative function is fulfilled by a two-place predicate Δ meaning 'exemplifies'. The concept-word 'red' thus turns out to be a singular term referring to a property. In other words, it is not merely when a predicate becomes subject that it is converted into a singular term. Even in a sentence like 'This apple is red', 'red' is construed as a singular term. Bealer thus accepts the claim that no conversion occurs. *The general term does not shift from one category to another when it becomes subject.* That is because it was already a singular term even before it became subject.

28. Or not much. Reification may turn out to be a matter of degree, as Vendler has suggested with his distinction between 'perfect' and 'imperfect' nominalizations. See Vendler 1967: chapter 5.

29. One possible reaction to this argument consists in rejecting it as flawed. Propositions, one might say, are not genuine 'objects'—at least not on the operator analysis. To say that John believes that S is not to say that a certain 'object' (the proposition that S) has a certain 'property' (the property of being believed by John). Hence, the objector might pursue, we cannot use the law that identical objects have all their properties in common to conclude, from the fact that the proposition that S is the same as the proposition that S', that John must believe that S' if he believes that S. Indeed we *know* that S and S' cannot be freely substituted under 'John believes that' even though they express the same proposition.

Such reaction would rest on a serious mistake. As Prior pointed out (1971: 53 ff), even if we do not reify propositions—even if we do not treat them as genuine objects—we can talk of propositional identity. Propositional identity itself may be construed as an operator. Thus we can use the dyadic operator $I =$ 'the proposition that ... is identical to the proposition that ...'. That connective makes a sentence out of two sentences, and the resulting sentence is true whenever the constituent sentences have the same content. In terms of this operator it will be possible to formulate laws of propositional identity similar to the ordinary laws of identity: *Every proposition is identical to itself* (that is, 'For every p, the proposition that p is identical to the proposition that p'), and *Identical propositions have all their properties in common* (that is, 'If the proposition that p is identical to the proposition that q, then δp if and only if δq'). The argument against hyperintensionality will therefore be statable without begging the question against the operator analysis.

30. A suitably qualified version of the Principle of Substitutivity can be found in Marcus 1993: 108.

Part II

1. See, e.g., Sperber and Wilson (1981: 306–311), Ducrot (1984: 210–213), Clark and Gerrig (1984), Walton (1990: 222–224), Perrin (1996: ch. 5), Clark (1996: 371 ff).

2. Bally describes the conditional in French as the 'mood of potentiality', as opposed to the indicative, which the mood of actuality (Bally 1965: 49).

3. That phrase comes from Leslie (1987), but I use it freely here.

4. This example comes from Dinsmore (1991: 84 ff). Dinsmore stresses the analogy between the simulative approach, inspired by Fauconnier's work on 'mental spaces' (Fauconnier 1985), and the use of assumptions in natural deduction.

5. See also Pratt (1990: 369) where the above type of reasoning is described as 'reasoning within the scope of an imagined cognitive predicament'.

6. These two things can easily be distinguished within a modal framework of the type described at the beginning of this chapter. See chapters 5 to 7 below.

7. Mackie 1973: 93; Ducrot 1972: 167–68. Similar theories of 'conditional assertion' can be found in Quine 1962: 12; von Wright 1963; and Belnap 1970. See also the 1971 symposium on Conditional assertion (with articles by D. Holdcroft and P. Long) in the *Proceedings of the Aristotelian Society*, suppl. vol. 45: 123–147.

8. Quine's position concerning indicative conditionals in natural language is different. The statement which is made 'under the supposition' is a genuine assertion, for Quine, just in case the antecedent is true. When the antecedent is false, "our conditional affirmation is as if it had never been made" (Quine 1962: 12). Thus indicative conditionals with true antecedents are true or false, while indicative conditionals with false antecedents are neither true nor false.

9. Ducrot (1972: 180) mentions one such example, but he does not seem to realize that it raises a problem for the simulation theory strictly understood.

10. This example and the following are borrowed from Lemmon 1965: chapter 1.

11. Unfortunately, as well shall see in §6.3, this distinction is not sufficient to account for the late emergence of conditionals and full-blown metarepresentations; for something very much like the more complex ability arguably also underlies overt pretense.

12. Retrojection is a special form of 'reflection' (§5.2).

13. One may be reluctant to construe the time as an argument of the relation, even though it is 'articulated' through the present tense. I cannot go into this issue here.

14. The polarity is useful because situations are partial. We cannot say that a situation supports a negative fact $\neg\sigma$ iff that situation does not support the fact σ; for a partial situation may well support neither σ nor $\neg\sigma$. So we cannot handle negative facts in the way we handle other molecular facts (i.e., through clauses like: 'A situation supports σ & σ' iff it supports σ and supports σ''). Hence the suggestion that there are two sorts of (atomic) facts: negative and positive. On this view there is no fact without a polarity. As an alternative to that type of treatment, we may consider that a situation is (associated with) a set of possible worlds (viz. all the worlds which realize the 'factual set' of the situation—see

below). A situation will be said to support a fact σ iff that fact holds in all the worlds in question. A situation will be said to support a negative fact $\neg\sigma$ iff the (positive) fact σ holds in none of the worlds in question. (Criticism of the possible-worlds approach to situations can be found in Perry 1986a and Barwise 1989: chapter 4.)

15. I owe this observation to R. Stalnaker.

16. We could also leave the support relation unrelativized and enrich the left-hand-side of the relation with a world parameter. Instead of '$s \vDash_w \sigma$' we would write: '$\langle s, w \rangle \vDash \sigma$'. The ordered pair $\langle s, w \rangle$ is what I will later refer to as a *thick* situation (a 'circumstance'). See §7.5 below. But the relation between thick situations and the facts which hold in them is not quite the support relation I've tried to characterize so far. The relation between *thin* situations and the facts they support is contingent; not so with thick situations. (If we used the alternative notation I have just suggested, we could of course easily define the relation between facts and thin situations in terms of the more basic relation between facts and thick situations.)

17. As Ingvar Johansson says, "ordinary things *are* states of affairs" (Johansson 1989: 34). I am indebted to Kevin Mulligan for drawing my attention to (and lending me) Johansson's book. Armstrong, who claims that every state of affairs is a particular, does not go as far as to acknowledge that particular themselves are states of affairs, but his notion of a 'thick' particular is a step in that direction (Armstrong 1997: §8.3).

18. Is it the case that a situation s support the fact that $\sigma \vee \sigma'$ iff s supports σ or s supports σ'? Maybe, but maybe not. One may argue that for a situation to support a disjunctive fact $\sigma \vee \sigma'$, each of the disjuncts must be 'defined' with respect to the situation, i.e., such that the situation either supports it or supports its negation. If that is the case, then, for a situation s to support the fact that $\sigma \vee \sigma'$, s must either support both disjuncts or support one of the two disjuncts and the negation of the other.

19. Although in this book I help myself freely to notions like 'belief world', 'fictional world', and so forth, I am aware that, because of their partiality, such 'worlds' cannot really be worlds because they are not sufficiently determinate: they too must ultimately be thought of as *sets* of worlds (see e.g., Hintikka 1973: 199; Ross 1997: 49–54).

20. One distinguishing characteristic of free indirect speech, as opposed to genuine indirect speech, is its hospitability to untransposed occurrences of indexicals. See chapter 16.

21. This is a first shot. An improved analysis will be provided in chapter 7.

22. This too will be qualified below (§6.4).

23. Note that the domain of a situation s (the set of entities which s comprises) may reach beyond the domain of the world to which s itself belongs. That will be so whenever the factual set of s, with respect to a given possible world w_1, contains a fact σ internally indexed to some other possible world w_2, i.e., whenever s

is or involves a 'representation' endowed with content. (In such cases the comprise relation between the representation and the imaginary situation it represents is not a genuine relation but a pseudo-relation.) This goes against treating worlds themselves as situations.

24. When we think of a situation/entity *e* as comprising other entities and containing facts involving them, we construe it *both* as an entity and as a situation: see §6.4 below.

25. On quantificational facts and what it is for a situation to support such a fact, see Recanati 1999: §4.1–2.

26. Bühler distinguishes two sorts of simulative presentification: either the subject mentally experiences the imagined situation as if that situation was actually present around him—as if it was (a part of) the *hic et nunc* situation; or he experiences the imagined situation as if his egocentric coordinates were displaced to that situation—as if he himself was in that situation:

To put it in the manner of a parable, either Mohammed goes to the mountain or the mountain goes to Mohammed. . . . What is imagined, especially when movable things such as people are concerned, often comes to us, that is, into the given order of actual perception, within which it can be localized, though not quite "seen." . . . The imagined thing that appears to the mind's eye . . . can receive a place in front of, next to or behind me, located directly among the things in the room in which I am, among the things that I in part perceive, in part imagine. . . . The exact opposite occurs in the second type, in which Mohammed goes to the mountain. . . . One is displaced in imagination abruptly, suddenly to the geographical place of what is imagined, one sees what is imagined in front of one's mind's eye from a certain reception point which one can identify and at which one is situated in imagination. If one turns around in imagination, one sees what was behind one's back, if one walks on, one sees the things again in imagination as one once saw them when really walking there. (Bühler 1934: 150–151)

Bühler mentions various experiments in support of this distinction and at several points refers to Jakob Segal's in-depth study of mental simulation (Segal 1916).

27. As the analytic philosopher A. M. MacIver pointed out in his pioneering paper on context-sensitivity (also written in the thirties), the use of names is ultimately grounded in the egocentric situation and must be resolvable into some deictic reference to entities given to our senses. Thus the proper name 'James Baldwin' can be explained as follows, MacIver says: "You see this bit of ground that we are now standing on. Well, it is part of a much larger piece of ground called England, which is all under one government; and the present executive head of that government is a man called Stanley Baldwin" (MacIver 1936: 32).

28. See, e.g., Cohen (1986), Ostler and Atkins (1992), Nunberg et Zaenen (1992), Pustejovsky (1995).

29. Here 'belief states' are construed holistically (as a person's total belief system at a given moment). But it may be preferable not to do so. On a non-holistic construal, belief states are like mental sentences in the belief box. If we take this line, we should represent 'John believes that *p*' not as

John's belief state $\models_@ p^j$

but as:

$(\exists x)(x$ is a belief-state $\&\ x$ belongs to John $\&\ x \models_@ p^j)$

30. One might think that, if the complex sentence is uttered in the living-room of the house, it will be true in the initial circumstance c consisting of the living room, the present time, and the actual world, iff S is true in a different circumstance c' resulting from shifting the place of c from the living-room to the kitchen. But that is not quite right. The exercised situation cannot be the living room—it must be an *expansion* containing both the living room and the kitchen (§6.5), for example the house. The initial circumstance with respect to which the complex sentence is evaluated will therefore consist of the house, the present time, and the actual world. The (unexpanded) situation of utterance can still play a role as *secondary* exercised situation, however. (This notion corresponds to what Barwise and Perry (1983) call a 'resource situation' and Recanati (1996) calls a 'local domain'). Thus in a statement like 'Three kilometers on the left, there is a huge castle', the exercised situation is an expansion containing both the place of utterance and the place where the castle is located, but the location of the castle itself is relative to the situation of utterance. Three spatial situations are therefore involved in the interpretation of this example. The phrase 'three kilometers on the left' is evaluated with respect to the place of utterance s_1: 'three kilometers on the left' is understood as 'three kilometers on the left of s_1'. The place thus determined is a situation s_2 where the castle is located (if the utterance is true). The complete sentence 'Three kilometers on the left, there is a huge castle' is evaluated with respect to an expansion s_3 containing both s_1 and s_2. It is true with respect to s_3 iff the internal sentence, 'There is a huge castle' itself is true with respect to s_2.

31. Among the characters I include the narrator and the (fictional) reader.

Part III

1. This does not mean that John entertains those very words; he may be *indirectly* related to them. As Quine pointed out, the difference between the direct-discourse form 'John says/thinks *Grass is green*' and the indirect-discourse form 'John says/thinks that grass is green' need not be construed as a difference in the *relata*: it may be construed as a difference in the relation. Thus 'John says that grass is green' can be analysed as 'John says-the-same-thing-as-I-would-say-if-I-were-now-to-utter: *grass is green*'. The words 'grass is green' are mentioned, much as they are in direct reports, but the relation between the ascribee and the words is indirect.

2. The criterion of singularity I have just used can be stated as follows:

(A)   A belief (or a statement) is singular iff:
There is an x such that the belief (or the statement) is true iff … x …

Both Forbes and Quine strongly objected to that criterion, so I must respond briefly to their criticisms before proceeding. (Forbes's and Quine's reactions were directed at a first version of this material, presented in the middle section of my paper 'Opacity and the Attitudes'.)

Forbes objects that the criterion is too weak. "If all we require is the same truth-value on the two sides of the 'iff' every true belief is singular since ... *x* ... can just be *x* = *x*" (Forbes, personal communication). But the second line in the criterion ('There is an *x* such that ...') must be understood as characterizing the *intuitive* truth-conditions of singular statements or beliefs. Now even if 'Cicero was bald' happens to be a true statement, expressing a true belief, that belief is not, intuitively, true iff Forbes is Forbes.

Quine objects that "if this is just meant to require that the belief contain some singular term, represented here by '*x*', then 'the shortest spy' is not excluded" (Quine 2000: 429). But a descriptive belief concerning 'the shortest spy' would not count as singular by (A), unless we use the description referentially (see below). If Robert Sleigh believes or asserts that 'the shortest spy is *F*', we cannot say that there is an object *x* such that Sleigh's belief or statement is true iff *x* satisfies *G*, whichever predicate we put in place of the schematic letter '*G*'. In particular, we cannot say that a certain person, namely Helen (who happens to be the shortest spy), is such that Sleigh's belief is true iff *she* is *F*. The condition 'being the shortest spy' must also be satisfied by her. Nor can we say that Helen is such that the belief is true iff she is both *F* and the shortest spy. Intuitively, *any* person's being *F* and the shortest spy—be it Helen or anybody else—would suffice to make the belief true. So the belief is not, intuitively, true *if and only if* Helen has those properties.

3. To say that they have a non-deviant referential use is compatible with saying that their referential use is not their normal semantic function. If their referential use was their normal semantic function, their non-referential uses would themselves be deviant. In Recanati (1993) I claimed that attributive and referential uses of descriptions are *both* non-deviant. (In contrast, only purely referential uses of singular terms are non-deviant.)

4. "If we say that there is someone of whom Othello believes that she is unfaithful, while we do not thereby put *ourselves* into any relation with anyone except Othello, we do thereby say that there is someone with whom *he* stands in the relation of believing her unfaithful" (Prior 1971: 135).

5. In 1956 Quine said that exportation—the step from '*a* believes that *t* is *F*' to '*a* believes of *t* that it is *F*'—"should doubtless be viewed in general as implicative" (Quine 1956: 190). Afterwards he was moved by the Sleigh/Kaplan example of the shortest spy (Sleigh 1968; Kaplan 1968): if exportation is valid, then we can go from 'John believes that the shortest spy is a spy' to '($\exists x$)(John believes *x* is a spy)', via 'John believes of the shortest spy that he is a spy'; but if that is accepted, an obviously notional belief report is treated as if it were relational. As Quine concludes, "we must find against exportation" (Quine 1977: 9). Indeed, insofar as exportation opens the way to existential generalization, it is clear that exportability must be restricted to those cases in which the relational reading is intuitively appropriate. It cannot be treated as generally permissible.

Still, I think Quine was right in the first place: exportation *is* generally valid, provided *t* is a genuine singular term. In the Sleigh/Kaplan example, it isn't. Of course, exportation also works when *t*, though not a singular term, is given scope over the epistemic operator. But that is not the case in the Sleigh/Kaplan example either. In the Sleigh/Kaplan example Ralph is said to accept 'The shortest spy is a spy'; he is not said to believe, of some particular individual known to him (and described by the speaker as 'the shortest spy'), that he is a spy.

6. Sentence (11) can also be interpreted as short for 'In the story, Santa Claus lives in the sky' (Lewis 1978). On that interpretation (11) is a metafictional statement, like (10).

7. I said earlier that the two distinctions are *orthogonal*. As Graeme Forbes noticed, that entails not only that some reports are both relational and opaque, but also that some are both notional and transparent. Forbes objects that "notional transparent examples ... will be tough to find if what makes them notional is that the subject's ways of thinking are adverted to" (Forbes, personal communication). But what defines a report as notional is not the fact that the believer's ways of thinking are adverted to (*that* characterizes opacity), but the fact that the reported belief is general rather than singular. An example of a notional-transparent report would be: 'James believes that the shortest oculist is shorter than the shortest spy', in a situation in which (i) the reported belief is clearly general (James is not acquainted with the shortest oculist), and (ii) the noun 'oculist' is known to be unknown to James, who only uses 'eye-doctor'. (To be sure, it is part of the standard notion of a 'notional' belief report, inherited from Quine, that the believer's ways of thinking are adverted to. If I am right, however, 'notional' in *that* sense cannot be opposed to 'relational'.)

8. Opacity could be handled in terms of scope if we admitted that some operators shift the 'context' rather than the circumstance of evaluation. Such operators are called 'monsters' in Kaplan 1989a. See chapters 12 to 17 for an extended discussion of that option.

9. I am using 'Wychnevetsky' as an arbitrary name for the word 'cat'.

10. As I pointed out on p. 8, the expression in question may differ from the enclosed word in gender or number. In ' "Cats" is plural', the first word of the sentence is singular, but the mentioned word ('cats') is indeed plural.

11. In §17.2, following Richard Grandy (1990), I will offer a different analysis of that sort of example. I will argue that the word 'cat' in (3) is not used deviantly, but normally. What is deviant on that use is only the character assumed by the *sentence*, not the character assumed by the individual word 'cat'.

12. The autonymous word need not be taken as self-referential, of course. Instead of having the word refer to itself, we can insist that it is the complex expression (word plus quotation marks) or the pair of quotation marks (construed as a demonstrative, in the manner of Prior (1971: 60–61) and Davidson (1979)) which refers to the quoted word.

13. The expression 'echo' (or 'echoic use') comes from Sperber and Wilson (1981). See also Rey-Debove (1978: chapter 6), Recanati (1979: chapter 4) and Davidson (1979: 80–81) for early studies of such uses.

14. In Recanati (1987: 63) I offered an example involving a definite description:

Hey, 'your sister' is coming over.

In that example the person who is coming over is not actually the addressee's sister, but is thought to be the addressee's sister by some person whom the speaker is ironically mimicking.

15. See Fine 1989: 221–5 for an analogous observation. Fine's excellent paper anticipates many of the points made in this chapter, including the distinction between the 'narrow' and the 'broad' contribution made by a term to the truth-conditions of the sentence in which it occurs (§10.4).

16. In Quine's framework, the first type of case (the case in which it is the singular term itself which is used non-purely referentially) can be reduced to the second type of case (the case in which it is the context or the position that generates opacity). For Quine takes an autonymous word to be a word that occurs in a special linguistic context, viz. 'within quotation marks'. Quine can thus get rid of non-purely referential occurrences or uses altogether and handle opacity entirely in terms of positions. Opaque or non-purely referential positions are linguistic contexts (e.g., quotation contexts or reflecting contexts) such that a singular term in that context is not subject to the Principle of Substitutivity. In this way a uniform treatment is provided for ' "…" is a three-letter word' and '… is so-called because of his size'. (Even so, there remains a big difference between the two types of case. In the first context the singular term is not used referentially—it is deviant—while it is used with its normal referential function in the second context.)

17. As Kit Fine has shown, we can make any non-referential occurrence of a singular term similarly substitutable merely by forming the disjunction of the sentence where it occurs with '$2 + 2 = 4$' (Fine 1989: 218).

18. See Forbes 1990; Crimmins 1992; Recanati 1993. The first after Quine himself to have drawn attention to the analogy between belief sentences and 'Giorgione' sentences was Brian Loar in his 1972 article.

19. Brian Loar also uses the word 'frame' in his 1972 article, but in a different sense.

20. That is, in effect, the 'hidden indexical theory' of belief reports, the first formulations of which can be found in Linsky (1967: 113) and Schiffer (1977: 32–33).

21. There are also cases in which the embedded sentence plays no role at all in that imputation. In §20.3 we shall see that not all forms of opacity (but only those that are 'echoic') can be analysed in the manner suggested in this chapter.

22. This counterfactual circumlocution is necessary because the speaker herself need not be Ψ-ing in uttering the embedded sentence.

23. Some will hasten to conclude that only the transparent reading is relevant to semantics, since semantics is supposed to deal with literal meanings and 'minimal' interpretations, without considering 'speaker's meaning'. (See, e.g., Salmon 1986.) I disagree. If we want our theory to keep in touch with our intuitions, we cannot disregard those aspects of meaning resulting from enrichment. Moreover, when we embed an utterance, we see that the aspects of meaning which result from contextual enrichment often become part of the minimal interpretation of the complex utterance, thereby making the intended segregation of the semantic from the pragmatic untenable. For more on those matters, see Recanati 1993, part II.

24. At this point a suggestion must be considered: can we not reduce the third form of context-sensitivity to the second one? Remember that in the opaque reading, there are two dimensions of variation. (i) Any change in the wording of the embedded sentence can, by changing the *demonstratum*, affect the semantic value of the sentential operator; (ii) even if the *demonstratum* is fixed, the manner of Ψ-ing which is tacitly referred to can vary depending on the aspects of the index that are considered relevant in the context at hand. Now we could consider the transparent reading as the special case in which the relevant aspect of the demonstrated utterance is nothing other than its semantic content—its truth-conditions—to the exclusion of any other properties of the embedded sentence.

I have two objections to this move:

• Instead of considering the opaque reading as an enrichment of the transparent reading, it construes the transparent reading as a limiting case of the opaque. But in analysing the opaque reading in terms of 'so-believing' or 'believing thus', I implicitly accepted the primacy of the transparent sense. If we use subscripts to distinguish the transparent sense from the opaque, then, on my analysis, to believe$_o$ that p is to believe$_t$ that p in such and such a manner. That is hardly consistent with analysing believing$_t$ that p as a variety of believing$_o$ that p.

• If we construe 'that'-clauses as singular terms, it is indeed tempting to view transparency as a limiting case of opacity. Thus we can say that a 'that'-clause always refers to some enrichment of the proposition expressed, where that proposition itself counts as the minimal or 'zero' enrichment. But such a move is much less tempting when, giving up the view that 'that'-clauses are singular terms, we construe the embedded sentence as a *bona fide* sentence. On that construal the semantic content of the embedded sentence (the proposition it expresses) is its contribution to the content of the global attitude report: the embedded sentence expresses a proposition, on which the sentential operator operates. The semantic content of the embedded sentence is thus given prior to and independent of whatever tacit reference to some manner of Ψ-ing the sentential operator may happen to convey.

25. Remember that the 'context' in which the prefix is tokened includes the words it is prefixed to.

Part IV

1. The distinction between context and world has been elaborated by a number of authors. Beside Kaplan 1989a (the *locus classicus*), see Stalnaker 1978, Lewis 1980, and Fillmore 1981.

2. See also Kaplan (1989a: 491): "The speaker refers to himself when he uses 'I', and no pointing to another or believing that he is another or intending to refer to another can defeat this reference."

3. This corresponds to Ducrot's three-prong distinction between the empirical author of the text, the projected 'speaker', and the *'énonciateur'* whose point of view is expressed (Ducrot 1984: 192ff).

4. A particularly striking example Kaplan gives is, "It is possible that in Pakistan, in five years, only those who are actually here now are envied." As Kaplan points out, "the circumstance, place, and time referred to by the indexicals 'actually', 'here' and 'now' are the circumstance, place, and time of the context, not a circumstance, place, and time determined by the modal, locational, and temporal operators within whose scope the indexicals lie" (Kaplan 1989a: 499).

5. We find similar remarks in Evans's paper 'Does tense logic rest on a mistake?' (Evans 1985: 357–358): "Suppose that there is a language exactly like English, save that it possesses two additional operators, 'To the right', and 'To the left', which can be prefixed to sentences in the first person. A sentence like 'To the left (I am hot)' as uttered by a speaker x at t is true iff there is at t on x's left someone moderately near who is hot." What Evans is describing as possible (but not actual) in this passage is a context-shifting operator.

6. Predelli (1996) attempts to dispose of that counterexample by using a notion of 'displaced assertion' which corresponds to my notion of a (free) context-shift. Though I like Predelli's general framework, I find his account unconvincing because it ignores the major difficulty raised by the example: the occurrence of 'never' at the beginning. Predelli treats that occurrence as semantically empty, thereby making life too easy for himself. (For more on Predelli's views concerning context-shifting, see Predelli 1997 and 1998.)

7. By 'opacity' here I mean that which is correlated with *intensional* substitution failures, not the weaker form of opacity which can be explained away in terms of circumstance-shift (chapter 8).

8. Whatever the context, the English sentence 'Quarks are called "quarks"' is bound to be true; but the truth which it expresses in a particular context (say, in our context) is far from necessary: quarks might have been called by another name.

9. Among the authors who have put forward what we may refer to as demonstrative theories of quotation (e.g., Austin, Searle, Prior, Davidson, Ducrot, Sperber and Wilson, and Clark), some, like Ducrot and Clark, emphasize the use of icons, hence the simulative nature of quotation; others, like Davidson and Prior, emphasize the fact that mentioning words is like pointing to something given to our senses.

10. To use an example from Searle (1969: 76), an ornithologist may say, 'The sound made by the California Jay is ...', and what completes the sentence is a sound, not a linguistic expression.

11. The name 'mixed quotation' comes from Cappelen and Lepore 1997. (Davidson, whom they follow in their discussion, speaks of "mixed cases of use and mention.") Mixed quotation will be extensively dealt with in later chapters (especially 14 and 19).

12. I owe this point to Benoît de Cornulier.

13. Kaplan 1973: 507; Lewis 1978: 266; Stalnaker 1978: 330. See also Vuillaume 1990 for more on this 'secondary fiction'.

14. The catchy phrase 'opaque interface' comes from Quine. See §12.4.

15. See Geach (1957: 10): "Nonsense cannot be turned into *oratio obliqua*.... An attempt to report that somebody judges nonsense is itself nonsense. A British pupil of Heidegger might say "Nothing noths" in a tone of conviction; assuming that this is nonsense, "He judged that Nothing nothed" would also be nonsense. (We ought rather to say: "He judged that 'Nothing noths' was the expression of a truth.")"

16. Indeed the expression 'semi-quotation' was introduced by Fillmore (1971) precisely to deal with instances of metalinguistic negation.

17. That is *not* the phenomenon which Ducrot calls 'polyphony'. In polyphony, an utterance does not describe the actual world, but the world as seen by someone (an 'énonciateur') other than the speaker. Thus polyphony is an instance of world-shift. Ordinary negation is essentially polyphonic, for Ducrot. But metalinguistic negation is something very special, characterized by a context-shift rather than by a world-shift.

18. In support of his claim, Horn adduces the following example in a note:

U need not even involve a specifically linguistic utterance, as seen by the function of metalinguistic negation in the following musical scenario:

(i) [Piano student plays passage in manner μ.]
   Teacher: It's not [plays passage in manner μ]—it's [plays same passage in manner μ'].

The teacher's use of *not* is clearly not assimilable to anything remotely resembling truth-functional propositional negation. (Horn 1989: 564)

But this particular example is not convincing. If, as I claimed, a demonstration D (whether linguistic, musical, or whatnot) can serve as a singular term referring to that which is demonstrated, then Horn's example can be analysed as 'It's not D_1—it's D_2', in which 'not' function in the same way as in the straightforward sentence 'It's not that—it's this'.

19. Horn works with a simple dichotomy between descriptive and metalinguistic negation, but Ducrot has urged that we should distinguish between three sorts of negation: descriptive, polemic, and metalinguistic. See Ducrot 1984.

20. This claim will be qualified below (§14.4).

21. This example too comes from Cappelen and Lepore (1997: 436).

22. I am using 'context' here in a broad sense. In that sense, glossed in Bar-Hillel (1954) and Kaplan (1978), one particular feature of the 'context' is the language being spoken. See §19.2–3.

23. It should even be further restricted so as to rule out cases in which the echoed person is not the ascribee. Example (3) from chapter 15 is an example of that sort.

24. The fact that the content sentence is 'demonstrated' (open quotation) does not *by itself* account for failures of intensional substitution. The substitution indeed affects the demonstratum, but this would have no effect on the truth-conditions of the utterance if a pragmatic process of enrichment did not also take place. For more on this issue, see chapter 20.

Part V

1. See §17.2 for an alternative analysis in terms of *partial* pretense.

2. That formulation is arguably not very felicitous. If Santa Claus does not exist, then no proposition can exist which contains him as a constituent; hence no such proposition can be expressed. But when I say that the utterance expresses the proposition involving Santa Claus 'with respect to a fictional context', I mean that it *fictionally* expresses the proposition in question. This is compatible with the non-existence of the proposition in question.

3. "One can indicate to others what behaviour is appropriate in a given situation simply by behaving in the appropriate way. A native of an exotic culture might inform his alien guests that the snake livers are to be eaten with the parrot's nest sauce by going ahead and doing so. If it is awkward or improper to discuss Harold's winning of a prize before it is officially announced, one way of indicating that the announcement has been made, that the subject of Harold's good fortune is now a properly discussable one, would be to begin discussing it. Doing something is sometimes a way of claiming that it is proper or acceptable to do it" (Walton 1990: 399).

4. "The appended phrase [= the prefix] is not itself uttered in pretense, it seems, nor does it contribute to specifying a kind of pretense. It serves merely to comment on the kind of pretense specified by the words to which it is attached" (Walton 1990: 422). That is not Walton's last word, however. See below his remarks on the 'secondary pretense' underlying the prefix.

5. "The point of postulating semantic pretense … is to answer the question, what is a sentence like that doing in a statement like this? We have a fairly strong opinion about the sort of claim that is made in the statement, and a fairly strong opinion about the sort of claim that the sentence, in virtue of its structure, is really suited to expressing, but these opinions clash: the sentence doesn't seem suited to expressing the sort of claim it actually is used to express." (Crimmins 1998: 7; I quote from an earlier version of the paper, whose formulation I find more accurate than that of the published version.)

6. That view has been argued for by many authors, including Plantinga (1974: 159), Currie (1990: 146ff), and Cresswell (1990: chapter 9).

7. We find a similar example in this passage from Flaubert's *Bouvard et Pécuchet*: "Le comte demanda d'où venait cette enfant; on n'en savait rien. Les faneuses l'avaient recueillie pour les servir pendant la moisson. Il haussa les épaules, et, tout en s'éloignant, proféra quelques plaintes sur l'immoralité de nos campagnes." I am grateful to Marcel Vuillaume for bringing that example to my attention.

8. That example, which I have used many times in my writings on the topic, originates from Authier 1979: 225.

9. On the continuity between direct speech and free indirect speech, see Bakhtine 1977 (chapters 10–11).

10. Here I assume the 'indexical' analysis of proper names put forward in Recanati 1993: §8.3. On that analysis, the linguistic rule which constitutes the 'character' of a proper name is the rule that it refers to its bearer. (There still is an important difference between proper names and standard indexicals, on that view: all proper names are associated with the same semantic rule, while standard indexicals are each associated with a distinctive rule.) Nothing hinges on that view, however. If one takes the name-bearer relation to be linguistic rather than contextual, one can still analyse (1) in terms of context-shift, provided one uses 'context' in a broad sense (see page 332, note 22, and chapter 19.)

11. An occurrence, for Kaplan (1989a: 522, 546), is a sentence-context pair, that is, "the mere combination of the expression with the context" (Kaplan 1989b: 584). This "is not the same as the notion, from the theory of speech acts, of an *utterance* of an expression by the agent of a context. An occurrence requires no utterance. Utterances take time, and are produced one at a time; this will not do for the analysis of validity. By the time an agent finished uttering a very, very long true premise and began uttering the conclusion, the premise may have gone false.... Also, there are sentences which express a truth in certain contexts, but not if uttered. For example, 'I say nothing'. Logic and semantics are concerned not with the vagaries of actions, but with the verities of meanings" (Kaplan 1989b: 584–5).

12. I am indebted to Benoît de Cornulier for insisting on that point.

13. That point will be qualified below (§17.4): I will argue that the function *d* is not 'contributed' by any expression, not even the quotation marks. It is an 'unarticulated' constituent of the interpretation.

14. Untransposed 'now' and 'here' can be found in oral speech, but those cases can be explained away by treating 'now' and 'here' as demonstratives rather than pure indexicals. I cannot go into this issue here.

15. Still, there is something special to the cases we are talking about (Grandy's example of metonymy, or the 'Quine' examples): in those cases the sentence has a 'normal' character, which is modified through the operation of the relevant contextual process (metonymy or context-shift). Because of the secondary nature of the contextual process, which transforms the normal character of the sentence

into a deviant one, many philosophers and linguists will be willing to deny that the deviant character in question deserves to be called 'the character of the sentence', hence they will deny that, in *those* cases, the character of the sentence is context-dependent. What depends on the context, they will argue, is what *the speaker* means, not what the sentence literally says (let alone its character). See below, for an elaboration of that view.

16. This should be qualified in order to account for cases like the Carnap/Agnew example from Kaplan (1978). What that example shows is that *only the proximal intention counts*. In the example, the relevant intention is the speaker's intention to refer to the man whose portrait hangs on the wall behind him—not his intention to refer to Rudolf Carnap. See Bach 1992 for the relevant distinction between several layers of intention.

17. They are more common in languages other than English. See Anderson and Keenan 1985, §4.

Part VI

1. It is a striking fact that, among Lacanians, which interpretation is offered of a particular Lacanian dictum—e.g., 'The unconscious is structured like a language' or 'There is no sexual intercourse'—does not really matter: the diversity of possible interpretations is admitted. The only thing which is sacrosanct and cannot be disputed is the belief that *what Lacan says is true*.

2. Arguably, that constraint goes back to Russell (1918: 218).

3. Sperber insists that a metarepresentation (e.g., 'Lacan says that the unconscious is structured like a language') can be fully propositional even though the object-representation is not. This stands in direct conflict to the Inheritance Principle (p. 189). But the Inheritance principle must be properly understood. It says that metarepresentational embedding *per se*, in the absence of quotational context-shift, is unable to turn nonsense into sense. That can be reconciled with Sperber's claim if we construe metarepresentations such as 'Lacan says that the unconscious is structured like a language' as involving a measure of *oratio recta*, hence as instances of mixed quotation (similar to Austin's example: 'I said that he was behaving badly and he replied that "the higher you get the fewer"'— Austin 1975: 97). See §18.5 below.

4. Austin's phatic/rhetic distinction roughly corresponds to that between character and content.

5. The same point was made on p. 247 in connection with the context-shifting function *d*. On the relation between context-shifting functions and the deferential operator, see chapter 19.

6. That is debatable. Maybe the only constraint is that the context actually contain a user of σ. In stating the felicity condition of the deferential operator, I said that a user of σ must be *referred to*. Is it possible to refer to a user of σ without entertaining mental representations concerning him or her—that is the question (a question I will not go into here).

7. Sentence (6) deferentially expresses the proposition that Cicero's prose is full of synecdoches (i.e., the proposition which (10) would express in the mouth of the teacher). That content is very different from the metarepresentational content of (11).

8. One of Woodfield's examples involves a non-Czech speaker looking at a menu written in Czech and uttering *For lunch I shall have 'kachna'*. 'Kachna' means *duck* in Czech, Woodfield tells us.

9. In §17.4, I argued that contextual shifts are linguistically 'unarticulated' even when there is explicit use of quotation marks. I maintain that claim: Deferential context-shifts are unarticulated in natural language—in contrast to circumstance-shifts, which may or may not be articulated. In this chapter, however, I am primarily concerned with the 'language of thought'. It is in that hypothetical language that deferential shifts can be 'syntactically articulated' by means of the deferential operator.

10. As Millikan puts it:

It is ... possible, indeed it is common, to have a substance concept entirely through the medium of language, that is, in the absence of any ability to recognize the substance in the flesh. For most of us, that is how we have a concept of Aristotle, of molybdenum, and, say, of African dormice. There, I just handed you a concept of African dormice, in case you had none before. Now you can think of them at night if you want to, wondering what they are like—on the assumption, of course, that you gathered from their name what sorts of questions you might reasonably ask about them.... In many cases there is not much more to having a substance concept than having a word. To have a word is to have a handle on tracking a substance via manifestations of it produced in a particular language community. Simply grasping the phonemic structure of a language and the rudiments of how to parse it enables one to help oneself to an embryo concept of every substance named in that language. (Millikan 1998, §6)

Similar remarks can be found in Kaplan's 'Afterthoughts':

The notion that a referent can be carried by a name from early past to present suggests that the language itself carries meaning, and thus that we can *acquire* meanings through the instrument of language. This ... provides the opportunity for an *instrumental* use of language to broaden the realm of what can be expressed and to broaden the horizons of thought itself....

Contrary to Russell, I think we succeed in thinking about things in the world not only through the mental residue of that which we ourselves experience, but also vicariously, through the symbolic resources that come to us through our language. It is the latter—*vocabulary power*—that gives us our apprehensive advantage over the nonlinguistic animals. My dog, being color-blind, cannot entertain the thought that I am wearing a red shirt. But my color-blind colleague can entertain even the thought that Aristotle wore a red shirt. (Kaplan 1989b: 604)

11. See Evans 1982: chapter 8 for illuminating remarks on this topic.

12. The qualification is needed in view of what will be argued in §19.5.

13. Cases like (3) are somehow intermediate and can be treated either way, depending on how proper names are analysed (see p. 333, note 10).

14. I may be wrong. It is not always easy to make sense of Kaplan's position regarding the nature of contexts. Lewis (1980: 98) interprets Kaplan differently.

15. 'Disambiguation' is a fourth function played by the pragmatic context. It raises special problems and I prefer to leave it aside in this survey.

16. As we shall see, the context can be shifted in these two roles. When such a shift occurs, one of the two occurrences of 'c' will be replaced. The resulting formula will be either $P(\sigma, c')(c)$ or $P(\sigma, c)(c')$.

17. Such a reanalysis may perhaps be dispensed with if, as Vuillaume believes, conservative context-shifts are made possible by specific literary conventions and are not a genuine option in the normal use of language.

18. Technically it would be possible to drop the second parameter (the agent x to whom we defer) by suitably enriching the first one: after all the agent of a context is as much a feature of that context as the language spoken or the spatio-temporal location of the agent. But this would be philosophically unilluminating. I think context-shifts must be understood in terms of deference *qua* social phenomenon, not the other way round.

19. This will be qualified below (§20.1–2). It will be shown that the content of the global utterance (though not the content of the demonstrated expression) may ultimately be affected through a further process of 'contextual enrichment'.

20. This corresponds to my (admittedly controversial) claim that the truth-conditional content of an utterance is 'available' to those who understand that utterance (Recanati 1993: ch. 13).

21. 'Unarticulated constituent' is Perry's (1986b) phrase (see §17.4 above). 'Pragmatic intrusion' is Levinson's (Levinson, in press). Kent Bach uses a related notion of 'expansion' (Bach 1994). My own term, 'enrichment', is borrowed from Sperber and Wilson (1986), who use it in a slightly different way.

22. Let me repeat that it is the content of the global utterance that is affected by the demonstration, on the contextual enrichment analysis; not the content of the demonstrated expression itself, nor even the content of the complex expression constituted by the demonstrated expression and the quotation marks. Thus the earlier view is compatible with the claim that in cumulative mixed quotation, the expressions in the sentence are used in the normal way as far as their content is concerned.

23. I am in full agreement with David Lewis when he says: "[Faced with] the belief sentences that show up as test cases in articles advocating one semantic analysis or another … I always want to say: 'in a sense that's true, in a sense false'" (Lewis 1994: 427).

References

Anderson, S., and E. Keenan (1985). Deixis. In T. Shopen (ed.), *Language Typology and Syntactic Description*, vol. 3, pp. 259–308. Cambridge: Cambridge University Press.

Armstrong, D. (1997). *A World of States of Affairs*. Cambridge: Cambridge University Press.

Austin, J. L. (1971). *Philosophical Papers*. 2nd ed. Oxford: Clarendon Press.

Austin, J. L. (1975). *How to Do Things with Words*. 2nd ed. Oxford: Clarendon Press.

Authier, J. (1979). Problèmes posés par le traitement du discours rapporté dans une grammaire de phrase. *Linguisticae Investigationes* 3: 211–228.

Bach, K. (1992). Paving the Road to Reference. *Philosophical Studies* 67: 295–300.

Bach, K. (1994). Semantic Slack: What Is Said and More. In S. Tsohatzidis (ed.), *Foundations of Speech Act Theory*, pp. 267–291. London: Routledge.

Bakhtine, M. (1977). *Le marxisme et la philosophie du langage*. Paris: Minuit.

Baldwin, T. (1982). Prior and Davidson on Indirect Speech. *Philosophical Studies* 42: 255–282.

Bally, C. (1965). *Linguistique générale et linguistique Française*. 4th ed. Bern: Francke.

Banfield, A. (1982). *Unspeakable Sentences: Narration and Representation in the Language of Fiction*. London: Routledge.

Bar-Hillel, Y. (1954). Indexical Expressions. *Mind* 63: 359–379.

Barwise, J. (1989). *The Situation in Logic*. Stanford: CSLI.

Barwise, J., and R. Cooper (1981). Generalized Quantifiers and Natural Language. *Linguistics and Philosophy* 4: 159–219.

Barwise, J., and J. Etchemendy (1987). *The Liar: An Essay on Truth and Circularity*. New York: Oxford University Press.

Barwise, J., and J. Perry (1981). Semantic Innocence and Uncompromising Situations. *Midwest Studies in Philosophy* 6: 387–403.

Barwise, J., and J. Perry (1983). *Situations and Attitudes.* Cambridge: MIT Press.

Bealer, G. (1982). *Quality and Concept.* Oxford: Clarendon Press.

Belnap, N. (1970). Conditional Assertion and Restricted Quantification. *Noûs* 4: 1–12.

Bigelow, J. (1978). Semantics of Thinking, Speaking and Translation. In F. Guenthner and M. Guenthner-Reuter (eds.), *Meaning and Translation*, pp. 109–135. New York: New York University Press.

Bowerman, M. (1986). First Steps in Acquiring Conditionals. In E. Traugott, A. Ter Meulen, J. Reilly, and C. Ferguson (eds.), *On Conditionals*, pp. 285–307. Cambridge: Cambridge University Press.

Bühler, K. (1934). *Theory of Language.* Eng. trans. by D. F. Goodwin. Amsterdam: John Benjamins, 1990.

Burge, T. (1978). Self-Reference and Translation. In F. Guenthner and M. Guenthner-Reuter (eds.), *Meaning and Translation*, pp. 137–153. New York: New York University Press.

Burge, T. (1979). Individualism and the Mental. *Midwest Studies in Philosophy* 4: 73–121.

Burge, T. (1982). Other Bodies. In A. Woodfield (ed.), *Thought and Object*, pp. 97–120. Oxford: Clarendon Press.

Cappelen, H., and E. Lepore (1997). Varieties of Quotation. *Mind* 106: 429–50.

Carnap, R. (1947). *Meaning and Necessity.* Chicago: University of Chicago Press.

Carston, R. (1988). Implicature, Explicature, and Truth-Theoretic Semantics. In R. Kempson (ed.), *Mental Representations: The Interface between Language and Reality*, pp. 155–181. Cambridge: Cambridge University Press.

Chastain, C. (1975). Reference and Context. In K. Gunderson (ed.), *Language, Mind, and Knowledge*, pp. 194–269. Minneapolis: University of Minnesota Press.

Clark, H. (1992). *Arenas of Language Use.* Chicago: University of Chicago Press and CSLI.

Clark, H. (1996). *Using Language.* Cambridge: Cambridge University Press.

Clark, H., and R. Gerrig (1984). On the Pretense Theory of Irony. *Journal of Experimental Psychology: General* 113: 121–126.

Clark, H., and R. Gerrig (1990). Quotations as Demonstrations. *Language* 66: 764–805.

Cohen, L. J. (1962). *The Diversity of Meaning.* London: Methuen.

Cohen, L. J. (1986). How Is Conceptual Innovation Possible? *Erkenntnis* 25: 221–238.

Cresswell, M. (1973). *Logics and Languages.* London: Methuen.

Cresswell, M. (1975). Hyperintensional Logic. *Studia Logica* 34: 25–38.

Cresswell, M. (1985). *Structured Meanings*. Cambridge: MIT Press.

Cresswell, M. (1990). *Entities and Indices*. Dordrecht: Kluwer.

Crimmins, M. (1992). *Talk about Belief*. Cambridge: MIT Press.

Crimmins, M. (1998). Hesperus and Phosphorus: Sense, Pretense, and Reference. *Philosophical Review* 107: 1–47.

Crimmins, M., and J. Perry (1989). The Prince and the Phone Booth. *Journal of Philosophy* 86: 685–711.

Currie, G. (1990). *The Nature of Fiction*. Cambridge: Cambridge University Press.

Davidson, D. (1968). On Saying That. Reprinted in his *Inquiries into Truth and Interpretation*, pp. 93–108. Oxford: Clarendon Press, 1984.

Davidson, D. (1979). Quotation. Reprinted in his *Inquiries into Truth and Interpretation*, pp. 79–92. Oxford: Clarendon Press, 1984.

Dinsmore, J. (1991). *Partitioned Representations*. Dordrecht: Kluwer.

Donnellan, K. (1966). Reference and Definite Descriptions. *Philosophical Review* 75: 281–304.

Donnellan, K. (1974). Speaking of Nothing. *Philosophical Review* 83: 3–31.

Donnellan, K. (1993). There Is a Word for That Kind of Thing: An Investigation of Two Thought Experiments. *Philosophical Perspectives* 7: 155–171.

Ducrot, O. (1972). *Dire et ne pas dire*. Paris: Hermann.

Ducrot, O. (1973). Les échelles argumentatives. In O. Ducrot, *La preuve et le dire*, pp. 225–285. Paris: Mame.

Ducrot, O. (1980). Analyse de texte et linguistique de l'énonciation. In O. Ducrot et al., *Les mots du discours*, pp. 7–56. Paris: Minuit.

Ducrot, O. (1984). Esquisse d'une théorie polyphonique de l'énonciation. In O. Ducrot, *Le dire et le dit*, pp. 171–233. Paris: Minuit.

Dummett, M. (1973). *Frege: Philosophy of Language*. London: Duckworth.

Dummett, M. (1993). *The Seas of Language*. Oxford: Oxford University Press.

Evans, G. (1977). Pronouns, Quantifiers, and Relative Clauses (I). Reprinted in M. Platts (ed.), *Reference, Truth, and Reality: Essays on the Philosophy of Language*, pp. 255–317. London: Routledge, 1980.

Evans, G. (1982). *The Varieties of Reference*. Edited by J. McDowell. Oxford: Clarendon Press.

Evans, G. (1985). Does Tense Logic Rest on a Mistake? In his *Collected Papers*, pp. 343–363. Oxford: Clarendon Press.

Fauconnier, G. (1985). *Mental Spaces*. Cambridge: MIT Press.

Field, H. (1978). Mental Representation. *Erkenntnis* 13: 9–61.

Fillmore, C. (1971). Types of Lexical Information. In D. Steinberg and L. Jakobovits (eds.), *Semantics: An Interdisciplinary Reader in Philosophy,*

Linguistics, and Psychology, pp. 370–392. Cambridge: Cambridge University Press.

Fillmore, C. (1975). *The Santa Cruz Lectures on Deixis.* Bloomington: Indiana University Linguistics Club.

Fillmore, C. (1981). Pragmatics and the Description of Discourse. In P. Cole (ed.), *Radical Pragmatics*, pp. 143–166. New York: Academic Press.

Fine, K. (1989). The Problem of De Re Modality. In J. Almog, H. Wettstein, and J. Perry (eds.), *Themes from Kaplan*, pp. 197–272. New York: Oxford University Press.

Fodor, J. A. (1975). *The Language of Thought.* New York: Crowell.

Forbes, G. (1990). The Indispensability of *Sinn. Philosophical Review* 99: 535–563.

Forbes, G. (1996). Substitutivity and the Coherence of Quantifying In. *Philosophical Review* 105: 337–372.

Frege, G. (1970). *Translations from the Philosophical Writings of Gottlob Frege.* Edited by P. Geach and M. Black. Oxford: Basil Blackwell.

Garver, N. (1965). Varieties of Use and Mention. *Philosophy and Phenomenological Research* 26: 230–238.

Geach, P. (1957). *Mental Acts: Their Content and Their Objects.* London: Routledge and Kegan Paul.

Geach, P. (1972). *Logic Matters.* Oxford: Basil Blackwell.

Gordon, R. (1986). Folk Psychology as Simulation. *Mind and Language* 1: 158–171.

Grandy, R. (1990). Understanding and the Principle of Compositionality. *Philosophical Perspectives* 4: 557–572.

Grover, D. (1992). *A Prosentential Theory of Truth.* Princeton: Princeton University Press.

Harman, G. (1973). *Thought.* Princeton: Princeton University Press.

Harris, P. (1989). *Children and Emotion.* Oxford: Basil Blackwell.

Heal, J. (1998). Co-cognition and Off-Line Simulation: Two Ways of Understanding the Simulation Approach. *Mind and Language* 13: 477–498.

Hintikka, J. (1962). *Knowledge and Belief.* Ithaca: Cornell University Press.

Hintikka, J. (1969). Semantics for Propositional Attitudes. In his *Models for Modalities*, pp. 87–111. Dordrecht: Kluwer.

Hintikka, J. (1973). Grammar and Logic: Some Borderline Problems. In J. Hintikka, J. Moravcsik, and P. Suppes (eds.), *Approaches to Natural Language*, pp. 197–214. Dordrecht: Kluwer.

Hintikka, J. (1975). *The Intentions of Intentionality and Other New Models for Modalities.* Dordrecht: Kluwer.

Horn, L. (1989). *A Natural History of Negation*. Chicago: University of Chicago Press.

Hugly, P., and C. Sayward (1996). *Intensionality and Truth: An Essay on the Philosophy of A. N. Prior*. Dordrecht: Kluwer.

Jackendoff, R. (1983). *Semantics and Cognition*. Cambridge: MIT Press.

Jacob, P. (1987). Thoughts and Belief Ascriptions. *Mind and Language* 2: 301–325.

Johansson, I. (1989). *Ontological Investigations*. London: Routledge.

Kahneman, D., and A. Tversky (1982). The Simulation Heuristic. In D. Kahneman, P. Slovic, and A. Tversky (eds.), *Judgment under Uncertainty: Heuristics and Biases*, pp. 201–207. Cambridge: Cambridge University Press.

Kaplan, D. (1968). Quantifying In. *Synthese* 19: 178–214.

Kaplan, D. (1973). Bob and Carol and Ted and Alice. In J. Hintikka, J. Moravcsik, and P. Suppes (eds.), *Approaches to Natural Language*, pp. 490–518. Dordrecht: Reidel.

Kaplan, D. (1978). Dthat. *Syntax and Semantics* 9: 221–243.

Kaplan, D. (1986). Opacity. In L. Hahn and P. A. Schilpp (eds.), *The Philosophy of W. V. Quine*, pp. 229–289. La Salle, Illinois: Open Court.

Kaplan, D. (1989a). Demonstratives. In J. Almog, H. Wettstein, and J. Perry (eds.), *Themes from Kaplan*, pp. 481–563. New York: Oxford University Press.

Kaplan, D. (1989b). Afterthoughts. In J. Almog, H. Wettstein and J. Perry (eds.), *Themes from Kaplan*, pp. 565–614. New York: Oxford University Press.

Kripke, S. (1977). Speaker's Reference and Semantic Reference. *Midwest Studies in Philosophy* 2: 255–276.

Kripke, S. (1980). *Naming and Necessity*. Oxford: Blackwell.

Lakoff, G. (1993). The Contemporary Theory of Metaphor. In A. Ortony (ed.), *Metaphor and Thought*, 2nd ed., pp. 202–251. Cambridge: Cambridge University Press.

Lakoff, G., and M. Johnson (1980). *Metaphors We Live By*. Chicago: University of Chicago Press.

Langacker, R. (1984). Active Zones. *Proceedings of the Annual Meeting of the Berkeley Linguistics Society* 10: 172–188.

Langacker, R. (1987). *Foundations of Cognitive Grammar*. Vol. 1. Stanford: Stanford University Press.

Lemmon, E. J. (1965). *Beginning Logic*. Sunbury-on-Thames: Thomas Nelson and Sons.

Lepore, E., and K. Ludwig (2000). The Semantics and Pragmatics of Complex Demonstratives. *Mind* 109: 1–42.

Leslie, A. (1987). Pretense and Representation: The Origins of "Theory of Mind." *Psychological Review* 94: 412–426.

Levinson, S. (in press). *Presumptive Meanings.* Cambridge: MIT Press.

Lewis, D. (1970). General Semantics. Reprinted (with postscripts) in his *Philosophical Papers,* vol. 1, pp. 189–232. New York: Oxford University Press, 1983.

Lewis, D. (1978). Truth in Fiction. Reprinted (with postscripts) in his *Philosophical Papers,* vol. 1, pp. 261–280. New York: Oxford University Press, 1983.

Lewis, D. (1980). Index, Context, and Content. In S. Kanger and S. Öhman (eds.), *Philosophy and Grammar,* pp. 79–100. Dordrecht: Reidel.

Lewis, D. (1986). *On the Plurality of Worlds.* Oxford: Blackwell.

Lewis, D. (1994). Lewis, David: Reduction of Mind. In S. Guttenplan (ed.), *A Companion to the Philosophy of Mind,* pp. 412–431. London: Blackwell.

Linsky, L. (1967). *Referring.* London: Routledge and Kegan Paul.

Loar, B. (1972). Reference and Propositional Attitudes. *Philosophical Review* 81: 43–62.

Long, P. (1971). Conditional Assertion. *Proceedings of the Aristotelian Society,* suppl. vol. 45: 141–147.

MacIver, A. M. (1936). Demonstratives and Proper Names. Reprinted in M. MacDonald (ed.), *Philosophy and Analysis,* pp. 26–32. Oxford: Blackwell, 1954.

Mackie, J. (1973). *Truth, Probability, and Paradox.* Oxford: Clarendon Press.

Marcus, R. (1993). *Modalities.* New York: Oxford University Press.

Mates, B. (1952). Synonymity. In L. Linsky (ed.), *Semantics and the Philosophy of Language,* pp. 111–136. Urbana: University of Illinois Press.

McCarthy, J. (1993). Notes on Formalizing Context. *Proceedings of the Thirteenth International Joint Conference on Artificial Intelligence,* vol. 1, pp. 555–560. San Mateo: Morgan Kaufmann Publisher.

McDowell, J. (1977). On the Sense and Reference of a Proper Name. Reprinted in A. W. Moore (ed.), *Meaning and Reference,* pp. 111–136. Oxford: Clarendon Press, 1993.

McKay, T. (1981). On Proper Names in Belief Ascriptions. *Philosophical Studies* 39: 287–303.

Millikan, R. (1998). A Common Structure for Concepts of Individuals, Stuffs, and Real Kinds: More Mama, More Milk, and More Mouse. *Behavioral and Brain Sciences* 21: 55–65.

Moltmann, F. (1997). On the Semantics of Clausal Complements. Ms.

Moltmann, F. (1998). Nonreferential Complements and Secondary Objects. Ms.

Moravcsik, J. (1998). *Meaning, Creativity, and the Partial Inscrutability of the Human Mind.* Stanford: CSLI Publications.

Neale, S. (1990). *Descriptions.* Cambridge: MIT Press.

Neale, S. (1993). Term Limits. *Philosophical Perspectives* 7: 89–123.

Nunberg, G. (1979). The Non-uniqueness of Semantic Solutions: Polysemy. *Linguistics and Philosophy* 3: 143–184.

Nunberg, G. (1991). Indexicals and Descriptions in Interpretation. Ms.

Nunberg, G. (1993). Indexicality and Deixis. *Linguistics and Philosophy* 16: 1–43.

Nunberg, G. (1995). Transfers of Meaning. *Journal of Semantics* 12: 109–132.

Nunberg, G., and A. Zaenen (1992). Systematic Polysemy in Lexicology and Lexicography. In H. Tommola, K. Varantola, T. Tolonen and J. Schopp (eds.), *Proceedings of Euralex 2*. University of Tampere.

Orenstein, A. (forthcoming). Propositional Attitudes without Propositions. In P. Kotatko and A. Grayling (eds.), *Meaning*. Oxford: Clarendon Press.

Ostler, N., and B. S. Atkins (1992). Predictable Meaning Shift: Some Linguistic Properties of Lexical Implication Rules. In J. Pustejovsky and S. Bergler (eds.), *Lexical Semantics and Knowledge Representation*, pp. 87–100. Berlin: Springer.

Parsons, C. (1990). *Events in the Semantics of English: A Study in Subatomic Semantics*. Cambridge: MIT Press.

Partee, B. (1973). The Semantics of Belief-Sentences. In J. Hintikka, J. Moravcsik, and P. Suppes (eds.), *Approaches to Natural Language*, pp. 309–336. Dordrecht: Reidel.

Perner, J. (1991). *Understanding the Representational Mind*. Cambridge: MIT Press.

Perrin, L. (1996). *L'ironie mise en trope*. Paris: Kimé.

Perry, J. (1986a). From Worlds to Situations. *Journal of Philosophical Logic* 15: 83–107.

Perry, J. (1986b). Thought without Representation. *Proceedings of the Aristotelian Society*, suppl. vol. 60: 137–151.

Perry, J. (1993). *The Problem of the Essential Indexical and Other Essays*. New York: Oxford University Press.

Plantinga, A. (1974). *The Nature of Necessity*. Oxford: Clarendon Press.

Pratt, I. (1990). Psychological Inference, Rationality, Closure. In P. Hanson (ed.), *Information, Language, and Cognition*, pp. 366–389. New York: Oxford University Press.

Predelli, S. (1996). Never Put Off until Tomorrow What You Can Do Today. *Analysis* 56: 85–91.

Predelli, S. (1997). Talk about Fiction. *Erkenntnis* 46: 69–77.

Predelli, S. (1998). Utterance, Interpretation, and the Logic of Indexicals. *Mind and Language* 13: 400–414.

Prior, A. (1963). Oratio Obliqua. Reprinted in his *Papers in Logic and Ethics*, pp. 147–158. London: Duckworth, 1976.

Prior, A. (1971). *Objects of Thought*. Edited by P. Geach and A. Kenny. Oxford: Clarendon Press.

Pustejovsky, J. (1995). *The Generative Lexicon*. Cambridge: MIT Press.

Putnam, H. (1975). The Meaning of 'Meaning'. In K. Gunderson (ed.), *Language, Mind, and Knowledge*, pp. 131–193. Minneapolis: University of Minnesota Press.

Quine, W. V. O. (1951). *Mathematical Logic*. 2nd ed. Cambridge: Harvard University Press.

Quine, W. V. O. (1953). Three Grades of Modal Involvement. Reprinted in Quine 1976, pp. 158–176.

Quine, W. V. O. (1956). Quantifiers and Propositional Attitudes. Reprinted in Quine 1976, pp. 185–196.

Quine, W. V. O. (1960). *Word and Object*. Cambridge: MIT Press.

Quine, W. V. O. (1961). *From a Logical Point of View*. 2nd ed. Cambridge: Harvard University Press.

Quine, W. V. O. (1962). *Methods of Logic*. 2nd ed. London: Routledge and Kegan Paul.

Quine, W. V. O. (1974). *The Roots of Reference*. La Salle, Illinois: Open Court.

Quine, W. V. O. (1976). *The Ways of Paradox and Other Essays*. 2nd ed. Cambridge: Harvard University Press.

Quine, W. V. O. (1977). Intensions Revisited. *Midwest Studies in Philosophy* 2: 5–11.

Quine, W. V. O. (1980). The Variable and Its Place in Reference. In Z. van Straaten (ed.), *Philosophical Subjects: Essays Presented to P. F. Strawson*, pp. 164–173. Oxford: Clarendon Press.

Quine, W. V. O. (1995). Reactions. In P. Leonardi and M. Santambrogio (eds.), *On Quine*, pp. 347–361. Cambridge: Cambridge University Press.

Quine, W. V. O. (2000). Response to Recanati. In A. Orenstein and P. Kotatko (eds.), *Knowledge, Language, and Logic: Questions for Quine*, pp. 428–430. Dordrecht, Kluwer.

Ramsey, F. (1990). *Philosophical Papers*. Cambridge: Cambridge University Press.

Recanati, F. (1979). *La transparence et l'énonciation*. Paris: Seuil.

Recanati, F. (1986). On Defining Communicative Intentions. *Mind and Language* 1: 213–242.

Recanati, F. (1987). Contextual Dependence and Definite Descriptions. *Proceedings of the Aristotelian Society* 87: 57–73.

Recanati, F. (1988). *Meaning and Force*. Cambridge: Cambridge University Press.

Recanati, F. (1993). *Direct Reference: From Language to Thought*. Oxford: Basil Blackwell.

Recanati, F. (1995a). The Alleged Priority of Literal Interpretation. *Cognitive Science* 19: 207–232.

Recanati, F. (1995b). Quasi-Singular Propositions: The Semantics of Belief Reports. *Proceedings of the Aristotelian Society*, suppl. vol. 69: 175–193.

Recanati, F. (1996). Domains of Discourse. *Linguistics and Philosophy* 19: 445–475.

Recanati, F. (1997a). Can We Believe What We Do Not Understand? *Mind and Language* 12: 84–100.

Recanati, F. (1997b). The Dynamics of Situations. *European Review of Philosophy* 2: 41–75.

Recanati, F. (1998). Talk about Fiction. *Lingua e Stile* 33: 547–558.

Recanati, F. (1999). Situations and the Structure of Content. In K. Murasugi and R. Stainton (eds.), *Philosophy and Linguistics*, pp. 113–165. Boulder: Westview.

Recanati, F. (forthcoming a). The Iconicity of Metarepresentation. In D. Sperber (ed.), *Metarepresentation*. New York: Oxford University Press.

Recanati, F. (forthcoming b). Opacity and the Attitudes. In A. Orenstein and P. Kotatko (eds.), *Knowledge, Language, and Logic: Questions for Quine*, pp. 367–406 Dordrecht: Kluwer.

Recanati, F. (forthcoming c). Relational Belief Reports. *Philosophical Studies*.

Recanati, F. (forthcoming d). Deferential Concepts. *Mind and Language*.

Reichenbach, H. (1947). *Elements of Symbolic Logic*. New York: Macmillan.

Rey-Debove, J. (1978). *Le métalangage*. Paris: Le Robert.

Richard, M. (1990). *Propositional Attitudes*. Cambridge: Cambridge University Press.

Richard, M. (1993). Articulated Terms. *Philosophical Perspectives* 7: 207–230.

Richard, M. (1996). Propositional Quantification. In J. Copeland (ed.), *Logic and Reality: Essays on the Legacy of Arthur Prior*, pp. 437–460. Oxford: Clarendon Press.

Ross, J. (1997). *The Semantics of Media*. Dordrecht: Kluwer.

Rundle, B. (1979). *Grammar in Philosophy*. Oxford: Clarendon Press.

Russell, B. (1905). On Denoting. *Mind* 14: 479–493.

Russell, B. (1910). *Philosophical Essays*. London: Longmans, Green, and Co.

Russell, B. (1918). Knowledge by Acquaintance and Knowledge by Description. In *Mysticism and Logic and Other Essays*, pp. 209–232. London: Longmans, Green, and Co.

Russell, B. (1940). *An Inquiry into Meaning and Truth*. London: George Allen and Unwin.

Russell, B. (1956). *Logic and Knowledge: Essays, 1901–1950*, ed. by R. Marsh. London: George Allen and Unwin.

Sainsbury, M. (1979). *Russell*. London: Routledge and Kegan Paul.

Salmon, N. (1986). *Frege's Puzzle*. Cambridge: MIT Press.

Salmon, N. (1991). The Pragmatic Fallacy. *Philosophical Studies* 63: 83–97.

Schiffer, S. (1977). Naming and Knowing. *Midwest Studies in Philosophy* 2: 28–41.

Schiffer, S. (1987). *Remnants of Meaning*. Cambridge: MIT Press.

Searle, J. (1969). *Speech Acts*. Cambridge: Cambridge University Press.

Searle, J. (1978). Literal Meaning. *Erkenntnis* 13: 207–224.

Searle, J. (1980). The Background of Meaning. In J. Searle, F. Kiefer, and M. Bierwisch (eds.), *Speech Act Theory and Pragmatics*, pp. 221–232. Dordrecht: Reidel.

Sechehaye, A. (1926). *Essai sur la structure logique de la phrase*. Paris: Champion.

Segal, J. (1916). *Über das Vorstellen von Objekten und Situationen: Ein Beitrag zur Psychologie der Phantasie*. Stuttgart: Spemann.

Sleigh, R. C. (1968). On a Proposed System of Epistemic Logic. *Noûs* 2: 391–398.

Sperber, D. (1975). *Rethinking Symbolism*. Cambridge: Cambridge University Press.

Sperber, D. (1985). Apparently Irrational Beliefs. Chapter 2 of *On Anthropological Knowledge*. Cambridge: Cambridge University Press.

Sperber, D. (1997). Intuitive and Reflective Beliefs. *Mind and Language* 12: 67–83.

Sperber, D., and D. Wilson (1981). Irony and the Use-Mention Distinction. In P. Cole (ed.), *Radical Pragmatics*, pp. 295–318. New York: Academic Press.

Sperber, D., and D. Wilson (1986). *Relevance: Communication and Cognition*. Oxford: Blackwell.

Stalnaker, R. (1968). A Theory of Conditionals. Reprinted in F. Jackson (ed.), *Conditionals*, pp. 28–45. New York: Oxford University Press.

Stalnaker, R. (1974). Pragmatic Presuppositions. Reprinted in S. Davis (ed.), *Pragmatics: A Reader*, pp. 471–482. New York: Oxford University Press, 1991.

Stalnaker, R. (1975). Indicative Conditionals. Reprinted in his *Context and Content*, pp. 63–77. Oxford: Oxford University Press, 1999.

Stalnaker, R. (1976). Propositions. In A. McKay and D. Merril (eds.), *Issues in the Philosophy of Language*, pp. 79–91. New Haven: Yale University Press.

Stalnaker, R. (1978). Assertion. *Syntax and Semantics* 9: 315–332.

Strawson, P. (1964). Identifying Reference and Truth-Value. Reprinted in Strawson 1977, pp. 75–95.

Strawson, P. (1974a). *Subject and Predicate in Logic and Grammar*. London: Methuen.

Strawson, P. (1974b). Positions for Quantifiers. Reprinted in his *Entity and Identity*, pp. 64–84. Oxford: Clarendon Press, 1997.

Strawson, P. (1977). *Logico-Linguistic Papers*. London: Methuen.

Strawson, P. (1997). Introduction. In his *Entity and Identity*, pp. 1–20. Oxford: Clarendon Press.

Talmy, L. (1996). Fictive Motion in Language and "Ception." In R. Bloom et al. (eds.), *Language and Space*, pp. 211–276. Cambridge: MIT Press.

Tasmowski-De Ryck, L. (1972). La négation en français et la formalisation de la grammaire. *Logique et Analyse* 15: 171–207.

Travis, C. (1975). *Saying and Understanding*. Oxford: Blackwell.

Travis, C. (1981). *The True and the False: The Domain of the Pragmatic*. Amsterdam: Benjamins.

Vendler, Z. (1967). *Linguistics in Philosophy*. Ithaca: Cornell University Press.

Von Wright, G. H. (1963). On Conditionals. In his *Logical Studies*, pp. 127–165. London: Routledge and Kegan Paul.

Vuillaume, M. (1990). *Grammaire temporelle des récits*. Paris: Minuit.

Walton, K. (1990). *Mimesis as Make-Believe: On the Foundations of the Representational Arts*. Cambridge: Harvard University Press.

Wierzbicka, A. (1974). The Semantics of Direct and Indirect Discourse. *Papers in Linguistics* 7: 267–307.

Wiggins, D. (1984). The Sense and Reference of Predicates: A Running Repair to Frege's Doctrine and a Plea for the Copula. In C. Wright (ed.), *Frege: Tradition and Influence*, pp. 126–143. Oxford: Blackwell.

Williams, C. J. F. (1981). *What Is Existence?* Oxford: Clarendon Press.

Woodfield, A. (forthcoming). Reference and Deference. To appear in *Mind and Language*.

Index

UNIVERSITY LIBRARY
NOTTINGHAM